SOCIALIST ECONOMIC SYSTEMS

Bernie Sanders' socialist advocacy in the United States, communist China's economic successes and a Marxist revival are inspiring many to muse about improved strategies for building superior socialist futures. *Socialist Economic Systems* provides an objective record of socialism's promises and performance during 1820–2022, identifies a feasible path forward and provides a rigorous analytic framework for the comparison of economic systems.

The book opens by surveying preindustrial utopias from Plato to Thomas More, and libertarian communal designs for superior living. It plumbs all aspects of the revolutionary and democratic socialist political movements that emerged after 1870 and considers the comparative economic, political and social performance of the USSR and others from the Bolshevik Revolution onward. The book also provides case studies for all revolutionary Marxist–Leninist regimes, and supplementary discussions of Mondragon cooperatives, Israeli kibbutzim, Nordic corporatism and European democratic socialism. It investigates the theoretical and practical complexities of command planning, reform communism, market communism, worker economic management and egalitarianism. It examines communism as an engine of economic growth and a mechanism for improving people's quality of existence, including living standards, labor self-governance, egalitarianism, social justice and prevention of crimes against humanity before addressing the perennial question of what needs to be done next. A suggested path forward is elaborated drawing lessons from the warts-and-all historical performance of socialist economies during 1917–2022 and failed socialist prophesy. The evidence indicates that the key to 21st-century socialism success lies in empowering workers of all descriptions to govern democratically for their mutual protection and welfare without the extraneous imposition of priorities imposed by other movements.

The book is essential reading for anyone interested in socialism, political economy, comparative economic systems, and political and social history.

Steven Rosefielde is Professor of Economics at the University of North Carolina at Chapel Hill, USA.

Routledge Frontiers of Political Economy

For more information about this series, please visit: www.routledge.com/Routledge-Frontiers-of-Political-Economy/book-series/SE0345

Socialist Economic Systems

21st Century Pathways

Steven Rosefielde

Routledge
Taylor & Francis Group

LONDON AND NEW YORK

First published 2023
by Routledge
4 Park Square, Milton Park, Abingdon, Oxon OX14 4RN

and by Routledge
605 Third Avenue, New York, NY 10158

Routledge is an imprint of the Taylor & Francis Group, an informa business

© 2023 Steven Rosefielde

British Library Cataloguing-in-Publication Data
A catalogue record for this book is available from the British Library

ISBN: 9781032443164 (hbk)
ISBN: 9781032443188 (pbk)
ISBN: 9781003371571 (ebk)

DOI: 10.4324/9781003371571

Typeset in Bembo
by Newgen Publishing UK

To my wife Susan and daughter Justine.

Contents

Illustrations

Figures

Tables

Illustrations

Preface

The subject is socialism. The concept means different things to different people. There is no consensus about laws, attributes and merit. Some find socialism attractive, others repellent on diverse grounds. Some seek utopia, others justice, liberty, equality or fraternity. Some believe or disbelieve on intuitive, philosophical, rational and aesthetic grounds, or blind faith. Some are impassioned. Others are impartial and analytic. Philosophy, literature and political identity guide and misguide socialist advocates and opponents.

Socialist Economic Systems: 21st Century Pathways narrates the historical manifestation of the socialist phenomenon during 1820–2022 in its various dimensions. It describes the concepts and principles shaping schools of socialist thinking, culture, politics and economics. It documents experiments, performance and consequences, providing a platform for gauging what comes next. It is an exercise in the application of rational choice to complex phenomena rooted in Abram Bergson's mathematical systems and welfare economic theory.

The approach reflects mixed influences. Loyd Easton taught me Hegelian philosophy and the young Marx. Lord Lionel Robbins, Alexander Gerschenkron and John Kenneth Galbraith introduced me to socialism from an institutionalist perspective. Abram Bergson, Wassily Leontief and Simon Kuznets trained me in neoclassical economic theory and its applications. Leonard Schapiro, Alec Nove and Richard Pipes instructed me about the political realities of the Soviet experiment. I had extensive hands-on experience in the USSR from 1967 to 1991. President Ford appointed me Coordinator of the US-USSR Joint Cooperative Research Program on Science and Technology during 1977--1981. I worked closely with the Central Economic and Mathematics Institute and became a member of the Russian Academy of Natural Sciences [Rossiiskaia Akademiia Estestvennykh Nauk (RAEN)] in 1997. I integrated these experiences into a unified perception of the socialist phenomena guided by Abram Bergson's systems and welfare theory.

This treatise is the culmination of a project begun more than 40 years ago in a contribution penned for the Abram Bergson festschrift, "Knowledge and socialism: deciphering the Soviet experience," addressing the difficulties impeding reliable assessments of Soviet socialist reality (Rosefielde, 1981). The USSR's demise, the collapse of Yugoslavian labor self-management and the post-Soviet repudiation of Marxist–Leninist–Stalinism by the Kremlin's former satellites have settled some, but not all issues regarding the competitive viability of Bolshevism. New Age planning, democratic socialism and the emergence of other socialist alternatives remain the possibilities. This volume provides insight into what we know about the socialist experience during 1820–2022 and what is apt to be a very different future.

Reference

Rosefielde, Steven. (1981). "Knowledge and Socialism: Deciphering the Soviet Experience." In S. Rosefielde (ed.), *Economic Welfare and the Economics of Soviet Socialism.* Cambridge: Cambridge University Press.

Acknowledgments

I thank all those who assisted me sorting out the socialist conundrum.

Executive Summary

Socialism is a phenomenon. It altered the course of history for more than a century starting with the second wave of Western industrialization circa 1870 until the Soviet Union's demise in 1991. It challenged feudal, monarchial, fascist and libertarian democratic orders in the streets, media, salons and at the ballot box, often spurring reform and in some instances revolution. It divided the world into communist and capitalist camps. Although, the socialist tide gradually ebbed at the end of the 1970s, many still believed that the future belonged to the revolutionary working class until the Soviet Union imploded.

Suddenly, socialism's political prospects plummeted. Marxist–Leninist and democratic socialist parties tried to soldier on during the ensuing 30 years, as did other collectivist movements. They survive, but are treading water.

A reversal of fortune is conceivable. However, a multitude of political and economic forces impair prospects for socialist revival. Socialists tend to impose extraneous requirements on their systems that impair competitive efficiency and diminish political appeal.

The historical record of 1820–2022 presented in this volume testifies to the unwillingness of most socialists to put science before philosophizing and politics. It demonstrates that:

1 While some 19th-century utopian communities briefly flourished, all eventually perished.
2 While some forms of communalism like the Mondragon federation of worker-cooperatives thrive, their appeal is circumscribed.
3 While revolutionary syndicalism has sometimes briefly seized state power, it never ruled effectively.
4 While guild socialism ("direct economic democracy") seemed promising circa 1918, Bolshevism swiftly overshadowed it.
5 While diverse socialist parties sometimes win democratic elections, none has transformed transient victory into durable democratic socialist rule.
6 While Marxist-Leninism reigned in the Soviet Union for 73 years, and continues to rule in North Korea, it failed to deliver the "full communism" prophesized in the *Communist Manifesto* or even a satisfactory quality of worker existence.

7   While Yugoslavian worker self-management inspired a legion of admirers during1960–1989, the idea today is moribund.
8   While numerous alternative socialist schemes exist, none has proven its mettle.
9   While post-Soviet socialism has been treading water, the West's blue-collar working class, once predicted by Marx to become the vast majority, has dwindled into a small minority, prompting politicians and activists to favor other constituencies.
10 While contemporary socialists support organized labor, politicians and activists today care little about ordinary workers. They have shifted their allegiance to other radical causes.
11 While contemporary socialism faces an uphill battle, its fortunes could improve by returning to basics. If socialism following Robert Owen means worker sovereign libertarian democracy prioritizing blue- and white-collar worker betterment, the goal is achievable because most Westerners are members of the working class.
12 There is no evidence that socialist politicians, activists and the working class appreciate that workers themselves should democratically determine socialist policy.

The last 200 years have taught many useful lessons. We now know that the utopian socialism of Fourier, Saint-Simon and Cabet never attracted large followings and vanished. Sorel's revolutionary syndicalism, George Douglas Howard Cole's libertarian Guild socialism and William Morris's "art and crafts" Fabianism suffered the same fate.

We now know with considerable confidence that Marxist-Leninism (including Tito's labor self-management and Fidel Castro's Cuban subcases) perished, or are on life support. We now know that hi-tech economic planning is almost certainly inferior to warts and all laissez-faire. We now know that while illiberal Marxist democratic socialism is feasible, it has difficulty competing with liberal free enterprise, welfare states and Nordic corporatism. We now know that while Xi Jinping's market communism is promising in several respects, its commitment to workers and Marx's full communist idea is suspect. We now know that despite two centuries of experience, socialist political rhetoric remains more about late-19th-century revolutionary social romanticism and hostility toward big business, private property, markets, privilege and inequity than scientific designs for better living. There is no ethical consensus on the optimal configuration of socialist ends, institutionalist agreement about how to construct efficient socialist systems or authoritative standards for assessing comparative merit.

We now know that while libertarian worker sovereign socialism is feasible, it has not yet gained political momentum.

Methodology

Socialism is a filial set of concepts for protecting workers and enhancing their quality of existence.

Each concept specifies goals, institutions and principles for transforming concepts into realities.

Feasible socialist concepts must be logically consistent.

Critical reason enables analysts to assess the comparative merit of rival socialisms.

Experimental and quantitative methods enable analysts to assess socialist economic, social and political performance and ideological predictions.

This treatise uses logic, critical reason, neoclassical economic theory, experience and statistics to assess socialist performance and evaluate merit.

Statistics are unreliable and misleading, but suffice to draw useful inferences about socialist economic, social and political performance and ideological predictions.

GDP statistics are incomplete indicators of the quality of existence.

They ignore crimes against humanity and other relationships affecting the merit of socialist systems.

Quality of existence is subjective.

The comparative merit of socialism partly depends on ethical judgments about the moral worth of society's utilitarian experiences.

Merit in all its aspects is assessable with systems and social welfare functions.

Abram Bergson formulated mathematical systems and social welfare functions in 1938.

His systems and welfare functions are inclusive, meaning that appraisals of socialist performance take utilitarian account of consumption, employment and human relations including democracy, free choice, egalitarianism and ethics.

There are no reductionist fallacies.

Socialism is a protean phenomenon as well as sets of concepts and theories.

Bergson's systems and social welfare function framework illuminates the merit of socialist concepts, theories and phenomena.

Introduction

Socialism is a mélange of protean visions of a liberated, just, abundant, harmonious and sublime secular society that transforms workers into masters of their own destiny (Bestor, 1948).[1] Socialism esteems workers. It is not utopia for oppressors, a haven for the idle rich (Wharton, 1920)[2] or a reformist refuge for Charles Dickens' poor (Dickens, 1837). It is a "one for all, all for one" cooperative paradise for productive laborers prophesized by post-French Revolution working-class advocates including Robert Owen, Henri de Saint-Simon, Karl Marx, Étienne Cabet, Pierre-Joseph Proudhon, Georges Eugène Sorel, William Morris and George Douglas Howard Cole.[3] Socialism harmonizes everyone's libertarian individualism for working community well-being.[4] Virtuous individualism is not enough. Socialists advocate mutually supportive, fair and equitable treatment for productive people.[5] Socialism is best for them, but not necessarily for other groups who may prefer alternative schemes. This raises a host of nettlesome moral and philosophical issues sidestepped in this treatise by focusing on systems that maximize worker's quality of existence.

Socialism can exist in classless and amicably stratified societies that prioritize worker welfare (Robert Owen) or more narrowly for Marxists, the proletariat (agricultural and industrial wageworkers) (Durkheim, 1962; Giddens, 1977).

Socialists believe classless or benignly stratified regimes that prioritize worker welfare will display virtuous characteristics and lifestyles, but practice may not always accord with theory. There may be good and bad socialisms. The same principle holds for democratic free enterprise and Nordic corporatism (Smith, 1759).[6] The proof is in the pudding.

Socialism is not a state of nature like atoms and subatomic particles. Its luminaries are worldly philosophers (Heilbroner, 1953), visionary political economists (Marx), politicians (Proudhon, 1960),[7] intellectuals (Vladimir Lenin), activists (George Sorel) and artists (William Morris), not mathematicians and scientists like Isaac Newton and Albert Einstein. Socialists frequently claim that their constructs are scientific, but have never formulated their systems' laws of motion mathematically and empirically proven them (Newton, 1687).[8] They shun hard science, preferring to rely on proto-scientific suppositions (based on direct perception, physical analogies, free imagination, sentiment and cherry-picked empirical

DOI: 10.4324/9781003371571-1

evidence) and convictions to compose imaginative havens for the downtrodden (Hartman, 1996).[9] Many are sophists.[10] Some like François Marie Charles Fourier are crackpots (Beecher and Richard Bienvenu, 1971).

Socialist visions, whether sublime (eutopic)[11] or prosaic (ameliorating the plight of the working class), are speculative abstractions providing ambiguous guidance for gleaning real-world essentials through a glass darkly (Plato's allegory of the caves) (Plato, 1992). They may appear incontrovertible to believers; however, faith, witnessing and tenacity do not assure socialist dreams will come true (Dover, 1970).[12]

Philosophers and politicians imagine socialism differently. They disagree about essential characteristics, methods and culture. Socialism for artist William Morris (1834–1896) meant liberty (universal personal libertarianism),[13] equality, justice, peace and harmony with a Pre-Raphaelite touch for new men and women of taste (Morris, 1890).[14] Karl Marx (1818–1883) stressed abolishing all forms of proletarian exploitation and touted working-class harmony. Joseph Stalin (1878–1953) and George Bernard Shaw (1856–1950) demanded the eradication of class enemies (Carthaginian Peace).[15] African and Arab socialists equate socialism with precolonialist traditional ways of life (Friedland and Rosberg, 1964; Devlin, 1975).

Socialists believe that the key to success is establishing requisite institutions.

Philosophers, scholars, pundits, politicians, political economists and economists divide socialism into an array of core types (varieties of socialism) based on ownership, mechanisms, institutions (North, 2005; Williamson, 1975, 1996; Acemoglu and Robinson, 2012; Olsen, 2000); social, political and cultural criteria (Lane, 2007; Mizobata, 2008; Tugan-Baranovsky, 1910). Some emphasize ownership and mechanisms like markets versus plans, but most are content to romanticize socialism as the topsy-turvy antithesis of capitalism and autocracy,[16] without pondering how eradicating these sources of economic injustice will fully resolve worker discontent (Orwell, 1949; Gray, 1947; Kahneman, 1994). They choose sides on ethical grounds disregarding the intrinsic antidemocratic, antilibertarian and anti-religious proclivities of many post-French Revolution socialist regimes, making a leap of faith that well-intended socialisms will save workers from oppression and cure humanity's ills. They embrace abstract principles confident that there will be no slip between the lip and the cup (Kahneman, 1994).[17] Socialism for them is variously a panacea, a secular paradise or a passion play inspiring struggle and empowering the communist party.[18]

Devotion to the cause suited leaders like Vladimir Lenin and Joseph Stalin. It freed them from having to design efficient economic and social systems. They merely fostered the belief that anti-capitalism, anti-tsarism and anti-colonialism led by the vanguard of the proletariat would assure happy socialist endings (Nietzsche, 1966; Schopenhauer, 2010; Lenin, 1917).

The vision of a sky-blue life for post-ancien régime toilers that inspired the Jacobins during the French Revolution still captivates legions, but faith in the socialist cause fluctuates. Socialism as a political, cultural and social phenomenon surged in 1870–1940, however, was setback by Nazism and fascism (racist national romanticism) during World War II (Marco Gervasoni, 2016; McDonald, 1912; Sorel, 1999).[19] It regained momentum in the postwar years through the 1970s, only to wane with prosperity, the USSR's abandonment of central planning in 1987 and the rise of radical progressivism in the 21st century. The Soviet Union's demise appeared to sound the death knell of Moscow's communist brand of socialism, but socialist sentiment and politics made a comeback after the 2008 global financial crisis (Dean, 2012). It is currently rising in the United States, and nostalgia for Soviet-style communism is increasing in Russia (Soviet, 2020).

Will the demise of Bolshevism in the Soviet Union and Eastern Europe ultimately consign socialism to the "dustpan" of history? Does Marxist-Leninism deserve a second chance? Do declining numbers of industrial and agrarian day-wage workers make Marx's proletariat irrelevant? (Butler, 2016).[20] Are workers no longer the darlings of the intelligentsia? Is socialism an inspired proto-scientific vision? Can socialist philosophy, Sartre's socialist existentialism (Sartre, 1968, 1974, 2004; Merleau-Ponty, 1955, 1973) and proto-scientific musings become hard science? Are socialist institutions sufficient to assure that society will be sublime? If not, what is required to complete the task? Does liberation transform workers into angels? Is socialism a William Morris enchanted forest? Have politicians hijacked the socialist movement (wolves in sheep clothing)? Were late 19th-century Marxist and syndicalist militant revolutionary socialisms mostly political pretexts for seizing authoritarian power? Is Eduard Bernstein's evolutionary socialism (peaceful nonrevolutionary socialist transformation) an oxymoron as Marxist–Leninists contend? Are some forms of pragmatic socialism more promising than nonsocialist alternatives (Nove, 1992)? Has socialism as a catalyst for social transformation lost its potency? Does the past offer insights into tomorrow's possibilities and political prospects? Was socialism mostly a rallying cry for radical change? Is socialism "much to do about nothing"?

This book provides a net assessment and assesses feasible 21st-century pathways. It documents, probes and evaluates the multipronged quest by diverse socialist philosophers, artists, activists, politicians, planners and economists to transform pipedreams and proto-scientific theories into practice from the early 19th century to the present. The net assessment is inclusive. It employs national income statistics to measure material performance and supplementary indicators to gauge quality of existence. It assesses the comparative merit of socialist systems vis-à-vis each other and nonsocialist alternatives and considers socialist prospects.

The exercise finds that although some socialist systems outperformed others, none performed superlatively or demonstrably better than nonsocialist alternatives (Reed, 1919).[21] The collapse of communism in the Soviet Union and Eastern Europe, the failure of the world communist movement and a broad disenchantment with state ownership of the means of production in 1990–2008 (Csaba, 2022), central planning, Tito's Yugoslav style labor management[22] and anarcho-communalist kibbutzim reflect the inferior performance of 20th-century socialist systems.

The survey clarifies why Marxist-Leninism and Marxist-Titoism were undesirable and considers the possibility that other socialist schemes may enjoy a better fate. The main contenders are Xi Jinping's Chinese market version of Marxist communism, democratic socialism and 21st-century libertarian socialism. Marxist-Leninism is not moribund. It survives in North Korea and may still prove its mettle. Democratic socialism (both Marxist and non-Marxist varieties) is treading water. Anarcho-socialism has a small, diminishing, but still enthusiastic collection of practitioners. Twenty-first-century libertarian socialism is on the drawing boards.

The inclusive net assessment method also illuminates another subtle change affecting the socialist project moving forward. Workers are no longer the apple of many visionary eyes. Radical intellectuals, activists and politicians are prioritizing progressive causes like minority empowerment over the plight of the working class, and many are abandoning socialism for independent street justice movements championing affirmative action (Sandel, 2020),[23] restorative justice, anti-racism, fourth-wave feminism (Chamberlain, 2017), radical environmentalism, anti-imperialism, anti-meritocracy and universal guaranteed minimum incomes. Socialism that marginalizes, distains or exploits workers is an oxymoron for Marxists and democratic socialists, and difficult to reconcile with the rest of the socialist tradition.

Socialism as a cultural and political phenomenon only became nationally and internationally important in the 1870s when Marxism hitched its star to the idea of a politically insurgent revolutionary proletariat. The term socialism did not enter the popular usage until 1840, shortly before the landmark 1848 French February Revolution.[24] Earlier in the 19th century, it was mostly an infatuation for progressive reformers, eccentrics, transcendentalists, dreamers, bohemians, radicals and a handful of leftist politicians (Crowe, 1967; Delano, 2004). Charles Fourier's amour-topia, Saint-Simon's and Robert Owen's libertarian socialisms and Étienne Cabet's authoritarian leaning communism all failed. If workers' political and cultural significance continues to fade, faith in socialism as civilizations' best future will evaporate.

Twenty-first-century socialism remains conceivable because workers in the developed west are the majority. A movement by them for their protection and benefit undistorted by other agendas might succeed, but will require a clean break with 19th- and 20th-century trade unions and political parties that co-opt rather than promote workers' well-being.

The road ahead for socialism is apt to be rocky. The main socialist contenders are Marxist-Leninism, Xi Jinping's market communism, democratic socialism and 21st-century libertarian socialism. All four are pragmatic with a utopian gloss. They will face stiff competition from the Nordic corporatist model, varieties of capitalism and contemporary street justice progressivism.

All four promise to meet worker needs, but champion different economic mechanisms and cultures. Marxist-Leninism makes state ownership, planning and Spartan revolutionary virtue their sine qua non. State asset leasing, prosperity and power are the lynchpins of Chinese market communism. Democratic socialism mixes state ownership, private property, entitlements, government-managed markets with progressive lifestyles and an ambivalent attitude toward a democratic social contract. Twenty-first-century libertarian socialism stresses worker sovereignty.

The big four transition paths also differ. Marxist–Leninists prioritize defending the revolution (repressing capitalism) and building a turnpike to the future, subordinating current consumption and civil liberties. They sacrifice consumption and democracy today to create utopia tomorrow. Xi Jinping-style market communism is consumer friendly, but defers democracy, worker entitlement and social justice, while democratic socialists emphasize state ownership, cooperatives, state management and social leveling over Shangri-la. Twenty-first-century socialism emphasizes worker democratic libertarianism. All except the latter pay lip service to a sky-blue life for workers under conditions of full abundance and insist that utopia's attainment is inevitable, even though each denies the viability of the others' strategies. None of the four main socialist contenders makes immediately communalizing personal property, wealth, sexual relationships, child-rearing and altruistic sharing the defining characteristic of its system.

The similarity between varieties of capitalist markets on one hand and those employed by democratic socialism and Xi Jinping's Chinese communism on the other obscures matters further, as do close correspondences between most capitalist, progressive and socialist ideals including social welfare transfers.

Although Marxist–Leninists, market communists and democratic socialists insist that socialism is the antithesis of capitalism, this is only accomplished by demonizing free enterprise, individual libertarianism and ignoring abusive state socialist practices (Aron, 1955). Socialism and capitalism are not polar opposites. Their means and ends overlap. Both can be good and sometimes are evil (Levy, 1979). Both are improvable by rediscovering the importance of inclusiveness and consciousness raising that allows people to discard cultures of bellum omnium contra omnes (Hobbes, 1642, 1651),[25] and substitute enlightened self-interest and empathetic consensus building for the grand purpose of enhancing people's quality of existence. Both are vulnerable to abusive economic power, politics and bureaucratic inefficiencies (Bergson, 1979). The same principle holds for progressivism. Street justice virtue signaling does not assure virtue doing.

The wild card is 21st-century libertarian socialism, the possibility that workers may create movements and parties focused on their democratic betterment, undistorted by others' hijacking labor advancement for ulterior purposes. This is the most promising pathway.

The net assessment undertaken in this volume shows that despite more than two centuries of experience, socialist political rhetoric remains more about late-19th-century revolutionary social romanticism (Gray, 1947; Lukacs,1937)[26] and anti-capitalism than scientific designs for better living. There is no ethical consensus on the optimal configuration of socialist ends (Bauman, 2000),[27] institutionalist agreement about how to construct efficient socialist systems (Behrent, 2022) or transcendental standards for assessing comparative merit (Rosefielde, 2022).

A system prioritizing a fair deal for workers over rival claimants remains a possibility, but has little contemporary political support. It faces strong head winds from radical progressivism.

Finally, it is worth noting that westerners have been seeking to improve their lot since the Dark Ages. Socialism is only one of many strategies for coping with future shock (Toffler, 1970).[28]

Notes

1 Robert Owen coined the word socialism, but he did not rigorously define it. Lexicographers first recorded it in a dictionary in 1848.

2 In Wharton's world, noblesse oblige softens competition. Wharton depicts Shangri-la for women and other groups with little or no reference to the working class.

3 One for all, all for one (Unus pro omnibus, omnes pro uno) is the motto of Alexander Dumas' Three Musketeers and the traditional motto of Switzerland.

4 Enlightenment advocates of individualism like Adam Smith stressed that self-seeking had to be constrained by duty. He was anti-hedonist and a supporter of virtue ethics.

5 Socialism can be libertarian if it prioritizes worker welfare as its highest priority.

6 Good capitalism is perfectly competitive and bound by social moral duty. Bad capitalism is predatory.

7 Proudhon became a member of the French Parliament after the Revolution of 1848. He also was a racist stating that "The Jew is the enemy of the human race. This race must be sent back to Asia, or exterminated."

8 Isaac Newton (1642–1727) invented the calculus in the mid to late 1660s and formulated the theory of universal gravity. His *Philosophiæ Naturalis Principia Mathematica* transformed natural philosophy into modern physical science. Vilfredo Pareto (1812–1882), Paul Samuelson (1915–2009) and others attempted to accomplish the same feat for the non-Marxian economics branch of the soft social sciences. Soviet economists applied mathematical methods to planning, but not to socialist "natural" law.

9 Socialists are uncomfortable with the prevailing order and seek regime changes consonant with their notions of the people's will.

10 Sophists were ancient Greek teachers of rhetoric and philosophy prominent in the 5th-century BC. Later philosophers (particularly Plato) described them as sham philosophers, out for money and willing to say anything to win an argument.

11 The prefex "eu" implies sublime as distinct from "u" meaning nowhere. Sir Thomas More made the distinction. Socialist eutopia conveys euphoria felt by enthusiasts who believe that socialism is a panacea that fulfills everyone's fantasies without conflict or contradiction promised by Marx and Cabet under full communism. The socialisms of Owen, Saint-Simon, Cabet, Proudhon, Sorel, Cole and Marx–Lenin–Stalin make no such promise. They mitigate labor exploitation and improve the working class' lot.

12 Aristophanes ridicules Socrates as the headmaster of "Thinkery" in much the same manner Socrates lampooned the sophists.

13 Morris was a left libertarian. He advocated individual freedom to pursue anti-traditional ethical objectives like free love.

14 The Pre-Raphaelite Brotherhood was a group of young British painters who banded together in 1848 in reaction against what they conceived to be the unimaginative and artificial historical painting of the Royal Academy. They were inspired by Italian art of the 14th and 15th centuries, before the time of Raphael.

15 Peace achieved by completely crushing the enemy. The term derives from the peace imposed on the Carthaginian Empire by the Roman Republic.

16 Topsy-turveydom is a one-act satirical operetta (1874) by Sir William Gilbert. It spoofs utopian idealism and 19th-century pastoralism. On socialist romanticism, see Gray, 1947.

17 Kahneman stresses the importance of deliberative and logical "slow thinking."

18 The Passion Play or Easter pageant is a dramatic presentation depicting the Passion of Jesus Christ: his trial, suffering and death, culminating in resurrection and salvation.

19 Some contend that Hitler's Third Reich was socialist because his Nazi Party (National Socialist German Workers' Party) had a working-class constituency, and the government ran a controlled economy. Nazism does not qualify as socialism in this treatise because Hitler was not primarily concerned with the plight of the proletariat. His party's principal goals were race-based national and imperial domination.

  Fascism poses a similar classificatory problem. It was rooted in George Sorel's advocacy of revolutionary syndicalism. The intention of syndicalism was to organize strikes to abolish capitalism, not to supplant it with state socialism, but rather to build a society of working-class producers. This Sorel regarded as "truly true" Marxism in the Leninist spirit. However, unlike Lenin, Sorel and later Mussolini de-emphasized workers and promoted the nation. The Bolsheviks assumed the role of proletarian vanguard; Mussolini ruled as Italy's nationalist leader (Deuce). He created a corporatist system that included private business and aristocracy.

20

  Although just 25% of people now work in routine and manual occupations, 60% of Britons regard themselves as working class, a phenomenon described as a "working class of the mind." Nearly half of people in managerial and professional occupations identify as working class. Those who identify as working class are more likely to be conservative on a range of social issues, including the death penalty, homosexuality and morality, as well as immigration.

  www.theguardian.com/society/2016/jun/29/most-brits-regard-themselves-as-working-class-survey-finds

21 The analysis depicts the socialist experience as is without white washing (cf. John Reed, 1919).

22 Josip Broz Tito (1892–1980) was President of the Socialist Federal Republic of Yugoslavia, famous for discarding Marxist–Leninist–Stalinism for a Marxist labor-managed system.

23 Proponents of anti-meritocracy contend that society has an obligation to provide for the needy, even when they are unworthy from the standpoint of virtue and consequentialist ethics. The obligation is deontological. Marxist–Leninists by contrast despise "parasites."

24 The Republican and nationalist belief that the people should rule themselves drove the February Revolution. It ended the constitutional monarchy of Louis-Philippe and led to the creation of the French Second Republic. The new government was headed by Louis-Napoleon, the nephew of Napoleon Bonaparte, who in 1852 staged a coup d'état and established himself as a dictatorial emperor of the Second French Empire.

25 Bellum omnium contra omnes, a Latin phrase meaning "the war of all against all," is the description that Thomas Hobbes gives to human existence in *De Cive* (1642) and *Leviathan* (1651).

26 Social revolutionary sentiment suffused high cultural circles throughout the 19th century, including Richard Wagner and Franz Liszt. Liszt was active among socialist German nationalists in Dresden during the late 1840s, regularly receiving such guests as the conductor and radical editor August Röckel and the Russian anarchist Mikhail Bakunin.

27 There are three types of ethics: virtue, consequentialist and deontological (logical positivism). Socialist theorists have not rigorously justified their schemes on any of these bases, and contemporary postmodernist ethics insists that agreement on "true" values is unattainable in contemporary societies.
28 Alvin Toffler, *Future Shock*, New York: Random House, 1970.

References

Acemoglu, Daron and James Robinson. (2012). *Why Nations Fail: The Origins of Power, Prosperity and Poverty*. New York: Crown Publishers.

Aron, Raymond. (1955). *The Opium of the Intellectuals*. Paris: Calmann-Lévy.

Bauman, Zygmunt. (2000). *Liquid Modernity*. Cambridge: Polity Press.

Beecher, Jonathan and Richard Bienvenu (eds.). (1971). *The Utopian Vision of Charles Fourier Selected Texts on Work, Love and Passionate Attraction*. Boston: Beacon Press.

Behrent, Michael. (2022). "Left and New Left Critiques of Liberalism." In András Sajó, Renáta Uitz and Stephen Holmes (eds). *Routledge Handbook of Illiberalism*. London: Routledge.

Bergson, Abram. (1979). "The Politics of Socialist Efficiency." *The American Economist*. Vol. 24, No. 2, 5–11.

Bestor, Jr., Arthur E. (1948). "The Evolution of the Socialist Vocabulary." *Journal of the History of Ideas*. Vol. 9, No. 3, 259–302.

Butler, Patrick. (2016). "Most Britons Regard Themselves as Working Class, Survey Finds." *Guardian*. www.theguardian.com/society/2016/jun/29/most-brits-regard-the mselves-as-working-class-survey-finds

Chamberlain, Prudence. (2017). *The Feminist Fourth Wave: Affective Temporality*. New York: Palgrave Macmillan.

Crowe, Charles. (1967). *George Ripley: Transcendentalist and Utopian Socialist*. Athens: University of Georgia Press.

Csaba, Laszlo. (2022). "Illiberal Economic Policies." Chapter 42, In András Sajó, Renáta Uitz and Stephen Holmes (eds.). *Routledge Handbook of Illiberalism*. London: Routledge.

Dean, Jodi. (2012). *The Communist Horizon*. New York: Verso.

Delano, Sterling. (2004). *Brook Farm: The Dark Side of Utopia*. Cambridge: The Belknap Press of Harvard University Press.

Devlin, John. (1975). *The Baath Party: A History from Its Origins to 1966*. Palo Alto: Hoover Institute Press.

Dickens, Charles. (1837). *Oliver Twist*. London: Richard Bentley

Dover, Kenneth. (1970). *Aristophanes: Clouds*. London: Oxford University Press.

Durkheim, Emile. (1962). *Socialism*. New York: Collier.

Friedland, Wiiliam and Carl Rosberg Jr. (eds.). (1964). *African Socialism*. California: Stanford University Press.

Gervasoni, Marco. (2016). "Mussolini and Revolutionary Syndicalism." In Spencer Di Scala, Emilio Gentile (eds.). *Mussolini 1883–1915: Triumph and Transformation of a Revolutionary Socialist*. New York: Palgrave Macmillan.

Giddens, Anthony. (1977). "Durkheim's Political Sociology." *Studies in Social and Political Theory*. London: Hutchinson.

Gray, Alexander. (1947). *Socialist Tradition Moses to Lenin*. London: Longmans, Green and Co. Ltd.. https://cdn.mises.org/The%20Socialist%20Tradition%20Moses%20to%20 Lenin_3.pdf

Hartmann, D. (1996). "Protoscience and Reconstruction." *Journal of General Philosophy of Science*. Vol. 27, 55–69.

Heilbroner, Robert. (1953). *Worldly Philosophers: The Lives, Times and Ideas of the Great Economic Thinkers*. New York: Simon &Schuster.

Hobbes, Thomas. (1642). *De Cive*.

Hobbes, Thomas. (1651). *Leviathan*.

Kahneman, Daniel. (1994). *Thinking: Fast and Slow*. New York: Farrar Straus & Giroux.

Lane, David (ed.). (2007). *The Transformation of State Socialism: System Change, Capitalism or Something Else?* Basingstoke: Palgrave MacMillan.

Lenin, Vladimir. (1917). *Imperialism: The Highest Stage of Capitalism (Империализм как высшая стадия капитализма)*. Saint Petersburg: Zhizn i Znaniye.

Levy, Bernard-Henri. (1979). *Le testament de Dieu*. Paris: Grasset & Fasquelle.

Lukacs, Georg. (1937). "Richard Wagner as a 'True Socialist'." Литературные теории XIX века и марксизм (Nineteenth Century Literary Theories and Marxism). Moscow: State Publishing House of the USSR.

McDonald, James Ramsay. (1912). *Syndicalism: A Critical Examination*. London: Constable & Co. Ltd.

Merleau-Ponty, Maurice. (1955). *Les aventures de la dialectique*. Paris: Gallimard.

Merleau-Ponty, Maurice. (1973). *Adventures of the Dialectic*. Evanston: Northwestern University Press.

Mizobata, Satoshi (ed.). (2008). *Varieties of Capitalisms and Transformation*. Kyoto: Center for Advanced Economic Analysis.

Morris, William. (1890). *News from Nowhere*. NA.

Newton, Isaac. (1687). *Philosophiæ Naturalis Principia Mathematica*. NA.

Nietzsche, Friedrich. (1966). *Beyond Good and Evil*. New York: Vintage Books.

North, Douglas. (2005). *Understanding the Process of Economic Change*. Princeton: Princeton University Press.

Nove, Alec. (1992). *The Economics of Feasible Socialism Revisited*. London: Routledge.

Olson, Mancur. (2000). *Power and Prosperity: Outgrowing Communist and Capitalist Dictatorships*. New York: Basic Books.

Orwell, George. (1949). *Nineteen-Eighty Four*. London: Secker & Warburg.

Plato. (1992). *The Republic*. New York: Everyman's Library.

Proudhon, Pierre-Joseph. (1960). "On the Jews." In Pierre Proudhon (ed.). *Carnets de P. J. Proudhon*. Paris: M. Rivière.

Reed, John. (1919). *Ten Days that Shook the World*. New York: Boni and Liveright.

Rosefielde, Steven. (2023). "Economic Systems: Nature, Performance, Prospects." In Bruno Dallago (ed.). *Handbook of Comparative Economic Systems*. London: Routledge, 69–80.

Sandel, Michael. (2020). *The Tyranny of Merit: What's Become of the Common Good?* New York: Macmillan.

Sartre, Jean Paul. (1968). *Ghost of Stalin*. New York: George Braziller.

Sartre, Jean Paul. (1974). *Between Existentialism and Marxism*. New York: William Morrow and Company.

Sartre, Jean Paul. (2004). *Critique of Dialectical Reason*, Vol. 1. London: Verso.

Schopenhauer, Arthur. (2010). *The World as Will and Representation*, Vol. I. Cambridge: Cambridge University Press.

Smith, Adam. (1759). *The Theory of Moral Sentiments*. London: Andrew Millar.

Sorel, Georges. (1999). *Reflections on Violence*. London: Cambridge University Press.

Soviet. (2020). "75% of Russians Say Soviet Era Was 'Greatest Time' in Country's History – Poll." *Moscow Times*. www.themoscowtimes.com/2020/03/24/75-of-russi ans-say-soviet-era-was-greatest-time-in-countrys-history-poll-a69735

Toffler, Alvin. (1970). *Future Shock*. New York: Random House.

Tugan-Baranovsky, Mikhail. (1910). *Modern Socialism in Its Historical Development*. London: Swann Sonnenschein.

Wharton, Edith. (1920). *Age of Innocence*. New York: D. Appleton & Company.

Williamson, Oliver. (1975). *Markets and Hierarchies: Analysis and Antitrust Implications*. New York: Macmillan.

Williamson, Oliver. (1996). *The Mechanisms of Governance*. New York: Oxford University Press.

Part I

Socialist Cross Currents (1820–1920)

1 Utopia

Philosophers have been pondering the possibility for designing utopian social orders and refuges for at least two and a half millennia (Nozick, 1974, 1978). Socrates, Plato, Aristophanes, Tao Yuanming and Thomas More probed the perplexities of human nature, government, institutions and laws needed to maximize society's quality of existence. Aristophanes lampooned the notion of a utopian feminist egalitarian city-state (Ecclesiazusae), and Tao Yuanming conjured a poetic dream of a naturally harmonious communalist Shangri-La (Peach Blossom Spring) especially appealing to Chinese and Japanese literati. It was a precursor of William Morris' late-19th-century Arts and Crafts socialism (Morris, 1890). The Renaissance statesman, Sir Thomas More, devised a utopian commonwealth governed by egalitarian humanist philosophers for the benefit of the Republic's slaveholders. All addressed a smattering of issues that concern contemporary socialists including communal ownership of the means of production and fair treatment for workers and women. They philosophized about how regimes might maximize rulers, elites and citizen life quality, but never considered the problem of empowering workers and the downtrodden. Liberation, social justice, class equality, entitlements, affirmative action, worker, women and transgender fulfillment were off their radar screens. The utopias of ancient sages strove to be ideal in various senses, but were nonsocialist because they served the august and did not seek to make workers masters of the realm. Imaginary natural laws allowed Tao Yuanming's Peach Blossom Spring communitarians to do as they pleased and contentedly consume. More's Utopia succeeded in a similarly facile way by persuading people to reduce their demand to match deficit supplies.

Plato's Republic and Laws

Plato expounds his views on the possibility of ideal government in the *Republic* and *Laws* (Pangle, 1980; Plato, 1968). Many have suggested that his Republic is sublime or aspires to be so because it improves the lot of everyone, but this conflates improvement with the best.

Plato did not ponder whether his Republic maximized its rulers' utility (quality of existence), was the best form of government for everyone, or the workers. He

DOI: 10.4324/9781003371571-3

limited himself to philosophizing about making the Athenian Republic prosperous, efficient, stable and sustainable for its privileged rulers, and the happiness
(eudaimonia) of everyone else, given the unstated premise that the happiness of
commoners depends on complying with their masters wishes (happy servants),
rather than maximizing their own well-being.

Athenian society was hierarchical. It had well-defined upper, middle and
lower classes and a separate stratum of slaves. Upper class male Athenians were
wealthy property owners. They were citizens, and often held high military ranks.
Most were men of leisure. The upper class was a small minority admired by the
European nobility in the 18th century (Clark, 1976), which distained commerce,
business and manual labor.

The middle class in Athens was mostly "metics" (resident aliens, including freed
slaves) who could not vote or own land. They were predominantly merchants or
traders.

The lower class was composed mostly of emancipated slaves. Many were from
very poor families. They were not citizens and had little political influence.

Slaves were commonplace. Even poor families owned one or two while
wealthy families had 50 or more. Slaves were unransomed war prisoners, stolen
as children from enemies, or imported from other countries. Their masters could
emancipate them.

Women were an appendage of their social class. Their husbands or families
determined their status. They were prohibited from working outside of their
homes, were not citizens and could neither vote nor own property.

Plato's ideal prosperous, efficient, stable and sustainable Republic accordingly
might have enhanced the happiness of the middle and lower classes, slaves and
women insofar as they benefited from a well-functioning hierarchical system,
but it precluded their being their own masters. He did not endorse universal
libertarianism.

Plato's communist advocacy for the upper classes had only trickle-down benefits
for the middle and lower classes, slaves and women. It did not include mass education, equality of income and status or women's liberation.[1] His sole purpose in
communizing wealth and improving the lot of elite women was to enhance the
efficiency of the Republican order by rationalizing the use of resources and curbing
moral hazards that might bias the judgment of philosophers governing Republican
affairs. Plato claimed that private property and family concerns induced rulers to
act unjustly diminishing happiness and spawning discontent. "Communism of
property and family" he opined would allow philosophers supported by state taxes
to efficiently and scrupulously govern for everyone's good.[2]

Plato considers the costs and benefits of a more egalitarian utopia that he
calls Magnesia in his discourse on the *Laws*. Magnesian philosophers pay closer
attention to the institutions and rules governing productive labor with an eye
toward fairness and efficiency. They treat the middle and lower classes of both
sexes better, but do not make their well-being Magnesia's central purpose. Once
again, Plato's primary concern is improving the elite's quality of existence. It treats
workers as means rather than ends and his utopia consequently is antisocialist.

Aristophanes "Assembly of Women"

Aristophanes (446–c. 386 BC) was an Athenian comic playwright whose life over-lapped Socrates (470–399 BC) and Plato (428–347 BC). His play the "Clouds" written in 432 BC ridicules Socrates caricaturing him as a sophist who beguiles his students by conflating wisdom with tomfoolery and trains them how to swindle simpletons.[3] It does not address egalitarianism or a commonwealth of property and family, but Aristophanes does caustically satirize Socrates' "communism for the elite" (as recounted by Plato in the Republic) in his comic farce "Ecclesiazusae" (Assembly of Women) written in 393 BC. The subject of the Assembly of Women is a communist gynocratic Republic (political rule of women) run amok.[4] The play's message is that egalitarian gynocracy is preposterous.

The play begins with Blepyrus' high status Athenian wife Praxagora organizing a feminist plot to usurp the male governed Assembly (parliament) and replace it with a gynocratic Republic. The conspirators wear false beards and men's clothing. Praxagora criticizes the Assembly Men for being unpatriotic and corrupt. She persuades them to turn control of the government over to the women because "after all, men employ women as stewards and treasurers in their households." She explains furthermore that women are superior to men because they are harder workers, devoted to tradition and do not bother with useless innovations. As mothers, women will be more protective of soldiers and feed them extra rations, and as shrewd bargainers will secure more funds for the city.

The Assembly of Men convinced by these arguments allows Praxagora to install a regime that bans all ownership of private wealth and establishes equality for all non-slaves. She justifies these reforms by explaining that people will no longer need personal wealth because state taxes levied on the middle and lower classes will cover all expenses. She adds furthermore that men and women will be entitled to have sex with anyone they desire, if they first sleep with uglier members of the opposite gender. There are no transgender references. The community will share parental expenses because children will no longer know their fathers. Slaves will work the fields.

Praxagora also observes that under her gynocratic Republic the elite will no longer be bothered with lawsuits for the repayment of debts because there can be no debt in a society without private wealth. There is no need to borrow, when the elite can freely tax the productive. Thievery will cease because citizens will receive fair shares. Everyone except slaves will reside, live and eat in common spaces, courthouses and porticos converted into communal dining halls. Prostitution will be superfluous for the upper echelon, but slaves can continue plying the sex trade among themselves.

Praxagora's communist gynocracy in Aristophanes' farce, however, did not improve Athenian life, despite her promises. It malfunctioned. The elite willingly feasted at the Republic's expense (supported by taxes on workers) but refused to transfer its wealth to the communal kitty and pay taxes. A young girl and her lover lament the new laws governing sex. They desire each other, but an old woman insists the young man obey the law and sleep with her first. As the young girl and the old woman fight over the boy, two more old women drag him away against his will.

In the final scene, Praxagora looks forward to sharing a feast together with her husband but sees Blepyrus strolling to the banquet arm-in-arm with two amorous nymphs. The farce concludes with the chorus praising the lavish feast awaiting Blepyrus and his paramours.

Aristophanes' play proves nothing about the pros and cons of communist gynocracy or modern socialist possibilities. It nonetheless serves as a salutary reminder that communist ideas involving commonwealths of property, equality, women and utopia are neither novel, nor intrinsically socialist in the post-French Revolution sense. Athenians were aware that Spartan attitudes toward various aspects of communal sharing differed from their own. They were acquainted with tales of mythical Amazon women, but none of this mattered from a socialist perspective because the ancient Greeks never contemplated designing practical or ideal regimes devoted to serving the needs of workingmen and women. Nor did Aristophanes and Socrates display the slightest interest in scientifically investigating the full utilitarian behavioral consequences of their schemes and constructs. They were philosophers and satirists content to suggest or oppose social reforms, who gave no serious thought to economic efficiency, worker welfare or socialist revolution.

Tao Yuanming's Peach Blossom Spring

The political and social organization of China's Eastern Zhou dynasty (770–256 BC) differed significantly from Plato and Aristophanes' contemporary Athens. It was clan and Confucian extended family-centric and remained so through the Eastern Jin dynasty (317–420 AD) when Tao Yuanming (365–427 AD) penned his poetic fable "Peach Blossom Spring" (421 AD) about an ethereal communitarian utopia where people led idyllic lives, oblivious to the outside world. The poem, which has inspired generations of communalist utopian romantics,[5] describes a lost paradise unperturbed for 600 years, hidden beyond a forest of blossoming peach trees, discovered fortuitously by an errant voyager.

The villagers greet him and explain that their ancestors escaped to their Peach Blossom Spring sanctuary during the civil unrest and despotism of the Qin dynasty (221–210 BC) and have thrived peacefully thereafter.

They live simply and contentedly together as a community of families where "enough is plenty." They are satisfied with their lot, have no natural enemies and are able to provide sufficiently for everyone to exist happily from the fruits of gratifying productive labor. There is no private property (capital assets). Land is abundant. Villagers farm individually or cooperatively as they fancy. Output is distributed and consumed as everyone desires without want or conflict. No one aspires to wealth, power or distinction. No one covets, steals, abuses or indulges in debauchery. Men and women live harmoniously together without rigid gender role assignments. Villagers do not have to cope with problems of class and tyranny because Tao's utopia has no private property, no castes, strata or classes, no exploitation and the people amicably rule themselves in accordance with the harmonious laws of nature. The Peach Blossom Spring is a spontaneous "natural" socialist Shangri-La where everyone is a productive communal worker, no one wants, and people live happily and peacefully together.

The commune's virtuous attributes rest on an assumption of natural harmony. Tao's utopia presumes that if people live in a classless environment where "enough is plenty," have no aspirations for more, and no insecurities, the resulting order will be naturally ideal. Denizens of the Peach Blossom Spring will not be tempted by immoral desires, bedevil themselves with greed, power-seeking and personal ambitions or micro-manage anything. They will instinctually shun life's snares (Buddhism's second noble truth), know the way (Taoism), adhere to Confucius' family precepts[6] and build their lives in accordance with the principles of Nongjia (Agrarian School of Tillers).[7]

Tao Yuanming's libertarian natural harmonist premises are appealing, but patently unrealistic. Individuals often desire more than enough. Immoral passions and power seeking mislead them. They grow weary of egalitarianism and must cope with scarcity and external threats. The natural law supporting Tao's vision is a figment of his poetic imagination. The Peach Blossom Spring is charming, but like Karl Marx's adolescent musings in the *Economic and Philosophic Manuscripts of 1844* (Marx, 1959), fanciful.

Thomas More's Happy Commonwealth of Virtue, Tolerance and Moderation

Sir Thomas More, Lord High Chancellor of England (1529–1532), a noted Renaissance humanist, social philosopher, statesperson and lawyer, was more practical than Tao Yuanming.[8] He did not pin his hopes on the goodness of human nature. His *Utopia*, published in 1516, 21 years before his beheading,[9] is a narrative fable that serves as a platform for satirizing the defects of 16th- century society and politics and illustrates the potential benefits of progressive Republican libertarian humanist reform. Sir Thomas More, like Plato two millennia earlier, does not contend that his Republican policy recommendations are ideal or wisest. He treats his utopia (literally "nowhere") as a "happy" (**eu**topian) alternative to the 16th-century European order.

The Utopia of More's parable is an island commonwealth Republic governed by a prince elected through a secret ballot, and philosophers of appropriate rank. Society is hierarchical and depends on the slave labor of prisoners of war, criminals and the poor. Every household has two slaves.

Utopia is not a spontaneous natural order. The prince and philosophers wisely command and persuade people how to conduct themselves best. Everyone obediently and appreciatively complies.

The wealth and produce of Utopia as the prince and philosophers decree belong the Republic (Commonwealth). Everyone consumes whatever goods he or she desires gratis from state warehouses, but the Republic's sumptuary laws prohibit ostentatious consumption. There is no scarcity or shortages because as in the

Peach Blossom Spring "enough is plenty." Citizens rotate houses among themselves every ten years, and houses are always unlocked. Everyone is required to live in the countryside, farming for two years at a time, with women doing the same work as men. Citizens also must learn at least one other essential trade: weaving (mainly done by the women), carpentry, metalsmithing and masonry. All able-bodied individuals must work at least six hours per day but can work longer at their discretion. Scholars of any social rank may become officials or priests.

Although many regard More's utopia as a socialist vision, they are mistaken. His Republic succors some of the poor, nationalizes wealth, distributes income according to need and modestly increases women's autonomy, but it retains slavery, social ranks and subordinates the proletariat to the kindness of its Renaissance social humanist masters. Workers are subservient, not self-governing socialist humanists.

More's utopia like its Athenian and Peach Blossom Spring predecessors is flawed. It displays some sympathy for the plight of the toiling masses but fails to consider whether the workers prefer sops from the elite in lieu of empowerment. It ignores the unwillingness of humanist rulers to accept the sacrifices Sir Thomas More imposes on them and the implausibility of the outcomes he promises.

Tao Yuanming's communal utopia, and Socrates, Plato, Aristophanes and More's aristocratic Republican communism are pleasant "Midsummer Night's Dreams" (Brooks, 1979).

Notes

1 Plato treated elite women as equals not for their own benefit but because he wanted the Republic to harness their services.
2 Plato's communism denies guardians' and soldiers' private property including house, land or gold and silver. They live in the state-managed barracks and eat in the common mess.
3 *The Clouds* (patron goddesses of beguiling rhetoric), published in 423 BC, caricatures Socrates. Plato suggests in his *Apology* that the caricature contributed to Socrates' trial and execution. Aristophanes ridicules Socrates as the head of "Thinkery" in the *Clouds* and the goddess sings hymns to his utopias.
4 Aristophanes frequently satirized women. The "Assembly of Women" is his only play that does so from the standpoint of utopian governance. Cf. Lysistrata and Thesmophoriazusae.
5 Tao Yuanming's poems urge readers to drop out of official life, move to the country and take up a cultivated life of wine, poetry and farming. By the Tang Dynasty, Tao was elevated to greatness as a poet's poet, revered by Li Bai and Du Fu.
6 Tao Yuanming's utopia does not stress Buddhist Enlightenment, Taoist spiritualism and magic or Confucian prosperity seeking.
7 The Agriculturalists (Nongjia) believed that Chinese society should emulate the example of the sage king Shennong, who worked in the fields with his subjects. They believed that agricultural development was the key to a stable and prosperous society.
8 More served Henry VIII as Lord High Chancellor of England from October 1529 to May 1532.
9 More was beheaded for "treason" on July 1535. The charges of high treason (violating the Treasons Act 1534 by challenging the King's Supremacy) related to More's malicious silence.

References

Brooks, Harold (ed.). (1979). *A Midsummer Night's Dream, The Arden Shakespeare, 2nd series.* London: Methuen & Co.

Clark, Kenneth. (1976). *The Romantic Rebellion: Romantic versus Classic Art.* London: Omega.

Marx, Karl. (1959). *Economic and Philosophic Manuscripts of 1844.* Moscow: Progress Publishers.

Morris, William. (1890). *News from Nowhere.* London: Longmans.

Nozick, Robert. (1974). *Anarchy, State, and Utopia.* New York: Basic Books.

Nozick, Robert. (1978). "Who Would Choose Socialism?" *Reason.* (May), 22–23.

Pangle, Thomas. (1980). *The Laws of Plato.* New York: Basic Books.

Plato. (1968). *The Republic of Plato.* (1968). Oxford: Oxford University Press.

2 Libertarian Socialism

The term socialism in the 1820s entered the European lexicon in 1848 (Bestor, 1948).[1] It was a post French Revolution philosophical concept that had no exact meaning, but was broadly perceived as an amalgam of utopian and pragmatic principles espoused by Charles Marie-Francois Fourier, Robert Owen, Count Claude Henri de Rouvroy de Saint-Simon, Étienne Cabet and the youthful Karl Marx. Fourier, Saint-Simonians and Cabet were utopian advocates of various communalist schemes. Owen also briefly sponsored communal experiments but primarily advocated giving workers a hand-up and making them self-reliant. All found aspects of industrialization and business repellent, but Saint-Simonians believed that markets could propel national prosperity. Some like Owen counseled progressive reform. Others sought retreat to counterculture communes. All were libertarian advocates of the Rights of Man (personal freedom) as protection against oppression, including the illiberal state. They were democrats.

Their shared attitudes suggested that the contradictions among the various schools could be reconciled to achieve a consensus about a libertarian form of socialism everyone agreed seemed practical and best, despite doctrinal differences. The consensus never materialized. Libertarian socialism remained plural reflecting fundamental disagreements about essential socialist characteristics and priorities. Charles Marie-Francois Fourier, Robert Owen, Count Claude Henri de Rouvroy de Saint-Simon, Étienne Cabet, the youthful Karl Marx and later thinkers failed to reach consensus by 1870. Illiberal Marxist-Leninism and revolutionary syndicalism superseded them 1871–1991.

Fourier (Amour-topia)

Charles Marie-Francois Fourier, the patron saint of hedonist socialism, led a Walter Mitty double life (Thurber, 1939). He cultivated the public persona of a nondescript traveling salesman, but was an enfant terrible and quack metaphysician driven by distain for petty commerce, delusions of grandeur and unrequited amorous fantasies (Manuel, 1965; Riasanovsky, 1969; Fourier, 1968a, 1971; Fourier and Franklin, 1901). He equated socialism with sensuality and was disinterested in workers, equality, justice and human solidarity.

DOI: 10.4324/9781003371571-4

Fourier was born in 1772 in Besancon France into a respectable commercial family. His father was a cloth merchant who introduced him to the business world at an early age with adverse consequences (Van Eck, 2010). According to his personal testimony, he swore an oath of eternal hatred against the chicanery and fraud of French trade when he was seven (Riasanovsky, 1969). Soon thereafter, he confessed to simony and precocious fornication (Manuel, 1965) and enjoyed secretly playing the role of a humanity's savior in his pipedreams and obscure writings.

Fourier's father died in 1781, leaving him an estate of 200,000 francs (40,000 dollars)[2] (Pellarin, 1920). In 1791 before the proclamation of the First French Republic, he lived in Lyon working for the merchant M. Bousquet, and fought on the side of monarchists against Third Estate insurrectionaries.[3] French revolutionary authorities arrested him. He barely escaped execution. From 1791 to 1816, Fourier worked as a commercial agent and itinerant salesperson in Paris, Rouen, Lyon, Marseille and Bordeaux. He neither married, nor fathered children leading a mundane bourgeois public existence.

Fourier, who never called himself a socialist (Bestor, 1948), devoted his energies 1808–1821 to writing books enlightening the world about the joys of "amour-topia" (New Amorous World) (Guarneri, 1991).[4] He sought high patronage for his communal schemes promising to make Napoleon, Czar Alexander I and Baron Rothschild, respectively, Omniarch (master of world), Tetrarch (master of a Continental Europe) and King of Jerusalem in return for their patronage. He died after a prolonged struggle with a bowel ailment in Paris in 1837 surrounded by a small band of antibusiness, communitarian disciples, who proselytized chaste versions of his amour-topia stressing the virtues of puritanical phalanx living, gender equality and the rational communal labor organization that threw the baby out with the bathwater. Socialism as Fourier understood it was inseparable from carnal rapture.[5]

Like all those who would subsequently call themselves socialists, he condemned poverty, corruption and injustice, but more than anything else was an apostle of libertinism (Feldman, 20046).[6] Although Fourier descried civilization's inequities and discontents, he did not place peasants and workers on a pedestal. He found industrialization repellent (as William Morris did later) and did not object to inequality if everyone had enough. He applauded women, homosexual and transsexual libidinous rights, but not other aspects of women, homosexual and transgender empowerment. He was neither a social justice nor class struggle crusader. He did not reject individualism, private property, markets, finance, stock exchanges and entrepreneurship. He lauded stratification and income inequality (by talent and blood) (Fourier, 1968a, 29, 32, 35, 251–252).[7] He was uninterested in economic efficiency, planning, technocracy, industrialization, growth, development, modernization, and displayed only a perfunctory concern for fair wages and prices (Tugan Baranovsky, 1910; Riasanovsky, 1969, 61–62).[8] Fourier never said that proletarian rule, state ownership of the means of production, egalitarianism, criminalization of markets, social leveling, cooperation, affirmative action, solidarity, equal opportunity, social welfare, restorative justice, human potential and individual happiness were indispensable attributes of socialism. His primary mission was encouraging communal swingers to revel in sensuality (Marquis de Sade, 2016; Nicolas Restif de la Bretonne, 1769),[9] subject to his harmonizing orchestration (Fourier, 1968b, 377–382).[10] Fourier's vision was a "fête galante" (French aristocratic bacchanal) for 18th-century nobles depicted in paintings by Nicolas Poussin, Nicolas Lancret and Antoine Watteau (White, 2021).[11]

Fourier was not the only socialist to advocate libertinism. Henri de Saint-Simon and Robert Owen endorsed free love, but Fourier alone made sensual pleasure socialism's raison d'être (Marcuse, 1955). Bacchanalian orgies were his socialist key. They propelled amour-topia to full socialism in the same way that Marx's historical dialectic drove capitalism to communism (Marx, 1959; Jordan, 1967; Thomas, 2008).[12] If Fourier harbored any doubts (Goldberg, 2001),[13] he did not betray them (Barrie, 1911).

Fourier never tested his theories. He found his fantasies sufficient. None of his disciples tried. Some antiseptic versions of Fourier's communalism succeeded during the 19th century, but all eventually perished.

Quack Science

Fourier was a quack proto-scientist (Hartmann, 1996; Heilbroner, 1999). He devised his theory on the premise that the natural laws governing physical and human relations discerned by inspired intuition, observation and logic were true without empirical verification. The first part of his premise was scientific in the spirit of Nicolaus Copernicus (1473–1543), Galileo di Vincenzo Bonaiuti de' Galilei (1564–1642), Isaac Newton (1643–1727) and Charles Darwin (1809–1882). Scientific hypotheses require facts, logic and intuition. Fourier was not a mystic. The second part, however, was quackery because Fourier presumed that his eccentric perceptions, intuitions and deductions sufficed to identify socialist laws without empirical confirmation (Rosefielde, 1976, 1980).[14]

Fourier believed that divine natural law compelled pleasure seekers to maximize their quality of existence through amorous utility seeking.[15] Amorous goods and services were the only variables in his objective function. The sublimity of amour-topia was fantasy.[16]

Marx's early writings were similar, although less bizarre. He promised full abundance, harmony and bliss because he claimed that intuited dialectical materialist natural law guaranteed full communism.

Contrived Natural Laws

Fourier mesmerized his acolytes by devising an amour-topic social welfare function based on numerological analogies making welfare depend on harmonizing relationships across personality types.[17] He identified 405 passions (without explanation) and divided them into three categories: luxury, amour and settings. Luxury contained five subcategories: visual, olfactory, auditory, gustatory and tactile-erotic. There were four varieties of amour: friendship, ambition, love and family, and three types of settings: composite, papillon (butterfly) and cabal (intrigue).

Luxury refers to voluptuous passions experienced through the five senses. Other goods and services enter his utility functions as by-products generated by fête galante. Amour involves sensual interpersonal relationships (carnal, platonic and spiritual). Settings provide contexts for trysts and encounters (Fourier, 1968a, 266–268).[18] "Composites" are mixed arrangements, papillon (butterflies) flutter and cabalists relish intrigue.

Fourier claimed that natural law harmonizes luxury, amour and settings and maximizes welfare in the present and across all futures (Fourier, 1968a, 143, 145, 151), adding that fête galante increase the sensual potentials of humans, plants, animals and celestial bodies. Amour-topians enjoy trans-ethereal vision and grow elegant simian tails (Fourier, 1968a, 77, 82–83, 122, 132; Fourier, 1968b, 253n, 254n).[19]

Harmonious Institutions

Fourier chose Phalanstère (grand hotels) for staging fête galante. Their size was determined by 405 passions manifested in at least two sexes interacting in no less than two settings (composite, papillon and cabal) determined its size (no less than 1,620 bacchants) (Fourier, 1968a, 5; Fourier, 1968b, 5, 308; Riasanovsky, 1969).[20] They produced ordinary goods and amorous services. Amorous goods included "animal magnetism and intercelestial electromagnetic aromal fluid consumed by the planets and other heavenly bodies. Grand hotels used labor, talent and capital to produce consumer goods (Fourier, 1968a; Riasanovsky, 1969, 61n). Technologies were surreal (Fourier, 1968a, 81). They included genetically engineered visual enhancement permitting people to observe intercelestial aromal copulation, ichthvo-nervism allowing members to overcome the sensation of pain (Fourier, 1968a, 186, 190–192) and Albino touch enabling bacchants to feel the cosmic fire (Fourier, 1968a, 190–192).

Fourier claimed that fête galante guaranteed full abundance because he was the "focus of social perfection" (Fourier, 1968a, 374–381). He predicted that his socialism would produce 37 million poets that equal of Homer, 37 million geometricians equal to Newton and 37 million comedians equal to Moliere (Riasanovsky, 1969, 91). He promised that anti-tigers would carry seven travelers at 25 miles per hour between Grand Hotels, and anti-crocodiles would kill crocodiles (Riasanovsky, 1969, 91). Saltwater seas would become lemonade.

Although Fourier states that there will be a bourse in every Grand hotel, transactions were not competitive. Numerical analogies determined terms of exchange (Riasanovsky, 1969, 53).[21] Markets were piquant games, rather than competitive vehicles for solving scarcity problems. Fourier's socialism from start to finish was delusional and worthy of Marx's ridicule (Fourier, 1968a, 377–383; Mason, 1928, 257).

Saint-Simon: Libertarian Market Socialism

Count Claude Henri de Rouvroy de Saint-Simon was the founder of libertarian market socialism for the national productive community (Bestor, 1948).[22] He designed his paradigm to foster rapid industrial modernization, development and economic growth. His socialism was a precursor of democratic socialism, blending laissez-faire, entrepreneurship, state-supported infrastructure building and reform club social assistance (Manuel, 1956, 134).[23] Saint-Simon's seminal idea was turning the reins of power held by the Ancien Régime in the 18th century over to productive citizens[24] and reform clubs protecting the public interest (Manuel, 1956, 134; Saint-Simon, 1803a, 1813; Goyau, 1912).[25] Entrepreneurs would pioneer new technologies transforming France's economic, political and social landscape ushering in an era of industrial prosperity with narrowly targeted state support (Locke, 1660, 1662; Manuel, 1956, 118). Reform clubs would devise progressive policies to deal with issues of liberté, égalité and fraternité.[26]

Libertarian socialism prevented the nobility from restoring the feudal order, living idly off peasant, worker, professional and entrepreneurial labor. It opposed their efforts to repress free enterprise (Mason, 1931, 648).[27] Saint-Simon, like Jean Jacques Rousseau (1712–1778) before him, felt that all humans are rational and should have equal opportunities (Rousseau, 1997). He saw the state as liberty's potential enemy and sought to prevent government from fettering and overtaxing business.[28] He was an unabashed meritocrat (Ryan, 2012; Sandel, 2020; Young, 1958).

Some contend that Saint-Simon's hostility toward state intrusion in business and cradle-to-grave social services proves that his system was anti-socialist, but this is mistaken. Saint-Simon believed that big government was apt to do more harm than good. He insisted that French entrepreneurs would avoid exploiting wage labor (Manuel, 1956, 134) and deserved what they earned (Manuel, 1956, 132–133). Unlike contemporary democratic socialists, Saint-Simon argued that competitive remuneration and prosperity took precedence over egalitarianism. There was a place for leveling in his libertarian socialism. He favored restrictions on passive private property (land, bonds and securities) (Bougle and Halevy, 1924, 52; Lichtheim, 1969, 43),[29] and contended that reform clubs would protect "la classe la plus nombreuse et la plus pauvre" (Saint-Simon, 1825). Saint-Simon believed that modest state industrial policies and parsimonious entitlements were best, even though Marxists insist this is not good enough (Gershenkron, 1969; Gerschenkron, 1962, 23—24; Mason, 1931; Markham, 1964; Tugan Baranovsky, 1910).[30]

Saint-Simon

Saint-Simon was of noble lineage. Born in Paris on October 17, 1760, he traced his ancestry to Charlemagne. His family, like other noblesse de l'epee (Nobility of the Sword), was impecunious, so Henri was compelled to seek his fortune in the military.[31] He saw action in the American War of Independence and became a member of the Society of Cincinnatus.[32] During the French Revolution, he collaborated with the Jacobins.[33] He renounced his title on September 20, 1793, adopted the peasant surname Bonhomme, engaged in a series of enterprises with international bankers, Dantonists[34] and Hebertists,[35] amassing a huge fortune in land speculations. Although arrested during the Reign of Terror, he avoided prosecution.

Saint-Simon led a licentious entrepreneurial and social activist life during French First Republic (1792–1804), presiding over a salon of bankers, politicians, intellectuals and artists. He was a French First Republic "mover and shaker."[36] It was in this affluent period that he wrote Lettres d'un habitant de Geneve (1803) that prefigured most of his later libertarian socialist ideas (Saint-Simon, 1803b).[37] By 1805, Saint-Simon had dissipated his fortune. Penniless, he turned his energies to philosophical and scientific projects during the French Empire (1804–1814), but gradually went insane. He was committed to a sanitarium in 1813.[38] Saint-Simon recovered his sanity sometime before 1814 and at the age of 54 began a new career as pamphleteer and apologist for the liberal, industrial haute bourgeoisie, participating in a circle of liberal economists that included Jean-Baptiste Say and Charles Dunoyer.[39] He published a series of major works during this period including "On Reconstruction of the European Community"(1814), L'Industrie (1817), Le Politique (1819), L'Organisateur (1819), Du susteme industrial (1821–1824) and Opinions litteraires philosophique et industrielles (1825). His writing (1819—1825) emphasized libertarian socialist entrepreneurship and state-supported industrial modernization. Shortly before his death in 1825, he expanded his socialist outlook championing the poorest class (Saint-Simon, 1825),[40] and by claiming that the death of leading nobles and officials of the French bureaucracy would have no adverse economic effect (Leroy, 1925; Manuel, 1956, 1965; Markham, 1964; Weill, 1896). The Bourbon authorities arrested him for incitement.[41]

School of Paris

Following Saint-Simon's death in 1825, his followers pressed libertarian socialism in new directions. The children of Saint-Simon in Frank Manuel's characterization altered his core economic libertarian socialist paradigm in three ways: (1) they elaborated the institutional structure and administrative functions of High Administration; (2) devised a mechanism excluding idlers from receiving unearned income and (3) adopted a collectivist social welfare agenda. High administrators under the revised order organized industries into trade associations coordinated and controlled by an industrial bank like contemporary Japanese keiretsu (Aoki, 1988; Aoki and Patrick, 1994).[42] The Central Bank supervised industrial banks with ownership gradually vesting with the state achieved by proscribing family inheritance (Barnes, 1958, 93; Mason, 1931, 665–667).[43] The abolition of passive ownership effectively made productive laborers (entrepreneurs and workers) sovereign, operating in society's interest. The Saint-Simonian social welfare agenda remained primarily libertarian socialist, but adopted an outlook compatible with championing the cause of "la classe la plus nombreuse et la plus pauvre" via Saint-Simonian business policy (Tugan Baranovsky, 1910).[44] The Soviet and Chinese communist rapid industrialization ethos echoed the Saint-Simonian credo.

The basic levers of Central Bank control were monetary and financial. Banks adjusted interest rates to pace capital accumulation (Mason, 1931, 680). Regulations and directives guided business, but not coercive central planning (Barnes, 1958, 103–105; Mason, 1931, 675–680; Manuel 1956, 177–178; Tugan Baranovsky, 1910, 113–116; Gray, 1947 168; Landauer, 1959, 31–35).[45]

The children of Saint-Simon also recommended harmonizing the interests of productive workers, managers and industrial bankers to maximize profit (Barnes, 1958, 79).[46] In sum, Saint-Simonians circa 1832, advocated employing coercive power through banking networks and private planning to control economic activity (Barnes, 1958, 93),[47] tapping the cooperative and creative forces of all productive laborers to achieve modestly egalitarian prosperity.

Pecqueur

Constantin Pecqueur (1801–1887) was a minor member of the disbanded Saint-Simonian circle in 1832, but his theory deserves mention because it turned libertarian market socialism on its head by blending meritocracy with egalitarianism (Cole, 1962, 179–182; Halevy, 1948, 51–54; Lichtheim, 1969; Tugan Baranovsky, 1910, 116).[48] Pecqueur's socialist model was a state indicatively planned, market industrial system founded on state ownership of the means of production that excluded idler classes and sought to produce a mix of goods and services in accordance with market place preferences (Pecqueur, 1842).[49] The French government employed a similar approach called dirigisme 1946–1988.[50] Pecqueur's indicative planners computed each industry's production target based on prior year performance (Nielsen, 2008; Tugan Baranovsky, 1910, 116),[51] an approach known as planning from the achieved level (Birman, 1978).

Pecqueur advocated distributing the national product equally to all citizens without regard to the value of their contributions. All that remained of Saint-Simon's meritocratic, competitive market libertarian socialism was an indicatively planned market with collective ownership of the means of production rewarding laborers at egalitarian wages (Tugan Baranovsky, 1910, 123),[52] and permitting them to shop with equal purchasing power (Tugan Baranovsky, 1910, 120–121).

Pecqueur arrived at his egalitarian solution because he disliked Saint-Simon's meritocratic ethic. Human merit he contended depends on good will, not the value of an individual's marginal product. He was not purblind. He recognized the need for penalties to discourage shoddy work (Tugan Baranovsky, 1910, 118), competency examinations (Tugan Baranovsky, 1910, 123)[53] and special assistance for the handicapped, sick, elderly and young (Tugan Baranovsky, 1910, 118). He even accepted inheritance based on labor earnings (Tugan Baranovsky, 1910, 120) and the principle of consumer choice (based on egalitarian purchasing power). He proposed to pay egalitarian wages with fiat money usable only for the purchase of consumer goods and services (Tugan Baranovsky, 1910, 120), with prices fixed by labor time, except when demand for scarce goods (rare) exceeded supply (Tugan Baranovsky, 1910, 121). Despite the cumbersome interjection of the labor theory of value, Pecqueur's aim was clear enough. He preferred egalitarian consumer choice to rationing. Given a set of prices, consumers maximized their utility by selecting the most desirable bundle of goods and services within their budget constraints.

Pecqueur's model has numerous defects. It severs the link between occupational preferences and factor rewards, reducing production potential. It distorts the terms of the labor-leisure trade-off and introduces a battery of inefficiencies impairing the system's social merit.

Robert Owen: Cooperative Socialism

Robert Owen (1771–1858) was the founder of cooperative socialism designed to tame laissez-faire for the benefit of vulnerable workers by constraining profit seeking, promoting cooperation, wage-fixing and public programs including unemployment assistance. He began as a reformer with progressive moral views, but ended as an advocate for a cooperative socialist system that prioritized worker welfare over competing concerns.

Robert Owen

Robert Owen, the son of a saddler and ironmonger, was a Welsh textile manufacturer, philanthropist social reformer and founder of cooperative socialism. In 1793, he joined the Manchester Literary and Philosophical Society and supported better factory working conditions as a Manchester Board of Health committee member.

In July 1799, Owen moved to Scotland where he purchased and benevolently managed the New Lanark spinning mill. He bought out his partners in order to raise wages and reduce hours. Owen refused to hire children under ten at his textile mill. He provided decent, sanitary housing, libraries and educational facilities free to his employees, devised schemes to ameliorate unemployment (Polanyi, 1968),[54] and instilled his workers with an appreciation for reason and rectitude.

New Lanark

The business prospered and he became rich (Siméon, 2017; Butt, 1971). New Lanark became a showplace for enlightened capitalism, visited by a host of dignitaries including Tsar Alexander I of Russia.[55] Owen moved to America in 1824 investing most of his fortune in an experimental cooperative community at New Harmony, Indiana. It failed. In 1828, he returned to London, where he continued to champion the working class, cooperatives and the trade union movement. He supported the passage of child labor laws and free coeducation (Harrison, 1968).

In 1832, Owen opened the National Equitable Labor Exchange, an institution that exchanged goods for notes denominated in labor time and led the Grand

National Consolidated Trade Union (GNCTU). Both ventures quickly failed (Owen, 1920; Cole, 1925; Harrison, 1969; Packard, 1968; Pollard, 1971). The only lasting result of Owen's social activism was the cooperative movement,[56] although his lifework inspired the Fabian and Guild socialism. He died penniless apart from an annual income provided by a trust established by his sons in 1844 (Cole, 1953). Fabian and Guild socialists consider Owen the spiritual founder of their movements (Cole, 1962). Marxists are less admiring (Gatrell, 1970, 7–86).[57]

Libertarian Cooperative Democratic Socialism

Owen never penned a socialist manifesto. Nonetheless, the sum and substance of his reformist activism is tantamount to a cooperative socialist model. Like most of his contemporaries, he viewed the world through Adam Smith's eyes at the turn of the 18th century. He considered private property, liberty and the pursuit of individual happiness natural rights. Everyone was entitled to freely choose vocations, relationships and spend incomes on whatever they desired. He was a democrat, comfortable with private property, profit seeking and markets, and had an 18th-century Enlightenment sense of moral duty. Individualism and social responsibility were complements.

Owen also believed that individuals and governments had a duty to devise and implement progressive institutional change.

> Any general character, from the best to the worst, from the most ignorant to the most enlightened, may be given to any community, even to the world at large, by the application of proper means; which means are to a great extent at the command and under the control of those who have influence in the affairs of men.
>
> (Owen, 1966, 14)

Had Owen been a devout Christian, which he was not,[58] he might have channeled his efforts at ameliorating laissez-faire's flaws through alms and Christian political action. Instead, he took it upon himself to mitigate harsh labor conditions by pioneering new forms of industrial management and advocating state-funded human capital development and employment security.[59] Owen emphasized humanitarian obligation and worker cooperation enabling everyone to flourish (Paine and Philip, 2008).[60] Had Owen anticipated Herbert Spenser's social Darwinism with its implicit tough love antipathy toward public social spending (survival of the fittest and natural selection), he still would have championed assisting workers "marked for extinction" (Dickens, 2000).[61] Owen was a compassionate pragmatist, not an austere evolutionary scientist.

His libertarian cooperative socialism had seven distinct components:

1. Equitable social transfers: fair wages and public assistance.
2. Social investment in human capital: free public education.
3. Cultivating communitarianism: cooperative communities.

4. Equitable exchange: fiat wage and price setting based on labor time (Martin, 1970).[62]
5. Unemployment safety net: cooperative communities as employers of last recourse.
6. Consumer and producer cooperatives: enhancing worker purchasing power by eliminating superfluous middle-persons.
7. Trade unionism: worker-based platform democratically lobbying for fair labor protection.

Six of these seven principles subsequently became pillars of Fabianism, Guild socialism, the labor movement and contemporary European democratic socialism. The exception was labor time-based wage and price fixing. The seven principles emphasized worker self-help and placed few demands on other segments of the polity. Entrepreneurs, managers, financiers, merchants, aristocrats, rentiers, professionals and civil servants were free to pursue their own interests, but encouraged to support worker benefit in accordance with their consciences. Owen was not a staunch egalitarian, an advocate of state ownership of the means of production or democratic syndicalism (workplace democracy). He was a competitive private market-friendly libertarian with a social conscience who advocated cooperative self-reliance and opposed dependency. He endorsed cooperative communalism like New Harmony for some, but communalism was not mandatory for everyone. He favored a government supporting the Benthamite pluralist end of "producing the greatest happiness to the greatest number; including those who govern and those who obey" (Owen, 1920 63).[63]

Owen would have disapproved of the modern cradle to grave democratic socialist welfare state, preferring to restrict his libertarian socialism to public support of universal education, modest housing, transportation, medical, unemployment and retirement assistance, aid for special needs (handicapped) and fostering cooperative self-reliance.

He considered his pluralist cooperative socialism beautiful because it protected labor without being unfair to others or inefficient. Contemporary European democratic socialism according to his taste would have seemed inefficient, inequitable and anti-socialist to the extent that it prioritizes privileged big businesses and progressive causes like affirmative action, restorative justice, anti-meritocracy, radical feminism, activist environmentalism and open immigration over fair treatment for the self-reliant working class. Owen was not the father of the welfare state and contemporary democratic socialism. He was the voice of the cooperative socialist opposition.

Cooperatives

Cooperatives are the distinguishing feature of Owen's brand of socialism. They provide a refuge from internal and external competition analogous to Confucian families and Japanese groups. Members produce cooperatively for internal consumption and competitively for the external market. They choose technologies (production functions), input acquisition, labor conditions, decision-making rules and set production goals on a consensus-building basis that places great stock in mutual support. Cooperation does not necessitate egalitarian remuneration, but Owen's rules inclined in this direction by rewarding labor for hours worked rather than for skill grade or marginal productivity. Productive members share enterprises profit paying investors a "normal return" on equity in a manner similar to Yugoslavia's egalitarian labor managed firms.

Owen, however, left the operating rules to community members. There is no written record of how New Harmony communal members proceeded, but the rapid failure of Owen's experimental American communities suggests that they were unable to reach amicable consensus. Eyewitness testimony supports the inference. Josiah Warren,[64] a participant at New Harmony, asserted that the community was doomed to failure for lack of personal property and sovereignty. In describing New Harmony, he explained:

> We had a world in miniature – we had enacted the French revolution over again with despairing hearts instead of corpses as a result…. It appeared that it was nature's inherent law of diversity that had conquered us… our 'united interests' were directly at war with the individualities of persons and circumstances and the instinct of self-preservation….
>
> (Warren, 1856)

Guild Socialism

The failure of Robert Owen's cooperative socialism went unaddressed until the advent of guild socialism in the 1890s (Carpenter, 1920, 1922; Cole, 1920a, 1920b; Hobson, 1914; Orage, 1917; Penty, 1906, 1919, 1920; Reckitt and Roberts, 1918; Russell, 1919; Taylor, 1919; Maeztu y Whitney, 1916; Webb and Sidney, 1965).[65] The solution that evolved assigned the task of economic governance to enterprise workers and their representatives in labor organizations called guilds that coordinated interindustrial activities on a democratic basis, while remaining mum about private ownership and nonindustrial actors. It proposed worker control over industrial production, distribution and public services, without nationalizing the means of production. Parliament democratically dealt with noneconomic matters.[66] Guild socialists believed that vesting authority in civic guilds reminiscent of preindustrial England and preserving libertarian democratic principles in noneconomic matters would mitigate the antidemocratic thrust of militant trade unions.[67] They opposed Marxist-Leninism 1890–1920, but some admired Stalin's USSR in the 1930s. George Douglas Howard Cole (1889–1959) was guild socialism's most eminent architect during and immediately after World War I.

George Douglas Howard Cole

Cole was an English libertarian Fabian socialist,[68] an advocate for the cooperative movement (Cole, 1944, 1951) and the voice of guild socialism in its heyday.

He became interested in Fabianism while studying at Balliol College, Oxford (Cole, 1971). Cole joined the Fabian Society's (club) executive under the sponsorship of Sidney Webb (1859–1947) and became a principal proponent of guild socialist ideas, a libertarian socialist alternative to Marxian political economy. He espoused these ideas in *The New Age* before and during the World War I[69] and *The New Statesman*, a weekly founded by the Beatrice Webb (1858–1943) and George Bernard Shaw (1856–1950). Cole was a leader of the second generation of Fabians between the wars.[70] He gradually drifted away from guild socialism toward democratic socialism after 1920. Cole began as a reformer with progressive moral views, but ended as an advocate for a cooperative socialist system in various forms that prioritized worker welfare over competing concerns.

Fabianism

Crafts persons in medieval England worked in self-regulating civic associations called guilds that assured goods and services met high professional standards. Arthur Penty (1875–1937) desiring to impart this spirit to 20th-century England's industrial order coined the term guild socialism linking paradise lost to modern times in 1906 (Penty, 1906).[71]

Cole's version of guild socialism was a Janus-headed late-19th-century socialist movement. It cast one eye backward toward an imaginary, harmonious preindustrial civic past (Carpenter, 1922; Cole, 1920a, 45; Cumming and Kaplan, 1991; Gray, 1947, 434; MacCarthy, 1994)[72] and another eye forward toward a postcapitalist future where workers and their representatives coordinate the economy on a democratic basis for the benefit of the working class (Morris, 1891).[73] The future Cole envisioned required replacing capitalism with a classless society of squires. Gentlemen and women are equals (Morris, 1891, 135). Neither private property nor conventional markets exist, goods are freely distributed, people work for the pleasure of labor and strive for a wholesome life. Guild socialism's watchwords were worker cooperative ownership, control, shared distribution and harmony achieved through direct participatory democracy based on the majority rule of equals (Tawney, 1920; Maeztu y Whitney, 1916).[74] Cole believed that his program would enable England to exchange its satanic mills for a utopia empowering worker-squires to actualize their human potential.[75]

Cole's utopia assumes that economic control belongs in the hands of pertinent functional units. Miners should control mining, railway personnel railways and teachers the schools. Recognizing that other groups, both workers and nonworkers also have stakeholder interests in various productive activities, he nonetheless maintained that factory worker interests were paramount (Cole, 1920a, 35).[76] Workers in all functional units should regulate their work environment. They should choose technologies, set hours of labor, wages and the product mix (Cole, 1920a, 73–74). In Cole's world, the factory is the fundamental unit of economic life. As far as possible, it must be self-governing and infused with the spirit of association. Each factory is a basic functional unit of guild industrial organization (Cole, 1920a, 48—49; Cole, 1920b, 1920c).[77]

Factories in the same sector collaborate in national guilds (Cole, 1920a, 46). Sectoral national guilds set general factory policy, including wages, but are careful to allow maximum member self-governance. The same principle applies at the regional level (Cole, 1920a, 48, 68–70).

Conflicts of opinion among workers at all levels in the guild hierarchy are resolved democratically. Factory workers via the ballot set policy and establish production routines. They elect their own members, or hire technocrats, managers and professionals to perform supervisory tasks and choose delegates to represent them at regional sectoral guild congresses. Regional sectoral guild congress members elect executive boards of the national sectoral guilds. Cole asserts that ultimate control in each industrial sector rests at the factory level because workers dissatisfied with their delegates can recall them. He acknowledges that representatives cannot perfectly adjudicate all conflicts, but argues that direct participatory democracy, where the majority always respects the opinions of comrades in the minority, is the fairest way to organize the national guilds to avoid anarchism.

Inter-sectoral (guild) activities are coordinated analogously. Industrial guilds for each sector elect delegates to congresses of national guilds charged with the task of resolving conflicting interindustrial production issues at the local, regional and national level via the ballot (Cole, 1920a, 68), including interindustrial pay scales in a manner that assures skilled workers receive equal pay regardless of their employer (Cole, 1920a, 71–72). Disputes are democratically settled.

Cole's guild socialist production scheme is comprehensive and coherent. Factory workers directly and indirectly are democratically in command of production, finance, technology and interindustrial input-output coordination.

The distribution of goods and services parallels production. Cole creates consumer guilds starting with households, expanded vertically and horizontally across individuals, localities, regions and the nation tasked to resolve competing distributive demands via the ballot (Carpenter, 1922, 183; Cole, 1920a, 1–23, 130).[78]

If supply determined by producer guilds equals consumer demand adjudicated by consumer guilds, no further adjustment is required. If not, presumably Cole would create a democratically elected reconciliation guild across workers, individuals, localities, regions and the nation tasked to equilibrate demand and supply in lieu of the invisible hand. This solution applies to a single moment. If workers and consumers change their preferences, everyone would have to revote, or satisfice.

Cole subordinated competitive negotiation to democratic rule because he believed that individual workers should defer to majority sentiment. He tried to ameliorate the damage to unfettered worker utility maximizing by expanding consumer cooperatives, which blended member democracy with the competitive acquisition of wholesale supplies, and by creating elected consumers' public goods guilds at the local, regional and national level to negotiate the acquisition of supplies from producer guilds (Cole, 1920a, 86–95). Neither adjustment was fundamental. Expanding consumer cooperatives left the deep problem of national demand and supply disequilibrium mostly unaddressed, and consumers' public goods guilds merely usurped democratic elected governments right to serve community needs with general tax revenues. Cole was unable to square the circle. Guild socialism benefitted workers at the expense of their free choice. Cole was convinced that this was in the people's best interest, that balloting was satisfactory enough to disregard guild socialism's deadweight inefficiency losses.

Guild socialism as Cole conceived it, substituting democratic balloting for the invisible hand (or linear programming) and marginalizing state government was not only institutionally impractical (Cole, 1920a, 120, 137),[79] it was extravagantly inefficient and unacceptable to excluded members of the British electorate. Cole's cooperative democratic socialist confection was a proto-scientific fantasy (Cole, 1920a, 35–36),[80] and a political nonstarter that would have caused economic, political and social mayhem had it been tried. Guild socialism was never a practical idea (Carpenter, 1922, 234; Cole, 1920a, 35–36; Gray, 1947, 454; Hobson, 1914, 1917).[81] It was never tested, swept aside by other socialist currents.

Socialist Refuges: Oneida and Icaria

Socialist communes strive to create counterculture lives based on cooperative labor and shared consumption of income and assets. Other characteristics like gender, race, ethnicity, social equality, polyamory and religion are secondary. Work and shared labor rewards from industrial and agrarian activity are primary.

Robert Owen's New Harmony experiment satisfies this definition. He funded and organized a cooperative socialist community in New Harmony, Indiana 1825–1827, where members shared work obligations and the fruits of their labor after deductions for other inputs costs, and Owen's capital services (normal profit). Members dealt with other aspects of cooperation and shared consumption from industrial and agricultural activities, as they preferred. Although, Owen's experiment quickly failed, this did not discourage imitators.

Christian socialists founded the Oneida Community, located in New York in 1848. Followers of the libertarian socialist Étienne Cabet established an Icarian Community at Nauvoo, Illinois, in 1849.

The Oneida Community

John Humphrey Noyes, a Christian perfectionist founded the Oneida Association (later Oneida Community) (Nordhoff, 1875, 259–301; Noyes and Foster, 2001).[82] The community believed that Jesus had already returned in AD 70, making it possible for them to create Jesus' millennial kingdom themselves, and be free of sin and perfect in this world, not just in Heaven (a belief called perfectionism). Noyes considered himself a utopian socialist because the Oneida Community communalized productive property, shared possessions and the fruits of member labor. Sexual relations and child rearing were communal. The Community, like New Harmony, was liberal with an authoritarian tinge. Noyes, like Fourier, was a master choreographer, especially with regard to polyamorous complex marriage.[83]

The Oneida community strongly believed in a system of free love – a term coined by Noyes – known as complex marriage, where any member was free to have sex with any other who consented (orchestrated by Noyes). Christian perfectionists frowned on possessiveness and exclusive relationships.

Complex marriage meant that everyone in the community was married to and had sexual relations with everyone else. The concept was functionalist, not erotic, based on command instead of amorous choice. The result of Noyes' rationing scheme, where he personally had first dibs, was a farce of the sort ridiculed by Aristophanes 2,300 year earlier with adolescent boys servicing lustful hags and vestal virgins lecherous old men.

Unlike Fourier's amour-topia, ecstasy was not the primary purpose of Oneida's perfectionist socialism. Complex marriage was an integral component of perfectionist Christian sharing, not a bacchanal.

Oneida's socialists could refuse functionalist group sex on one pretext or another (headaches), but were shamed to acquiesce despite a host of moral and practical issues. "Free love" might cause women to be perpetually pregnant, burdening the Community with unwanted mouths to feed. Noyes solved the problem to his own satisfaction by requiring "male continence," where men avoided ejaculation. The system worked well in this regard (Claeys and Sargent, 2017), but libertarian and moral problems caused serious dissention (Kern, 1981).[84] Many found sex on Noyes command repugnant,[85] and members disagreed about the age of consent (Roach, 2001).[86] Noyes himself received notice of an impending arrest warrant for statutory rape and fled the country to Ontario, Canada in 1879.[87] Shortly thereafter, the Community abolished complex marriage.

Mandatory indoctrination also impaired libertarian free thought and choice. Every member of the community was subject to criticism by committee or the community as a whole, during obligatory general meetings. The goal was to eliminate undesirable character traits. Various contemporary sources contend that Noyes himself was the subject of criticism, although less often and of probably less severe criticism than the rest of the community (Nordhoff, 1875, 292–293).

In accordance with Christian perfectionist socialist principle, all community members worked, each according to his or her abilities and shared equally in communal consumption. Women tended to do many of the domestic duties (Kern, 1981). Skilled positions tended to become the perquisites of high-status members. Noyes assigned unskilled jobs in communal halls, fields or industries to everyone else. As Oneida prospered, it began hiring outsiders to work in these positions. The Community was a major local employer, providing jobs for approximately 200 outsiders in 1870 in the manufacture of leather travel bags, the weaving of palm frond hats, the construction of rustic garden furniture, game traps and tourism. Silverware production for which Oneida subsequently became famous began in 1877 (Hays, 1999).

The Oneida Community dissolved itself in 1880 transferring much of the common property to a joint-stock company renamed Oneida Community Ltd. (Robertson, 1972, 301–311). Its socialist cadre transformed themselves into capitalist shareholders, and never looked back.

Icaria

Icaria is a fictional country, reminiscent of Sir Thomas More's "utopia" (happy commonwealth of virtue, tolerance and moderation) romanticized by Étienne Cabet (1788–1856) in his 1839 communist utopian novel *Voyage et aventures de lord William Carisdall en Icarie* (Travel and Adventures of Lord William Carisdall in Icaria) (Hilquit, 1903).[88] Cabet subsequently evoked the utopian aura of his mythical paradise to symbolize his concept of a sublime communist society. He coined the term communism in 1839 (nine years before Marx and Engel's *Communist Manifesto*) using it in the sense of a social order based on egalitarianism and the common ownership of property for all productive people, including mid-level bourgeois professionals. The Icarian Community at Nauvoo, Illinois attempted to test his Icarian dream for national communism led by Cabet himself cast as Moses (elected dictator) shepherding his followers to the promised land. His Icarian script proscribed private property, markets, inequality, authoritarianism to foster prosperity, stable employment and the spirit of communist community.[89] Cabet believed that Icaria would resurrect the ethos of early Christian egalitarianism without the Catholic Church's feudal influence (Cabet, 1846).

He discussed his Icarian project with Robert Owen in the 1830s and sought his advice about where to locate his American colonies in 1847 (Sutton, 1994).[90] Cabet respected Owen's socialist intentions, but aspired to go beyond his advocacy of cooperatives. Cabet considered them half measures (Johnson, 1966, 2008). He did not believe that they would revolutionize social relations. Although, Cabet did not comment on the Oneida Community, he believed that Icaria alone represented humanity's communist future, and would not have considered Noyes' heterodox perfectionist Christianity a serious rival.

History failed to validate his self-confidence. The Icarian Community at Nauvoo embraced his communist institutions but did not succeed.

Étienne Cabet

Étienne Cabet was born in Dijon, France in 1788 to a middle-class family of artisans. His father was a cooper. He attended a Roman Catholic secondary school and earned a Doctor of Law degree in 1812, but chose to devote his energies to politics and journalism. Following the fall of Napoleon Bonaparte in 1815, Cabet campaigned for republicanism under monarchical tutelage. He was a prominent member of the republican insurrection committee[91] and played a leading role in the Revolution of 1830.

Cabet wrote a four-volume history of the French Revolution and served as a deputy to the lower chamber of the National Assembly in 1834, emerging as a fierce opponent of the Orléanist conservative regime and a potential revolutionary leader. King Louis Philippe retaliated against Cabet's outspoken criticism by exiling him for five years. He went to England where he drafted *Voyage et aventures de lord William Carisdall en Icarie*, returning in 1839. Readers received the book well, treating it as a blueprint for a glorious future.

In 1841, Cabet revived the journal *Populaire*, which he founded in 1833. It was widely read by French workers. An estimated 400,000 people considered themselves Icarians in 1847. In May 1847, Le Populaire carried a lengthy article entitled "Allons en Icarie" (Let Us Go to Icaria), proposing the establishment of an American colony based on Icarian communist political and economic ideals and calling for volunteers. Icarians harkened to the call and set sail in February 1848. They expected to succeed under Cabet's visionary guidance (Johnson, 1966, 2008).

Communist Order

The Nauvoo Icarian Community adopted Cabet's *Voyage en Icarie* charter. Cabet was its elected president, but governed in an authoritarian manner. He appointed officers to administrate finance, farming, industry and education without consultation. Charter members were required to donate all their world goods to the colony. They agreed to live in communally owned housing and work cooperatively without pay. They shared the fruits of their collective labor equally. New applicants required approval by the majority of adult males, after living in the commune for four months, forfeiting all personal property, and pledging $80. Two rooms were allotted to each family in an apartment building with identical furnishing. Children lived with their parents until the age of four. They lived in a boarding school thereafter, and visited their families on Sundays; arrangements intended to foster a love for the community "without developing special affection for parents." Icarians practiced no religion, voluntarily gathering instead in "Cours icarien" to discuss Cabet's writings and Christian morals and ethics. Marriage was the norm. Divorce was acceptable, providing couples swiftly remarried.

The Nauvoo Icarian village consisted of a dwelling of individual apartments, two schools (one for girls and the other for boys), two infirmaries, pharmacy, one large community kitchen with dining hall, a bakery, a butchery and a laundry room. A steam-powered flour mill, a distillery, pigsty and sawmill were added. Icarians traded with outsiders. They sold their handmade shoes, boots, dresses, lumber and alcoholic beverages.

Work was gender specific. Men were tailors, masons, wheelwrights, shoemakers, mechanics, blacksmiths, carpenters, tanners and butchers. Women worked as cooks, washerwomen and ironers. Men and women participated equally in weekly community assemblies, voting on constitutional changes and the election of the officer in charge of clothing and lodging.

Education was Icaria's highest social priority, followed closely by culture. The community held several concerts and theatrical productions for the entertainment of its members. The Nauvoo Community library contained over 4,000 books. Icaria also published *Colonie Icarienne*, a biweekly newspaper.

Communist Content

Cabet ideal communist solution for humanity's woes proscribed private property, markets, inequality, authoritarianism and established old world administrative institutions to foster prosperity, stable employment and the spirit of communist community. Icaria accomplished some of these things. It abolished private property, and there was rough equality in consumption, but this did not usher in the promised era of harmonious prosperity. There was full employment, but this was hardly surprising because per worker dividends were adjustable. When times were hard, members automatically cut their own wages (Weitzman, 1986). Cabet promised self-sufficiency, but Icaria traded with outsiders. He praised democracy, but commanded obedience. Icaria honored equality more in word than deed. Some members held permanent superior jobs. Women did not enjoy equal job opportunities and status. They voted on some matters, but not on others. Icaria was disharmonious.

Performance

Icaria sought to maximize members' quality of existence by substituting shared ownership, labor, living quarters, dining, education and other consumption activities for free choice. Cabet's communism was a form of voluntary family business where members empathetically set the terms of endearment through trial and error, with an asset forfeiture clause imposed on those who defected. Members believed that "two could live more cheaply than one" and that the benefits of a shared labor and community outweighed constraints on individual freedom. Those who chose Icaria hoped that the benefits of communism would surpass its costs, anticipating a happy-ending. Cabet's followers were not doubting Thomas. They were committed to the project, prepared to adjust their behavior and make personal sacrifices to increase Icaria's chances for success, but discovered that net benefits were insufficient. Icaria disappointed member expectations, failed to eradicate discord and caused enough discomfort that members chose to exit (paying the forfeiture) and disband rather continue. The failed experiment falsified the presumption that communist institutions, in a capitalist free environment would empower members to behave angelically. Icaria failed to create a sustainable communist order, or purge humanity of its flaws. Cabet was wrong on both scores. Institutions were not determinative and people were not divine.

There is no evidence that the Nauvoo Icarian experiment would have fared better had Cabet been more democratic. More member inclusive Icarian projects ended badly. Nonetheless, many blame the man, instead of his communism. Cabet prohibited talking in workshops, banned the use of tobacco or alcohol and sought to increase his authority by constitutionally granting elected presidents control over all aspects of the community's government in 1855. A strong majority initially supported his position, but the minority remained disgruntled, perpetuating the factional battle and ending in a formal split. Icaria expelled the Cabetists. Cabet led about 170 of his followers out of Nauvoo in October 1856, heading downstream along the Mississippi to establish a new colony near Saint Louis. Shattered by the loss of 40% of its members and no longer able to raise financial support in France, the remnant Nauvoo Community disbanded in 1860.

Cabet's authoritarianism doubtlessly contributed to the Nauvoo Community's demise. Like Vladimir Lenin, his belief that workers could not build a sustainable socialist society without vanguard's guidance caused dissension. This, however, obscures the fundamental issue. Icaria's great lesson is that communist institutions and vanguard guidance do not validate Cabet's and Lenin's premises and promises. Communist institutions and liberation did not transform people into angels. They did not guarantee the fulfillment of communist dreams for believers and those forced to obey, and it is unreasonable to suppose that they will ever do so. Icaria suggests that given their druthers most people prefer private property, markets, free work choice and personal consumption to communist ownership, restrictive labor assignment and egalitarian rationing.

Human Ingenuity and Solidarity

Nineteenth-century libertarian socialism boiled down to the conviction that human ingenuity and solidarity assured the existence of one or more designs for social living capable of greatly improving the well-being of productive men and women even though those calling themselves socialists disagreed about its characteristics, and all schemes failed. This faith persists to the present day for some, but became outdated after 1870 when activists decided that politics offered a faster road to the future than libertarian socialist utopianism (Hayek, 1952).

Notes

1 Robert Owen is often credited with coining the word socialism, but he did not define it clearly or use it consistently. Lexicographers first recorded it in a dictionary in 1848.
2 The dollar figure represents 2020 prices, based on 1800 French prices.
3 The Third Estate in France included peasants, urban workers, merchants and professionals. They constituted 98% of the population.
4 Fourier envisioned a "New Amorous World" that would give full scope to human sexual "attractions" by organizing love in a series of graded "corporations" ranging from "vestalic" virginity to complete promiscuity, both heterosexual and homosexual. Albert Brisbane, the foremost American Fourier acolyte, simply omitted the New Amorous World from his associations.
5 Carnality included eroticism, Sadism, sadomasochism, bestiality and sensual love. It was compatible according to Fourier's taste with other types of affection.
6 A libertine is one devoid of most moral principles, a sense of responsibility or sexual restraints. It is an extreme form of hedonism.
7 Fourier contended that socialist stratification was the joint consequence of passionate attraction and genetic gradation, asserting that passionate temperaments, talents, nobility and potentials differ, as do the passions themselves. He explained that touch-rut and taste are superior passions related to the cardinal hyper-minor love, and hyper-major ambition, and informs us that they give rise to two distinct pleasures in material love, copulation and kissing.

8 Amour-topia sets factor prices for labor, capital and talent in proportion to the 12 passions: five luxuries, four affectives and three settings. Labor is given 5/12, capital 4/12 and talent 3/12. Riasanovsky tells us that although 5/12 of the factor bill goes to the payment of labor and 4/12 to capital, these shares are distributed unequally to members of each class reflecting the unpleasantness of work and types of capital.

9 Sadism is a psychosexual disorder in which sexual urges are gratified by inflicting pain on another person. The term alludes to the Marquis de Sade, an 18th-century French nobleman who chronicled his own behavior. Restif was a pornographer. He describes himself as a communist.

10 Under Harmony there will exist eight basic types of sexual relations. The cardinal accords of consanguinity begin with delphigamous (pentagamous) relations, followed by the phanerogamous orgy in which several genteel and well-bred coteries engage in intercourse where all the men and all the women have had each other.

Omnigamous love brings into intercourse masses composed of many thousands of individuals who have frequently never seen each other, and who nonetheless are known to sympathize from the first day of meeting, at the end of two hours, in a compound order, in a spiritual as well as material tie.

11 Bacchanalia (or Bacchanal/Carnival) were Roman festivals of Bacchus based on various ecstatic elements of the Greek Dionysia. They seem to have been popular and well organized throughout the central and southern Italian peninsula. Masquerade balls had similar amorous connotations. The neoclassical style was a rejection of renaissance idealism. Jean-Antoine Watteau, The Embarkation for Cythera (1717) depicts a departure from the island of Cythera, the birthplace of Venus, thus symbolizing the temporary nature of human happiness. The painting portrays a fête galante is an amorous celebration or party enjoyed by the aristocracy of France after the death of Louis XIV, which is generally seen as a period of dissipation and pleasure, and peace, after the somber last years of the previous reign.

12 Fourier's amour-topia promises perpetual ecstasy.

13 Performance art is a form of expression that emerged in 1916 parallel to dadaism, under the umbrella of conceptual art. Tristan Tzara, one of the pioneers of Dada, led the movement. Western culture theorists have set the origins of performance art in the beginnings of the 20th century, along with constructivism, Futurism and Dadaism.

14 Fourier's enumeration and classification was not positivist. He did not document and statistically test behavioral correspondences. His method was completely nonempirical.

15 Goods and services inadvertently generated in Fourier's fête galante do not appear in linear programs because these activities do not receive inputs on a competitive basis.

16 See Appendix 1 for an example of a scientifically constructed social welfare function where goods and services are variables, not by-products.

17 Context does effect consumer utilities, but is not a substitute for it. See Bergson's system welfare function in Appendix 1.

18 Fourier wrote: "Such is, however, the precious effect which springs from the societary system, and from the mechanism of the settings; to have a passion for work, through the love of work itself, and without the receipt of pecuniary pay."

19 Co-solar vision is the ability of the eye to gaze eagle like, uninterruptedly into the sun. Trans-ethereal vision permits people to see objects in the milky way as accurately as one sees any ordinary visual object. These properties will be physically acquired by the human race as soon as it enters harmony. Other interesting acquired acuities include diaphanic vision or X-ray vision and co-aromal vision that permits Harmonians to observe intercelestial aromal communication including interplanetary copulation.

20   The notion that passions are sex specific is gleaned from Fourier's discussion of the "Integrality of the Soul": "The 810 characters of the integral scale, their proportions, functions, and relations are represented by 810 muscles of the human couple, male and female." Charles Fourier, *The Passions of the Human Soul*, II. Account also should be taken of the affective passions and the age distribution of the phalanx member.

21   In every phalanx there are negotiated every day at the bourse at least eight hundred meeting for work, meals, gallantry, journeys and other purposes. Each of these meetings requires debate among ten, twenty and sometimes a hundred persons; there are at least twenty thousand intrigues to disentangle in a bourse within one hour.

22   Robert Owen coined the word socialism, but he did not define it clearly or use it consistently. Lexicographers first recorded it in a dictionary in 1848.

23   The Reform Club was a British forum for radical ideas founded in 1836. Saint-Simon sometimes euphemistically referred to his reform club concept as "professors in administration" of the "high administration of society."

24   Ancien Régime was the political and social system of the Kingdom of France from the Late Middle Ages (circa 15th century) until the French Revolution of 1789, which led to the abolition (1792) of hereditary monarchy and of the feudal system of the French nobility.

25   Saint-Simon's works demonstrate his faith in science as a means to regenerate society. He envisioned a society in which science and industry would take the moral and temporal power of medieval theocracy.

26   The French Revolutionary motto liberté, égalité, fraternité was not institutionalized until the Third Republic (1870–1940) at the end of the 19th century. The philosophes (French for philosophers) were the intellectuals of the 18th-century Enlightenment. They strongly endorsed progress and tolerance and distrusted organized religion (most were deists) and feudal institutions. They faded away after the French Revolution reached a violent stage in 1793.

27   Saint-Simon does not explain how this will be accomplished. Edward Mason: "The decline of these unearned incomes must be expected to be the result only of an improvement in the productive processes."

28   He even went so far as to oppose civilian police services on the grounds that the people are their own best protectors.

29   Celestin Bougle and Elie Halevy,

> It is evident that the right of property as it exists, must be abolished, because by giving to a certain class of men the chance to live on the labor of others and in complete idleness, it preserves the exploitation of one part of the population, the most useful one, that which works and produces, in favor of those who only destroy.

30   Tugan Baranovsky denies that Saint-Simon was a socialist.

31   The Nobles of the Sword (French: noblesse d'épée) were the noblemen of the oldest class of nobility in France dating from the Middle Ages and the Early Modern. It was originally the knightly class. They played an important part during the French revolution.

32   The Society of the Cincinnati is a fraternal, hereditary society with 13 constituent societies in the United States and one in France, founded in 1783, to perpetuate the remembrance of American Independence.

33   The Society of the Friends of the Constitution renamed the Society of the Jacobins, Friends of Freedom and Equality after 1792 and commonly known as the Jacobin Club (Club des Jacobins), was the most influential political club during the French

Revolution of 1789. The period of its political ascendancy includes the Reign of Terror. The Jacobins saw themselves as constitutionalists, dedicated to the Rights of Man.

34 Georges-Jacques Danton was a French Revolutionary leader and orator, often credited as the chief force in the overthrow of the monarchy and the establishment of the First French Republic (September 21, 1792). He later became the first president of the Committee of Public Safety, but his increasing moderation and eventual opposition to the Reign of Terror led to his own death at the guillotine.

35 The Hébertists or Exaggerators associated with the populist journalist Jacques Hébert came to power during the Reign of Terror.

36 The term "Movers and shakers" was coined by Arthur O'Shaughnessy in his 1874 poem Ode. The phrase is commonly used to describe powerful and worldly individuals and groups who make great accomplishments.

37 He called for the creation of a religion of science with Isaac Newton as a saint.

38 The Marquis de Sade suffered a similar fate. He was arrested for his works Justine and Juliette and was later transferred to the Charenton insane asylum without a trial after his opponents declared him insane. He remained in the sanitarium 1801 until his death in 1814.

39 Jean-Baptiste Say (1767–1832) was a liberal French economist and businessman who argued in favor of competition, free trade and lifting restraints on business. He is best known for Say's law. Charles Dunoyer Barthélemy-Charles-Pierre-Joseph Dunoyer de Segonzac (1786–1862) was a pioneer business cycle theorist.

40 Saint-Simon wrote "The whole of society ought to strive towards the amelioration of the moral and physical existence of the poorest class; society ought to organize itself in the way best adapted for attaining this end." This principle became the watchword of the entire Saint-Simon school of thought.

41 The Bourbon Restoration was the period of French history following the fall of Napoleon in May 3, 1814 to the July Revolution of July 26, 1830. The brothers of the executed Louis XVI, namely Louis XVIII and Charles X, successively mounted the throne and instituted a conservative government aiming to restore the proprieties, if not all the institutions, of the Ancien Régime. Exiled supporters of the monarchy returned to France.

42 A keiretsu is a set of companies with interlocking business relationships and shareholdings.

43 "A new order is now being established. It consists in the transference of the right to inheritance, today still confined to the domestic family, to the state, which has become the association of workers."

Barnes quotes Saint-Simon, "If as we have proclaimed, mankind moves toward a state in which all individuals will be classed according to their ability and rewarded according to their work, it is evident that property, as it exists now, must be abolished; for in giving a certain class of men the right to live in idleness from the work of others property supports the exploitation of one part of the population, namely the most useful one which works and produces, for the profit of those who know only how to destroy". Mason interprets inheritance differently, arguing that the Saint-Simonian principle of abolishing inheritance conflicted with its tenant of merit-based remuneration because it constrains rational choice.

44 Mikhail Tugan Baranovsky, *Modern Socialism in Its Historical Development*. London: S. Sonnenschein & Co, 1910.

45   Tugan Baranovsky interprets Saint-Simonian doctrine differently. He identifies the Central Bank with the State as a religious-communal form, planned in an authoritarian fashion based on strict hierarchical subordination and need-based redistribution. Although, Tugan Baranovsky does not cite his source, confirmation can be found in a letter from Enfantin and Bazard addressed to the Chamber of Deputies on October 1, 1830. Gray quotes Saint-Simon

> Ils demandent que tous les instruments du travail, les terres et les capitaux, qui forment aujord'hui le fonds morcele des proprieties particulieres, soint reunis en un fond social, et que ce fonds soit exploite par association et HIERARCHIQUEMENT, de maniere a ce que la tache de chacun soit l'expression de sa capacite et sa richesse le mesure de ses oeuvres."

46   Barnes writes,

> Saint Simon has shown us the definitive goal towards which all human capacities must converge: the complete abolition of antagonism and attainment of universal association by and for the constantly progressive amelioration of the moral, physical and intellectual condition of the human race.

47   The egalitarianism stems from banning private ownership of passive income earning assets.

48   Charles Constantin Pecqueur was a French economist, socialist theoretician and politician. He participated in the Revolution of 1848 and influenced Karl Marx. In 1830 he joined the followers of Saint-Simon. He contributed to Le Globe and other Saint-Simonian papers, but left the Saint-Simonian school in 1832, dissatisfied with the religious direction in which Prosper Enfantin was taking it. Until 1836 he belonged to the school of Fourier and joined a phalanstère or Fourierist community. He wrote a biography of Fourier in 1835 and contributed to various Fourierist journals. In 1836 he left the Fourierists, publishing a critique of their system, and developed his own theories. He remained close, however, to some of his friends from the Saint-Simonian and Fourierist schools, such as Pierre Leroux and Victor Considerant. In contrast to these theorists, Pecqueur was one of the earliest French socialists to advocate collective ownership of the means of production, distribution and exchange. He is sometimes called the "father of French collectivist socialism." Tugan Baranovsky writes, "This last labor of reforming and improving Saint Simonism has chiefly been performed by Pecqueur, the father of modern collectivism." Consumers had choice, but their pre-income transfer demand did not govern output supplies.

49   Consumer demand determines both the production and distribution of goods under perfect competition without state intermediation. Pecqueur's model distorted both forms of supply by prohibiting competitive wages and transferring above-average to below-average income recipients.

50   Dirigisme or dirigism is an economic doctrine in which the state plays a strong directive role as opposed to a merely regulatory or noninterventionist role over a capitalist market economy.

51   Indicative planning aims to coordinate private and public investment and output plans through forecasts or targets.

52   Pecqueur argued that after receiving a minimum income, people would naturally seek to work to their capacity in their chosen field of employment without pecuniary incentive because they had a psychological need to perform useful labor of recognized

excellence. Access to professions was based on competence examinations. See Mikhail Tugan Baranovsky, *Modern Socialism in Its Historical Development*. London: S. Sonnenschein & Co, 1910, p.123.

53 Society is expected to vote on whether applicants deserve prestigious positions.

54 During the Napoleonic Wars, England's factories had become mechanized turning out large quantities of manufactured articles. At the end of the conflict in 1815, demand fell causing massive layoffs. Owen suggested addressing the problem by creating many small communities with population of 500 to 1,500, built by individuals, parishes, counties or the national government. Owen argued that his solution would eliminate existing programs supporting the poor (Speenhamland system).

55 The visit of Alexander I in 1814 to England was not a state visit. By 1818, Owen had completed a couple of his major communitarian projects for the village in the Institute for the Formation of Character and the School and wanted to show his model industrial community to the world. The many eminent visitors to New Lanark included Grand Duke Nicolas of Russia, the brother of the Emperor, who himself was to become Tsar Nicolas I in 1825. Robert Owen opened up the Russian market shortly after his arrival in New Lanark in 1800.

56 Although a failure, the Equitable Labor Exchange served as a model for the successful experiment of the Rochdale Pioneers in 1844, which established consumer cooperatives as an enduring movement.

57 Gatrell insists that Owen is a feudal socialist. Owen was not a revolutionary, but a conciliator, who sought to restore England to some mythical preindustrial social harmony.

58 Owen was a religious free thinker. He was critical of organized religion, such as the Church of England believing that religion was a barrier to peace and harmony.

59 Owen advocated a system of labor communes to alleviate the unemployment problem. He spent a considerable sum publicly advertising its virtues, but parliament reject it, prompting him to set off for America to prove his theory.

60 In the closing chapters of Rights of Man, Paine addresses the condition of the poor and outlines a detailed social welfare entitlement program, asserting that citizens have an inherent right to receive welfare. Paine (1737–1809) declares welfare is not charity. It is an irrevocable right. He published the pamphlet *Agrarian Justice* (1797), discussing the origins of property and introduced the concept of a guaranteed minimum income through a one-time inheritance tax on landowners.

61 Charles Darwin (1809–1882) published his theory of evolution in 1859, a year after Owen's death. Herbert Spenser (1820–1903) applied Darwin's survival of the fittest concept to human societal evolution in the 1870s.

62 Josiah Warren, who participated in Robert Owen's New Harmony cooperative communalist experiment, established a "labor for labor store" called the Cincinnati Time Store in downtown Cincinnati in 1827. All the goods offered for sale in Warren's store were offered at the same price the merchant himself had paid for them, plus a small surcharge, in the neighborhood of 4% to 7%, to cover store overhead. Between 1827 and 1830, the store proved successful.

63 Jeremy Bentham was one of Owen's partners in New Lanark.

64 Josiah Warren (1798–1874) was an American anarchist, inventor, musician, printer and author. He published four-page weekly paper *The Peaceful Revolutionist* in 1833. Warren took his place as one of 900 or so Owenites in New Harmony, Indiana in 1825.

65 Guild socialism was a movement that included a substantial diversity of opinion regarding the state and consumer sovereignty in the new social order. George Douglas

Howard Cole (1889–1959) was its most articulate exponent. Other major figures include Samuel George Hobson (1870–1940), Arthur Penty (1875–1937), Maurice Benington Reckitt and Carl Eric Bechhofer Roberts (1894–1949), Bertrand Russell, George Robert Sterling Taylor, Ramiro de Maeztu y Whitney (1875–1936), Alfred Richard Orage (1873–1934), Fisher Unwin (1917) and Niles Carpenter (1891–1971).

66 The Reform Act of 1832 granted representation to cities, small landowners, tenant farmers, shopkeepers, householders who paid a yearly rental of £10 or more and some lodgers. Only qualifying men were able to vote. The 1867 Reform Act and the 1928 Representation of the People Act accelerated British democratization.

By the mid-1860s, Parliament was in the process of extending the vote to the working class. The Second Reform Act, 1867 granted the franchise to propertied male adults over 21 years of age (4% of the total population).

The Parliamentary Reform Act of 1867, which franchised renters, increased the electorate to almost 2.5 million.

The Representation of the People Act of 1918 gave the vote to all men over 21, whether they owned property or not. The act gave the vote to women over the age of 30 who met a property qualification, or whose husband did. This represented 8.5 million women – two thirds of the total population of women in the UK.

The Representation of the People Act, 1928 franchised women on the same terms as men. All adults over 21 could vote.

67 The Labour Representation Committee was established in 1900. It was the product of a coming together of Fabian Society and trade unions. The first Labour prime minister was Ramsay MacDonald, who was in office in 1924 and again in 1929–1935. Ramsay MacDonald was determined that the party should have a broad, national appeal – firmly progressive, but also committed to individual freedom, and to the securing of power through the existing democratic, parliamentary methods.

68 The Fabian Society is a British socialist organization founded in 1884 whose purpose is to advance the principles of democratic socialism via gradualist and reformist effort in democracies, rather than by revolutionary overthrow. The Fabian Society founded the London School of Economics and Political Science in 1895. Today, the society functions primarily as a think tank and is one of 21 socialist societies affiliated with the Labour Party. The Fabian Society was named – at the suggestion of Frank Podmore – in honor of the Roman general Quintus Fabius Maximus Verrucosus. His strategy sought gradual victory against the superior Carthaginian army under the renowned general Hannibal through persistence, harassment and wearing the enemy down by attrition rather than pitched, climactic battles.

69 The *New Age* was a British weekly magazine (1894–1938), inspired by Fabian socialism, and credited as a major influence on literature and the arts during its heyday from 1907 to 1922. Alfred Richard Orage was the editor.

70 The Second-Generation Fabians included Richard Henry Tawney (1880–1962) and Harold Laski (1893–1950). Laski served as the chairman of the British Labour Party from 1945 to 1946 and was a professor at the London School of Economics from 1926 to 1950. He pinned his hopes on Joseph Stalin's Soviet Union.

71 Penty favored a Christian socialist form of the medieval guild, as an alternative basis for economic life.

72 John Ruskin and William Morris' rejection of the tawdry industrial manufacture of decorative arts and architecture in favor of a return to hand-craftsmanship (arts and crafts movement) and, late-19th-century nostalgia for a romanticized medieval past

shaped Coles looking backward. William Morris' influence as the founding spirit of guild socialism is widely acknowledged.

73 William Morris influenced Cole's vision of the future.
74 Ramiro de Maeztu y Whitney (1875–1936) developed the functionalist concept of participatory democracy in the guild socialist context.
75 Cole, like Morris and the early Karl Marx, believed capitalist institutions prevented people from being truly human.
76

> But, it will be said, surely to a great extent everything is everybody's concern. It is certainly not the exclusive concern of miners ... On the other hand the coal industry clearly concerns the minor and education the teacher in a way different from that ins which they concern the rest of the people; for, whereas for the latter coal is only one among a number of commodities,, and education one among several civic services, to the miner or the teacher his own calling is the most important single concern in his social life.

77 "The factory or place of work will be the natural unit of guild life."
78 Cole thought that regional guild decision making would be the most impart component of direct democracy.

> These needs can only be met by the method of regional organization, and, without developing the full case for regionalism here, I propose to assume that Guild Society will adopt, in response to an evident need, a regional basis of organization.

> The full case for regionalism is elaborated in Cole, *Social Theory*, chapter 10. For a contrary opinion stressing the local aspect of Cole's guild socialism, see Carpenter.

79 Cole argued that government would lose its traditional role as sovereign and become a loose association of guilds and councils in the form of a national commune. Cole, *Guild Socialism Restated*, wrote:

> We can then safely assume that not only will the present political machine lose its economic and civic functions to new bodies, but that the task of coordinating these functions will also pass out of its hands. It will thus, at least "wither away" to a very considerable extent, and I have no hesitation in saying that in my belief, it will disappear altogether, either after a frontal attack, or by atrophy following upon dispossession of its vital powers.

80 Almost allergic to higher mathematics (he did not understand algebra) Cole distrusted science, as it was being used to quantify things that were best left to interpretation.
81 Cole's version of guild socialism was more akin to stateless anarcho-syndicalism than Robert Owen's cooperative socialism. Alexander Gray argues that insofar as national laws are binding on guilds and councils, the concept of state and sovereignty has not really been exercised, so that guild socialism may in fact be institutionally dualistic. Carpenter considered Cole's scheme impractical. "Its relative indifference to economic considerations has been seen to constitute a distinguishing characteristic of the guild idea." Carpenter raises the following political objection to Cole's construct: (1) the hazard of anarchy, (2) the trend toward collectivism, (3) communal impotence and (4) failure to provide a party system. He also notes that factor and commodity prices cannot be efficiently set outside the market context. No mechanism exists for determining the interest rate in accordance with time preference and

inter-temporal opportunity costs. No entrepreneurial incentive is provided for innovation and industriousness.

82   The community's original 87 members grew to 172 by February 1850, 208 by 1852 and 306 by 1878. There were smaller Noyesian communities in Wallingford, Connecticut; Newark, New Jersey; Putney and Cambridge, Vermont.

83   Group marriage or conjoint marriage is a marital arrangement where three or more adults enter into sexual, affective, romantic or otherwise intimate short- or long-term partnerships, and share in any combination of finances, residences, care or kin work. Group marriage is considered a form of polygamy. While academic usage has traditionally treated group marriage as a marital arrangement, more recent usage has expanded the concept to allow for the inclusion of nonconjugal unions. Colloquial usage of group marriage has also been associated with polyamory and polyamorous families.

84   A woman's right to satisfying sexual experiences was recognized, and women were encouraged to have orgasms. However, a woman's right of refusing a sexual overture was limited depending on the status of the man who made the advance.

85   Young men in the community would practice with the women of the community who had already gone through menopause, until they were able to control their ejaculation. Only Noyes and a few other men had the skills and self-control necessary to participate in sexual intercourse with the young women of the community. Sexual intercourse was communal; it was based on consent, and all sexual unions were documented and regulated. Sexual intercourse was spiritual, and the pairing of man and woman for sexual intercourse in the community had to be approved by a committee, although most of the virgin females of the community were reserved for Noyes. Noyes did believe that women had the right to choose if and when to bear a child, which was not a common belief at the time.

86   Within the commune, there was a debate about when children should be initiated into sex, and by whom. There was also much debate about its practices as a whole. The founding members were aging or deceased, and many of the younger communitarians desired to enter into exclusive, traditional marriages.

87   John Humphrey Noyes was informed by trusted adviser Myron Kinsley that a warrant for his arrest on charges of statutory rape was imminent. Noyes fled the Oneida Community Mansion House and the country in the middle of a June night in 1879, never to return to the United States.

88   A rough translation by Cabet was serialized in Icarian periodicals of the 1850s; an additional translation by academic specialist Robert Sutton has been deposited with the Library of Congress, although it remains unpublished. A plot outline was published by Morris Hillquit in 1903. The first part of the book contains a glowing account of the blessings of the cooperative system of industry of the Icarians, their varied occupations and accomplishments, comfortable mode of life, admirable system of education, high morality, political freedom, equality of sexes and general happiness. The second part contains a history of Icaria. It appears that the social order of the country had been similar to that prevailing in the rest of the world, until 1782, when the great national hero, Icar, after a successful revolution, established the system of communism. This recital gives Cabet the opportunity for a scathing criticism of the faults of the present social structure, and also to outline his favorite measures for the transition from that system to the new regime. The last part of the book is devoted to the history of development of the idea of communism, and contains a summary of the views of almost all

known writers on the subject, from Plato down to the famous utopians of the early part of the 19th century.

89 Icarians established a series of other egalitarian communes in the states of Texas, Illinois, Iowa, Missouri and California. All failed.

90 Both were born in 1788. They met in England in the later 1830s when Cabet was living in exile. Cabet turned to his friend Robert Owen for advice, traveling to London in September 1847 to consult with him. Owen recommended colonization in the new American state of Texas, a location reckoned to possess vast tracts of inexpensive unoccupied land.

91 The republicans were led by secret societies formed of the most determined and ferocious members of their movement. These groups planned to provoke riots similar to those that had led to the 1830 July Revolution against the ministers of Charles X. The "Society of the Rights of Man" was one of the most instrumental. It was organized like an army, divided into sections of 20 members each (to evade the law that forbade the association of more than 20 persons), with a president and vice president for each section.

References

Aoki, Masahiko (1988). *Information, Incentive, and Bargaining in the Japanese Economy: A Microtheory of the Japanese Economy*. London: Cambridge University Press.

Aoki, Masahiko and Hugh Patrick. (1995). *The Japanese Main Bank System*. London: Clarendon.

Barnes, Harry Elmer. (1958). *The Doctrine of Saint-Simon: An Exposition: First Year, 1828–1829*. Boston: Beacon Press.

Barrie, James. (1911). *Peter Pan and Wendy*. New York: Charles Scribner's Sons.

Bestor, Jr., Arthur. (1948) "The Evolution of the Socialist Vocabulary." *Journal of the History of Ideas*. Vol. 9, No. 3, 259–302.

Birman, Igor. (1978). From the Achieved Level. *Soviet Studies*. Vol. 30, No.2, 153–172.

Bougle, Celestin and Elie Halevy (eds.). (1924). *Exposition de la Doctrine du Saint-Simon*. Paris: Marcel Rivière & Cie..

Butt, John. (1971). *Robert Owen, Prince of Cotton Spinners*. London: Newton Abbot, David and Charles.

Cabet, Étienne. (1846). *Le vrai christianisme suivant Jésus Christ ("The real Christianity according to Jesus Christ")*. Paris.

Carpenter, Niles. (1920). "The Literature of Guild Socialism." *Quarterly Journal of Economics*. Vol. 34, No. 4, 763–776.

Carpenter, Niles. (1922). *Guild Socialism*. New York: Appleton.

Claeys, Gregory and Lyman Sargent. (2017). *The Utopia Reader*. New York: New York University Press.

Cole, George Douglas Howard. (1920a). *Guild Socialism Restated*. London: L. Parsons.

Cole, George Douglas Howard. (1920b). *Self-Government in Industry*. London: G. Bell..

Cole, George Douglas Howard. (1920c). *Social Theory*. London, Methuen and Co., Ltd., chapter 10.

Cole, George Douglas Howard. (1925). *Life of Robert Owen*. London: Ernest Benn Ltd.

Cole, George Douglas Howard. (1944). *A Century of Co-operation*. Oxford: George Allen & Unwin Ltd.

Cole, George Douglas Howard. (1951). *The British Co-operative Movement in a Socialist Society*. London: Routledge.

Cole, George Douglas Howard. (1962). *A History of Socialist Economic Thought*, Vol. 1. London: Macmillan.

Cole, Margaret. (1953). *Robert Owen of New Lanark*. London: Batchworth Press.

Cole, Margaret. (1971). *The Life of G. D. H. Cole*. London: St. Martin's Press.

Cumming, Elizabeth and Wendy Kaplan. (1991). *Arts and Crafts Movement*. London: Thames & Hudson.

Dickens, Peter. (2000). *Social Darwinism: Linking Evolutionary Thought to Social Theory*. Philadelphia: Open University Press.

Feldman, Fred. (2004). *Pleasure and the Good Life: Concerning the Nature, Varieties, and Plausibility of Hedonism*. London: Clarendon

Fourier, Charles. (1968a). *Passions of the Human Soul and Their Influence on Society and Civilization*. Vol. I. New York: Augustus M. Kelley.

Fourier, Charles. (1968b). *Passions of the Human Soul and Their Influence on Society and Civilization*. Vol. II. New York: Augustus M. Kelley.

Fourier, Charles. (1971). *Design for Utopia: Selected Writings of Charles Fourier*. New York: Schocken Books.

Fourier, Charles and J. Franklin. (1901). *Selections from the Works of Fourier*. London: S. Sonnenschein & Co.

Gatrell, V.A.C. (1970). *Report to the County of Lanark A New View on Society*. Baltimore: Pelican Classics. (Penguin Classics).

Gerschenkron, Alexander. (1962). "Economic Backwardness in Historical Perspective." In A. Gerschenkron (ed.). *Economic Backwardness in Historical Perspective* (pp. 5–30). Cambridge: Belknap Press.

Gerschenkron, Alexander. (1969). "History of Economic Doctrines and Economic History." *AER Proceedings*. Vol. 59, No. 2, 1–17.

Goldberg, Rose. (2001). *Performance Art: From Futurism to the Present (World of Art)*. New York: Thames & Hudson.

Goyau, G. (1912). "Saint-Simon and Saint-Simonism." In *The Catholic Encyclopedia*. New York.

Gray, Alexander. (1947). *The Socialist Tradition: Moses to Lenin*. London: Longmans, Green.

Guarneri, Carl. (1991). *The Utopian Alternative: Fourierism in Nineteenth-Century America*. Ithaca: Cornell University Press.

Halevy, Elie. (1948). *Histoire du socialism europeen*. Paris: Librairie Gallimard.

Harrison, John. (1968). *Utopianism and Education*. New York: Columbia University Press.

Harrison, John. (1969). *Quest for the New Moral World*. New York: Scribner.

Hartmann, D. (1996). "Protoscience and Reconstruction." *Journal of General Philosophy of Science*. Vol. 27, 55–69.

Hayek, Friedrich. (1952). *The Counter-Revolution of Science: Studies on the Abuse of Reason*. New York: Liberty Fund.

Hays, Constance (1999). "Why the Keepers of Oneida Don't Care to Share the Table, Section 3." *The New York Times*.

Heilbroner, Robert. (1999). *The Worldly Philosophers: The Lives, Times and Ideas of the Great Economic Thinkers*. New York: Touchstone.

Hillquit, Morris. (1903). *History of Socialism in the United States*. New York; London: Funk & Wagnalls Co.

Hobson, Samuel George. (1914). *National Guilds*. London: G. Bell.

Hobson, Samuel George. (1917). *Guild Principles in War and Peace*. London: G. Bell.

Johnson, Christopher. (1966). "Etienne Cabet and the Problem of Class Antagonism." *International Review of Social History*. Vol. 11, No. 3, 403–443.

Johnson, Christopher. (2008). *Etienne Cabet and the Problem of Class Antagonism.* London: Cambridge University Press.

Jordan, Z. A. (1967). *The Evolution of Dialectical Materialism.* London: Macmillan.

Kern, Louis. (1981). *An Ordered Love: Sex Roles and Sexuality in Victorian Utopias–The Shakers, the Mormons, and the Oneida Community.* Chapel Hill: The University of North Carolina Press.

Landauer, Carl. (1959). *European Socialism: A History of Ideas and Movements.* Berkeley: University of California Press.

Leroy, Maxime. (1925). *La Vie veritable du Comte Henri de Saint-Simon.* Paris: Bernard Grasset.

Lichtheim, George. (1969). *The Origins of Socialism.* London: Weidenfeld & Nicolson.

Locke, John. (1660). *First Tract of Government.* London: Awnsham Churchill.

Locke, John. (1662). *Second Tract of Government.* London: Awnsham Churchill.

MacCarthy, Fiona. (1994). *William Morris.* London: Faber and Faber.

Maeztu y Whitney, Ramiro de. (1916). *Authority, Liberty and Function.* London: George Allen and Unwin.

Manuel, Frank. (1956). *The New World of Henri Saint-Simon.* Cambridge: Harvard University Press.

Manuel, Frank. (1965). *The Prophets of Paris.* New York: Harper Torch.

Marcuse, Herber. (1955). *Eros and Civilization.* Boston: Beacon Press.

Markham, Felix (ed.). (1964). *Henri de Saint-Simon: Social Organization, the Science of Men and Other Writings.* New York: Harper and Row.

Marquis de Sade. (2016). *The 120 Days of Sodom.* London: Penguin Books.

Martin, James. (1970). *Men against the State: The Expositors of Individualist Anarchism in America, 1827–1908.* Colorado Springs: Ralph Myles Publishers.

Marx, Karl. (1959). *Economic and Philosophical Manuscripts of 1844.* Moscow: Progress Publishers.

Mason, Edward. (1928). "Fourier and Anarchism." *Quarterly Journal of Economics.* Vol. 42, No. 4, 228–262.

Mason, Edward. (1931). "Saint-Simonism and the Rationalization of Industry." *Quarterly Journal of Economics.* Vol. 45, 641–683.

Morris, William. (1891). *News from Nowhere.* London: Reeves and Turner.

Nielsen, K. (2008). "Indicative Planning." In S.N. Durlauf and L. Blume (eds), *The New Palgrave Dictionary of Economics.* London: Palgrave Macmillan.

Nordhoff, Charles. (1875). *The Communistic Societies of the United States: From Personal Visit and Observation.* London: John Murray.

Noyes, George Wallingford and Lawrence Foster. (2001). *Free Love in Utopia: John Humphrey Noyes and the Origin of the Oneida Community.* Urbana: University of Illinois Press.

Orage, Alfred Richard. (1917). *An Alphabet of Economics.* London: T. Fisher Unwin.

Owen, Robert. (1920). *The Life of Robert Owen.* London: G. Bell and Sons.

Owen, Robert. (1966). *A New View of Society.* New York: Dutton.

Packard, Frederick. (1968). *Life of Robert Owen.* New York: Augustus M. Kelly.

Paine, Thomas and Mark Philp. (2008). *Rights of Man, Common Sense, and Other Political Writings.* London: Oxford University Press.

Pecqueur, Constantin. (1842). *Theorie Nouvelle d'Economie Sociale et Politique, ou Etudies sur l'Organization des Societies.* Paris: Capelle Libraire.

Pellarin, C. (1920). *The Life of Charles Fourier.* New York: Francis Geo. Shaw.

Penty, Arthur. (1906). *The Restoration of the Guild System.* London: Swan Sonnenschein and Co.

Penty, Arthur. (1919). *Guilds and the Social Crisis.* London: George Allen and Unwin.

Penty, Arthur. (1920). *A Guildman's Interpretation of History.* London: George Allen and Unwin.

Polanyi, Karl. (1968). *The Great Transformation.* Boston: Beacon Press.

Pollard, Sidney. (1971). *Robert Owen, Prophet of the Poor.* London: Macmillan.

Reckitt, Maurice Benington and Carl Eric Bechhofer Roberts. (1918). *The Meaning of National Guilds.* London: C. Palmer & Hayward.

Restif de la Bretonne, Nicolas. (1769). Review of Joseph-Alexandre-Victor Hupay de Fuveau, *Project for a Philosophical Community.*

Riasanovsky, Nicholas. (1969). *The Teaching of Charles Fourier.* Berkeley: University of California Press.

Roach, Monique. (2001). "The Loss of Religious Allegiance among the Youth of the Oneida Community." *The Historian.* Vol. 63, No. 4, 787–806.

Robertson, C. N. (1972). *Oneida Community, the Breakup, 1876–1881.* Syracuse: Syracuse University Press.

Rosefielde, Steven. (1976). "Operational Economic Theory in the Excluded Middle between Positivism and Rationalism." *Atlantic Economic Journal.* Vol. 4, No. 2, 1–8.

Rosefielde, Steven. (1980). "Post Positivist Scientific Method and the Appraisal of Nonmarket Economic Behavior." *Quarterly Journal of Ideology.* Vol. 3, No. 1, 23–33.

Rousseau, Jean Jacques. (1997). *The Social Contract' and Other Later Political Writings.* Cambridge: Cambridge University Press.

Russell, Bertrand. (1919). *Proposed Roads to Freedom.* New York: Hold.

Ryan, Alan. (2012). *On Politics,* Book II. New York: Liveright.

Saint-Simon, Claude-Henri de. (1803a). *Introduction aux travaux scientifiques du XIXe siècle* (Introduction to scientific discoveries of the 19th century).

Saint-Simon, Claude-Henri de. (1803b). *Lettres d'un habitant de Genève à ses contemporains.*

Saint-Simon, Claude-Henri de. (1813). *Mémoire sur la science de l'homme* (Notes on the study of man).

Saint-Simon, Claude-Henri de. (1825). *Nouveau christianisme* (New Christianity). Paris.

Sandel, Michael. (2020). *The Tyranny of Merit: What's Become of the Common Good?* New York: Farrar, Straus and Giroux.

Schumpeter, Joseph. (1954). *History of Economic Analysis.* London: Allen & Unwin.

Siméon, Ophélie. (2017). *Robert Owen's Experiment at New Lanark: From Paternalism to Socialism.* London: Palgrave Macmillan.

Sutton, Robert. (1994). *Les Icariens: the utopian dream in Europe and America.* Urbana: University of Illinois Press.

Tawney, Richard Henry. (1920). *The Sickness of an Acquisitive Society.* London: Fabian Society.

Taylor, George Robert Sterling. (1919). *The Guild State: Its Principles and Possibilities.* London: George Allen and Unwin.

Thomas, Paul. (2008). *Marxism and Scientific Socialism: From Engels to Althusser.* London: Routledge.

Thurber, James. (1939). "The Secret Life of Walter Mitty." *New Yorker.*

Tugan Baranovsky, Mikhail. (1910). *Modern Socialism in Its Historical Development.* London: S. Sonnenschein & Co.

Van Eck, Steve. (2010). "Fourier, Charles." In H. K. Anheier and S. Toepler (eds.). *International Encyclopedia of Civil Society.* New York: Springer.

Warren, Josiah. (1856) *Periodical Letter II.* Boston.

Webb, Beatrice and Sidney. (1965). *Industrial Democracy.* New York: Kelly.

Weill, George. (1896). *Un Precuseur du socialism, Saint-Simon et son oeuvre.* Paris.

Weitzman, Martin. (1986). *The Share Economy; Conquering Stagflation.* Cambridge: Harvard University Press.

White, Katie. (2021). "Watteau's Beloved Depiction of Dreamy Aristocratic Love Is a Rococo Gem. Here Are 3 Things You May Not Know about It." https://news.art net.com/art-world/watteau-3-things-embarkation-for-cythera-1989754?utm_ content=from_&utm_source=Sailthru&utm_medium=email&utm_campa ign=7%2F31%20Saturday&utm_term=Daily%20Newsletter%20%5BALL%5D%20 %5BMORNING%5D

Young, Michael. (1958). *The Rise of Meritocracy.* London: Pelican.

3   Socialist Utopian Fiction

Nineteenth-century socialists from Robert Owen to George Douglas Howard Cole focused their attention on improving workers quality of existence (Cabet, 1840).[1] Second-generation socialists stressed idealist possibilities and social justice after 1870 (Surtz and Hexter, 1965, 20),[2] aided by two seminal works of socialist utopian fiction: Edward Bellamy's *Looking Backward* (1888) and William Morris' *News from Nowhere* (1892). Both spotlighted utopia's horn of plenty, lifestyle, secular spirit and sundry virtues, which might apply in any economic system, while glossing over the importance of fair wages, job security and working-class empowerment. Socialism for workers and their leaders meant eradicating drudgery and oppression; for socialist utopians, it promised a secular sky blue life (Bowman, 1958).[3]

Edward Bellamy

Edward Bellamy (1850–1898) was an American author, journalist and political activist famous for his utopian novel, *Looking Backward: 2000–1887*. He considered himself a "nationalist" and distained socialism (Bowman, 1958, 114),[4] but inadvertently popularized it by romanticizing state ownership of industry. His utopia captured the public imagination and catapulted Bellamy to literary fame. By the end of the 19th century, *Looking Backward* had sold almost as many copies as Harriet Beecher Stowe's, *Uncle Tom's Cabin*.

Bellamy's sci-fi vision of a carefree country unburdened by competition and private property appealed to a generation of intellectuals alienated from the dark side of Gilded Age America (Twain and Charles Warner, 1873).[5] It inspired people to imagine a happy land (utopia) without war, poverty, crime, prostitution, corruption, money, taxes, politicians, lawyers, merchants and soldiers. Workdays were short, vacations long, labor joyous and everyone retired at 45, enabling humanity to recover its lost innocence. Healthy lifestyles would purge worldly woes, eradicating greed, maliciousness, untruthfulness and neurosis.

Bellamy's novel inspired admirers to create nationalist clubs promoting utopia. They made a political splash for three years, but the vogue swiftly faded into

DOI: 10.4324/9781003371571-5

oblivion. Bellamy wrote a sequel to *Looking Backward* elaborating the various aspects of utopia titled *Equality* in 1897 shortly before his death.

Looking Backward tells the sci-fi "Rip Van Winkle" tale of Julian West who toward the end of the 19th century falls into a hypnosis-induced slumber and wakes up 113 years later.[6] He finds himself in what most readers consider a socialist utopia. The remainder of the book outlines Bellamy's thoughts about a better tomorrow. The major themes include nationalizing industry and creating an industrial army to organize production and distribution, without forsaking aspects of personal liberty.

Doctor Leete elaborates all the advances of the new age to West, from drastically reduced working hours to the egalitarian distribution of consumer goods on demand. People dine in public kitchens and receive sermons and music by cable telephone. Workers performing skilled, dangerous or tedious jobs labor fewer hours. There is little crime and few incorrigible criminals, thanks to the development of miraculous medical therapies. Women receive equal job opportunity in Bellamy's sequel *Equality*.

Both Bellamy's novels are pulp fiction, but struck a chord in a woke Golden progressive era yearning to storm utopia through radical institutional and technological change loosely connected with state economic management and the eradication of capitalism (private property, markets, individual entrepreneurship and money).[7] The promise of universal happiness dominates Bellamy bright shining future, without any discussion of whether there is a special place for the working class in utopia.

William Morris

William Morris (1834–1896) was a British textile designer, craft factory owner, poet, artist, novelist, translator and socialist activist associated with the British Arts and Crafts Movement.[8] He dabbled with anarchism (befriending Sergey Mikhailovich Stepnyak-Kravchinsky and Peter Kropotkin),[9] embraced Marxism in the 1880s when socialism had only a few hundred adherents (MacCarthy, 1994; Mackail, 1899; Mackail, 1901; Thompson, 1955),[10] and founded the Socialist League in 1884 (MacCarthy, 1994, 504; Mackail, 1899, 131–132, 140; Mackail, 1901; Thompson, 1955, 366). Morris read Henry George's *Progress and Poverty*, Alfred Russel Wallace's *Land Nationalization* and Karl Marx's *Das Kapital*, although Marx's economic analysis of capitalism gave him "agonies of confusion on the brain" (MacCarthy, 1994, 472). He helped author a Democratic Federation manifesto, *Socialism Made Plain*, with Ernest Belfort Bax demanding improved housing for workers, free compulsory education for all children, free school meals, an eight-hour working day, the abolition of national debt, nationalization of land, banks and railways and the organization of agriculture and industry under state control and cooperative principles.[11] He met Friedrich Engels and composed *Revolutionary International Socialism*, advocating proletarian internationalism and world revolution. Morris avoided the Fabian Society, judging it too middle-class, but mended fences in the late 1890s. He oversaw production of the Socialist League's newspaper, *Commonweal* founded in 1885, serving as its editor for six years, during which time he kept it financially afloat. Engels, George Bernard Shaw,[12] Paul Lafargue (Marx's son-in-law),[13] Wilhelm Liebknecht[14] and Karl Kautsky were contributors.[15] Morris serialized his socialist novel, *News from Nowhere* in *Commonweal*. It became a classic among Europe's socialist community. His literary contributions helped socialism win acceptance in *fin de siècle* Great Britain.

Morris' magnum opus was *News from Nowhere* (Morris, 1891), a work combining utopian socialism and Arts and Crafts nostalgia. It tells yet another Rip Van Winkle yarn of a contemporary socialist, William Guest, who falls asleep and awakes in the early 21st century, discovering a future society based on common ownership and democratic control of the means of production. There is no private property, no big cities, no authority, no monetary system, no divorce, no courts, no prisons and no class system. It is Morris' socialist Shangri-la.

The novel is an aesthete fairy tale. It explores the details of utopia's organizations and relationships. Morris fuses Marxism and Arts and Crafts romanticism, presenting himself as an enchanted figure. The protagonist William Guest searches for love, fellowship, transfiguration and beatitude revealed through a series of encounters with utopia's venerable people. Old Hammond is a communist educator and romantic sage. Dick and Clara are good comrades and the married lovers who aid Morris in his wanderings. The journey on the Thames is a search for socialism's secular soul, symbolized by the unattainable working-class Ellen (Dante's Beatrice).[16] The book conveys Morris' belief that socialism will integrate liberty, art, love, life, beauty and work by making labor creative and pleasurable. Morris' utopia is the antithesis of Bellamy's shallow egalitarian Disneyland (Morris, 1889).[17]

Morris' criticism of Bellamy social vision is apt, but *News from Nowhere* not only misrepresents the secular spirit of 19th-century socialist salons, it also is discordant with his Marxist rhetoric of 1880–1890. Morris' heroes are artisans, not industrial laborers shunning the machine age for rustic utopia. His brave new world where the pursuit of beauty governs work, production, distribution, consumption, leisure, art and human bonding is consistent with socialism insofar as it abolishes class status, inequality and some aspects of traditional moral obligation, but only works because empathy and taste compel everyone to do what Morris dubiously considers the right thing. For example, women in his enchanted realm enjoy full sexual, political, educational and professional freedom, but Morris expects them to behave like Madonna,[18] respected as mothers, beloved companions and devoted housekeepers (Levitas, 1996). Women do what they can do best and what they like best and the men are neither jealous nor injured by it (Morris, 1889).

Morris contends that the practice of women serving men is justified because

It is a great pleasure to a clever woman to manage a house skillfully, and to do so that all house-mates about her look pleased and are grateful to her. And then you know everybody likes to be ordered about by a pretty woman...

(Levitas, 1996)

Morris also reports that utopians practice monogamy even though there are no marital contracts because good taste restrains their impractical instincts.[19]

Life in Morris' socialist utopia is a bowl of cherries from his perspective because he believes that discarding industrialization and retreating to nature transfigures humanity. Going back to the future guided by the pursuit of beauty makes his utopia spiritually rich, suffused with love, high-minded, empathetic, compassionate, happy, productive and cooperative.

The mood and spirit of Morris' enchanted cottage utopia is reminiscent of Tao Yuanming's "Peach Blossom" and Confucian literati artist communities still flourishing today.[20]

Socialism with a Thousand Faces

George Bellamy and William Morris tried in vain to identify socialism distinctive essence (Cabet, 1842; Hertzka, 1890; Howells, 1894; Balodis, 1898).[21] They had no difficulty counterposing plans and markets, cooperation and competition, egalitarianism and rank, but failed to show how these characteristics captured the essence of socialism because planning, rationing, cooperation and egalitarianism are not exclusively socialist attributes. Many nonsocialist communities are egalitarian.

Moreover, nonsocialist communities can be spiritually rich, suffused with love, high-minded, empathetic, compassionate, happy, productive and cooperative if it is assumed this is how enlightened humans want to behave. Morris and Marx found it convenient to believe that planning, communal ownership, egalitarianism and cooperation would transfigure and beatify human relations, but there is no compelling evidence that they were right.

Socialism is neither singular nor sublime. It is a set of speculative constructs pioneered by Owens, Saint-Simon, Marx, Cabet, Proudhon, Sorel and Cole designed to protect the working class from exploitation by powerful capitalists, professionals and the state. Systems that satisfy this criterion can employ multiple means to seek diverse utopian socialist ends preferred by Bellany, Morris or other visionaries confident that their values are best for the working class. Utopias for everyone including free riders and free loaders are not socialist (Breme, 1848; Lane, 1880).

Socialist utopian fiction is no more coherent and practical than Charles Marie-Francois Fourier, Count Claude Henri de Rouvroy de Saint-Simon, Étienne Cabet and the youthful Karl Marx's libertarian schemes. They only echo the conviction that human ingenuity and solidarity assure the existence of one or more designs for social living capable of greatly improving the well-being of productive men and women. Utopia sentimentality persists, but it is no longer a serious part of the socialist conversation.

Notes

1 Étienne Cabet's *The Voyage to Icaria* is mostly about the organization of work, sharing, virtue and politics. It does not delve into the emotional and spiritual benefits of a social way of life.

2 In his 1516 work Utopia, Thomas More claimed that his imaginary island of that name was a eutopia, translated as "happy land" in the Yale edition of his works.
3 Between 1860 and 1887, no fewer than 11 similar works of fiction were produced in the United States by various authors dealing with the questions of economic and social organization.
4

> Every sensible man will admit there is a big deal in a name, especially in making first impressions. In the radicalness of the opinions I have expressed, I may seem to out-socialize the socialists, yet the word socialist is one I never could well stomach. In the first place it is a foreign word in itself, and equally foreign in all its suggestions. It smells to the average American of petroleum, suggests the red flag, and with all manner of sexual novelties, and an abusive tone about God and religion, which in this country we at least treat with respect. [...] [W]hatever German and French reformers may choose to call themselves, socialist is not a good name for a party to succeed with in America. No such party can or ought to succeed that is not wholly and enthusiastically American and patriotic in spirit and suggestions.
> (Letter from Edward Bellamy to William Dean Howells, June 17, 1888)

5 The "Gilded Age" refers to America's patrician society 1870–1900 and broadly coincides with the mid-Victorian era in Britain and the Belle Époque in France. The phrase is the title of Mark Twain and Charles Dudley Warner, *The Gilded Age: A Tale of Today*. The novel satirizes serious social problems masked by a thin gold gilding during the era. Cf. Edith Wharton, *The Age of Innocence*. New York: D. Appleton & Company, 1920.
6 Rip Van Winkle is a short story by the American author Washington Irving, first published in 1819. Rip Van Winkle falls asleep in the Catskill Mountains, awakening 20 years later to a very changed world, having missed the American Revolution.
7 The Progressive Era (1896–1916) was a period of widespread social activism and political reform across the United States of America that spanned the 1890s to the 1920s. Progressive reformers were typically middle-class society women or Christian ministers.
8 The Arts and Crafts movement was an international trend in the decorative and fine arts that developed earliest and most fully in the British Isles and subsequently spread across the British Empire and to the rest of Europe and America. The movement flourished between 1880 and 1920 and later morphed into the Art Nouveau movement. It stood for traditional craftsmanship and often used medieval, romantic or folk styles of decoration. It advocated economic and social reform and was anti-industrial.
9 Stepniak was a Russian revolutionary mainly known for assassinating General Nikolai Mezentsov, the chief of Russia's Gendarme corps and the head of the country's secret police in St Petersburg in 1878. Peter Alekseyevich Kropotkin (1842–1921) was a Russian revolutionary and geographer, the foremost theorist of the anarchist movement.
10 Henry Hyndman founded Britain's first socialist party, the Democratic Federation (DF) in 1881. He was a Marxist. Morris joined the DF in January 1883.
11 Fiona MacCarthy, *William Morris: A Life for Our Time*. London: Faber & Faber, 1994, p. 472.
12 George Bernard Shaw (1856–1950) was a gradualist Fabian in the 1890s and after World War I an admirer of both Mussolini and Stalin.

13 Paul Lafargue (1842–1911) was a French revolutionary Marxist socialist, political writer, journalist, literary critic and activist. He was Karl Marx's son-in-law having married his second daughter, Laura. He wrote *The Right to Be Lazy*. At the age of 69, he and 66-year-old Laura committed suicide.

14 Wilhelm Martin Philipp Christian Ludwig Liebknecht (1826–1900) was a German socialist and one of the principal founders of the Social Democratic Party of Germany (SPD).

15 Karl Johann Kautsky (1854–1938) was a Czech-Austrian philosopher, journalist and Marxist theoretician. Kautsky was one of the most authoritative promulgators of orthodox Marxism after the death of Friedrich Engels in 1895 until the outbreak of World War I in 1914. He founded the socialist journal Neue Zeit.

16 Beatrice "Bice" di Folco Portinari (1265–1290) was the principal inspiration for Dante Alighieri's Vita Nuova and Dante's guide in the last book of the Divine Comedy (La Divina Commedia), Paradiso. She is the incarnation of beatific love and represents divine revelation.

17 Morris reviewed *Looking Backward* in the *Commonweal* on June 21, 1889. He condemns Bellamy's utopia as a misrepresentation of socialism.

> In short a machine life is the best which Mr. Bellamy can imagine for us on all sides; it is not to be wondered at then that this, his only idea for making labor tolerable is to decrease the amount of it by means of fresh and ever fresh developments of machinery.

18 A Madonna is a representation of Mary, either alone or with her child Jesus. These images are central icons for both the Catholic and Orthodox churches.

19 Jane Morris, the wife of William Morris, was Dante Gabriel Rossetti muse. Their romantic relationship is reputed to have started in 1865 and lasted, on differing levels, until his death in 1882. Morris broke with Rossetti over the romance, despite his expressed endorsement of free love.

20 Literati are scholars in China and Japan whose poetry, calligraphy and paintings reveal their cultivation and express their personal feelings rather than demonstrate professional skill. The concept of literati painters was first formulated in China in the Bei (Northern) Song dynasty but was codified in the Ming dynasty by Dong Qichang. Tao Yuanming's utopia served them as an inspired ideal.

21 Soviet, East European, Chinese and Vietnamese communists tried to depict socialism in their literatures and visual arts but never go beyond glorifying revolutionary intrepidness.

References

Balodis, Kārlis. (1898). *The Future State: Production and Consumption in the Socialist State. (Der Zukunftsstaat: Produktion und Konsum im Sozialstaat)*. Stuttgart: J.H.W.Dietz Nachf.

Bowman, Sylvia. (1958). *The Year 2000: A Critical Biography of Edward Bellamy.* New York: Bookman Associates.

Breme, Fredrika. (1848). *Sibling Life or Brothers and Sisters* (Swedish: *Syskonlif*). New York: Harper & Brothers.

Cabet, Étienne. (1840) *The Voyage to Icaria*. Paris: Souverain.

Hertzka, Theodor (1890). *Freeland.*

Howells, William Dean. (1894). *A Traveler from Altruria*. New York: Harper Brothers.

Lane, Mary Bradley. (1880). *Mizora*. Cincinnatti: Cincinnati Commercial.

Levitas, Ruth. (1996). "Who Holds the Hose? Domestic Labor in the Work of Bellamy," Gillman, and Morris –Ebasco Host. *Academic Search Premier* 6.

MacCarthy, Fiona. (1994). *William Morris: A Life for Our Time*. London: Faber & Faber.

Mackail, J. W. (1899). *The Life of William Morris: Volume One*. London, New York, and Bombay: Longmans, Green & Co.

Mackail, J. W. (1901). *The Life of William Morris: Volume Two*. London, New York, and Bombay: Longmans, Green & Co.

Morris, William. (1889). *Bellamy's Looking Backward*. The William Morris Internet Archive Works.

Morris, William. (1891). *News from Nowhere*. Boston: Reeves & Turner.

Surtz, Edward and J. H. Hexter (eds.). (1965). *The Complete Works of St. Thomas More*, Vol. 4. New Haven: Yale University Press.

Thompson, E. P. (1955). *William Morris: Romantic to Revolutionary*. London: Lawrence & Wishart.

Twain, Mark and Charles Dudley Warner. (1873). *The Gilded Age: A Tale of Today*. New York: American Publishing Company.

Wharton, Edith. (1920). *The Age of Innocence*. New York: D. Appleton & Company.

4 Prelude to the Marxist–Leninist Moment

Robert Owen, Count Claude Henri de Rouvroy de Saint-Simon and Étienne Cabet were libertarian institutionalists concerned primarily with designing and building better economic systems for workers. Libertarian institutionalism dominated socialist thinking until 1848, when Karl Marx and Friedrich Engel's *Communist Manifesto* issued a clarion call to revolution. Like their predecessors, Marx and Engels had a design for utopia. It was harmonious, self-regulating communalism, a shared regime where members worked and consumed cooperatively because there were no private property rights enabling them to market labor and goods. Harmonious communalism they proclaimed was a lost natural state easily restored by eradicating private property, markets and entrepreneurship. *Paradise Lost, Paradise Regain'd* (Milton, 1667, 1671; Graeber and Wengrow, 2021). Their harmonist sentiment accorded with Jean Jacques Rousseau's primitivist romanticism (noble savage) and was the antithesis of Sigmund Freud's concept of civilization's intrinsic discontents (Freud, 1930).

This made the *Communist Manifesto* the pivotal moment in socialism's 19th-century evolution. After 1847, the class struggle and political activism, not utopian designs, became the keys to worker betterment. At first, Marxists paid little attention to how the class struggle would cancel capitalism. Some thought it would be democratic, others violent. During the subsequent decades, both paths seemed plausible. One way or another, Marxists were confident that historical dialectic assured capitalism's demise and communism's triumph.

Karl Marx changed course in 1871. He concluded that strategic patience was a mistake because justice delayed was justice denied (Marx, 1970, 13–30; Johnstone, 1971, 447–462). Friedrich Engels concurred. Both urged shortening the birth pangs of socialism by seizing power and promptly installing proletarian dictatorships. Vladimir Lenin eventually heeded Marx's call to arms. Eduard Bernstein opposed (Gay, 1952), choosing peaceful Marxist democratic socialism as the wisest strategy. The choice between these alternatives was fundamental. It affected the substance of the class struggle and attitudes toward postcapitalist governance. Marx not only advocated proletarian insurrection, he also urged proletarian authoritarian rule as long as needed to foreclose capitalist counterrevolution. This was the path blazed

DOI: 10.4324/9781003371571-6

by Lenin and Stalin. Bernstein opted for parliamentary democracy to achieve and preserve socialist rule via the ballot box.

Both paths were risky, if dialectical materialism failed to provide ironclad assurance that the future belonged to socialism. The Marxist–Leninist–Stalinist route canceled capitalism, but did not guarantee harmonious communalism. Social democratic policies bettered workers lots, but might not establish socialist rule. Politics provided a tool empowering socialist policy, without assuring desirable results.

Karl Marx and Friedrich Engel's clarion call to class struggle and political activism drove a wedge between socialists who supported and opposed the state, worker participation in public affairs and libertarianism. Owen, Saint-Simon and Cabet were libertarians. They never considered dictatorships of the proletariat or comprehensive public policymaking attractive tools for advancing the socialist cause. Anarcho-socialists like Pierre-Joseph Proudhon (1809–1865) (Proudhon), Mikhail Bakunin (1814–1876) and Peter Kropotkin (1842–1921) concurred. They loathed the state and shunned national state politics.

Marxists of all persuasions fought for illiberal authority, and the primacy of the state (pending full communism). The rest of the socialist community rejected their ambitions (Proudhon, 1840). Professions to the contrary, notwithstanding, Marxists opposed local worker self-management pending capitalism's complete eradication.

The majority initially disapproved Marxist-Leninism, but the tide gradually turned in its favor. A series of historical transformations created the foundation for workers seizure of state power, including the rise of nationalism, the first wave of globalization 1870–1913 (Ferguson, 2003), a revolution in heavy industry and transportation, burgeoning trade unionism, urbanization, waning aristocratic authority, emerging representative democracy, expanding education, World War I and the Bolshevik Revolution. The appeal of Marxist and anarcho-syndicalist revolutionary politics steadily grew, and the Fabian alternative (G. D. H. Cole's version of Guild Socialism) gradually became anachronistic (Cole, 1920).

The moment-of-truth for Marxist-Leninism arrived on November 7, 1917. The great experiment began. Lenin's subsequent consolidation of Bolshevik power on January 18, 1918, made his brand of revolutionary socialism the gold standard. Democratic and Fabian socialism remained speculative possibilities, while Lenin put Marx and Engel's revolutionary communism to the test. He criminalized private property, markets and entrepreneurship, canceled capitalism, and Stalin subsequently installed comprehensive central planning for the working classes' benefit. Lenin attempted to humble critics by demonstrating that "Proletarian democracy was a million times more democratic than any bourgeois democracy; and Soviet power a million times more democratic than the most democratic bourgeois republic" (Lenin, 1918).

The Great Challenge was on. It lasted 73 years and ended conclusively on December 25, 1991, in Marxist-Leninism's defeat, tempered by some renewed interest in libertarian democratic socialism and Chinese market communism.

Marxist-Leninism's failure did not seal the fate of other early-20th-century socialisms. There were two other important rival schools, 1885–1917: democratic socialism (including Fabianism and the labor union movement in England)[1] and revolutionary anarcho-syndicalism. On the eve of World War I, it seemed that the future might belong to the Fabians in England, Marxist socialist democrats in Germany and revolutionary syndicalism in Southern Europe, but contemporary prospects for all three are unpromising.[2]

Notes

1 The German Social Democratic Party (Sozialdemokratische Partei Deutschlands, SPD) was founded on May 23, 1863, by Ferdinand Lassalle under the name Allgemeiner Deutscher Arbeiterverein (ADAV, General German Workers' Association). In 1869, August Bebel and Wilhelm Liebknecht founded the Sozialdemokratische Arbeiterpartei (SDAP, Social Democratic Workers' Party of Germany), which merged with the ADAV at a conference held in Gotha in 1875, taking the name Socialist Workers' Party of Germany (SAPD). At this conference, the party developed the Gotha Program, which Karl Marx criticized in his *Critique of the Gotha Program*. Through the Anti-Socialist Laws, Otto von Bismarck had the party outlawed for its pro-revolution, anti-monarchy sentiments in 1878; but in 1890 it was legalized again. That year – in its Halle convention – it changed its name to Sozialdemokratische Partei Deutschlands (SPD), as it is known to this day.
2 Marxist socialist democratic parties before World War I were ambivalent about violent revolution. Even though they labeled themselves democratic, they were not committed to an orderly peaceful construction of socialism. The Fabians alone staunchly supported democracy over revolution. After the Bolsheviks seized power in Russia, several formerly revolutionary Marxists condemned Lenin. In late 1918, the Czech-Austrian Marxist Karl Kautsky authored an anti-Leninist pamphlet condemning the antidemocratic nature of Soviet Russia, to which Lenin replied. German Marxist Rosa Luxemburg echoed Kautsky's views, while the Russian anarchist Peter Kropotkin described the Bolshevik seizure of power as "the burial of the Russian Revolution." These critiques took on a life of their own in subsequent discussions of Soviet socialism, but do not mean that Europe had a mature and viable democratic socialist alternative. The Mensheviks similarly were ambivalent Marxist democratic socialists inclined toward workers' state domination.

References

Cole, George Douglas Howard. (1920). *Guild Socialism Re-stated*. London: L. Parsons.
Ferguson, Niall. (2003). *Empire: The Rise and Demise of the British World Order and the Lessons for Global Power*. New York: Basic Books.
Freud, Sigmund. (1930). *Das Unbehagen in der Kultur*. Wien: Internationaler Psychoanalytischer Verlag.
Gay, Peter. (1952), *The Dilemma of Democratic Socialism: Eduard Bernstein's Challenge to Marx*. New York: Columbia University Press.
Graeber, David and David Wengrow. (2021). *The Dawn of Everything: A New History of Humanity*. New York: Farrar, Straus and Giroux.

Johnstone, Monty. (1971). "The Paris Commune and Marx's Conception of the Dictatorship of the Proletariat." *The Massachusetts Review.* Vol. 12, No. 3, 447–462.

Lenin, Vladimir. (1918). "The Proletarian Revolution and the Renegade Kautsky." www. marxists.org/archive/lenin/works/1918/prrk/democracy.htm

Marx, Karl. (1970). "Critique of the Gotha Programme, 1875." In *Marx/Engels Selected Works, Volume Three.* Moscow: Progress Publishers.

Milton, John. (1667). *Paradise Lost.* London: Simmons.

Milton, John. (1671). *Paradise Regain'd.* London: Simmons.

Proudhon, Pierre-Joseph. (1840). *What Is Property? An Inquiry into the Principle of Right and of Government.* Paris: Brocard.

Part II
Marxist-Leninism (1917–1991)

5   Bolshevik Revolution

The period between the assassination of Tsar Alexander II in 1881 and the outbreak of World War I witnessed a transformative double movement. There was a dazzling rise of urban industrialization founded on libertarian democracy (the Gilded Age, Belle Époque, laissez-faire capitalism)[1] and an equally impressive Marxist socialist challenge (anti-capitalism).[2] Both claimed the future.

Socialists divided into four camps in the 1880s. Fabians advocated the trade union movement. Anarchists plumbed for self-governing communes. Democratic socialists sought ballot box victories and revolutionary Marxists and anarcho-syndicalists violent regime change.

The revolutionary Marxist moment arrived in Russia on January 19, 1918, when the Bolsheviks forcibly closed the democratically elected Constituent Assembly and seized the Russian state in the name of the "vanguard of the proletariat." Revolutionary Marxists had been plotting for this day since 1871 (Marx, 1871, 1875), paying no serious attention to the problem of designing and managing a statist socialist order, content to imagine that having canceled capitalism they could install state socialism. This entailed vanquishing trade unions, revolutionary syndicalism, anarchists and other opponents of one-party Bolshevik rule as stepping stones to Marxist–Leninist planning and command.

Vladimir Lenin and Joseph Stalin rose to the challenge of 1917–1928, fighting tactical battles in multiple theaters to maintain political power and create a centrally planned economy based on state ownership, control and management of the means of production, free of private propriety, markets and entrepreneurship. Marxist–Leninist–Stalinist command plan communism began in late 1928. The founding fathers were triumphal (Appendix 2).

Road to Power and Planning

The Marxist portrayal of the Bolshevik revolution is a creation myth concocted by John Reed to persuade the world that proletarian revolutionary will was the foundation stone of Soviet power (Reed, 1919).[3] The workers did not storm the Winter Palace on November 7, 1917, and the majority of Russian citizens

DOI: 10.4324/9781003371571-8

preferred other political parties. The Bolshevik seizure of power was a coup d'état against the democratically elected Constituent Assembly on January 19, 1918. It represented Lenin's will to rule in the name of proletariat, not the workers' will to have the Bolsheviks rule them in the name of the vanguard of the proletariat. It was revolution from above.

The Bolshevik's road to power illuminates the importance of political will in determining the architecture of revolutionary Marxist socialist systems. The story briefly starts with the February Revolution. War-weary Russian workers and soldiers of Petrograd deposed Tsar Nicholas II on March 8–15, 1917.[4] Vladimir Lenin (1870–1924) hastened home to Russia from Switzerland after the German authorities agreed to permit his passage through Germany to neutral Sweden. Berlin hoped that Lenin's return to Petrograd would undermine the Russian war effort.

Lenin arrived in Petrograd on April 16, 1917 one month after Tsar Nicolas II abdicated, at a moment when Russia was being temporarily governed by an imperially appointed Provisional Government composed of the Cadet (liberal), Menshevik (democratic socialist) and social revolutionary (agrarian socialist) parties,[5] together with supporters of the imperial family.[6]

On his return to Russia, Lenin denounced the Provisional Government and tried to subvert it by demanding "All power to the Soviets" (irregular committees of workers, soldiers and peasants). He ordered an armed assault on the Provisional Government administration on November 7, 1917, from a hideout in Helsinki and proclaimed that state power had passed into the hands of the Soviets. The Constituent Assembly elected on October 20, 1917, by 36 million voters as the permanent successor of the Provisional Government ignored the Bolsheviks and continued ruling as Russia's only legitimate government (Khrushchev, 1956).[7] Although, Lenin argued that the election was unfair, the newly elected Russian Constituent Assembly convened in Petrograd in January 1918. Lenin's Council of People's Commissars (Sovnarkom) then forcibly disbanded the Constituent Assembly, imposing a Bolshevik "dictatorship of the proletariat" on January 19, 1918. At their seventh Congress March 1918, the Bolsheviks changed their official name from the Russian Social Democratic Labor Party to the Russian Communist Party. This ended the pretense that the Bolsheviks were democratic socialists. The Bolsheviks always were revolutionary Marxists.

On November 18, 1917, Lenin's illegitimate Soviet Government passed Decrees on Peace and Land. The Decree on Land ratified the actions of the peasants who throughout Russia seized private land from the nobility and redistributed it among themselves.

Lenin's Council of People's Commissars (Sovnarkom) simultaneously adopted six other fundamental decrees:

The self-proclaimed Bolshevik government seized all private property.
It nationalized all Russian banks.
It confiscated all private bank accounts.
It seized the Church's properties (including bank accounts).

It repudiated all foreign debts.
It assigned control of the factories to the soviets (ad hoc worker councils).

Lenin's opponents strenuously resisted these illegal seizures, prompting an Ivan the Terrible style reign of terror and despotism in the name of the proletariat. After the Bolsheviks disbanded the Constituent Assembly and seized government power on January 19, 1918, Communist revolutionaries under Yakov Yurovsky shot the Russian Imperial Romanov family (Emperor Nicholas II, his wife Empress Alexandra and their five children: Olga, Tatiana, Maria, Anastasia and Alexei) in Yekaterinburg on the night of July 16–27, 1918.[8] The Bolsheviks took their bodies to the Koptyaki forest, stripped and mutilated them. According to Leon Trotsky's diaries, Lenin supported killing the Tsar and his family (Trotsky, 1986).

All these events illuminate Marx's mature concept of ruthlessly destroying established power (capitalist, tsarist, democratic) through insurrectionary state seizure by a self-anointed communist leader (vozhd) in the name of the toiling masses, buttressed with terror and policies that criminalized private ownership, markets and entrepreneurship and substituting state coercion, bureaucratic administration, planning and revolutionary zealotry (Marx, 1871, 1875, 1880; Lenin, 1902).

Foundations of the Marxist–Leninist–Stalinist Order

Leninists equated cancelling Russia's embryonic libertarian capitalism with the establishment of socialism without bothering to figure out how to construct a well-functioning socialist regime. Lenin and Karl Marx never understood general competitive consumer sovereign economic theory (Lenin, 1899),[9] and consequently the Bolsheviks did not have a feasible blueprint for socialist construction on the morrow of the revolution. Lenin described what he thought should be done in *State and Revolution* (1917) written in exile. He suggested running the economy like a post office, where consumers requested goods by mail, and factory directors posted them back gratis (Lenin, 2017; Evans, 1987; Barfield, 1971). Nikolai Bukharin and Evgeny Preobrazhensky tried to fill the void in their *ABCs of Communism* (1918) that celebrated the destruction of money (Bukharin and Preobrazhensky, 1969), but patchwork implementation of these schemes quickly proved catastrophic.

Revolutionary Transition 1918–1921

Vladimir Lenin was the cofounder of the Marxist Russian Social Democratic Labor Party (RSDLP), a revolutionary socialist political party formed in 1898. He became the leader of the Bolshevik faction at its Second Party Congress in 1903.[10] Bolsheviks actively participated on a minority basis in factory worker organizations called soviets (councils) that played a major role in the 1905 Russian Revolution (public demonstrations).[11] The soviets disappeared after the revolution of 1905, but reemerged during the revolution of 1917.

The dissolution of the Constituent Assembly by the Council of People's Commissars (Sovnarkom) on January 19, 1918 under the slogan "All Power to the Soviets" marked the start of Communist Party rule in Russia. The Bolshevik regime's legitimacy, rested on the fiction that the soviets represented the will of the working class, and that the Bolshevik wing of the Marxist Russian Social Democratic Labor Party now self-rebranded as the Communist Party, was the "vanguard of the proletariat" (wage earning workers and peasants).

Lenin's task thereafter was to transform the Bolshevik's claim to legitimacy into reality by commandeering the state government apparatus from the National Assembly and using it under new Bolshevik names to rule the polity, military, police, economy and society after nationalizing the means of production, criminalizing markets and entrepreneurship. The Bolshevik state owned the nation's natural resources, land and the entire industrial and administrative means of production including housing, gold and other valuable assets by the November 18, 1917, decree.[12] Non-agrarian laborers were state employees, when they could find jobs (Hutchings, 1967).[13] The state set wages. Workers were powerless whenever the Bolsheviks chose to disregard trade unions and worker councils (soviets). The rule of men prevailed, not the rule of law, and there was no planning.

Circumstances compelled Lenin to improvise. Russia and Germany were at war. The Bolshevik government surrendered to Berlin[14] and redeployed its troops (renamed the Red Army) to fight various forces including foreign armies (British, French, American and Japanese) contesting Soviet power (Trickey, 2017).[15] Lenin had to feed his administrators and provision the population. The Red Army commanded by Leon Trotsky (1879–1940) dragooned workers and compelled them to operate factories under military command after former private owners fled. Trotsky and other Bolshevik officials commandeered supplies and rationed them as the Communist Party dictated. The Bolsheviks compelled remnants of the tsarist era bureaucracy to work under its direction. Many urbanites returned to the countryside, and the peasants mostly operated under traditional agrarian communal organizations (mir and obshchina).[16]

The Bolshevik strategy during the revolutionary transition 1918–1921 was vanquishing political and military foes and eradicating all vestiges of capitalism (private ownership, markets and social influence) by direct action. Lenin could have focused on military victory first, and then gradually transformed markets to planned economy, but revolutionary Marxist logic ruled out orderly transition. Lenin was confident that the Bolsheviks could efficiently command factor allocation, production, distribution and consumption in natural terms, that is, physical units of measure, without money and competitive prices. He believed that accounting would suffice.

Accounting and control-these are the chief things necessary, for the organizing and correct functioning of the first phase of Communist society. All citizens are here transformed into hired employees of the state "syndicate" (trade union). All that is required is that they should work equally, should regularly do their share of the work, and should receive equal pay (in kind).

(Lenin, 2017)

Lenin expected workers and peasants to run expropriated economic institutions according to their ability in return for equal compensation in kind under the guidance and control of the Bolshevik dictatorship of the proletariat pending a transition to proletarian communal self-management. He appointed the Sovnarkom, Council of People's Commissars (economic cabinet) and the VSNKh (Supreme Council of the National Economy) setup on December 15, 1917, before the Bolshevik putsch against the National Assembly to act as commanders overseeing various political and economic portfolios. Both institutions, together with the STO (Labor and Defense Council) had broad mandates to get the job done using whatever means necessary,[17] meaning "prodrazverstka" (forced requisitioning of foodstuffs, with or without compensation, and physical distribution to intermediate input use, or final consumption). The same principle applied to other goods, and encompassed dragooning hapless souls into Leon Trotsky's Red Labor Army and otherwise compelling state employees to work on terms they often considered abusive.

Lenin prioritized decision making based on revolutionary fervor (redness) instead of competitive efficient rational choice and promoted radical policies like hyperinflation, creating a de facto money-free economy and accelerating the spontaneous development of worker and peasant self-managed collective and communal organizations. The administrative economic control mechanism was a top-down command structure. Worker, peasant and local party official activities were horizontal. Lenin sought complete top-down administrative adherence to his command and wanted horizontal actors to do the right communist things, but decisions throughout the transition regime were mostly ad hoc, discordant, inefficient and destructive.

The situation was chaotic due to the civil war, foreign military intervention, nationalization of the means of production, the criminalization of markets and entrepreneurship, radical Bolshevik revolutionary policies and economic incompetence, but the word chaos exaggerates the disarray. There was order in the mayhem. There were competing power centers, not a power vacuum. Gray and black markets replaced tsarist rent-granting and competitive laissez-faire. The importance of regional and local institutions increased vis-à-vis the center. The economy devolved into weakly connected networks of inefficient state administrators and self-sufficient collective and communist entities.

There was considerable talk of astonishing communist successes (Bolshevik utopian delirium) amid industrial unemployment and material catastrophe. Industrial output during War Communism fell 69% and agrarian output plummeted 40%, causing widespread famine (Nove, 1972, 68). The population deficit 1918–1923 was 19.7 million (Rosefielde, 2002, 1164; Volkov, 1930; Davies, Harrison and Wheatcroft, 1994; Wheatcroft, 1994, 62–64).[18] Lenin tried his best to ignore the destruction as the economy collapsed,[19] but called a strategic retreat.[20] He announced a pause at the Tenth Party Congress in March 1921,[21] temporarily legalizing some private market and competitive interstate enterprise activities.

Lenin did not view his decision as a verdict on transition period top-down and horizontal institutions. The pause only indicated his dissatisfaction with the revolutionary transition mechanism that had haphazardly evolved and recognition that central planning was a prerequisite for reliable Communist Party command. He also may have mused about blending markets with communist administrative command planning, but never said anything explicitly about it (Erlich, 1960; Cohen, 1971).

Lenin was able to avoid acknowledging the catastrophic failure of his methods with the slogan "one step back, two steps forward," but the Communist Party never really considered reverting to a strategy of spontaneous ad hoc coercion. His successors chose instead to forge a planning system to guide top-down administration, tightened central control and pitched revolutionary proletarian self-management into the garbage can of history (until Mao revived it during the Cultural Revolution 1967–1976).

New Economic Policy 1921–1928

Lenin's pause was the crux of the Bolshevik's New Economic Policy (NEP) announced at the Tenth Party Congress in March 1921. It permitted peasants and other state agents some degree of freedom in producing, distributing, pricing and marketing their goods and services to the public and state purchasers. NEP was not a blue print for a mixed economy, but gradually moved in that direction by permitting various forms of private and state entrepreneurship (Deng Xiaoping's crossing streams one stone at a time strategy).

The Bolsheviks sought to improve asset use in the agrarian, industrial and commercial sectors. The state owned the means of production including the land by decree. Some assets were returned to their prerevolutionary owners, but in principle the state retained the freehold right.[22] The Bolsheviks permitted citizens, including former owners beginning July 7, 1921 to lease facilities from the state, resuming old business, or starting new ones on the proviso that they hired no more than 20 employees (Nove, 1972, 106). The only mixed system consistent with the Communist Party's aversion to private property was one that allowed peasants, workers, managers and entrepreneurs to use state assets in whole or part for private purposes (leasehold markets). The vast majority of party members were willing to tolerate peasants, workers, managers and entrepreneurs using state property for private purposes as a temporary expedient, but attitudes varied.

Some like Leon Trotsky and Evgeny Preobrazhensky were NEP minimalists. They disliked private individual material self-seeking and were willing to make only minor concessions to ensure Bolshevik survival. Both urged ending the pause swiftly, and moving forward to comprehensive central planning purged of private individual material self-seeking. Nikolai Bukharin by contrast encouraged the Party to foster market-oriented agrarian initiatives, and contemplated a transition beyond NEP to democratic market socialism.[23] Stephen Cohen believed that ignoring Bukharin's democratic socialist advocacy was Bolshevism tragic error, but democratic socialism was never a serious possibility in 1917–1953 because the party was under the thrall of the Revolutionary Marxist mindset (Cohen, 1971).

The reality of the NEP system, given the Communist Party's monopoly of political and social power, lay between these extremes. The Bolsheviks granted peasants greater latitude in using state land and marketing crops (Narodnoe khoziaistvo za 60 let, 1977, 9; Nove, 1972, 136–137),[24] but simultaneously sponsored collective (kolkhoz) and state (sovkhoz) farms as surrogates for peasant communes (Narodnoe khoziaistvo za 60 let, 1977, 8; Narodnoe khoziaistvo SSSR za 70 Let, 1987, 35).[25] The Communist Party gave peasants freedom with one hand and gradually strangled them with the other.

Commercial and industrial liberalization followed the same pattern. The Bolsheviks permitted individuals (called NEP men) to peddle wares. They were intermediaries. They allowed craftspeople (kustars) and small private firms employing five or fewer laborers to manufacture and market their goods to consumers and state purchasing agents (Narodnoe khoziaistvo za 60 let, 1977, 98).[26] They posed a potential "capitalist threat" to Bolshevik authority, but only a minor one because NEP men constituted a small share of the labor force, and VSNKh (Supreme Economic Council) became more effective.

It organized enterprises into trusts and coordinated their activities. It professionalized enterprise management, transforming activists into competent state business administrators. This enhanced state industrial discipline on one hand, but also increased managerial discretionary authority. VSNKh authorized managers to competitively purchase intermediate inputs and other supplies and determine product assortments hoping to improve efficiency and productivity. Although, it did not command enterprise managers to maximize profits, reducing costs and increasing revenue enhanced the performance of the transition model (Nove, 1972, 68).

The devolution of authority had a darker side from the Communist Party's perspective. It made it possible for Bolshevik managers to serve themselves at the same time they served the state. NEP rules not only encouraged managers to purchase inputs and sell products to NEP men, they tacitly permitted managers to act as private entrepreneurs using state assets. They could enter into sweetheart deals with outside NEP men and become inside entrepreneurs acting as independent contractors, raising the specter of capitalist capture. Instead of producing to meet the state's needs, managers could service consumer demand directly and supplement their own income as derivative independent contractors. They wore two hats. The Communist Party doublemindedly wanted the economy to serve the proletariat but abhorred managers enriching themselves by using state assets.

Official statistics report that NEP enabled Russia to fully recover from its War Communist hyper-depression and surpass the 1917 level of production by 1926, growing after recovery at double digits rates, 1926–1928. Bolshevik leaders, however, did not consider this performance good enough (Narodnoe khoziaistvo za 60 let, 1977, 9, 12, 167; Gregory, 1994).

The Communist Party debated whether NEP's material benefits were worth imperiling Bolshevik power and ideological sensibilities through the prism of Marxist–Leninist specters such as the "scissors crisis" and "cry wolf" fears of imminent industrial collapse (Erlich, 1960; Preobrazhensky, 1926).[27] There were no serious scientific assessments of NEP's comparative economic merit, including the Feldman-Preobrazhensky model (Ellman, 1990, 2004, 2008; Kontorovich, 2013; Day, 1975; Dobb, 1966; Domar, 1957; Engerman, 2003, 2009; Ehrlich, 1978; Fel'dman, 1964; Gregory, 2004; Preobrazhensky, 1979; Rutland, 1985).

Stalin unilaterally settled the debate and terminated NEP in September 1928. The data suggest that he made a faulty decision. The NEP mixed command-market economy was performing splendidly on paper and the capitalist class was shrinking rapidly. Perhaps, the data were wrong. The truth here is inessential because right or wrong, the Soviet Communist Party decided to terminate its experiment with a mixed command-market economy 1921–1928. It concluded that central planning was more promising.[28]

The Bolsheviks never looked back until Mikhail Gorbachev's arenda (leasing) and perestroika experiments 1987–1991. Gorbachev did not revert to either the revolutionary transition period or NEP, but Castro tried both during 1959–2021 with similar unsatisfactory results. Some supporters of the "Workers Opposition" (Daniels, 1960),[29] revolutionary romantics and avant-garde artists consider the revolutionary transition regime of 1917–1921 to be paradise lost.[30] Class warfare, martyrdom and sexual liberation fire their imagination (Manaev and Chalyan, 2018).

Notes

1 Libertarians, including many socialists favored the sanctity of private property and the right to engage in business (Fourier, Owen, Saint-Simon and then later George Douglas Howard Cole). Karl Marx opposed but supported other aspects of free rational choice.

2 Left libertarians supported individual freedom except when this harmed the working class. The difference between traditional and left libertarianism concerns appropriate restrictions on individual freedom. Capitalist libertarianism is unacceptable to the left.

3 BONI & Liveright was the publishing house of the Communist Party, the United States. John Reed was a founding member. John "Jack" Silas Reed (1887–1920) was an American journalist, poet and Communist activist. Reed first gained prominence as a war correspondent during World War I, and later became best known for his coverage of the November Revolution in Petrograd, Russia. Reed is buried in the Kremlin Wall Necropolis. The Soviets made a film version of John Reed's book, *October: Ten Days That Shook the World*. It is a celebratory 1928 dramatization of the 1917 October Revolution written and directed by Sergei Eisenstein and Grigori Aleksandrov.

4 On September 1, 1914, after the outbreak of World War I, the Imperial government renamed the city Petrograd meaning "Peter's city." On January 26, 1924, five days after the death of Vladimir Lenin, it was renamed Leningrad. On September 6, 1991, a city-wide referendum restored the original name, Saint Petersburg.

5 The intention of the provisional government was the organization of elections to the Russian Constituent Assembly and its convention. The provisional government lasted approximately eight months.

6 The Provisional Committee of the State Duma formed the Provisional Government in Petrograd in 1917. The State Duma was the more representative chamber of the two in the Russian parliament established after the Revolution of 1905 and was led first by Prince Georgy Lvov (1861–1925) and then by Alexander Kerensky (1881–1970). It replaced the Imperial institution of the Council of Ministers of Russia. The last ruling Russian Emperor Nicholas II (1868–1918) abdicated in February 1917 in favor of his youngest brother, the Grand Duke Michael (1878–1918), who agreed that he would accept after the decision of the Russian Constituent Assembly. The Provisional Government was unable to make decisive policy decisions due to political factionalism and a breakdown of state structures. The Provisional Government's chief adversary on the left was the Petrograd Soviet, which gradually gained control of the Imperial Army, local factories and the Russian Railway.

7 Khrushchev said:

> Nevertheless, three weeks after the Communist coup November 7, 1917, 36 million Russians voted in free elections for an All-Russian Constituent Assembly, gave only a fourth of their votes to the Communists and a clear majority to the agrarian, democratic Socialist Revolutionaries. Lenin, Trotsky, Stalin and their associates dispersed the Assembly by force on January 19, 1918.

8 Yakov Yurovsky (1878–1938) was a Russian Old Bolshevik, revolutionary and Soviet Chekist (secret policeman).

9 The book is journalistic Marxist political economy assembling data showing the gathering crisis of Russian capitalism before Russia became a capitalist economy.

10 Alexander Bogdanov cofounded the Bolshevik faction. The word Bolshevik means majority, but Lenin's faction was actually the minority. The Mensheviks faction (literally minority) was actually the majority. The misnomers result from a tactical maneuver at the Second Party Congress in 1903.

11 The Russian Revolution of 1905 was a wave of mass political and social unrest that spread through the Russian Empire. It included worker strikes, peasant unrest and military mutinies. It led to constitutional reform (the "October Manifesto"), including the establishment of the State Duma, the multiparty system and the Russian Constitution of 1906. Russia's defeat in the Russo-Japanese War triggered the 1905 public protests.

12 The peasants, however, acted as if the land were theirs and did not pay explicit ground rent to the state.

13 Of the 1,352,800 registered unemployed at the beginning of 1928, 263,900, or nearly 20%, were new male industrial job seekers. There was little unemployment among skilled workers.

14 He signed a peace treaty with the Kaiser. The Treaty of Brest-Litovsk (also known as the Treaty of Brest in Russia) was a separate peace treaty signed on March 3, 1918, between the new Bolshevik government of Russia and the Central Powers (German Empire, Austria-Hungary, Bulgaria and the Ottoman Empire), that ended Russia's participation in World War I.

15 The American Expeditionary Force, Siberia (AEF in Siberia) was a formation of the United States Army involved in the Russian Civil War in Vladivostok, Russia, after the October Revolution, from 1918 to 1920.

16 The mir was a community consisting of former serfs, or state peasants and their descendants, settled in a single village. The mir owned the land. Members of the mir had the right to cultivate their allotments.

   Obshchina were agricultural communities.

17 The Council of Labor and Defense established in November 1918 was responsible for the central management of the economy and production of military materiel in the Russian Socialist Federative Soviet Republic and in its successor state, the Soviet Union. During the Russian Civil War of 1917–1922, the council served as an emergency national economic cabinet, issuing emergency decrees in an effort to sustain industrial production for the Red Army. The Council included Lenin, Trotsky and Stalin.

18 The population deficit is the difference between the demographically projected and actual population resulting from a combination of unexpected changes in mortality and natality. Russia's population in 1917 was 144 million. The underlying source of Volkov's estimate is uncertain because of the poor quality of the data, and assumptions about trends in natality and mortality. However, there is broad agreement that Volkov's estimate is in the ballpark. Since the Russians surrendered to Germany on March 3, 1918, few population deficit casualties are ascribable to World War I.

19 The Soviet regime was rattled by the Kronstadt rebellion, peasant revolts in the provinces, angry food queues in the cities, strikes by hungry workers and factionalism within the Communist Party.

20 The term War Communism misleadingly suggests that Lenin's revolutionary institutions and economic policies would have proved their mettle if there had not been a civil war.

21 The formal decree that introduced the NEP was "On the replacement of prodrazverstka [grain requisitioning] with prodnalog (a fixed tax)." Unit commander decided prodraverska quotas during war communism. Peasants retained more of their output under NEP.

22 Of the tens of thousands of enterprises confiscated prior to May 1921, only 76 were returned to their former proprietors by the presidium of VSNKh. Provincial authorities restored some others, but denationalization never happened.

23 Note that five years earlier Bukharin had been a radical anti-market revolutionary Marxist–Leninist.

24 The state share of gross agricultural output in 1928 was 3.3%.

25 1.7 percent of agricultural household were collectivized in 1928. There were 2.9 million collective farm workers in 1928.

26 There were 4.6 million people classified as bourgeoisie, landowners, traders and kulaks in 1928.

27 Under War Communism, industrial production fell more steeply than agriculture, causing industrial and agricultural prices to diverge. The peak disparity occurred in 1923, and then reversed. The scissors image was concocted by plotting terms of trade in alternative denominators, so that one series rose, and the other fell. The episode had no intrinsic economic importance, but Stalin used it as a bogyman to justify forced collectivization by claiming that markets discouraged peasant grain marketing. Leon Trotsky coined the term "scissors crisis." Evgeny Preobrazhensky and Leon Trotsky contended that the peasants had to be forcibly collectivized so that the Bolsheviks could squeeze them sufficiently to provide a "primitive socialist capital accumulation" critical for rapid socialist industrialization. They asserted with the primitive socialist

capital accumulation, the Soviet capital stock would crumble, putting Bolshevik power in Jeopardy. This was scare talk masquerading sound economic theory.

28 The State Planning Agency, Gosplan, was established on February 22, 1921. *Voprosy Ekonomiki* (Questions of Economics) and *Planovoe khoziaistvo* (Planned Economy), both scientific planning journals were launched in the early 1920s.

29 The Workers' Opposition was a faction of the Russian Communist Party that emerged in 1920 as a response to the perceived over-bureaucratization that was occurring in Soviet Russia. They advocated the transfer of national economic management to trade unions. Alexander Shlyapnikov, Sergei Medvedev, Alexandra Kollontai and Yuri Lutovinov were leading members. It existed until 1922, when it was defeated at the 11th Congress of the Russian Communist Party.

30 Sergei Eisenstein's film *Battleship Potemkin* exemplifies the use of avant-garde cinematography to stir revolutionary outrage.

References

Barfield, Rodney. (1971). "Lenin's Utopianism: State and Revolution." *Slavic Review.* Vol. 30, No. 1, 45–56.

Bukharin, Nikolai and Yegeny Preobrazhensky. (1969). *The ABC of Communism.* London: Pelican classics.

Cohen, Stephen. (1971). *Bukharin and the Bolshevik Revolution: A Political Biography, 1888–1938.* London: Oxford University Press.

Daniels, Robert. (1960). *The Conscience of the Revolution: Communist Opposition in Soviet Russia.* Cambridge: Harvard University Press.

Davies, R. W., Mark Harrison and Stephen Wheatcroft. (1994). *The Economic Transformation of the Soviet Union* 1913–1945. Cambridge: Cambridge University Press.

Day, Richard. (1975). Preobrazhensky and the Theory of the Transition Period. *Soviet Studies.* Vol. 27, No. 2, 196–219.

Dobb, Maurice. (1966). *Soviet Economic Development Since 1917.* New York: International Publishers.

Domar, Evsey. (1957). "A Soviet Model of Growth." In Evsey Domar (ed.). *Essays in the Theory of Economic Growth* (pp. 223–261). New York: Oxford University Press.

Ellman, Michael. (1990). "Grigorii Alexandrovic Fel'dman." In John Eatwell, Murray Milgate and Peter Newman (eds.). *Problems of the Planned Economy* (pp. 109–112). New York: Norton.

Ellman, Michael. (2004). "Soviet Industrialization: A Remarkable Success?" *Slavic Review.* Vol. 63, No. 4, 841–849.

Ellman, Michael. (2008). "The Political Economy of Stalinism in the Light of the Archival Revolution. *Journal of Institutional Economics.* Vol. 4, No. 1, 99–125.

Engerman, David. (2003). *Modernization from the Other Shore: American Intellectuals and the Romance of Russian Economic Development.* Cambridge: Harvard University Press.

Engerman, David. (2009). *Know Your Enemy: The Rise and Fall of America's Soviet Experts.* New York: Oxford University Press.

Erlich, Alexander. (1960). *The Soviet industrialization debate, 1924-1938.* Cambridge: Harvard University Press.

Erlich, Alexander. (1978). "Dobb and the Marx-Fel'dman Model: A Problem in Soviet Economic Strategy." *Cambridge Journal of Economics.* Vol. 2, 203–214.

Evans, Alfred. (1987). "Rereading Lenin's State and Revolution." *Slavic Review*. Vol. 46, No. 1, 1–19.

Fel'dman, Grigory. (1964). "On the Theory of Growth Rates of National Income." In Nicolas Spulber (ed.). *Foundations of Soviet Strategy for Economic Growth* (pp. 304–331). Bloomington: Indiana University Press.

Gregory, Paul. (1994). *Before Command: An Economic History of Russia from Emancipation to the First Five-Year*. Princeton: Princeton University Press.

Gregory, Paul. (2004). *The Political Economy of Stalinism, Evidence from the Soviet Secret Archives*. Cambridge: Cambridge University Press.

Hutchings, Raymond. (1967). "The Ending of Unemployment in the USSR." *Soviet Studies*. Vol. 19, No. 1, 29–52.

Khrushchev, Nikita. (1956). *Crimes of the Stalin Era. Special Report to the 20th Congress of the Communist Party of the Soviet Union*. New York: New Leader.

Kontorovich, Vladimir. (2013). "The Preobrazhenskii-Feldman Myth and the Soviet Industrialization." https://scholarship.haverford.edu/cgi/viewcontent.cgi?article=1172&context=economics_facpubs

Lenin, Vladimir. (1899). *The Development of Capitalism in Russia*. St. Petersburg: Bodovozovoi.

Lenin, Vladimir. (1902). *What Is to Be Done?* St. Petersburg: Iskra.

Lenin, Vladimir. (2017). *State and Revolution*. Moscow: International Publishers.

Manaev, Georgy and Daniel Chalyan, (2018). "How Sexual Revolution Exploded (and Imploded) across 1920s Russia." *Russia Beyond*. www.rbth.com/history/328265-russian-sexual-revolution

Marx, Karl. (1871). *The Civil War in France*. London.

Marx, Karl. (1875).*Critique of the Gotha Program*. London.

Marx, Karl. (1880). *Socialism: Utopian and Scientific*. London.

Narodnoe khoziaistvo SSSR za 70 Let. (1987). Moscow: Finansy I Statistika.

Narodnoe khoziaistvo za 60 let, iubileinyi statisticheskii ezhegodnik. (1977). Moscow: Finansy I Statistika.

Nove, Alec. (1972). *An Economic History of the U.S.S.R.* Baltimore: Pelican.

Preobrazhensky, Evgeny. (1926). *Novaya ekonomika (New Economy)*. Moscow.

Preobrazhensky, Evgeny. (1979). *The Crisis of Soviet Industrialization: Selected Essays*. White Plains: M. E. Sharpe.

Reed, John. (1919). *Ten Days that Shook the World*. New York: BONI & Liveright, Inc.

Rosefielde, Steven. (2002). "Premature Deaths: Russia's Radical Economic Transition in Soviet Perspective." *Europe-Asia Studies*. Vol. 53, No. 8, 1159–1176.

Rutland, Peter. (1985). The *Myth of the Plan: Lessons of Soviet Planning Experience*. La Salle: Open Court.

Trickey, Erick. (2017). "The Forgotten Story of the American Troops Who Got Caught up in the Russian Civil War." *Smithsonian Magazine*.

Trotsky, Lev. (Троцкий, Лев). (1986). Дневники и письма (Diary and Letters). Эрмитаж.

Volkov, E.V. (1930). *Dinamika naseleniya SSSR za vosem' desyat let*. Moscow.

Wheatcroft, Stephen. (1994). "The crooked mirror of Soviet economic statistics." In Davies, Harrison and Wheatcroft (eds.). *The Economic Transformation of the Soviet Union, 1913—1945* (pp. 24–37). Cambridge: Cambridge University Press.

6 Planning

A babushka asks a commissar "Who invented communism – the communists or scientists?" "The commissar proudly responds – the communists, of course!" "That's what I thought," the babushka says. "If the scientists had invented it, they would have tested it first on dogs!"

(CIA, 2013)[1]

How do we know that Adam and Eve were Soviet citizens? They had one apple between the two of them, they had no clothes, and they believed they were living in paradise.

(Aron, 2019)

Revolutionary communists insist that scientific socialism is synonymous with the efficient allocation of resources to best proletarian economic use by Communist Party leaders in lieu of market production, distribution and transfers. Planning in their view is superior to markets because it efficiently and equitably maximizes worker welfare undistorted by capitalist profiteering and labor exploitation.

The Soviet Union set about transforming this scientific socialist ideal into practice in 1928 after Joseph Stalin terminated Lenin's New Economic Policy (NEP). Marxists expected the Soviet planned economic order to endure until in accordance with the *Economic and Philosophical Manuscripts of 1844* and the *Communist Manifesto* (1848): the state withered into a harmonious self-regulating system without masters or markets. Karl Marx believed that planning and self-governing communalism were reconcilable, but if Stalin was aware of this possibility, he ignored it, favoring comprehensive authoritarian top-down command planning and implementation (Burkett, 2005; Marx, 1871).[2]

The Soviet economic planning and control mechanism was supposed to be superlative. The Kremlin-treated scientific paper plans as exact analogues of perfectly competitive market outcomes improved with socialist tax-transfers. Soviet plan implementation likewise was supposed to be perfect, assuring the unity of theory and practice. Robert Dorfman, Paul Samuelson and Robert Solow's duality theorem proved the equivalence of perfectly competitive and perfectly planned economic systems (Dorfman, Samuelson and Solow, 1958).

DOI: 10.4324/9781003371571-9

The Soviet economic planning and control mechanism, however, did not match its theoretical potential. It was not computopic (Neuberger, 1966). Stalin's system deliberately divorced state supply from worker household demand and labor self-management to facilitate rapid industrialization, development and military modernization (Rosefielde, 2007, 201–255; Gregory and Harrison, 2005; Ellman, 2008; Kontorovich, 2013; Samuelson, 2000).[3]

Soviet planning sought to mobilize resources and orchestrate national factor allocation, production, investment, innovation, distribution, international trade, finance, wage and price setting and monetary policy on a rational utility maximizing basis for the workers' benefit. It involved computing paper plans not as forecasts or guidelines (Saint-Simonian/European Union indicative planning) but as legally binding assignments. Soviet authorities did not just publish national plans. They implemented them.

Plans were prepared and implemented at two distinct levels, centrally in Moscow and in Soviet enterprises. The term central planning often obscures this reality for novices and experts alike. They erroneously infer that the State Planning Agency (Gosplan) computed 27.5 million micro-production assignments and the administrative apparatus implemented them on a command basis. This misrepresents the deep logic of Soviet planning practice.

Central planners did not compute enterprise micro-directives. They prepared control targets for 150 sectoral product categories like automotive products, chemicals, machinery, textiles and food using time series data. They had no knowledge of enterprise production functions, forcing them to estimate (forecast) sectoral targets rather than objectively compute them based on engineering production potentials. Their estimates took pragmatic account of intersectoral primary and intermediate input transfers required to support alternative GDP output assortments.

Gosplan then forwarded its draft composite good plan (forecast) to Stalin for his approval. If he was displeased, he demanded revisions. Gosplan complied, and the approval process continued until Stalin was satisfied. Once he signed off, Gosplan notified ministers in 30 principal industrial sectors of Stalin's production goals (supported by Gosplan's calculations).

Gosplan also provided guidance to the State bank (Gosbank), the State wholesale distribution authority (Gossnabysbyt) and labor assignment agencies on the allocation of funds, labor and resources supporting the implementation of sectoral production targets. Gosplan, with Stalin's approval told industrial ministers how much to produce and took steps to assure that primary factors and intermediate inputs were allocated for these purposes.

The Communist Party controlled the commanding heights. Stalin determined the broad composition of the gross domestic product (guns and butter) and backed up his commands by preventing resources from being diverted to dispreferred uses.

Stalin was command socialism's Olympian strategist and overlord. He pondered Soviet output possibilities from on high, partly guided by expert technical advice, and then decided how to deploy resources and manage his troops. He was the economic sovereign purportedly on the workers' behalf. His decisions became legal supply directives binding on enterprise managers, and supply chains subject to stern punishments for noncompliance. This made the system top-down and rigid. Pertinent information percolated bottom-up from enterprises, ministries, the central statistical agency (Goskomstat), but these stale data only supported Stalin's strategic choices. He received no information directly from households. There were no consumer demand back channels and no cybernetic interplay between state planning functionaries, laborers and consumers. The economic system unlike perfectly competitive markets was a Procrustean bed without Walrasian and Marshallian automatic disequilibrium adjustment mechanisms (Adam Smith's invisible hand) to cope with unforeseen contingencies.[4]

Both central and peripheral planning operations were rational. Aggregate input (factor) and output supply were responsive to Stalin's demand. His preferences determined sectoral production and the allocation of factor supplies, but not the enterprise micro-production and micro-distribution of 27.5 million specific products.

Enterprise managers conversant with their firms' engineering production function independently micro-planned output volumes and assortments within the sectoral control targets fixed by Gosplan, supervised by appropriate supervisory ministries. Ministries and their departments (glavks) told subordinate enterprises to employ assigned resources as efficiently as they could within Gosplan aggregate parameters. For example, the food sector minister tasked candy factory managers to compute the mix of sweets that enabled them to comply with the Gosplan aggregate composite supply target, subject to micro-output quotas and input constraints. Candy factory managers accomplished this assignment with tekhpromfinplan (technical, industrial, financial) planning techniques, including linear programming. Mathematical methods allowed them to estimate the effect of allocating factors to alternative use in multiproduct firms, given enterprise production functions to determine satisfactory communist results (Rosefielde, 2007).

Tekhpromfinplan supply calculated with these techniques was economically rational insofar as it responded to Stalin's aggregate sectoral demand, and additionally to minister micro judgments, multiproduct output quotas and input constraints. The determination of micro-production targets combined enterprise-level computations and face-to-face negotiations between ministers and managers. Enterprise managers sent tekhpromfinplan preliminary results to ministerial supervisors who then suggested revisions mimicking the macro-planning approval protocol between Stalin and Gosplan. Red enterprise directors responded by computing fresh counterplans, initiating a process that continued until everyone was satisfied. Just as Stalin iteratively negotiated with Gosplan, ministries attempted to harmonize enterprise micro-production based on their notion of Stalin's intentions.

Tekhpromfinplan supply was inferior to perfect market competition because factor and output prices were determined on a fiat basis (Marxist labor theory of value) disconnected from equilibrium supply and demand. Managers computed enterprise multiproduct linear program solutions, but the results were necessarily disequilibrium outcomes because the prices employed were false. The Soviet micro-production system was in chronic disequilibrium with no exit (Yaremenko, 1981).

Soviet planning was inefficient. Enterprise managers were engineers. They knew how to manufacture products and had no difficulty computing tekhpromfinplans. Gosplan aided by other input supply agencies controlled their activity levels by rationing inputs to alternative sectoral use, and Stalin controlled aggregate economic demand by setting Gosplan aspirational targets. State managerial incentive setting agencies and the State Price Bureau supplemented these controls by rewarding red directors for complying with minister and Stalin's goals. They received bonuses for fulfilling and overfulfilling plan targets.

Ministries authorized enterprises to negotiate intersectoral intermediate input supply contracts subject to their final approval. The state bank (Gosbank) strictly monitored enterprise payments to prevent malfeasance. When push came to shove, enterprises informally bartered scarce material with the aid of "pushers" (tolkachi) (Beissinger, 1988; Ledeneva, 1998, 2006).[5] The state inspectorate, the state bank, courts local authorities and military and secret police (NKVD/KGB) officials always intervened when they saw fit.

The enterprise micro-planning and administrative regulation mechanism (khozraschyot) was perpetually perturbed by exogenous shocks. Managers and ministers muddled through. The mechanism was neither second best, nor second worst. It crudely supported Stalin's primary macro objectives (Rosefielde, 2015, 30–44; Rosefielde, 2020).

Figure 6.1 maps the communist planning system. Stalin is the sovereign (vanguard of the proletariat), represented impersonally for generic purposes as the State Economic Directorate (topmost center box). He is the mastermind of top-level strategic resource allocation (rationing). Washington plays a similar strategic role in the American economy through its tax, transfer, budgeting and regulatory activities.

Stalin set the main sectoral plan directives with the State Planning Agency's (Gosplan) guidance (topmost box on the right)[6] and commanded the Council of Economic Ministers (second box down the central chain of command) to carry out his orders. The State Economic Directorate processed Stalin-approved sectoral plan directives and transmitted them to ministries (boxes labeled Ministry A and Ministry B). Each of the 30 ministries during the 1930s sorted the plan directives by product type and forwarded the results to main departments (boxes labeled Department 1, Department 2, Department 3 and Department 4) responsible for overseeing individual enterprises (boxes labeled Firm 1, Firm 2, Firm 3 and Firm 4). The main departments disaggregated sectoral plan directives into micro-plan assignments for the firms under their jurisdiction using enterprise microdata from the achieved production of the preceding year. These departments were responsible collectively for transforming Stalin's 150 sectoral-composite good plans into 27.5 million micro-plan directives, based on approved prior year enterprise tekhpromfinplan (enterprise micro-plan) results and consultations with enterprise managers with updated micro-plan information. Tekhpromfinplans were counterplans that micro-optimized multiproduct production possibilities

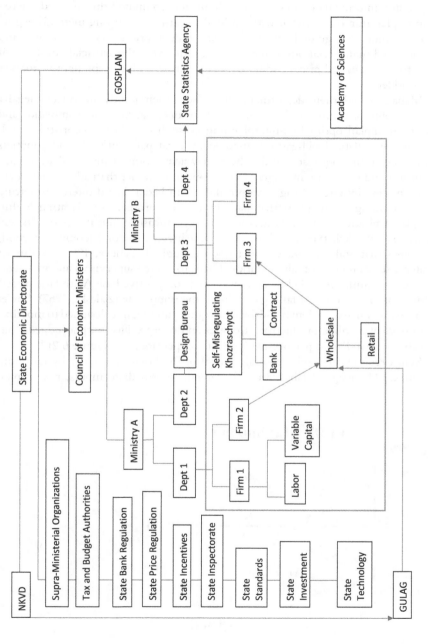

Figure 6.1 Soviet Command Planning System

guided by state-imposed bonus incentive schemes (like profit maximizing given state fixed prices and wages) subject to state rationed primary and interministerial negotiated intermediate input supplies. Managers computed this updated micro-counterplanning information with optimal linear programming methods beginning in the1960s, guided by official fiat product prices, state set wages and profit-based managerial bonus incentives. Profits were the artificial construct of state fixed wages and prices and bore no correlation with the competitive market value added.

Managers and their department supervisors then jointly negotiated legally binding enterprise micro-plan assignments reconciling Gosplan commands and tekhpromfinplan optimal counterplanning possibilities. These negotiations took account of collateral obligations imposed by local party officials and contracts with other ministries essential for the timely acquisition of intermediate inputs. Ministers and enterprise managers were cooperators rather than adversaries operating in a family circle (krugovaya poruka). Both had a shared interest in setting legally binding micro-plans that had some small prospect of placating Stalin. Gosplan aspirational macro targets were always infeasible, but if supervisors and managers colluded, they stood a chance of achieving sectoral (composite good) outcomes that Stalin might consider good enough (Ledeneva, 1998).[7] Stalin set strategic sectoral plans on an aspirational basis to coerce supervisors and managers to micro-optimize from below on a simulated competitive basis (with false prices) while making excuses for failing to achieve the impossible (Zaleski, 1967). Soviet planning was an excess demand-driven disequilibrium regime designed to mobilize resources, overutilize productive capacities and overproduce output judged from the competitive Pareto perspective (perfect competition) (see Figure 6.2).[8]

Stalin retained strategic sectoral control of the Soviet economy by rationing resources. He assigned labor, variable capital, intermediate inputs, new capital

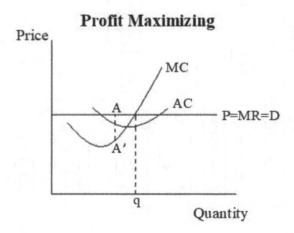

Figure 6.2 Profit Maximizing

formation and technologies to various composite good activities. Investment and defense sectors received ample supplies, while consumer sectors starved, with production in all sectors micro-optimized subject to state price and wage fixing. Firm directors executed their assignments under this two-level planning scheme by acquiring inputs, raw materials and intermediate inputs, producing goods and delivering them to the state wholesale agency (box labeled Wholesale) for top-level planned distribution to enterprises and households, all in accordance with Stalin's master sectoral plans. The command chain (Figure 6.1, central column) was comprehensively top-down for factor allocation, intermediate good assignment and product distribution at the sectoral level, and simultaneously micro-optimized horizontally by managers in multiproduct firms. Implementation was always on a satisficing basis throughout the system.

Stalin claimed that he set supply and distribution obligations at the top in the workers' best interest. Managers fulfilled production plans, and wholesalers (Gossnabsbyt) delivered the outputs to various intermediate input and retail recipients. Main departments and banking authorities (box in the central column labeled Bank) monitored enterprise performance to ensure that red directors fulfilled their assignments. The State Bank (Gosbank) transferred credit and issued cash only for completed tasks stipulated in enterprise tekhpromfinplans, preventing managers from producing for their own account and embezzling funds as they had under NEP.

The Soviets claimed top-down command planning was superior because Stalin's preferences were socialist and took full account of scientifically computed opportunity costs. They falsely asserted further that plans were ideal because the Academy of Sciences (lowest entity on the right-hand column in Figure 6.1) devised advanced planning and statistical forecasting methods; State Statistical Agency data were reliable, and the plan variants computed for Stalin by Gosplan were state of the arts.

Nonetheless, even if these false proficiency claims had been true, unforeseeable events might upset the applecart. Neither Stalin nor Gosplan were clairvoyant. They operated with stale data,[9] inflexible methodologies and protocols. The Soviets addressed the problem by allowing ministers, department heads and managers to improvise when circumstances required, guided by managerial and worker performance incentives (Bergson, 1944), and Communist Party situational priorities and interventions. Managerial and labor incentives encouraged red director and worker exertion when plans were feasible and allowed red directors to suboptimize otherwise. Prompt political intervention allowed the Party to address unforeseen contingencies on an ad hoc basis. Stalin assigned Communist Party and NKVD officers to every enterprise. They pressured and terrorized management and workers wherever material incentives and revolutionary zeal did not suffice (Rosefielde, 2010).

The state wholesale network improvised too, juggling the distribution of supplies with a crude technique called material balances that identified potential gaps in intermediate goods supply and demand plans (Gregory and Stuart, 2003, 127; Montias, 1959), attempting to correct imbalances through rationing. No one made rational choices based on real-time scarcities and technological possibilities, not Stalin, not Gosplan, not ministerial expediters. Soviet planning from above was an exercise designed solely to provide rule-of-thumb directive guidance to economic ministries, main departments (glavks) and enterprises (Birman, 1978), lofty claims to the contrary notwithstanding. It was better than War Communism, but not very good. It may have been inferior to NEP.

The Soviet top-down planning process was analogous to American federal budgeting. The White House, Senate, Congress, departments and myriad lobbyists assisted by the Congressional Budget Office, the Office of Management and Budget and the Treasury hammer out America's annual federal budget, financed by taxes and borrowing. The document provides funding for all federally approved programs and subprojects. Federal agencies have broad discretion in implementing subprograms and have the right to request supplementary funding. The government at its discretion can sequester appropriations.

Soviet top-down central planning worked the same way, but rationed physical resources instead of money, supplemented by state bank (Gosbank) credit controls. Both the American and Soviet top-down command-programming mechanisms function effectively in the sense that they provide agencies with the resources needed for their missions (in the Soviet case including enterprises). Consumers (recipients of public goods and services), however, have to take it, or leave it. Decisions are made about the assortment and quantities of public services produced and delivered on an ad hoc patchwork basis without global optimization. There is no competitive test, only hollow declarations by public officials that they do their job right, even though they disregard consumer micro demand.

The Soviet version of federal budget management (top-down planning) was extraordinarily detrimental because it was unaccountable to workers and the electorate and there was no automatic market or democratic adjustment mechanisms. Kremlin's top-down central planning unlike American federal programs determined the production of household goods. Soviet authorities fixed wages and prices. They selected technologies, designed goods, rationed inputs and outputs, micro-planned products, set goals, established managerial bonuses and worker incentives and used motivational campaigns and stern discipline, including terror tactics to strengthen managerial and worker compliance with plan directives. America overregulates the production of goods for private consumption too, but Soviet directive control was more stifling.

The vertical panel on the left-hand side (regulatory authorities) of Figure 6.1 and the central khozraschyot box (tekhpromfinplan and interministerial intermediate input coordination submechanism) depict the incentive-guided self-regulating component of Stalin's top-down command system. The term khozraschyot (economic cost accounting) describes a domain in the lower register of the top-down command model where managers compute and implement enterprise input and output micro-plans (tekhpromfinplans) on output maximizing and accounting cost minimizing basis,[10] guided by government incentives and controls (left vertical panel) (Bergson, 1964). It simulates the competitive market cybernetic supply and demand mechanism.

The principal performance criteria mandated by the state incentive bureau were the gross volume of physical output, revenue and profit measured at fixed fiat state prices set by Goskomtsen (State Price Bureau). In the simplest case, managers received ruble bonuses for exceeding their physical output assignments.[11] When bonuses depended on revenue, red directors maximized sales receipts and ignored costs. When profit determined bonuses, managers maximized revenues and minimized accounting costs at state fixed fiat prices (subject to inter-enterprise contract obligations and Gosbank oversight) (Rosefielde, 2007).[12]

Khozraschyot (Soviet simulated micro cybernetic supply and demand mechanism) served worthy purposes. It allowed red directors to enhance efficiency, productivity and growth by fine-tuning Stalin's choices, without compromising the principle of top-down command because tekhpromfinplan adjustments were guided by the state management mechanism (Rosefielde and Pfouts, 1988, 1997, 21–38), not the preferences of managers, workers or consumers.[13] Khozraschyot was a micro-planning and adaptation management tool, not a black market mechanism. Ministerial departments approved all revisions of Stalin's original plan and forwarded them to Gosplan for use in the next round of the central planning cycle.

Stalin's two-level (vertical/horizontal) planning and khozraschyot cybernetic bureaucratic regulatory scheme was successful on paper. The official Soviet statistical handbook *Narodnoye Khoziaistvo SSSR* reported that there was no unemployment in the Soviet Union after September 1929. Soviet central planning (more precisely two-level planning) buttressed by Stalin's resource mobilization priorities, despite dire predictions by naysayers overfully employed the population, overutilized the engineering production capacity of the capital stock and propelled rapid industrialization by building new and better factories (new capital formation). There are no credible grounds for believing that these Marxist–Leninist–Stalinist accomplishments were illusory, although growth rates were certainly slower than officially proclaimed, and the prioritization of guns over butter did little to improve the quality of working-class existence.

It is easy to understand why communists felt that overfull employment (including forced labor),[14] industrialization and rapid GDP growth employed in its war on economic backwardness validated their claim that scientific planning was superior to both monopoly and competitive market capitalism. Soviet foreign trade even passed the Heckscher-Ohlin test (Rosefielde, 1973a, 1973b, 1974, 1976).[15] There was no Leontief Paradox (Leontief, 1953).[16] Appearances, however, are deceptive.[17] These accomplishments satisfied Stalin's goals, not those of the workers. Stalin was the Soviet economic sovereign, not his drudges. He wanted control in his own hands and the hands of the Communist Party, secret police and military. The people wanted a high material quality of existence, democracy and civil liberties.

Scientific socialism behind the triumphant Marxist–Leninist veneer of full employment exaggerated rapid economic growth (Table 6.1). It did not efficiently allocate resources to what workers considered their best economic uses (Gregory and Harrison, 2005). Planning proved to be inferior to competitive

Table 6.1 USSR Comparison of CIA Estimates of Overall Growth with Official and Unofficial Soviet Estimates, 1961–1987

	CIA Estimates		National Income Produced		National Income Used	
					Percent average annual rates	
	GNP[a]	NMP[b]	Official[c]	Selyunin and Khanin[d]	Official[e]	Aganbegyan
1951–1960	5.2	6.7	10.3	7.2	NA	NA
1961–1965	4.8	4.9	6.5	4.4	5.7	NA
1966–1970	4.9	5.2	7.8	4.1	7.2	5.5
1971–1975	3.0	3.3	5.7	3.2	5.1	3.9
1976–1980	1.9	1.8	4.3	1.0	3.8	2.1
1981–1985	1.8	1.6	3.6	0.6	3.1	0.3
1986–1987	2.7	2.4	3.2	2.0	2.4	NA
1951–1985	3.8	4.3	6.9	3.9	NA	NA
1966–1985	2.9	3.0	5.3	2.2	4.8	2.9

[a] Based on value added at 1982 factor cost.
[b] GNP excluding services that do not contribute directly to material.

Source: Measures of Soviet Gross National Product in 1982 Prices, Joint Economic Committee of Congress, Washington, DC, 1990.

markets because it diminished workers' material and human welfare by paying them subsistence wages (state exploitation of labor) without adequate compensation for their value added and by compelling them to overwork. It drove millions from farms to factories and forced millions to toil in concentration camps, thwarted career aspirations, prohibited entrepreneurship and compelled consumers to accept perpetual shortages of shoddy goods. Marxist–Leninist–Stalinist top-down planning discouraged innovation, repressed democracy and civil liberties (including religious freedom) and terrorized the masses. Full employment, industrialization and economic growth benefitted Stalin and the Communist Party, but could not provide workers with a higher quality of existence than competitive market democracies because Soviet planning by design precluded job and consumer satisfaction. It generated perpetual overemployment, consumer good shortages and shoddy merchandise (Birman, 1983; Rosefielde, 1988). The claim that Bolshevik planning adequately served the people is false.

This should be obvious because the Communist Party prohibited workers from negotiating hours of employment and wages (USSR incorporated was sole employer), assigned and rationed jobs, restricted educational access, banned entrepreneurship, prohibited enterprise managers from negotiating with consumers (customized production and prices), underproduced household goods, ignored consumer taste and time preference, criminalized democracy, repressed civil liberties and terrorized opponents. The Party steadfastly refused to create institutions empowering the workers. It created the illusion, but not the reality of socialist progress.

Recapitulating, the system disempowered workers and consumers. Soviet citizens could not own productive assets, start their own business, invest, innovate, obtain the education and training they desired, search out the best employment opportunities, self-employ, refuse work assignments, negotiate wages, share management activities, travel without internal passports and permission, emigrate, influence product supply, characteristics, distribution or negotiate prices. They were straitjacketed, dependent on the communist order, defenseless and could not improve their lot through democratic action. They were pawns, not liberated masters of their own fate as Marx promised.

Notes

1 The allusion is to Pavlov's conditioned response experiments on dogs.
2 Associationist-planning is discussed in *The Civil War in France*, 1871. Marx and Engels endorsed consensus building, harmonious cooperation and planning to eliminate the risk of market exploitation, but failed to appreciate that proscribing the invisible hand let the wolf in the back door. Without Adam Smith's invisible hand, there are no trustworthy whistleblowers. Factors can be intercommunally misallocated and workers can shirk their duties. Communes can satisfice with obsolete technology and shun innovation. Shoddy goods can be fobbed off as luxuries, communards can be forced to consume products that they do not want and planners can flagrantly mismanage intercommunal relations. Communal consensus building, harmonious cooperation and central planning sound charming, but their consequences are malign. Intercommunal planning institutions cannot cope satisfactorily with moral hazard, and planners cannot do more than primitively satisfice.
3 Vitaly Shlykov concurs. Personal conversation with Shlykov and Lennart Samuelson in Stockholm.
4 Procrustes was a rogue smith and bandit from Attica who attacked people by stretching them or cutting off their legs to fit the size of an iron bed oblivious of the consequences. He was punished by Theseus who "fitted" him to his own bed.
5 The tolkachi used informal connections to enable production managers to meet or manipulate targeted outputs imposed by the central economic plan. They exchanged favors (blat). By 1937, the tolkachi had come to occupy a key position mediating between the enterprises and the commissariat.
6 Gosplan use "material balance" techniques to manage intermediate input imbalances that inevitably emerged when planned growth varied across sectors.
7 The term variously means "family circle" or mutual responsibility.
8 Figure 6.2 illustrates perfectly competitive enterprise profit maximizing. Equilibrium occurs at point E where marginal revenue equals marginal cost. The corresponding production point on the abscissa fully employs workers and variable capital. The Soviet Price Committee (Goskomtsen) deliberately set output prices above competitive equilibrium levels illustrated in Figure 6.2 to induce profit maximizing enterprise mangers to overproduce and over-fully employ primary factors of production. Aspirational plans drove resource mobilization at the apex of the command system. Soviet pricing fixing rules spurred it at the enterprise level.

9 Stalin and Gosplan worked with historical data prepared by Goskomstat (the State Statistical Committee), input-output tables and consolidated information compiled by ministries from draft enterprise tekhpromfinplans (technical industrial financial plans).

10 In the Hungarian context plan bargaining as Kornai noted was used to increase costs in order to increase state procurement prices and reduce output quotas.

11 The state reluctantly subsidized some Soviet firms out of necessity to bail out the negative operating and net cash flow in order to keep the supply chains going and minimize bottlenecks. It was a negative feedback of output quotas across the supply chains. Cross-subsidies were also built-in in procurement and supply prices over the supply chains based on priorities such as to promote energy-intensive manufacturing.

12 See Rosefielde, *Russian Economic from Lenin to Putin* for mathematic and graphic details.

13 Goskomsten Marxist labor time price fixing was an aspect of this state management mechanism. They guided tekhpromfinplan adjustments, not equilibrium red director, or consumer prices.

14 Overfull employment was achieved from above by Stalin's overambitious macro-sector plans and from below by administratively setting bonus to reward managers for overproduction.

15 Heckscher-Ohlin theory predicts that the capital-rich countries will be capital intensive and imports will be labor intensive. The Soviet economy satisfied the criterion, America did not.

16 The Leontief Paradox refers to Wassily Leontief's discovery that capital-rich America exported labor-intensive goods.

17 The Soviet foreign trade organization bought and sold goods abroad at global market prices. The State Price Committee set the domestic ruble prices of goods selected for import and export in accordance with Marxist labor-value theory. The foreign trade organization chose low ruble cost exportables for sale abroad and high domestic priced goods that planner desired for import. They comprehensively chose rationally to import planner preferred goods at least domestic ruble cost. The criterion was sound, from the standpoint of planners' sovereignty, but was divorced from the consumer utility standard.

References

Aron, Leon. (2019). "Russian Jokes Tell the Brutal Truth." *AEI*, November 29. www. aei.org/op-eds/russian-jokes-tell-the-brutal-truth/?mkt_tok=eyJpIjoiTkRGbVltWTB OV0k1WVdNdyIsInQiOiJFcVhpT1wvWVVWNmF1OFYyYzJkWFhIeXE5NHB5U mJLRFZFdFB2UVc0ek1TY2VkUEhGWEtiUjlXYU40OUd3WTBCOFZTWFwvS0 5ZcFVEbk9OaGwzanFDTlVGVW5VVlhmTHJLYzZoYkhuTklXWlBITUtjakZjR UhZXC9RSjNYZ005dFQzQiJ9
Beissinger, Mark. (1988). *Scientific Management, Socialist Discipline, and Soviet Power*. Cambridge: Harvard University Press.
Bergson, Abram. (1944). *The Structure of Soviet Wages*. Cambridge: Harvard University Press.
Bergson, Abram. (1964). *The Economics of Soviet Planning*. New Haven: Yale University Press.
Birman, Igor. (1978). "From the Achieved Level." *Soviet Studies*. Vol. 30, No. 2, 153–172.
Birman, Igor. (1983). Экономика недостач (*Economy of Shortage*). Нью-Йорк: Chalidze publications.
Burkett, Paul. (2005). "Marx's Vision of Sustainable Human Development." *Monthly Review*. Vol. 57, No. 5, 34–62.

CIA. (2013). "Soviet Jokes for the DDCI." www.cia.gov/library/readingroom/docs/CIA-RDP89G00720R000800040003-6.pdf

Dorfman, Robert, Paul Samuelson and Robert Solow. (1958). *Linear Programming and Economic Analysis*. New York: McGraw Hill.

Ellman, Michael. (2008). "The Political Economy of Stalinism in the Light of the Archival Revolution." *Journal of Institutional Economics*. Vol. 4, No. 1, 99–125.

Gregory, Paul and Mark Harrison. (2005). "Allocation under Dictatorship: Research in Stalin's Archives." *Journal of Economic Literature*. Vol. 43, No. 3, 721–761.

Gregory, Paul and Robert Stuart. (2003). *Comparing Economic Systems in the Twenty-First Century*. Boston: Houghton Mifflin.

Kontorovich, Vladimir. (2013). "The Preobrazhenskii-Feldman Myth and the Soviet Industrialization." http://ssrn.com/abstract=2200184

Ledeneva, Alena (ed.). (1998). *Russia's Economy of Favours: Blat, Networking and Informal Exchange*. Cambridge: Cambridge University Press.

Ledeneva, Alena. (2006). *How Russia Really Works: The Informal Practices That Shaped Post-Soviet Politics and Business*. Ithaca: Cornell University Press.

Leontief, Wassily. (1953). "Domestic Production and Foreign Trade; The American Capital Position Re-Examined." *Proceedings of the American Philosophical Society*. Vol. 97, No. 4, 332–349.

Marx, Karl. (1871). *The Civil War in France*. www.marxists.org/archive/marx/works/1871/civil-war-france/

Montias, John Michael. (1959). "Planning with Material Balances in Soviet-Type Economies." *American Economic Review*. Vol. 49, No. 5, 963–985.

Neuberger, Egon. (1966). "Libermanism, Computopia, and Visible Hand: The Question of Informational Efficiency." *The American Economic Review*. Vol. 56, No. 1, 131–144.

Rosefielde, Steven. (1973a). *Soviet International Trade in Heckscher-Ohlin Perspective*. Heath-Lexington.

Rosefielde, Steven. (1973b). "The Embodied Factor Content of Soviet International Trade: Problems of Theory, Measurement and Interpretation." *Association of Comparative Economic Systems Bulletin*. Vol. XV, No. 2–3, 3–12.

Rosefielde, Steven. (1974). "Factor Proportions and Economic Rationality in Soviet International Trade 1955–1968." *American Economic Review*, Vol. 64, No. 4, 670–681.

Rosefielde, Steven. (1976). "Foreign Trade Ruble Prices and the Heckscher-Ohlin Interpretation of Soviet Foreign Trade." *Association for Comparative Economic Studies Bulletin*. Vol. 8, No 3, 31–38.

Rosefielde, Steven. (1988). "The Soviet Economy in Crisis: Birman's Cumulative Disequilibrium Hypothesis." *Soviet Studies*. Vol. 40, No. 2, 222–244.

Rosefielde, Steven. (2007). *Russian Economy from Lenin to Putin*. New York: Wiley.

Rosefielde, Steven. (2010). *Red Holocaust*. London: Routledge.

Rosefielde, Steven. (2015). "Economic Theory of the Second Worst." *Higher School of Economics Journal (HSE), (Moscow)*. Vol. 19, No. 1, 30–44.

Rosefielde, Steven. (2020). *Putin's Russia: Economic, Economy, Defence and Foreign Policy*. Singapore: World Scientific Publishers.

Rosefielde, Steven and R. W. Pfouts. (1988). "Economic Optimization and Technical Efficiency in Soviet Enterprises Jointly Regulated by Plans and Incentives." *European Economic Review*. Vol. 32, No. 6, 1285–1299.

Rosefielde, Steven and R. W. Pfouts. (1997). "Economic Optimization and Technical Efficiency in Russian Enterprises Jointly Regulated by Profits and State Incentives." *Ekonomicheskii Zhurnal (Journal of Economics)*. Vol. 2, No. 2, 21–38.

Samuelson, Lennart. (2000). *Plans for Stalin's War Machine: Tukhachevskii and Military-Economic Planning, 1925–1941.* Basingstoke and London: Macmillan Press.

Yaremenko, Yuri. (1981). *Strukturnye izmeneniya v sotsialisticheskoi ekonomike.* Moscow: Mysl'.

Zaleski, Eugene. (1967). *Planning Reforms in the Soviet Union, 1962–1966.* Chapel Hill: University of North Carolina Press.

7 Perestroika

Almost 70 years ago, our Leninist party raised over the nation the victorious banner of the socialist revolution, the struggle for socialism, freedom and equality, for social justice and societal progress, against oppression and exploitation, poverty and national subjugation.

For the first time in human history, the interests and needs of the workers were placed at the center of the state's agenda. There have been many successes during the socialist construction of the Soviet Union in the political, economic, social and spiritual realms. Under party guidance, the Soviet people have built socialism, defeated fascism in the Great Patriotic war, established and strengthened the national economy and transformed their homeland into a great power.

Our achievements have been immense and indisputable, and the Soviet people are justifiably proud of their successes. They are the true guarantee of the realization of the current plan and our future dream (Narodnoe Khoziaistvo SSSR za 70 Let, 1987, 6–7).[1]

Communist Party leaders boasted on the eve of the 70th anniversary of the Bolshevik revolution that the Soviet people had built socialism, established and strengthened the national economy, and transformed their homeland into a great power. No dark clouds threatened the communist dream.

On June 30, 1987, barely five months after the Communist Party Plenum, Mikhail Gorbachev sabotaged top-down command planning and charted a radical new socialist course, although at the time this was still ambiguous (Gorbachev, 1987, 1988; Gates, 1988; Aslund, 1989; Bergson, 1989a, 1989c, 1991).[2] He told ministers and supervisors that although they had an obligation to oversee managers, they had to defer to them. The contradiction destroyed the Communist Party's ability to command. The decision was rash because even though the Party enacted a law enterprise empowering red directors to exploit tekhpromfinplanning for private purposes (abrogation of planners sovereignty) (Gorbachev, 1988; Kurashvili, 1989; O korennoi perestroike, 1987), and another mandating worker-red director comanagement (Torkanovskii, 1989; Zakon, 1985, 5–12), it failed to resolve inherent contradictions. Gorbachev conflated lofty declarations of progressive intent with practical measures to improve centralized oversight and assured

DOI: 10.4324/9781003371571-10

responsible enterprise self-regulation. He failed to empower workers, equitably restore private ownership and create rule-of-law-abiding competitive markets.

The new enterprise law did not establish links between consumers and suppliers, foster competition or create contract law protecting buyers and sellers. There was no revised state guidance governing the leadership, planners, ministers and management priorities. The Communist Party did not reconfigure the State Economic Directorate (SED) control mechanism (see Chapter 6), and embed managerial liberalization in a viable transition program shepherding the economy from a Marxist–Leninist command planning system to a market-assisted economic system (perestroika) or perekhod (full transition to a market) (Abalkin, 1989a, 1989b; Korostelev, 1989; Palterovich, 1989; Kulikov, 1989; Aven and Shironin, 1989). Gorbachev's inattention to detail may have reflected the influence of western market shock therapists like Jeffrey Sachs on a coterie of presidential advisors (Sachs and Pistor, 1997), especially Stanislav Shatalin who contended that laissez-faire heals all wounds (Aslund, 1987; Schroeder, 1987).[3]

The new enterprise law disoriented top-down command planning by transforming plan obligations into murky guidance, terminating strict top-down planned-command control over the allocation of labor, capital and intermediate inputs (Berliner, 1992; CIA, 1987). It allowed red directors broad discretion over enterprise funds and obligated ministerial supervisors to cooperate (and implicitly collude). The tekhpromfinplan approval process continued, as did State Bank oversight, but it no longer had teeth to compel red directors (now called managers) to place state interest above personal self-seeking.[4] The State Economic Directorate lost control over selfish red director impulses and stoked the flames of moral hazard,[5] leaving the Soviet economy vulnerable to destructive misconduct.[6]

The new law on the enterprise at first seemed benign, but was not. Gorbachev erroneously assumed that red directors would prioritize society's interest over their own in exercising expanded managerial freedom, and that the State Economic Directorate would continue safeguarding Soviet workers from managerial exploitation. However, it soon became apparent that this was the triumph of hope over common sense. Red directors abused their expanded authority and the State Economic Directorate gradually lapsed into a deep vegetative state that exacerbated absurdities already embedded in the command planning system (Kesey, 1962). The system went from a state of endemic microeconomic disequilibrium (economy of consumer shortage and shoddy goods) and macroeconomic over full employment (forced labor) to a micro economy with anticompetitive insider-markets and deficient aggregate effective demand.

The Soviet rational choice and control system (Gosplan, tekhpromfinplanning, khozraschyot and ministerial oversight) functioned poorly under normal conditions. It tolerated numerous absurdities including value subtracted[7] and precycling (Winiecki, 1988). It permitted illegal colored markets (Katsenelinboigen, 1977; Grossman, 1977) and corruption (Belova, 2001). It over-employed labor, capital and resources. It created consumer shortages (Kornai, 1980). It fostered structural militarization (Rosefielde, 2007) and produced things few wanted (Rosefielde, 1989c). It allowed wage and wealth inequality (McCauly, 1981;

Bergson, 19944; Bulgakov, 2016),[8] gender and ethnic inequality (McCauly, 1981), social privilege and injustice, educational, health and residential inequalities, labor and travel immobility.[9] It restricted opportunities and liberties, stoked civic insecurities (Conquest, 1991) and political repression (Schapiro, 1955, 1970, 1972; Fainsod, 1963).[10]

The new law on the enterprise expanded these disorders rendering top-down command planning and control defenseless against managerial misconduct. It desensitized the State Economic Directorate to the diversion of resources from Communist Party strategic top-down macroeconomic objectives and vital interindustrial use. Modern industry depends critically on the timely acquisition of parts and components (supply chains). Soviet planning created interministerial coordinators and intersectoral contracting to prevent intermediate input supply disruptions. Gorbachev's law on the enterprise scuttled both mechanisms by allowing red directors to divert resources to projects that enriched them at their enterprise's expense.

There were solutions. Gorbachev could have improved interactive two-level cybernetic planning in the State Economic Directorate that allowed ministries or other centralized bodies to strengthen the regulation of managerial operations in lieu of face-to-face negotiations. He could have methodically built the institutional foundations for a competitive, rule-of-law-abiding,[11] democratic socialist market to assist communist top-down command planning (Dewatripont and Gerard Roland, 1997).[12] He could have constructed an integrated mixed economy (strategically macro-planned above and competitive market below) (Boycko, Shleifer, and Vishny, 1996) or an orderly transition to competitive market economy, but he did none of these things.[13]

Before July 1, 1987, one-man-rule (Communist Party sovereignty) prevailed throughout the two-level planning system. Soviet law required red directors to fulfill ministry-approved enterprise tekhpromfinplans and prohibited them from purchasing other goods and services for personal gain. Gosbank strictly monitored and controlled tekhpromfinplan compliance (Belkin and Ivanter, 1969).[14] Red directors could not circumvent Gosbank's oversight because the state bank held their financial assets. Gosbank debited purchaser and credited vendor accounts for approved tekhpromfinplan transactions. There were no interenterprise cash payments (Fedorov, 1989), and therefore no opportunities for diverting enterprise funds to private red director purposes. These rational control protocols in support of State Economic Directorate and ministerial authority prevented red directors from abusing and embezzling enterprise funds. They could not sell their products to unauthorized buyers. They could not purchase goods, services and assets for own use at home or abroad, nor misappropriate state funds without risking draconian criminal sanctions. The principle of hard top-down one-man-rule was inviolate in all these regards.

On July 1, 1987, everything changed. Red directors became state asset managers (nominally cogoverning with worker collectives),[15] freed from hard tekhpromfinplan directives and hard Gosbank financial controls in the State Economic Directorate interest. The new enterprise law encouraged managers to decide themselves how best to use company funds for the good of the Soviet people, including purchasing assets and borrowing funds abroad, presumably on the premise that they would do the right thing. Surely, one can always trust comrades to put collective above individual private interest, but Gorbachev should not have done so.

Red directors-cum-managers ceased fulfilling their duty and became self-interested rational choice actors. This was a new twist on revolutionary Marxist creative destruction (Reinert, 1994; Schumpeter, 1994, 82–83).[16] Gorbachev persuaded himself that discarding directive planning would ensure communism's triumph (Rosefielde, 1986, 1989a, 1989b, 1989c, 1990a, 1990b, 1991a; Rosefielde and Pfouts, 1991) if his officially stated intentions were sincere. The danger that indicative planning implemented at the enterprise's discretion without adminis-trative or market discipline might compromise communism's goals (Kornai, 1979, 1986, 2000, 2001; Kornai, Maskin and Roland, 2003)[17] did not perturb him. He was unconcerned that enterprise managers and supervisors might rent-seek (Krueger, 1974), embezzle and privatize state assets to themselves (Rosefielde, 2001). He was unafraid that the perestroika might create an anti-socialist, mixed economy (Maskin and Xu, 2001; Majumdar, 1998; Goldfeld and Quandt, 1990; Frydman, Gray, Hessel and Rapaczynski, 2000; Freixas, Guesnerie and Tirole, 1985; John Earle and Saul Estrin, 1998) or neo-capitalist regime (Rosefielde, 1991a, 1991b, 1991c, 1994, 1995, 1999; Rosefielde and Mills, 1990).

The Chinese faced a similar challenge in the early 1990s and resolved it suc-cessfully by leasing state assets to various groups with appropriate safeguards, while retaining freehold ownership. See Chapter 16. Gorbachev's solution was to whistle past the graveyard.

Red director self-empowerment was not instantaneous. It was a slow-motion adverse learning-by-doing process. Encouraging managers to decide for them-selves how to use enterprise funds held on a custodial basis by Gosbank did not make them private owners or free ministerial agents. The ministries retained the right to fire, hire and discipline subordinates for flagrant misconduct and had an implicit obligation to oversee enterprise operations. The State Economic Directorate had the right to set the economy's main goals with Gosplan assistance and counsel subordinates on how to implement them. The Communist Party had the right and power to intervene anywhere it wished down the administra-tive chain of command. The state kept its regulatory controls over prices, wages, standards, inspection, taxation, subsidies and investment, but the new law on the enterprise prevented zombie authorities from saving hard top-down command planning. Although they saw what was happening, and had the power to react, the lack of clear party guidance (and Gorbachev double-speak) led ministers and supervisors to gradually abandon their duty and join managers in pillaging the state.

Gorbachev was unruffled. He pressed forward as Stalin before him under the slogan "there is no fortress that Bolsheviks cannot storm" (McClelland, 1980; Foss, 2006). He launched a program permitting cooperatives of no more than five members to lease state facilities (*arenda*) for dividend-sharing ventures like restaurants (extended to individuals in 1989) (Korostelev, 1989)[18] and permitted similar joint ventures with foreign companies such as McDonalds (Hertzfeld, 1991). Gorbachev authorized collective (kolkhoz) and state (sovkhoz) farms at their discretion to grant leasing privileges to groups, families and individual peasants (Moskoff, 2019). The Soviets also began experimenting with ruble convertibility and price and wage flexibility in burgeoning leasing markets. All these initiatives yielded positive results from the public perspective. The quantity, quality and variety of consumer goods improved. Life in Moscow and Leningrad briefly was better for the nimble few.

However, these gains were more than offset by the termination of legally compulsory central plans in 1987, and the accelerated disintegration of communist top-down command control. Insiders at all levels of the administrative hierarchy, although lacking the will to administratively fix perestroika under pressure from Gorbachev's market liberalizers, were able to rouse themselves enough to desert the sinking ship. Ministers and their subordinates ceased waiting for Communist Party guidance, and started looting state assets independently and in partnership with managers, wherever possible pirating the funds abroad (capital flight) (Tihomirov, 1997; Goldman, 2003).[19] They spontaneously privatized enterprises and other assets hoping that authorities ultimately would recognize their squatter claims (Johnson, 1991; Johnson and Heidi Kroll, 1991; Hansen, 1990). Once sharks smelled blood, red directors, ministers and institute directors disregarded short-term economic performance despite the bonuses they provided and devoted their energies to asset acquisition, plunder and foreign transfers. Legal privatization introduced in 1990 accelerated the looting as did state price decontrol (Leonard and Pitt-Watson, 2013; Shleifer and Treisman, 2000; Appel, 1997; Blasi, Kroumova and Kruse, 1997; Boycko, Shleifer and Vishny, 1995; McFaul and Perlmutter, 1995; Sutela, 1994; Frydman, Rapaczynski and John Earle, 1993). The Ministry of Defense's prolong war fighting strategic mineral reserves vanished abroad, much of it shipped through the Japanese port of Maizuru, contributing to the worldwide natural resource price bust of the early 1990s.[20]

There was a battle of conflicting incentives. On one hand, the khozraschyot bonus mechanism incentivized managers to overproduce (due to guaranteed state wholesale purchase at profitable fixed prices), and overfully employ workers. On the other hand, windfall gains reaped by managers, ministers and institute heads from pillage and spontaneous privatization numbed the State Economic Directorate to disintegrating interindustrial dependencies, falling production, spiraling inflation (Economic Survey of Europe, 2003; Filatochev and Bradshaw, 1992)[21] and rising unemployment (Rosefielde, 2000).[22] At first in 1987, 1988 and much of 1989, managerial bonus incentives outweighed windfall gains from looting and spontaneous privatization, especially in the military industrial complex (Filatotchev, Buck and Wright, 1993),[23] but by the end of 1989 pillage became the main force governing the Soviet system. GDP nose-dived 3% in 1990 and 5% in 1991. Weapons production fell 90%.[24] The downward momentum continued after the dissolution of the Soviet Union on December 25, 1991, and did not hit rock bottom at 42% below the 1989 level until 1996 (Economic Survey of Europe, 2003), five years after Boris Yeltsin officially killed communist command economy by terminating guaranteed state purchases. A handful of insiders privatized the people's assets to themselves, leaving workers holding worthless vouchers (company shares) as the workers reward for 73 years of communist service (Goldman, 2003). Gorbachev willy-nilly had sabotaged the system, precipitating katastroika (Zinoviev, 1990; Ellman, 1994), and Yeltsin finished the job by ending khozraschot and guaranteed state output purchases, plunging Russia into hyper-depression (Rosefielde, 1989a, 1991b, 1991d, 1991e, 1991f, 1992, 1994, 1998; Rosefielde, Danilin and Kleiner. (1994)), decimating its conventional military power, and leaving the Kremlin with a shell of nuclear deterrence to ensure national security (Rosefielde, 2005). The Bolsheviks discovered the hard way that extricating the nation from the Marxist–Leninist command planning was costly.[25]

Blame or credit for wrecking the Soviet socialist command economy rests squarely on Gorbachev's shoulders (Ellman and Kontorovich, 1998). The new law on the enterprise and supporting perestroika reforms were his initiatives. He could have called a moratorium to spontaneous privatization, and restored the pre-July 1, 1987 State Economic Directorate administrative control mechanism in 1989 when the Soviet economy reported the first GDP decline in the postwar period. If Stalin's ghost had taken charge on the eve of the Soviet Union's dissolution, December 24, 1991, it could have restored the status quo ante in short order with a signature terror campaign. The siloviki (power services) including Putin who despised Gorbachev would have jumped at the opportunity to liquidate Marxist-Leninism's enemies.[26]

Why did Gorbachev destroy command planning? (Miller, 2020). Why did he simultaneously abet the formation of rival intraparty factions, facilitate republican secession, de-constitutionalize the Communist Party political monopoly, renounce the Brezhnev doctrine[27] and destroy Soviet military power (Rosefielde, 2005), culminating in the dissolution of the Soviet Union?

There are myriad explanations (Ellman and Kontorovich, 1998; Gorbachev, 2021), but the truth remains illusive. Three explanations seem plausible. First, Gorbachev who publically trumpeted his fidelity to communism may have privately considered Marxist–Leninist command planning and communist authoritarianism a great Satan (Gorbachev, 1987). The possibility is compatible with his close advisor Stanislav Shatalin's declaration on November 1991 that it did not matter if it took "500 days, or 500 years to transition to the market, as long as communism was destroyed!" (Hertzfeld, 1991; Holloway, 1989; Shatalin, 1990).[28] Elements of the Soviet elite called the "Children of the Twentieth Party Congress" craved a freer and more affluent way of life.[29]

Gorbachev's decision to end the Communist Party's constitutional political monopoly on February 7, 1990 (Dobbs, 1990) and subsequent actions to dismantle the Soviet empire (Brown, 2020, 2021) also support the supposition that he considered the prevailing Soviet order reprehensible. Chinese intelligence sources in the late 1980s considered Gorbachev a CIA useful idiot or collaborator (Zubok, 2021).[30]

Second, Gorbachev was an intrepid. He may have believed there was no fortress that Bolsheviks could not storm; that if he doubled-down on perestroika and new thinking he could integrate top-down command planning with leasing markets (*arenda*) and create an amicable post-Cold War international order (Nove, 2004). New thinking here meant living harmoniously with capitalism and trusting German and NATO's good intentions. Many Western analysts including George Kennan, Peter Reddaway and Robert Tucker sympathize with this interpretation (Kennan, 1988; Reddaway, 1988; Tucker, 1987; Dallin, 2004a).[31]

Third, Gorbachev may have been a Dr. Jekyll and Mr. Hyde split personality, desiring simultaneously to destroy top-down command planning and to redeem communism.

The first and third explanations do not require elaboration. Conspiracies and double-mindedness happen. The second explanation for soldiering ahead with perestroika, pressing democracy and burying the hatchet with the West, however, raises an intriguing political economic issue. Could Gorbachev have been a closet neo-Bukharinite apostle of democratic market socialism? (Brown, 2004; Timofeyev, 2004; Lapidus, 2004; Dallin, 2004a, 2004b; Cohen, 2000). Although Gorbachev never publicly mused about the possibility, the answer is probably yes (Hansen, 2003; Kurian, 2011; Bloom, 1946; Surin, 1990),[32] but his flawed transitioned strategy prevented democratic market socialism from happening (Leeds, 2019).[33]

The conundrum of why Gorbachev destroyed top-down command planning, diminished the authority of the KGB, abetted republican secession, de-constitutionalized the Communist Party's political monopoly, renounced the Brezhnev doctrine, decimated Soviet military power and trusted the assurances of America, Germany and NATO is important. However, it is inessential for rendering a verdict on Marxist-Leninism. Communist command planning always was a shallow and pernicious idea. It prohibited consumer (worker) demand from influencing the State Economic Directorate, ministerial and red director supply decisions. Disequilibrium prices, arbitrary constraints and hodgepodge incentives prevented the State Economic Directorate, ministers and red directors from efficiently producing supplies that satisfied the Communist Party's own demands, to say nothing about worker consumer sovereignty. Dispersed rational choice making capabilities at the ministerial and enterprise levels were primitive. Hard command planning was resistive to constructive reform and vulnerable to catastrophic decay.

Marxist–Leninist socialism is micron shallow because blind faith in dogmatic methods warped the Bolshevik mindset (Gollwitzer, 1990, 2012; French II and Chang, 2016).[34] Party idealists conjured an alluring utopia, and inspired heroic enthusiasm, but concealed the truth that zeal is a poor substitute for principled rational choice in a pluralist world constrained by scarcity. Communist Party leaders before 1987 refused to believe that their ideologically straitjacketed economic supply mechanism could not adequately satisfy socialist promises, allowing them to persevere on treadmill of sterile reform with perverse consequences.

Command socialism fostered structural militarization and the production of shoddy things few wanted. It created acute consumer good shortages, other supply and demand disequilibria, value subtracted, pre-cycling, illegal colored markets, corruption, over-employment of labor, capital and resources; wage and wealth inequality, gender and ethnic inequality, social privilege and injustice, educational, health and residential inequalities, labor and travel immobility, restricted opportunities and liberties, civic insecurities, terror, political repression and oppression. It failed to empower deep worker self-governance or provide a superior quality of socialist existence.

Command planning could have survived, but as Abram Bergson and CIA's assessments of Soviet growth retardation indicated (see Chapters 6 and 15), it could never have fulfilled Marxist–Leninist promises or effectively competed with democratic free enterprise (Bergson, 1987, 1989a, 1989b, 1989c, 1991, 1994). Household consumption, public services and other utilities (Figure A4.4) could never have been satisfactory, absolutely, or in comparison with other socialist alternatives because of Bolshevik dogmatism.

The Plenum of the Communist Party Central Committee, January 27–29, 1987, drew the opposite conclusion. It boldly declared that its Leninist party had placed the workers' interests and needs at the center of the state agenda, scoring victory after victory in the struggle for socialism, freedom, equality, social justice and societal progress against oppression and exploitation, poverty and national subjugation. Many believed (Sherman, 1969) and some still do that the glass of Soviet socialism was more than half-full (Mendel-Gleason, 2019).

They prize the benefits of eradicating capitalism, defending the revolution against Western imperialism. They are impressed by Soviet economic development and modernization, full employment, price stability, economic growth (based on "lipstick on a pig" official statistics) (Rosefielde, 2003), affordable (substandard) healthcare, Marxist education, Spartan public transportation and shoddy housing (social safety net), sexual freedom (licentiousness), advocacy of women and minority rights (but not their effective implementation) and discount the negatives.

Their judgment reflects both an unwillingness to deconstruct Soviet communism (Degenaar, 1990) and adherence to revolutionary communist dogma. Bolshevism made it seem as though the success or failure of Soviet socialism depended on progress in the class war against capitalism (in one country without capitalist ownership of the means of production) and imperialism and a handful of socioeconomic indicators including employment, price stability, public services, rising living standards, Gini coefficients and the social safety net.

The success of the Soviet experiment only partly depended on these metrics. Worker self-governance also was essential. Stalin's cynical claim that the Communist Party was the highest form of worker self-management was false. Canceling capitalism did not deter the Communist Party from exploiting workers. Liberating workers from capitalist oppression did not facilitate the actualization of their human potential or create harmonious social relations. Top-down command planning straitjacketed workers and shackled them to pauper communism (Jean-Louis Panné, Andrzej Paczkowski, Karel Bartosek, Jean-Louis Margolin and Nicolas Werth, 1999). Proletarian romanticism made good propaganda, but condemned Soviet workers to a meager existence. Western social democrats understood this and jumped promptly on Gorbachev's new thinking bandwagon. Think tanks were aflutter heralding a new age that never materialized (Levgold, 1988).

Beauty is in the eye of the beholder. Straitjacket pauper socialism was good enough and better than the capitalist alternative for the Plenum of the Communist Party Central Committee before June 30, 1987. Some Western scholars still see things this way (Fitzpatrick, 1992, 1999; Getty, 2013; Davies, 1987; Dobb, 1966; Ghodsee, 2018). If one is satisfied with a mess of pottage, and sustained by an unfounded belief in the system's utopian potential, then communist top-down command planning may seem a great triumph and the harbinger of a bountiful future. If one judges a meager existence insufficient, then Marxist-Leninism is the debacle of hope over reason.

Notes

1 *Materials from the Plenum of the Communist Party Central Committee,* January 27–29, 1987, Politizdat, 1987, pp.6–7. Quoted in *Narodnoe Khoziaistvo SSSR za 70 Let,* Iubileinyi Statisticheskii Ezhegodnik, Finansy I Statistika, 1987, p.12. (Author's translation).
2 Gorbachev declared that he was a communist. Perestroika: New Thinking for Our Country and the World was written before the Communist Party Plenum indicating that Gorbachev's team intended to purge communist party technocrats and Marxist–Leninist ideologues under the banner of liberalization and democratization well before the Communist Party Plenum. Declassified CIA documents reveal that while the agency was aware that trouble was afoot, it did not fully grasp the distinction between liberals, technocrats and Marxist–Leninist politburo ideologues.
3 Gorbachev's main economic advisors were Academicians Abel Aganbegyan, Oleg Bogomolov, Tat'yana Zaslavskaya, Corresponding Member Leonid Abalkin and Nikolai Petrakov. The neoliberal debate over Chile's transition from state control to the market may have percolated into the circle of Gorbachev's advisors.
4 Red directors did not have free access to cash. The state deposited the revenues from tekhpromfinplan approved sales directly into enterprise accounts at the State Bank. Gosbank only permitted payments to approved vendors designated in approved tekhpromfinplans. The protocol prevented embezzlement.
5 Systemic risk is the risk of collapse of an entire financial system or entire economic mechanism, as opposed to risk associated with any one individual entity, group or component of a system that can be contained without harming the entire system.
6 One or more drafters of the new law on the enterprise may have deliberately sought to sabotage Marxist–Leninist central planning.
7 Processing that reduces the value of raw materials or intermediate inputs. Some mistakenly define value subtracted more broadly to include the production of domestic goods from raw materials that have higher value abroad. But, this phenomenon is flawed trading. As long as the domestic value of the fabricated good exceeds the domestic raw material cost, value is added, not subtracted.

8   Women received only 61% of the average male wage. They received the same wage for the same job, but were shunted into low-paying jobs. Wage disparities across skill levels and occupations were comparatively small by international standards, but still significant. Freehold personal wealth was mostly abolished, but insiders enjoyed the usufruct of the state's wealth.

9   Gulag forced labor and domestic and foreign travel prohibitions.

10 The Communist Party banned competitors.

11 Rule of law, the mechanism, process, institution, practice or norm that supports the equality of all citizens before the law secures a nonarbitrary form of government and more generally prevents the arbitrary use of power.

12 This rule-of-law-abiding socialist market system would be a co-sovereign regime ruled by the Communist Party and other economic actors.

13 The epithet "harebrained schemer" was widely used to describe Nikita Khrushchev. www.globalsecurity.org/military/world/russia/khrushchev-hare-brained.htm Gorbachev was cut from the same cloth.

14 I discussed the issue with Ivanter at length in 1988.

15 Worker collectives met once annually to approve managers' action. This was inadequate, and managers remained kings of their roost.

16 Creative destruction is a concept in economics which since the 1950s has become most readily identified with the Austrian economist Joseph Schumpeter who derived it from the work of Karl Marx and popularized it as a theory of economic innovation and the business cycle.

17 Soft directive planning is analogous to what Janos Kornai calls soft budget constraints in mixed economies where the state controls enterprise managers' behavior through the regulation of their budgets instead of plans.

18 The Law on Individual Labor Activity, issued on November 19, 1986, sought to encourage private entrepreneurship "based exclusively on the personal labor of citizens and members of their families." This law was followed in early 1987 by a series of decrees (consolidated eventually in the Law on Cooperatives of May 26, 1988) that put self-financing, self-managed and profit-and-market-oriented cooperatives on the same basis as state enterprises with their members enjoying the same social rights as state employees. By the end of 1987, approximately 150,000 people worked in some 13,921 cooperatives of the new type.

19 Red directors and their superiors transferred assets abroad through many nefarious channels, purchasing assets abroad in the state's name, then changing title and by underreporting export receipts, leaving the residual overseas in their personal accounts.

20 Vitaly Shlykov, personal discussion. Port master of Maizuru, personal conversation.

21 Consumer prices rose 5.2% in 1989, 160% in 1990 and 1,528.7% in 1991.

22 Unemployment rose but was concealed because Goskomstat only reported registered unemployment. This excluded unpaid furloughed workers.

23 Personal conversations with Vitaly Shlykov.

24 Personal conversations with Vitaly Shlykov and CIA.

25 Boris Yeltsin sought to transform Russia to a competitive market economy but failed in 1991–2000. Vladimir Putin introduced some constructive reforms, but Russia remains a soft authoritarian martial police state.

26 Gorbachev's chief of staff, Valery Boldin; Oleg Baklanov, first deputy chairman of the USSR defense council; Oleg Shenin, secretary of the Central Committee of the Communist Party of the Soviet Union (CPSU); and Gen. Valentin Varennikov, chief of the Soviet Army's ground forces, accompanied by KGB Gen. Yury Plekhanov, chief

of security for party and state personnel, attempted a coup d'etat to reverse perestroika on August 18, 1991 in the name of the State Committee for the State of Emergency in the USSR.

27 Foreign policy put forth by Soviet leader Leonid Brezhnev in 1968, calling on the Soviet Union to intervene – including militarily – in countries where socialist rule was threatened.

28 Duke University lecture. Shatalin's assertion responded to my (Rosefielde) question. 500 Days Program was an ambitious program to overcome the economic crisis in the Soviet Union by means of transition into market economy. The program was proposed by Grigory Yavlinsky and further developed by a work group under the direction of Stanislav Shatalin (an economic advisor to Mikhail Gorbachev). Before beginning work on the project, Shatalin had been assured by Gorbachev that he was serious about radically reforming the Soviet economy.

29 The "Children of the Twentieth Party Congress" were communists whose view of the world was shaped by the party congress of 1956 at which Nikita Khrushchev delivered his famous "Secret Speech" denouncing Stalin's crimes. The Children of the Twentieth Party Congress believed in communism – in state control of the means of production, in central economic planning, in the social guarantees granted by the Soviet constitution, in the Soviet Union as a genuine "brotherhood of nations." But at the same time, they felt that the system was not living up to its promise. They believed that Stalinism had overcentralized and over-bureaucratized Soviet society, stifling initiative, breeding corruption and creating a severe disconnect between the claims of Soviet propaganda and the realities on the ground. The solution was to return to Leninist norms, whatever those might be, putting the USSR back on track to a bright communist future.

30 Zubok mentions a variety of conspiratorial theories involving the CIA compatible with the Chinese claim.

31 Tucker states,

> Under Gorbachev's leadership the Soviet Union has embarked on major domestic reforms and proclaimed the need for new political thinking in international relations. This new thinking, which Gorbachev set out most recently last December in his speech to the United Nations, embraces a number of propositions about the nature of international relations in the modern world: human interests take precedence over the interests of any particular class; the world is becoming increasingly interdependent; there can be no victors in a nuclear war; security has to be based increasingly on political rather than military instruments; and security must be mutual, especially in the context of U.S.-Soviet relations, since if one side is insecure it will only make the other side insecure too. This new thinking rejects many basic assumptions of earlier Soviet foreign policy, and should be understood primarily as a response to the crisis in foreign relations to which Leonid I. Brezhnev's policies had brought the Soviet Union by the early 1980s.

32 "Withering away of the state" is a Marxist idea that, with realization of the ideals of socialism, the social institution of a state will eventually become obsolete and disappear.

33 Yaremenko was one of the principal economic advisers to Mikhail Gorbachev. Yaremenko warned that simply discontinuing central planning and opening the country to foreign trade would lead to collapse of consumer goods sectors, which could not compete with imports. Rather, the system of priorities should first be used to transform the economy's structure to something approximating that of market

economy. This advice was not heeded, and the consequences were much as he had anticipated. In the 1990s, Yaremenko was sharply critical of the policies adopted by the Russian government. He was not at all opposed to an orderly transition to a market economy but felt that the "shock therapy" approach was needlessly costly. Yaremenko who was Director of the Institute of Economic Forecasting discussed the matter at length with Vitaly Shlykov and me in 1993. He considered conditions in Moscow in 1993 worse than the siege of Leningrad, September 8, 1941–January 27, 1944.

34 A mindset is a set of assumptions, notions and methods held by one or more people or groups of people that govern without critical rational management. It leads to "group think," mental inertia and a refusal to credence counterevidence and disproofs.

References

Abalkin, Leonid. (1989a). "Restructuring New Thinking in Soviet Economics." In Anthony Jones and William Moskoff, *Perestroika and the Economy: New Thinking in Soviet Economics*. New York: M.E. Sharpe, 91–98.

Abalkin, Leonid. (1989b). "A New Conception of Centralism." In Anthony Jones and William Moskoff (eds.). *Perestroika and the Economy: New Thinking in Soviet Economics*. New York: M. E. Sharpe, 91–98.

Appel, Hilary. (1997). "Voucher Privatization in Russia: Structural Consequences and Mass Response in the Second Period of Reform." *Europe-Asia Studies*. Vol. 49, No. 8, 1433–1449.

Aslund, Anders. (1987). "Gorbachev's Advisors." *Soviet Economy*. Vol. 3, 246–269.

Aslund, Anders. (1989). *Gorbachev's Struggle for Economic Reform: The Soviet Reform Process, 1985–1988*. Ithaca: Cornell University Press.

Aven, Petr and V. M. Shironin. (1989). "The Reform of the Economic Mechanism." In Anthony Jones and William Moskoff (eds.). *Perestroika and the Economy: New Thinking in Soviet Economics*. New York: M. E. Sharpe, 251–267.

Belkin, Victor and V. V. Ivanter. (1969). *Ekonomicheskoe upravlenie i bank*. Moskva: Izd-vo Ekonomika.

Belova, Eugenia. (2001). "Economic Crime and Punishment." In Paul R. Gregory (ed.). *Behind the Façade of Stalin's Command Economy: Experience from the Soviet State and Party Archives*. Stanford: Hoover Institution Press, 131–58.

Bergson, Abram. (1984). "Income Inequality under Soviet Socialism." *Journal of Economic Literature*. Vol. 22, 1052–1099.

Bergson, Abram. (1987). "Comparative Productivity: The USSR, Eastern Europe and the West." *American Economic Review*. Vol. 77, No. 3, 342–357.

Bergson, Abram. (1989a). "Economics of Perestroika: An Inauspicious Beginning." *Challenge*. Vol. 32, No. 3, 10–15.

Bergson, Abram. (1989b). *Planning and Performance in Socialist Economies*. Boston: Unwin and Hyman.

Bergson, Abram. (1989c). "Soviet Economic Reform under Gorbachev Trials and Errors." In William Kern (ed.). *From Socialism to Market Economy: The Transition Problem*. Kalamazoo: Upjohn Institute, 35–52.

Bergson, Abram. (1991). "The USSR before the Fall: How Poor and Why?" *Journal of Economic Perspectives*. No. 5, 29–44.

Bergson, Abram. (1994). "The Communist Efficiency Gap: Alternative Measures." *Comparative Economic Studies*. Vol. 36, No. 1, 1–12.

Berliner, Joseph. (1992). "Reconstructing the Soviet Planned Economy." In William Kern (ed.). *From Socialism to Market Economy: The Transition Problem*. Kalamazoo: Upjohn Institute, 53–73.

Blasi, Joseph, Maya Kroumova and Douglas Kruse. (1997). *Kremlin Capitalism: Privatizing the Russian Economy*. Ithaca: ILR Press.

Bloom, Solomon. (1946). "Withering Away of the State." *Journal of the History of Ideas*. Vol. 7, No. 1, 113–121.

Boycko, Maxim, Andrei Shleifer and Rob Vishny. (1995). *Privatizing Russia*. Cambridge: MIT Press.

Boycko, Maxim, Andrei Shleifer and Rob Vishny. (1996). "A Theory of Privatisation." *Economic Journal*. Vol. 106, No. 435, 309–319.

Brown, Archie. (2004). "The Rise of Non-Leninist Thinking about the Political System." In Archie Brown (ed.). *The Demise of Marxist-Leninism in Russia*. London: Palgrave MacMillan, 19–40.

Brown, Archie. (2020). *The Human Factor: Gorbachev, Reagan, and Thatcher and the End of the Cold War*. London: Oxford University Press.

Brown, Archie. (2021). "Then and Now." *Russia in Global Affairs*. No. 3. https://eng.global affairs.ru/articles/then-and-now/

Bulgakov, Mikhail. (2016). *The Master and Margarita*. London: Penguin.

CIA. (1987). "Restructuring the Soviet Workplace: The New Enterprise Law." *SOVA*. www.cia.gov/library/readingroom/docs/DOC_0000499785.pdf

Cohen, Stephen. (2000). *Failed Crusade America and the Tragedy of Post-Communist Russia*. New York: W. W. Norton & Company.

Conquest, Robert. (1991). *The Great Terror: A Reassessment*. London: Oxford University Press.

Dallin, Alexander. (2004a). "The Rise of New Thinking on Soviet Foreign Policy." In Archie Brown (ed.). *The Demise of Marxist-Leninism in Russia*. London: Palgrave MacMillan, 178–191.

Dallin, Alexander. (2004b). "The Development of New Thinking about World Communism." In Archie Brown (ed.). *The Demise of Marxist-Leninism in Russia*. London: Palgrave MacMillan, 192–206.

Davies, Robert. (1987). *Soviet History in the Gorbachev Revolution: The First Phase*. Birmingham: Centre for Russian and East European Studies.

Degenaar, Johan. (1990). "Marxism and Deconstruction." *Journal of Literary Studies*. Vol. 6, No. 3, 164–172.

Dewatripont, Mathias and Gerard Roland. (1997). Transition as a Process of Large Scale Institutional Change." In David Kreps and Ken Wallis (eds.). *Advances in Economic Theory*. New York: Cambridge University Press, Vol. 2, 240—278.

Dobb, Maurice. (1966). *Soviet Economic Planning Since 1917*. New York: International Publishers.

Dobbs, Michael. (1990). "Soviet Party Votes to Drop Monopoly on Power." *Washington Post*, February 9.

Earle, John and Saul Estrin. (1998). *Privatization, Competition, and Budget Constraints: Disciplining Enterprises in Russia*. SITE Working Paper 128. Stockholm: Stockholm Institute of Transition Economics and East European Economies.

Economic Survey of Europe. (2003). Geneva, United Nations, No.1, tables B1, B2, B3, B4, B5 and B8.

Ellman, Michael. (1994). "The Increase in Death and Disease under 'Katastroika'." *Cambridge Journal of Economics*. Vol. 18, No. 4, 329–355.

Ellman, Michael and Vladimir Kontorovich (eds.). (1998). *The Destruction of the Soviet Economic System: An Insiders' History.* London: Routledge.

Fainsod, Merle. (1963). *How Russia Is Ruled.* Cambridge: Harvard University Press.

Fedorov, Boris. (1989). "Reform of the Soviet Banking System." *Communist Economies.* Vol. 1, No. 4, 455–461.

Filatochev, Igor and Roy Bradshaw. (1992). "Soviet Hyperinflation: Its Origins and Impact throughout the Former Republics." *Soviet Studies.* Vol. 44, No. 5, 739–759.

Filatochev, Igor, Trevor Buck and Mike Wright. (1993). "The Military-Industrial Complex of the Former USSR: Asset or Liability?" *Communist Economies and Economic Transformation.* Vol. 5, No. 2, 187–204. https://doi.org/10.1080/14631379308427752

Fitzpatrick, Sheila. (1992). *The Cultural Front. Power and Culture in Revolutionary Russia.* Ithaca: Cornell University Press.

Fitzpartick, Sheila. (1999). Everyday Stalinism: Ordinary Life in Extraordinary Times: Soviet Russia in the 1930s. New York: Oxford University Press.

Foss, Clive. (2006). *The Tyrants: 2500 Years of Absolute Power and Corruption.* London: Quercus Publishing.

Freixas, Xavier, Roger Guesnerie and Jean Tirole. (1985). Planning under Incomplete Information and the Ratchet Effect. *Review of Economic Studies.* Vol. 52, 173–191.

French II, Robert and Heewon Chang. (2016). "Conceptual Re-imagining of Global Mindset: Knowledge as Prime in the Development of Global Leaders." *Journal of International Organizations Studies.* Vol. 1, No.1, 49–62. http://journal-iostudies.org/sites/journal-iostudies.org/files/JIOS-ReviewEssay_GlobalMindset.pdf

Frydman, Roman, Andrzej Rapaczynski and John Earle. (1993). *The Privatization Process in Russia, Ukraine and the Baltic States.* Budapest: Central European University Press.

Frydman, Roman, Cheryl Gray, Marek Hessel and Andrzej Rapaczynski. (2000). "The Limits of Discipline – Ownership and Hard Budget Constraints in the Transition Economies." *Economics of Transition.* Vol. 8, No. 3, 577–601.

Gates, Robert. (1988). "The Gorbachev Era: Implications for U.S. Strategy." American Association for the Advancement of Science Colloquium on Science, Arms Control and National Security. www.cia.gov/library/readingroom/docs/CIA-RDP89G00720R000800150010-6.pdf

Getty, J. Arch. (2013). *Practicing Stalinism: Bolsheviks, Boyars, and the Persistence of Tradition.* New Haven: Yale University Press.

Ghodsee, Kristen. (2018). *Why Women Have Better Sex under Socialism: And Other Arguments for Economic Independence.* New York: Nation Books.

Goldfeld, S. M. and Richard Quandt. (1990). "Output Targets, the Soft Budget Constraint and the Firm under Central Planning." *Journal of Economic Behavior and Organization.* Vol. 14, No. 2, 205–222.

Goldman, Marshall. (2003). *The Piratization of Russia: Russian Reform Goes Awry.* London: Routledge.

Gollwitzer, Peter. (1990). "Action Phases and Mind-sets." In E. Tory Higgins and Richard Sorrentino (eds.). *The Handbook of Motivation and Cognition: Foundations of Social Behavior,* Vol. 2. New York: Guilford Press, 52–92.

Gollwitzer, Peter. (2012). "Mindset Theory of Action Phases." In Paul Van Lange, Ari Kruglanski and E. Tory Higgins (eds.). *Handbook of Theories of Social Psychology,* Vol. 1. Thousand Oaks: Sage, 526–545.

Gorbachev, Mikhail. (1987). *Perestroika: New Thinking for Our Country and the World.* New York: Harper & Row.

Gorbachev, Mikhail. (1988). *General Secretary of the CPSU Central Committee, Documents and Materials.* Moscow: Novosti Press Agency Publishing House.

Gorbachev, Mikhail. (2021). "Perestroika and New Thinking: A Retrospective." *Russia in Global Affairs*. https://eng.globalaffairs.ru/articles/perestroika-and-new-thinking/

Grossman, Gregory. (1977). "The Second Economy of the USSR." *Problems of Communism*. Vol. 26, No. 5, 25–40.

Hansen, Phillip. (1990). "Property Rights in the New Phase of Reforms." *Soviet Economy*. Vol. 6, No. 2, 95–124.

Hansen, Phillip. (2003). *The Rise and Fall of the Soviet Economy: An Economic History of the USSR from 1945*. London: Pearson Education.

Hertzfeld, Jeffrey. (1991). "Joint Ventures: Saving the Soviets from Perestroika." *Harvard Business Review*.

Holloway, David. (1989). "Gorbachev's New Thinking." *Foreign Affairs*. Vol. 68, No. 1, 66–81.

Johnson, Simon. (1991). "Spontaneous Privatization in the Soviet Union: How, Why and for Whom." *World Institute for Development Economics Research of the United Nations University*. www.wider.unu.edu/sites/default/files/WP91.pdf

Johnson, Simon and Heidi Kroll. (1991). "Managerial Strategies for Spontaneous Privatization." *Soviet Economy*. Vol. 7, No. 4, 281–316.

Katsenelinboigen, Aron. (1977). "Colored Markets in the Soviet Union." *Soviet Studies*. Vol. 29, No. 1, 62–85.

Kennan, George. (1988). "The Gorbachev Prospect." *New York Review of Books*. 3–7. www.nybooks.com/articles/1988/01/21/the-gorbachev-prospect/

Kesey, Ken. (1962). *One Flew over the Cuckoo's Nest*. New York: Viking Press.

Kornai, János. (1979). "Resource-Constrained versus Demand-Constrained Systems." *Econometrica*. Vol. 47, No. 4, 801–812.

Kornai, János. (1980). *The Economics of Shortage*, 2 vols. Amsterdam: North-Holland.

Kornai, János. (1986). *Economics of Shortage*. Amsterdam: North-Holland.

Kornai, János. (2000). "Ten Years after the Road to a Free Economy: The Author's Self Evaluation." In Boris Pleskovic and Nicolas Stern (eds.). *Annual Bank Conference on Development Economics*. Washington: The World Bank, 49–66.

Kornai, János. (2001). "The Soft Budget Constraint." *Kyklos*. Vol. 39, No. 1, 3–30.

Kornai, János, Eric Maskin and Gerard Roland. (2003). "Understanding the Soft Budget Constraint." *Journal of Economic Literature*. Vol. 41, No. 4, 1095–1136.

Korostelev, V. A. (1989). "The Rebirth of Small-Scale Commodity Production." In Anthony Jones and William Moskoff (eds.). *Perestroika and the Economy: New Thinking in Soviet Economics*. New York: M. E. Sharpe, 45–59.

Krueger, Anne. (1974). "The Political Economy of the Rent-Seeking Society." *American Economic Review*. Vol. 6, No. 3, 291–303.

Kulikov, V. V. (1989). "The Structure and Forms of Socialist Property." In Anthony Jones and William Moskoff (eds.). *Perestroika and the Economy: New Thinking in Soviet Economics*. New York: M. E. Sharpe, 217–232.

Kurashvili, Boris. (1989). "Restructuring and the Enterprise." In Anthony Jones and William Moskoff (eds.). *Perestroika and the Economy: New Thinking in Soviet Economics*. New York: M. E. Sharpe, 21–44.

Kurian, George Thomas (ed.). (2011). "Withering Away of the State." *Encyclopedia of Political Science*. Washington: CQ Press.

Lapidus, Gail. (2004). "Transforming the 'National Question': New Approaches to Nationalism, Federalism and Sovereignty." In Archie Brown (ed.). *The Demise of Marxist-Leninism in Russia*. London: Palgrave MacMillan, 119–177.

Leeds, Adam. (2019). "Administrative Monsters: Yurii Yaremenko's Critique of the Late Soviet State." *History of Political Economy*. Vol. 51, No. 1, 127–151.

Leonard, Carol and David Pitt-Watson. (2013). *Privatization and Transition in Russia in the Early 1990s.* Oxford: Routledge.

Levgold, Robert and The Task Force on Soviet New Thinking. (1988). *Gorbachev's Foreign Policy: How Should the United States Respond? Foreign Policy Association.* No. 284, 1–67.

Majumdar, Sumit. (1998). "Slack in the State-Owned Enterprise: An Evaluation of the Impact of Soft-Budget Constraints." *International Journal of Industrial Organization.* Vol. 16, No. 3, 377–394.

Maskin, Eric and Chenggang Xu. (2001). "Soft Budget Constraint Theories: From Centralization to the Market." *Economics of Transition.* Vol. 9, No. 1, 1–27.

McCauly, Alastair. (1981). *Women's Work and Wages in the Soviet Union.* London: Allen and Unwin.

McClelland, James. (1980). "Utopianism versus Revolutionary Heroism in Bolshevik Policy: The Proletarian Culture Debate." *Slavic Review.* Vol. 39, No. 3, 403–425.

McFaul, Michael and Tova Perlmutter (eds.). (1995). *Privatization, Conversion, and Enterprise Reform in Russia.* Boulder: Westview Press.

Mendel-Gleason, Gavin. (2019). "Soviet Socialism More Popular than Ever among Russians." *People's World.* www.peoplesworld.org/article/soviet-socialism-more-popular-than-ever-among-russians/

Miller, Chris. (2020). *Mikhail Gorbachev and the Collapse of the USSR.* Chapel Hill: UNC Press.

Moskoff, William (ed.). (2019). *Perestroika in the Countryside: Agricultural Reform in the Gorbachev Era.* London: Routledge.

Narodnoe Khoziaistvo SSSR za 70 Let. (1987). *Materials from the Plenum of the Communist Party Central Committee,* January 27–29. Politizdat: Statistika.

Nove, Alec. (2004). "The Rise of Non-Leninist Thinking on the Economy." In Archie Brown (ed.). *The Demise of Marxist-Leninism in Russia.* London: Palgrave MacMillan,.41–50.

O korennoi perestroika. (1987). *O korennoi perestroike upravleniia ekonomikoi: sbornik dokumentov.* Moscow: Politizdat.

Palterovich, D. (1989). "Competition and Democratization." In Anthony Jones and William Moskoff (eds.). *Perestroika and the Economy: New Thinking in Soviet Economics.* New York: M. E. Sharpe, 60–67.

Panné, Jean-Louis, Andrzej Paczkowski, Karel Bartosek, Jean-Louis Margolin and Nicolas Werth. (1999). *The Black Book of Communism: Crimes, Terror, Repression.* Cambridge: Harvard University Press.

Reddaway, Peter. (1988). "The Battle for Moscow." *New Republic.* Vol. 198, No. 5, 34–38.

Reinert, Hugo. (1994). *Creative Destruction in Economics: Nietzsche, Sombart, Schumpeter: The European Heritage in Economics and the Social Sciences.* New York: Springer, 55–85.

Rosefielde, Steven. (1986). "Regulated Market Socialism: The Semi-Competitive Soviet Solution." *Soviet Union/Union Sovietique.* Vol. 13, Part 1,1–21.

Rosefielde, Steven. (1989a). "Ruble Convertibility: Promise or Threat?" In Simon Serfaty (ed.). *The Future of U.S.¬Soviet Relations: Twenty American Initiatives for a New Agenda.* Baltimore: Johns Hopkins University Press.

Rosefielde, Steven. (1989b). "State-Directed Market Socialism: The Enigma of Gorbachev's Radical Industrial Reforms." *Soviet Union/Union Sovietique.* Vol. 16, No. 1, 1–22.

Rosefielde, Steven. (1989c). "The Distorted World of Soviet-type Economies: Review Article." *Atlantic Economic Journal.* Vol. 17, No. 4, 83–86.

Rosefielde, Steven. (1990a). "Market Communism at the Brink." *Global Affairs.* Vol. 5, No. 2, 95–108.

Rosefielde, Steven. (1990b). "Soviet Market Socialism: An Evolutionary Perspective." *Research on the Soviet Union and Eastern Europe*. Vol. 1, 23–43.

Rosefielde, Steven. (1991a). "Democratic Market Communism: Gorbachev's Design for Utopia." *Shogaku-Ronshu (Fukushima Journal of Commerce, Economics and Economic History)*. Vol. 59, No. 3, 15–23.

Rosefielde, Steven. (1991b). "Gorbachev's Transition Plan: Strategy for Disaster." *Global Affairs*. Vol. 6, No. 2, 1–21.

Rosefielde, Steven. (1991c). "Les limites du liberalisme economique sovietique: la perestroika va-t-elle passer a la trappe?" (The Limits of Soviet Economic Liberalism: Perestroika in Limbo). *Revue D'Etudes Comparatives Est-Ouest*. Vol. 22, No. 2, 59–70.

Rosefielde, Steven. (1991d). "The Grand Bargain: Underwriting Catastroika." *Global Affairs*. Vol. 7, No. 1, 15–35.

Rosefielde, Steven. (1991e). "The New Soviet Foreign Trade Mechanism: East West Trade Expansion Possibilities under Perestroika." In Eric Stubbs (ed.). *Soviet Foreign Economic Policy and International Security*. M. E. Sharpe, 75–86.

Rosefielde, Steven. (1991f). "The Soviet Peace Dividend and the Transition to Market Socialism." In Roy Allison (ed.). *Military and Strategic Issues in the Contemporary USSR*. London: Macmillan, 60–69.

Rosefielde, Steven. (1992). "Beyond Catastroika: Prospects for Market Transition in the Commonwealth of Independent States." *Atlantic Economic Journal*. Vol. 20, No. 1, 1–8.

Rosefielde, Steven. (1994). "Retreat from Utopia: The Reconfiguration of Russian Socialism." *Atlantic Economic Journal*. Vol. 22, No. 2, 1–12.

Rosefielde, Steven. (1995). "Eastern Economic Reform: Transition or Mutation?" *Atlantic Economic Journal*. Vol. 23, No. 4, 323–332.

Rosefielde, Steven. (1998). "Who Lost Russia?" *Japan Times*. September 24.

Rosefielde, Steven. (1999). "Russia's Warped Transition: The Destructive Consequences of Ethically Unconstrained Utility Seeking." *Eastern Economic Journal*. Vol. 25, No. 4, 459–476.

Rosefielde, Steven. (2000). "The Civilian Labor Force and Unemployment in the Russian Federation." *Europe-Asia Studies*. Vol. 52, No. 8, 1433–1447.

Rosefielde, Steven. (2001). "Klepto-Banking: Systemic Sources of Russia's Failed Industrial Recovery." In Howard Stein, Olu Ajakaiye and Peter Lewis (eds.). *Deregulation and the Banking Crisis in Nigeria: A Comparative Study*. Basingstoke: Palgrave, 193–210.

Rosefielde, Steven. (2003). "The Riddle of Postwar Russian Economic Growth: Statistics Lied and Were Misconstrued." *Europe-Asia Studies*. Vol. 55, No. 3, 469–481.

Rosefielde, Steven. (2005). *Russia in the 21st Century: The Prodigal Superpower*. Cambridge: Cambridge University Press.

Rosefielde, Steven. (2007). *Russian Economy from Lenin to Putin*. London: Blackwell.

Rosefielde, Steven and Quinn Mills. (1990). "Transition Shock: Can the East Get There From Here?" *California Management Review*. Vol. 32, No. 4, 9–21.

Rosefielde, Steven and Ralph Pfouts. (1991). "Market Communism: The 'Organic' Strategy." *Communist Economies*. Vol. 3, No. 1, 93–104.

Rosefielde, Steven, Vyachaslav Danilin and Georgii Kleiner. (1994). "Deistvuiushaya Model' Reform i Ugroza Giperdepressii." (The Russian Reform Model and the Threat of Hyperdepression). *Russian Economic Journal (Rossiiskii Ekonomicheskii Zhurnal)*. No. 12, 48–55.

Sachs, Jeffrey and Katharina Pistor. (1997). *The Rule of Law and Economic Reform in Russia* (John M. Olin Critical Issues Series (Paper)). Denver: Westview Press.

Schapiro, Leonard. (1955). *The Origins of the Communist Autocracy.* London: G. Bell and Sons.

Schapiro, Leonard. (1970). *The Communist Party of the Soviet Union.* New York: Random House Publishers.

Schapiro, Leonard. (1972). *Totalitarianism: Key Concepts in Political Science.* Ann Arbor: The University of Michigan.

Schroeder, Gertrude. (1987). "Anatomy of Gorbachev's Economic Reform." *Soviet Economy.* Vol. 3, 219–241.

Schumpeter, Joseph. (1994). *Capitalism, Socialism and Democracy.* London: Routledge.

Shatalin, Stanislav (1990). *Transition to the Market: 500 Days,* pt. 1. Moscow: Arkhangelskoe.

Sherman, Howard. (1969). *The Soviet Economy.* Boston: Little, Brown and Company.

Shleifer, Andre and Daniel Treisman. (2000). *Without a Map: Political Tactics and Economic Reform in Russia.* Cambridge: MIT Press.

Surin, Kenneth. (1990). "Marxism(s) and 'The Withering Away of the State'." *Social Text.* No. 27, 35–54.

Sutela, Pekka. (1994). "Insider Privatization in Russia: Speculations on Systemic Change." *Europe-Asia Studies.* Vol. 46, No. 3, 417–435.

Tihomirov, Vladimir. (1997). "Capital Flight from Post-Soviet Russia." *Europe-Asia Studies.* Vol. 49, No. 4, 591–615.

Timofeyev, Igor. (2004). "The Development of Russian Liberal Thought since 1985." In Archie Brown (ed.). *The Demise of Marxist-Leninism in Russia.* London: Palgrave MacMillan, 51–118.

Torkanovskii, E. (1989). "The Participation of Working People in the Management of Production as a Factor in Heightening Labor Activism." In Anthony Jones and William Moskoff (eds.). *Perestroika and the Economy: New Thinking in Soviet Economics.* New York: M. E. Sharpe, 78–90.

Tucker, Robert. (1987). "Gorbachev and the Fight for Soviet Reform." *World Policy Journal.* 183–206.

Winiecki, Jan. (1988). *The Distorted World of Soviet-Type Economies.* Pittsburgh: University of Pittsburgh Press.

Zakon. (1985). Zakon o trudovykh kollektivakh v deistvii", Sovetskoe gosudarstvo i pravo 6 (June), 5–12.

Zinoviev, Alexander. (1990). *Katastroika: Legend and Reality of Gorbachev.* London: Claridge.

Zubok, Vladislav. (2021). *Collapse: The Fall of the Soviet Union.* New Haven: Yale University Press.

8   Worker Self-Management

Gorbachev's decision to free red directors (nominally co-governing with worker collectives)[1] from tekhpromfinplan directives and Gosbank financial controls without adequate institutional adjustments destroyed communist top-down command planning. Managers and corrupt State Economic Directors exploited Gorbachev's radical reform causing a chain reaction and toppling the system. Suppose that Gorbachev foreseeing the danger bypassed red directors and entrusted worker collectives to manage enterprises in their own best interest. Could the Soviet experiment have had a happy ending? Could worker self-management have changed the course of history?

The Yugoslavian experiment with labor self-governing market socialism of 1952–1988 sheds useful light on Gorbachev's perestroika and the viability of worker self-management (Bartlett and Uvalić, 1986).[2] It demonstrates that although worker collectives have some interesting behavioral features, they are not a panacea (Estrin and Uvalić, 2008),[3] and do not validate Marx's claim in the *Economic and Philosophical Manuscripts* of 1844 that if private property and markets are abolished, workers will efficiently and equitably manage the economy (Marx, 1932).

Yugoslavian Worker Self-Governing Socialism

Josip Bronz Tito, President of Yugoslava, 1953–1980, and President of the League of Yugoslav Communists, 1939–1980 tried to improve the communist top-down command plan model by empowering worker collectives to codirect enterprise operations with state-appointed red directors (Uvalić, 2019; Estrin, 1983).[4] The power of worker collectives varied widely, but economists curious about the theoretical potential of worker self-governing revolutionary socialism (with state freehold ownership of the means of production, planning and markets) investigated the microeconomic and macroeconomic possibilities of an egalitarian labor management system, assuming that working collectives maximized egalitarian dividends instead of profits. They found that if worker collectives had complete authority to manage state enterprises, the socialist character of Soviet top-down command planning would have been transformed without necessarily

DOI: 10.4324/9781003371571-11

eradicating shortages, enhancing equity or assuring a smooth transition from Marxist–Leninist central planning to worker freehold owned market socialism. Gorbachev from this perspective was right to presume that enterprise worker collectives would seek to improve their quality of existence within an indicative Soviet planning framework, but wrong to wager on worker egalitarian altruism.

This finding was counterintuitive to Marxist political economists who believed that a dialectical historical struggle between capitalists and workers would culminate in communist prosperity and economic justice. Marxists claimed that most people were poor, and society was unjust because capitalism depressed productivity and exploited the masses. It seemed plausible to infer therefore that if labor were in command, living standards would rise and consumption would be more equitable, but Yugoslavian and Western economists found to their surprise that self-interested worker collectives might not improve productivity or equity. Although Marx and Engel's *Communist Manifesto* implied that labor self-governing socialism should be prosperous and just because workers were altruistic, economists discovered that workers might reserve their effort and foster inegalitarianism.

They stumbled on this revelation by assuming that workers in Yugoslav enterprises would organize production efficiently, and negotiate with ministerial supervisors in "family circles" to devise optimal worker benefit sharing enterprise plans. Western economists supposed that workers would maximize group utility.

Advocates of worker-managed socialism contended that replacing red directors with working collectives would make soft communist top-down command planning more responsive to worker preferences through the "family circle" mechanism, making the workplace would more congenial, fairer and productive, even though these benefits were local rather than trans-communal.

Ben Ward discovered shortly after Tito's experiment in market syndicalism began in the mid-1950s, however, that labor and other resources might be underemployed in worker-managed communist systems that paid members equal shares of enterprise net revenue in lieu of red director bonuses (Ward, 1957, 1958; Estrin, 1983).[5] This finding held for all egalitarian labor-managed firms (ELMF) that rewarded worker collective members with equal dividends (Ward, 1958; Domar, 1966; Vanek, 1970; Furubotn and Pejovic, 1970).[6]

The aberration was an artefact of the Yugoslav decision to foster egalitarianism through worker net revenue sharing instead of lump-sum tax transfers (Mankiw, Weinzierl and Yagan, 2009).[7] Under the Yugoslav dividend sharing protocol, members received the average enterprise net revenue (revenue minus nonlabor factor costs) instead of wages equal to the value of each worker's marginal product. This meant that workers who generated above average net revenue could increase their dividend by ejecting members whose net revenue was below average. The majority of worker collective members had to decide whether above-average net revenue contributors should maximize their utility by expelling under-contributors, or charitably share net revenue in some measure with members whose productivity was subpar. ELMF advocates insisted that solidarity would prevail, but if the majority in accordance with rational choice theory decided otherwise, Yugoslav and Soviet ELMFs would necessarily underemploy workers and underproduce both from the communist and Western competitive market perspectives. Tito and Gorbachev, if they grasped the issue, would then have to judge whether improvements in the workplace democracy, congeniality, fairness and worker enthusiasm outweighed the underemployment and underproduction effects of ELMFs.

The perplexing effects of ELMF were not restricted to underemployment and underproduction. Closer investigation revealed other anomalies. If scientific and technological progress increased ELMF productivity, or prices rose, augmenting net revenue, then employment and output would contract instead of expanding as it must in competitive market and communist top-down command planning systems (Rosefielde and Pfouts, 1996; Domar, 1966).[8] Technological progress and higher product prices would likely increase average net revenue more than marginal net revenue (Domar, 1966; Saul Estrin, Derek Jones and Jan Svejnar, 1987; Furubotn and Pejovic, 1970; Vanek, 1970), prompting the majority to eject subpar net revenue contributors. Vice versa, if prices fell, the majority would readmit expelled members. If macroeconomic policymakers stimulated demand to increase employment, and prices rose, then employment would contract. Vice versa, if they increased ELMF tax to cool the economy, employment would expand. If the risk of default rose, ELMFs would add members to spread the debt burden, but in the process expand output (Meade, 1972, 1989). Vice versa, if default risk fell, they would expel members and contract output.[9]

Moreover, if above-average net revenue contributors elected to augment their utility by reserving their labor (substituting leisure for effort) until their contribution fell to the average net revenue, average net revenue would decline. This would create a new group of above-average net revenue contributors who could then reserve their effort, triggering serial bouts of effort reservation until the ELMF dividend fell to the subsistence level (Rosefielde and Pfouts, 1998) (see Chapter 20).

All these anomalous intra-ELMF effects caused adverse inter-ELMF spillovers. Expelled members from high-dividend ELMFs found new jobs mostly in low-dividend-paying ELMFs, and the mobility of superior dividend contributors in poor ELMF was impaired. The best workers in a Yugoslav communist syndicalist economy were concentrated in rich ELMFs and everyone else in poor worker collectives. Paradoxically, from a socialist perspective, while intra-ELMF net revenue sharing fostered egalitarianism locally, it intensified inegalitarianism across system (Milanović, 1990, 1998).[10] See Chapter 20 for further insight into the special character of Yugoslavia's egalitarian strategy.

Transition from a top-down command planning regime to a socialist mixed-plan market or a syndicalist market economic system not only risked destabilizing pre-transition top-down command plan controls, but also raised the specter of aggravating inegalitarianism (Uvalić, 1964).[11]

Soviet red directors and their overseers degraded the khozraschyot mechanism after 1987 by misusing enterprise revenues, spontaneously privatizing assets to themselves and transferring ill-gotten gains abroad in lieu of bonus maximizing.

In doing so, they transferred productive wealth from the state (people's ownership) to themselves with severe inegalitarian consequences. Yugoslav worker collectives, 1980–1991, behaved similarly, albeit with some important differences, 1980–1991. First, worker collectives in Yugoslav ELMFs mostly operated as leasehold proprietorships of the people's assets (social ownership) rather than freeholders.[12] They sought to enrich themselves primarily from the usufruct of the people's property with relatively limited concern for long-term future earnings that would have occurred by switching to freehold ownership (present discounted value) (Uvalić, 1992).[13] ELMFs operated with "soft budgets" that allowed them to overborrow and accumulate debt some hoped never to repay (Kraft and Milan Vodopivec, 1992).

They held non-indexed financial assets and liabilities in an inflationary environment that drastically redirected income to worker collectives in the manufacturing sector.[14] High investment and inflation should have spurred GDP growth and full employment, but did not do so. Growth stagnated in 1977–1989, before plummeting catastrophically in 1990–1991. Unemployment in 1980s ran as high as 16%. The average annual inflation rate rose from 30% in 1980 to triple-digit figures in 1987–1988 and reached hyperinflation in 1989 at an annual rate of 1,252% (Uvalić, 2010). Restrictive income policies in combination with rising inflation led to declining living standards: between 1980 and 1984, there was a 34% drop in real net wages. There were also mounting social tensions. This led the government to relax income controls, which in turn further contributed to rising inflationary pressures. The various stabilization programs implemented during the 1981–1989 period were unsuccessful.

Second, burgeoning inequality spawn by both transition strategies (more pronounced in Russia than Yugoslavia) affected Soviet and Yugoslav politics differently (Kimp and Novokmet, 2018; Novokmet, Piketty, and Zucman, 2017). The Gorbachev faction of the Communist Party and Russian successors tried to placate workers by portraying the inequities of spontaneous privatization as the price for progress, whereas authorities in Bosnia and Herzegovina, Croatia, North Macedonia, Montenegro, Serbia, Slovenia and Kosovo had to improvise according to circumstances. The Soviet-Russian approach eventually led to the restoration of the power vertical (Monaghan, 2011);[15] the Yugoslav alternative split the country politically, partly due to severe regional income inequality (Uvalić, 1993),[16] and culminated in the abandonment of ELMFs across the Balkan syndicalist space.

ELMFs were not the sole cause of Yugoslavia's disintegration in 1991.[17] The behavioral aberrations of egalitarian worker collective dividend maximizing exposed by Ward, Domar and Vanek depended on assumptions that did not fully capture the realities of Yugoslavia's labor-managed syndicalist economy (Horvat, 1967, 1972, 1982). Even if they had, subsequent contributors to the ELMF literature showed that reforms could have mitigated many potential inefficiencies (Estrin, Derek Jones and Jan Svejnar, 1987; Nuti, 1992; Sapir, 1980; Drèze, 1976, 1989).

Nonetheless, it is undeniable that ELMFs and syndicalism more broadly failed to save Yugoslavia's communist core. ELMFs and syndicalism neither prevented Yugoslavia's dissolution, nor led Bosnia and Herzegovina, Croatia, North

Macedonia, Montenegro, Serbia, Slovenia and Kosovo to the socialist future.[18] Yugoslavian communism from start to finish failed to provide its citizens with a decent quality of existence. Belgrade quickly became dissatisfied with communist top-down command planning. ELMF and later syndicalist reforms fared no better. Yugoslavia like the Soviet Union was an endemic economy of shortage. Material well-being, including the utility of substandard public services, remained stubbornly low. The Communist Party suppressed democracy and circumscribed personal and civil liberties. It repressed capitalism but did not eradicate exploitation, unemployment, inflation and insecurity. It embarked on an egalitarian quest that enthralled advocates of labor self-management, equity and workplace democracy for three decades, only to end in disappointment.

Tito's "Third Way" was a flop (Koyama, 2022).[19]

Notes

1 Worker collectives met once annually to approve managers' action. This was inadequate, and managers remained kings of the roost.
2 For a survey of the literature, see Bartlett and Uvalić. Yugoslavia was a country in Southeastern and Central Europe for most of the 20th century. It began in 1918 after the fall of the Austro-Hungarian Empire as the Kingdom of Serbs, Croats and Slovenes. The official name became Kingdom of Yugoslavia on October 3, 1929. Josip Bronz Tito's communist government abolished the Kingdom in November 1945 and renamed the successor the Federal People's Republic of Yugoslavia the Socialist Federal Republic of Yugoslavia (SFRY) in 1963. The SFRY disintegrated into six countries after Tito's death in 1980: Bosnia and Herzegovina, Croatia, North Macedonia, Montenegro, Serbia, Slovenia and Kosovo.
3 Yugoslavia's specific economic features based on self-management and increasing reliance on the market mechanism inspired a vast literature on market socialism and the labor-managed economy. Yugoslavia's unique economic system stimulated considerable academic interest for several reasons. First, the Yugoslav experience suggested the possibility of a third way, a view enhanced by President Tito's global role as one of the leaders of the nonaligned movement. Second, many felt that the extension of the principles of democracy to enterprise decision making was intrinsically virtuous.
4 The Communist Party initially appointed enterprise managers who collaborated with worker collectives. Later worker collectives elected enterprise managers. This, however, did not exclude the state. The Communist Party maintained a pervasive presence throughout and served as guardian of the state's interest. The new economic model introduced in 1950 assigned the direct management of public property to the workforce of enterprises, as contained in the Basic law on the administration of state enterprises by workers' collectives of July 2, 1950. This Law ended the centralized economic system and introduced the principle of self-management into the economy. The Law entrusted the administration of enterprise state property to the workers in most sectors – manufacturing, mining, communications, transport, trade, agriculture, forestry. The introduction of enterprise self-management did not change the property regime. The Yugoslavia market socialist experiment is divisible into three epochs: the "Visible Hand" period from 1952 to 1965, the "Market Self-Management" era from 1965 to 1972 and the "Social Planning" period after 1974.

5   Yugoslav workers received wages differentiated by skill, supervised by the state. This does not alter Ward's core finding. Yugoslav workers received egalitarian dividends in addition to fixed wages.

6   The theoretical drawbacks of egalitarian labor-managed firms (ELMF) were inefficient labor allocation due to perverse responses to changes in product price, technology and capital rents; restrictive employment policies; monopolistic behavior due to maximization of monopoly profit per man instead of total profit; and excessive risk taking.

   LMFs also used variable capital inefficiently and tended to underinvest due to limited property rights. When workers do not have full property rights over the firm's assets ("non-owned" assets), they cannot recover the principal of their investment at the end of their time horizon when they leave the firm, whereas investment in individual savings accounts in banks (or "owned" assets) ensures the recovery of both the principal and interest. In considering whether to invest earned income in the firm or in personal savings accounts, workers will prefer the latter. This caused ELMFs to underinvest.

7   A lump-sum tax is a fixed tax paid by everyone and the amount a person is taxed remains constant regardless of income or owned assets. Because the tax remains constant, an individual's incentives and a firm's incentives will not fluctuate, as opposed to a graduated income tax that taxes people more for earning more. In competitive market economies, factors including labor are reward in accordance with the value of their marginal products. Residual income, if any, is a windfall to shareholders. In the ELMFs, members only receive equal shares of net revenue after deducting nonlabor factor costs, not the value of each worker's marginal product.

8   The inverse correlation between price increases and ELMF membership stems from the assumption that dividends (net revenue) contain both variable and fixed costs (including fixed labor costs). When prices rise, fixed costs are unchanged, but revenues rise with prices. Marginal net revenue, which omits fixed costs, increases less rapidly, providing a rational choice basis for expelling underproductive members.

9   The 1970s reforms tried to reduce the concentration of economic power in part to mitigate abusive worker cooperative borrowing. Banks were transformed into "service" agencies of enterprises operating under their direct control, and new methods of mobilizing savings were introduced that would not necessarily require banks' intermediation. A 1971 law on securities diversified financial instruments, introducing both standard instruments (such as bonds, treasury bills and promissory notes) and those adapted to the Yugoslav system (so-called pooling of labor and resources that permitted direct investment of one enterprise into another).

10 Yugoslav income distribution was egalitarian compared with the global norm. Overall income distribution in socialist countries was more egalitarian than in most market economies, though in Yugoslavia the Gini coefficient was somewhat higher due to wide interregional differences in average income. Nevertheless, the Gini coefficient in Yugoslavia, using the per capita method, ranged between 0.32 and 0.35, while using total household revenue, it ranged between 0.33 and 0.34; these values were relatively stable over the 1973–1983 period, placing Yugoslavia among the countries with a moderate level of income inequality. As other socialist countries, Yugoslavia had a strong welfare state that provided free education and health care, social support to citizens in need and specific housing policies that secured the working population a place to live, usually giving them tenants' rights (not privately owned apartments).

11 Planning was also a permanent feature of the Yugoslav economic system used in combination with various other nonmarket mechanisms of allocation of resources.

12 The property regime in Yugoslavia was based on the system of social property, officially defined for the first time in the 1953 Constitution as the property of the whole society.

13 Yugoslavian LMFs were granted the right to invest their profits and did so even though they had no secure claim on future earnings. Firms were able to choose their own investment projects, as well as the proportion of profits to be allocated to investment.

14 Kraft and Vodopivec attribute ELMF overborrowing to the pursuit of job and wage security.

15 The term refers to the hierarchical political control of Russia by the power services (siloviki).

16 The gap between the Social Product per capita of the most developed Slovenia and the least developed Kosovo actually widened, from 5:1 in 1955 to 8:1 in 1989 (based on official statistics).

17 After Yugoslavia's breakup in 1991, there have been very different interpretations and explanations of the causes of the country's disintegration, sometimes attributing all the ills that had affected the country to the system of self-managed socialism. The crucial factor that pushed toward the country's breakup was the renewal and explosion of nationalist sentiment fed by the political myopia of leaders such as Milošević or Tudjman who believed that the key national objectives could be successfully resolved by the disintegration of the federation.

18 At the time of Yugoslavia's breakup, in mid-1991, its five successor states inherited very similar institutional features, but thereafter followed different trajectories.

19 Yoji Koyama suggests that the Soviet Union's demise accelerated Yugoslavia's disunion. Tito had persuaded federation members that unity was essential to parry Stalin's designs on the nation. The case against secession weakened when the USSR dissolved.

References

Bartlett, Will and Milica Uvalić, (1986). "Labour-Managed Firms, Employee Participation and Profit-sharing: Theoretical Perspectives and European Experience." *Management Bibliographies and Reviews*. Vol. 2, No. 4, 3–66.

Domar, Evsey. (1966). "The Soviet Collective Farm." *American Economic Review*. Vol. 56, No. 4, 734–757.

Drèze, Jean. (1976). "Some Theory of Labor Management and Participation." *Econometrica*. Vol. 44, 1125–1139.

Drèze, Jean. (1989). *Labor Management, Contracts and Capital Markets: A General Equilibrium Approach*. Oxford: Blackwell.

Estrin, Saul. (1983). *Self-Management: Economic Theory and Yugoslav Practice*. Cambridge: Cambridge University Press.

Estrin, Saul, Derek Jones and Jan Svejnar. (1987). "The Productivity Effects of Worker Participation: Producer Cooperatives in Western Economies." *Journal of Comparative Economics*. Vol. 11, 40–61.

Estrin, Saul and Milica Uvalić. (2008). "From Illyria towards Capitalism: Did Labor-Management Theory Teach Us Anything about Yugoslavia and Transition in Its Successor States?" *Comparative Economic Studies*. Vol. 50, 663–696.

Furubotn, Eric and S. Pejovic. (1970). "Property Rights and the Behaviour of the Firm in a Socialist State: The Example of Yugoslavia." *Zeitschrift fur Nationaloekonomie.* 431–454.

Horvat, Branko. (1967). "A Contribution to the Theory of the Yugoslav Firm." *Economic Analysis.* Vol. 1, No. 1, 288–293.

Horvat, Branko. (1972). "Critical Notes on the Theory of the Labour-Managed Firm and Some Macroeconomic Implications." *Economic Analysis.* Vol. 6, 291–294.

Horvat, Branko. (1982). *The Political Economy of Socialism.* Armonk, New York: M. E. Sharpe.

Kimp, Natasa and Filip Novokmet. (2018). "Top Incomes in Croatia and Slovenia, from 1960s until Today." Wideworld Working Paper Series, No. 2018. https://wid.world/document/top-incomes-in-croatia-and-slovenia-from-1960s-until-today-wid-world-working-paper-2018-8/

Koyama, Yoji. (2022). *What Was Soviet and East European Socialism: Its Historical Lessons and Future Society.* Tokyo: Logos.

Kraft, Evan and Milan Vodopivec. (1992). "How Soft Is the Budget Constraint for Yugoslav Firms?" *World Bank,* Policy Research working papers; No. WPS 937. http://documents.worldbank.org/curated/en/512871468759856715/How-soft-is-the-budget-constraint-for-Yugoslav-firms

Mankiw, Gregory, Matthew Weinzierl and Danny Yagan. (2009). "Optimal Taxation in Theory and Practice." *Journal of Economic Perspectives.* Vol. 23, No. 4, 147–174.

Marx, Karl. (1932). *Economic and Philosophical Manuscripts of 1844.* Moscow: International Publishers.

Meade, James. (1972). "The Theory of Labor-Managed Firms and of Profit-Sharing." *Economic Journal.* Vol. 82, 401–428.

Meade, James. (1989). *Agathopia: The Economics of Partnership.* Ann Arbor: University of Michigan Press.

Milanović, Branko. (1990). *Ekonomska nejednakost u Jugoslaviji* (Economic Inequality in Yugoslavia). Belgrade: Ekonomika and the Institute of Economic Sciences.

Milanović, Branko. (1998). *Income, Inequality and Poverty during the transition from Planned to Market Economy.* Washington: The World Bank, Regional and Sectoral Studies.

Monaghan, Andrew. (2011). "The Russian Vertikal: The Tandem, Power and the Elections." *Chatham House,* Russia and Eurasia Programme Paper REP 2011/01. www.chathamhouse.org/sites/default/files/19412_0511ppmonaghan.pdf

Novokmet, Filip, Thomas Piketty and Gabriel Zucman. (2017). "From Soviets to Oligarchs: Inequality and Property in Russia 1905–2016." *Vox.* https://voxeu.org/article/inequality-and-property-russia-1905-2016

Nuti, Domenico Mario. (1992). "On Traditional Cooperatives and James Meade's Labor-Capital Discriminating Partnerships." *Advances in the Economic Analysis of Participatory and Labor-Managed Firms.* Vol. 4, 1–26.

Rosefielde, Steven and R. W. Pfouts. (1996). "The Firm in Illyria: Market Syndicalism Revisited." *Journal of Comparative Economics.* Vol. 10, No. 2, 160—170.

Rosefielde, Steven and R. W. Pfouts. (1998). "Egalitarianism and Production Potential in Postcommunist Russia." In Steven Rosefielde (ed.). *Efficiency and the Economic Recovery Potential of Russia.* Ashgate, 245–263.

Sapir, Andre. (1980). "Economic Growth and Factor Substitution: What Happened to the Yugoslav Miracle?" *The Economic Journal.* Vol. 90, No. 358, 294–313.

Uvalić, Milica. (1992). *Investment and Property Rights in Yugoslavia: The Long Transition to a Market Economy.* Cambridge: Cambridge University Press.

Uvalić, Milica. (1993). "The Disintegration of Yugoslavia: Its Costs and Benefits." *Communist Economies & Economic Transformation.* Vol. 5, No. 3, 273–293.

Uvalić, Milica. (2010). *Serbia's Transition. Towards a Better Future.* Basingstoke: Palgrave Macmillan.

Uvalić, Milica. (2019). "The Rise and Fall of Market Socialism in Yugoslavia." *DOC Research Institute.* March 27. https://doc-research.org/2018/03/rise-fall-market-social ism-yugoslavia/

Uvalić, Radivoj. (1964). "Functions of the Market and Plan in the Socialist Economy." In Radmila Stojanovic (ed.). *Yugoslav Economists on Problems of a Socialist Economy.* New York: International Arts and Sciences Press, 140–147.

Vanek, Jaroslav. (1970). *The General Theory of Labor Managed Market Economies.* Ithaca: Cornell University Press.

Ward, Ben. (1957). "Workers Management in Yugoslavia." *Journal of Political Economy.* Vol. 65, 373–386.

Ward, Ben. (1958). "The Firm in Illyria: Market Syndicalism." *The American Economic Review.* Vol. 48, No. 4, 566–589.

9   Maoism

Mao Zedong proclaimed the establishment of the People's Republic of China (PRC) under the control of the Communist Party of China (CPC) on September 21, 1949. The CPC was a Marxist–Leninist vanguard party founded in 1921 that embraced democratic centralism,[1] and world revolution. Soviet political, martial and economic successes under Joseph Stalin's helmsmanship (1928–1953) confirmed Mao's faith in Marxism-Leninism. Stalin's USSR became Mao's archetype for transforming China into an advanced industrial communist society (Rue, 1966). Mao and Zhou Enlai adopted the Soviet political economic governance model. China became a one-party state with a dependent judiciary and internationalist ambitions supported by its power services (military and secret police). The state owned the means of production including agriculture on a freehold basis with various subtle qualifications (Ho, 2005; 2) Chen, 2012,[2] and managed them with command economic planning.

The First Five-Year Plan began in 1953. China's version of command planning was softer than the Soviet prototype.[3] See Figure 6.1. Red directors had more discretion over production and often subcontracted informally for intermediate inputs instead of operating through the chain of command and the wholesale system (Wang and Chen, 2017).[4] The state price bureau fixed important commodity prices. Local communist authorities set the rest. Bonuses and honorary rewards stimulated red director effort (Hoffmann, 1964).

The CPC was China's sole economic sovereign (1953–1966). Its authority spanned branches and sectors, including agriculture. It did not share economic sovereignty with workers and peasants in production or consumption, although people could advise party officials.

The Great Proletarian Cultural Revolution (1966–1976) changed China's economic system. "Super-soft" indicative planning with inspired revolutionary committee management replaced soft command economic planning (MacFarquhar and Schoenhals, 2006).[5] Planning continued (Rosefielde and Latane, 1980; Robinson, 1969), but compliance was voluntary.[6] Similar to French indicative planning designed for market economies (Hansen,1969; Black, 1968),[7] principals and agents in Mao's planning regime familiarized themselves with the Five-Year Plan, but were free to decide what to do.

DOI: 10.4324/9781003371571-12

During the Cultural Revolution, the CPC, Chinese Red Army, workers and peasants guided by the Five-Year Plan determined production and consumption, not central planners. The CPC, while remaining China's ultimate political authority, deputized revolutionary committees, consisting of representatives from the party, workers and the Chinese People's Liberation Army to manage enterprises.

Mao's cultural revolution economy shares many traits with Lenin's War Communism (1917–1921),[8] including Communist Party sovereignty, state ownership, criminalization of markets, suppression of private entrepreneurship, military participation, revolutionary zeal, worker participation, distain for professional enterprise management, however, it does so in a fresh context (Malle,1985; Sakwa, 1988).[9] The goal of Soviet War Communism was to lay the foundations for socialism by canceling capitalism and the aristocracy. The CPC had accomplished these objectives in the 1950s. Mao's Cultural Revolution sought to purge the CPC of fifth column, corrupt counterrevolutionary "capitalist roaders" (Wheelwright and McFarlane, 1971; Rosefielde, 1980), and build a revolutionary Chinese socialist economy on situational communist initiative, given people's ownership of the means of production, CPC economic sovereignty, and inspired revolutionary party, worker and military management.

Mao's "politics in command" strategy assumed that communism required revolutionary Marxist–Leninist fervor. Cultural Revolution had two keys (Kraus, 2012). First, Mao claimed that revolutionary ethics and zeal were more important than technocratic expertise. They counteracted bureaucratic inertia (Hearn, 1978), safeguarding the revolution from moral hazard and counterrevolution (Mirrlees, 1999).[10] The Marxist–Leninist–Stalinist top-down command planning model was sound as Mao perceived it, but not foolproof and needed to be defended by communist stalwarts against technocrats, bureaucrats and red directors. Mao felt that socialist ideals and inspired workers were more important than hollow promises made by technocrats, bureaucrats and red directors. The moral imperative of defending the revolution outweighed other considerations.

Second, Mao contended that party, worker and military management made supersoft command planning a superior engine of material progress.[11] He claimed that socialist revolutionary wisdom assured productive efficiency, faster economic growth, a more equitable distribution of income and superior cultural benefits. In Mao's opinion moral benefits of the Cultural Revolution outweighed material sacrifices incurred in the unlikely case that repressing experts impaired productivity, distributional efficiency and economic growth. He contended that gains in revolutionary cultural utilities including equality, social justice and liberation would exceed losses in consumption and public services (see Appendix 4). The repression of experts was essential for completing the communist revolution and providing the Chinese people with a high quality of existence.

Looked at from another angle, Mao's Cultural Revolution can be construed as an attempt to improve the communist model by substituting co-sovereign labor-party-military governance for centralized CPC rule hampered by subversive technocrats without incurring the risks associated with Yugoslavian labor self-management (see Chapters 8 and 20). Although there is no evidence that

Mao gave serious thought to Yugoslavian labor self-management, the preservation of state-fixed wages should have avoided the dangers of egalitarian dividend maximizing. Chinese workers had no egalitarian dividend-sharing motive for reserving effort to augment personal utility. Inspired by Mao's socialist ideals, workers were obliged to exert themselves together with the party, managers and the People's Liberation Army for the people's benefit.

The suppression of expert rational choice did not oblige three-in-one cultural revolutionary committees to be a rational. They considered opportunity costs, but duty compelled them to prioritize cultural revolutionary goals. The merit of Mao's scheme hinged on three-in-one committees' ability to strike the right balance, avoiding the twin temptations of morally hazardous expertness and red (anarcho-socialist) overzealous. Mao presumed that the three-in-one committees were up to the task insisting that cultural revolutionaries were technologically proficient and politically insightful. Like Lenin, they would discern "what should be done?" (Lenin, 1961).

The notion that the right thing to do is discernable, even when reason proved to be a fallible guide (Kant, 1993; Sandel, 2010) is a staple of many belief systems. Confucius, grasping the limitations of pure reason (Wittgenstein, 1922),[12] helped his disciples cope by combining sage precepts (aphorisms) with exemplification (Bonevac and Stephen Phillips, 2009; Schuman, 2015; Ames, 1999). Mao adopted the same strategy. He compiled his own precepts in a *Little Red Book* to guide China's Cultural Revolutionaries (Mao, 1965). The right thing for three-in-one committees was to act in accordance with Mao's thought. When the context required prudence, three-in-one committees would act conservatively. When radicalism was required, three-in-one committees would smite counterrevolutionaries and martyr themselves for the socialist cause.

The context and rhetoric of the Cultural Revolution required three-in-one committees to unmask and liquidate counterrevolutionary experts, repudiate hedonistic bourgeois individualist values, struggle for material and social egalitarianism and implement the CPC's shifting economic development policies. Mao-think compelled three-in-one committees to be bloody, resolute and bold, pressing forward toward victory unconcerned about collateral damage.

There is ample evidence that three-in-one committees and the Red Guard movement more broadly hearkened to Mao's thought (Chong, 2002; Frederick Teiwes, 2010),[13] and Mao's "cult of personality" (Leese, 2011 Gill, 1980; Bonnell, 1999).[14] Red Guards confronted, harassed, intimidated, killed suspected "capitalist roaders," and had them exiled and interred in laogai and laojiao "re-education" labor camps (Courtois and Jean-Louis Margolin, 1999; Thurston, 1987; Rosefielde, 2010).[15] Three-in-one committees organized "struggle sessions" to badger and bully opponents until they acknowledged their folly and embraced Maoist policies (Lipman and Harrell, 1990).[16] Confucius was content to let his followers interpret aphorisms for themselves. Mao refused to leave things to chance. He compelled followers to fight themselves (Mao, 2014, 111–112).

The combination of paragon leadership and terror made the Cultural Revolution doubly radical. Mao not only concluded that persuasion, compromise and consensus building were inadequate tools for building communism, he insisted that unrelenting class war and self-struggle were indispensable for saving socialism from counterrevolution.[17] The communist command planning crisis that precipitated the Cultural Revolution in Mao's eyes was endemic. CPC's failure to devise counterrevolution resistant institutions led Mao to conclude that permanent revolution from below was essential for keeping fifth column anti-communist self-seekers at bay (Trotsky, 2010).[18]

Perhaps, Mao was right.

However, all that is known with certainty is that three-in-one committees guided by Mao's *Little Red Book* fared no better than Yugoslav worker collectives in transforming communist command planning into a well-functioning labor participatory socialist economic system. The Cultural Revolution was an economic failure from a material and doctrinal perspective (Perkins, 1991).[19] The hardships it wrought, like the Great Leap Forward (1958–1962)[20] and Pol Pot's Cambodian version of China's Cultural Revolution,[21] caused immense suffering that convinced high CPC officials that Maoism should never be repeated (Table 9.1).

Table 9.1 Communist Superindustrialization Surges: Maddison's GDP Series (Thousand 1990 International Geary-Khamis Dollars)

Period	Year	USSR	China	Cambodia
Holodomor	1931	275.2		
	1932	254.4		
	1933	264.9		
	1934	290.9		
Great Terror	1935	334.8		
	1936	361.3		
	1937	398.0		
	1938	405.2		
	1939	430.3		
	1940	420.1		
Great Leap Forward	1959		464.0	
	1960		448.7	
	1961		368.0	
	1962		368.0	
	1963		403.7	
Cultural Revolution	1966		553.7	
	1967		537.0	
	1968		525.2	
	1969		574.7	
Year Zero	1974			5.0
	1975			4.3
	1976			4.7
	1977			5.0
	1978			5.5
	1979			5.6

Source: Angus Maddison, *The World Economy: Historical Statistics*, OECD: Geneva, 2003, Table 3b, p. 98; Table 5b, pp. 174, 178.

Maoism survived his death in 1976, but Jiang Qing (Mao Zedong's fourth wife), Zhang Chunqiao, Yao Wenyuan and Wang Hongwen (the Gang of Four), Mao's most ardent supporters, closely associated with the Cultural Revolution were arrested and removed from power in 1977. After a lengthy trial in 1981, the people's court found the Gang of Four guilty of usurping state power,[22] abusing party leadership and persecuting 750,000 people, 34,375 of whom died during the period 1966–1976 (Yan and Gao, 1996; Rosefielde, 2010).[23] Jiang Qing serving a life prison sentence committed suicide in May 1991 (Kristof, 1991).

The Cultural Revolution was an ideological catastrophe from the Marxist–Leninist–Stalinist–Maoist viewpoint. Its excesses spurred Dong Xiaoping's economic reforms during the 1980 and early 1990s that scuttled China's command planning and paved the way for Xi Jinping's market communism (Rosefielde and Leightner, 2017). Mao appears to have misread the "end of history" (Fukuyama, 1992).

Perhaps, he is to blame for Xi's counterrevolution. He misappraised the situation, or botched the war on capitalist roaders. Perhaps, Deng Xiaoping's triumph of experts over reds was inevitable, or next time will be different (Reinhart and Rogov, 2009). In the final analysis, the fault most likely lay in two false assumptions: Maoist fervor was sustainable; and revolutionary zeal provides a sound fast track to a superior communist life.

Notes

1 Democratic centralism is a Leninist procedure for recording member agreement with communist party policy. It obligates member to abide by the party line, regardless of personal feelings.

2 The word freehold means unrestricted ownership. The Chinese people are the freehold owners of the means of production, under the stewardship of the state and Communist Party. The state as custodian of the people's freehold assets has the right to lease and apportion privileges to decentralized authorities, enterprises and individuals. Some argue that rural collectives are freeholder owners, but the state can rescind this authority. Other leasees may also act like freehold owners, but from a legal and ideological point of view they own nothing without the sufferance of the CPC. Rural private land ownership was effectively abolished through Land Reform, leaving the land in the hands of the state or the collective. China's Land Reform (1950–1952) was one of the largest examples of land expropriation in world history. Between 200 and 240 million acres of arable land were redistributed to approximately 75 million peasant families.

3 To implement the First Five-Year Plan, Mao followed the Soviet model by making a single person responsible for each factory. Productivity, skill and expertise determined remuneration.

4 Contracting later became a centerpiece of Chinese economic management.

5 Revolutionary committees were tripartite bodies established during China's Cultural Revolution to facilitate government by three mass organizations – the people, the PLA and the Party. They were replaced the old Party apparatus, but quickly became subordinate to it.

6 The Soviet Union ran its economy with indicative plans during the New Economic Policy (NEP) period until they became mandatory under Gosplan's auspices in 1929.

7 Indicative planning is a form of economic planning implemented by a state to solve the problem of imperfect information in market and mixed economies. When utilizing indicative planning, the state exerts influence via subsidies, grants and taxes to support goals but does not compel. Indicative planning is the antithesis of mandatory planning, where a state sets quotas and mandatory output requirements.

8 War Communism is a term for Bolshevik economic policy during the period of the Russian Civil War (1918–1920).

9 Soviet "war communism" included forced requisitioning of foodstuffs, redistribution of land, nationalization of industry, state management of production, centralization of resource allocation, state monopolization of trade, partial suspension of money transactions and the introduction of strict labor discipline. It is also associated with the radicalization, militarization and bureaucratization of politics, the institutionalization of the one-party state, increased exertion of party discipline, the repudiation of the political and cultural autonomy of civil society and the intensification of repression in a vigorous class war.

10 Moral hazard arises in a principal–agent problem, where one party, called an agent (technocrats, bureaucrats and red directors), acts on behalf of another party (CPC), called the principal. The agent usually has more information about his or her actions or intentions than the principal does because the principal usually cannot completely monitor the agent. The agent may have an incentive to act inappropriately (from the viewpoint of the principal) if the interests of the agent and the principal are not aligned.

11 Factories were entrusted to revolutionary committees consisting of representatives from the party, the workers and the Chinese People's Liberation Army, whose members often had little knowledge of either management or the enterprise they were supposed to run. Virtually all engineers, managers, scientists, technicians and other professional personnel were "criticized," demoted, "sent down" to the countryside to "participate in labor," or even jailed, all of which resulted in their skills and knowledge being lost to the enterprise.

12 Wittgenstein pointed out that logically consistent theories disconnected from reality are not true. They are tautologies.

13 Red Guards were a mass student-led paramilitary social movement mobilized and guided by Chairman Mao Zedong in 1966 and 1967, during the first phase of the Chinese Cultural Revolution. According to a Red Guard leader, the movement's aims were as follows: "Chairman Mao has defined our future as an armed revolutionary youth organization … So if Chairman Mao is our Red-Commander-in-Chief and we are his Red Guards, who can stop us?" Mao used Red Guards to destroy symbols of China's pre-communist past, including ancient artifacts and gravesites of notable Chinese figures.

14 Mao was referred to as "the great leader Chairman Mao" in public and "the great leader", the great supreme commander, the great teacher and the great helmsman in Cultural Revolution. Elements of his cult of personality continue to exist. Mao's personality cult manifested itself in the ubiquitous wearing of badges depicting Chairman Mao, and people carrying around a Little Red Book with the writings of Mao.

15 Laogai means "reform through labor" and refers to PRC camps for convicts and political prisoners that employ penal labor. Láojiào refers to similar facilities for people who commit minor offenses.

16   A struggle session is a form of public humiliation and torture used by the Communist Party of China during the Cultural Revolution to shape public opinion and humiliate, persecute or execute political rivals and those deemed class enemies. Red guards force victims of a struggle sessions to admit various crimes before a crowd of people.

17   Mao called for a mobilization of the people to cleanse the communist party of capitalist saboteurs at all levels, including the top (specifically Liu Shaoqi and Deng Xiaoping). University and middle school students responded to this call and formed groups of "Red Guards."

18   Leon Trotsky argued that the proletariat needed to take power in a process of uninterrupted and permanent revolution in order to implement socialism.

19   Industrial production plummeted 14% in 1967.

20   The Great Leap Forward of the People's Republic of China (PRC) was an economic and social campaign by the Communist Party of China (CPC) from 1958 to 1962. The campaign led by Chairman Mao Zedong aimed to transform the country from an agrarian economy into a socialist society through rapid industrialization and collectivization. These policies led to social and economic disaster, hidden by deceitful reports. Food production plummeted causing tens of millions of deaths in the Great Chinese Famine.

21   Pol Pot reformed Cambodia as a new, one-party state called Democratic Kampuchea. Seeking to create an agrarian socialist society, his government forcibly relocated the urban population to the countryside to work on collective farms. He mass killed enemies of the new government, including Buddhist monks and ethnic minorities. Between 1.5 and 2 million people, more than 20% of Cambodia's population died.

22   The Gang of Four was a political faction composed of four Chinese Communist Party officials who came to prominence during the Cultural Revolution (1966–1976). Premier Hua Guofeng latter indicted for series of treasonous crimes. The gang's leading figure was Jiang Qing (Mao Zedong's last wife). The other members were Zhang Chunqiao, Yao Wenyuan and Wang Hongwen.

23   These figures are too low.

References

Ames, Roger. (1999). *The Analects of Confucius: A Philosophical Translation (Classics of Ancient China).* New York: Ballantine Books.

Black, John. (1968). "The Theory of Indicative Planning." *Oxford Economic Papers New Series.* Vol. 20, No. 3, 303–319.

Bonevac, Daniel and Stephen Phillips. (2009). *Introduction to World Philosophy.* New York: Oxford University Press.

Bonnell, Victoria. (1999). *The Iconography of Power: Soviet Political Posters under Lenin and Stalin.* Berkeley: University of California Press.

Chen, Albert. (2012). "The Law of Property and the Evolving System of Property Rights in China." In Guanghua Yu (ed.). *The Development of the Chinese Legal System – Change and Challenges.* London and New York: Routledge.

Chong, Woei Lien (ed.). (2002). *China's Great Proletarian Cultural Revolution: Master Narratives and Post-Mao Counter-narratives.* London: Rowman & Littlefield Publishers.

Courtois, Stéphane and Jean-Louis Margolin. (1999). *The Black Book of Communism: Crimes, Terror, Repression.* Cambridge: Harvard University Press.

Fukuyama, Francis. (1992). *The End of History and the Last Man Standing.* New York: Free Press.

Gill, Graeme. (1980). "The Soviet Leader Cult: Reflections on the Structure of Leadership in the Soviet Union." *British Journal of Political Science*. Vol. 10, 167.

Hansen, Niles. (1969). "French Indicative Planning and the New Industrial State." *Journal of Economic Issues*. Vol. 3, No. 4, 79–95.

Hearn, Francis. (1978). "Rationality and Bureaucracy: Maoist Contributions to a Marxist Theory of Bureaucracy." *The Sociological Quarterly*. Vol. 19, No. 1, 37–54.

Ho, Peter. (2005). *Institutions in Transition: Land Ownership, Property Rights, and Social Conflict in China: Land Ownership, Property Rights, and Social Conflict in China*. Oxford: Oxford University Press.

Hoffmann, Charles. (1964). "Work Incentive Policy in Communist China." *The China Quarterly*. Vol. 17, 92–110.

Kant, Immanuel. (1993). *Grounding for the Metaphysics of Morals*. New York: Hackett.

Kraus, Richard. (2012). *The Cultural Revolution: A Very Short Introduction*. London: Oxford University Press.

Kristof, Nicholas. (1991). "Suicide of Jiang Qing, Mao's Widow, Is Reported." *New York Times*.

Leese, Daniel. (2011). *Mao Cult: Rhetoric and Ritual in China's Cultural Revolution*. Cambridge: Cambridge University Press.

Lenin, Vladimir. (1961). "What Is to Be Done? Burning Questions of Our Movement." *Lenin's Collected Works*. Vol. 5. Moscow: Foreign Languages Publishing House, 347–530.

Lipman, Jonathan and Stevan Harrell (eds.). (1990). *Violence in China: Essays in Culture and Counterculture*. New York: SUNY Press, 154–157.

MacFarquhar, Roderick and Michael Schoenhals. (2006). *Mao's Last Revolution*. Boston: Belknap Harvard.

Malle, Silvana. (1985). *The Economic Organization of War Communism, 1918–1921*. New York: Cambridge University Press.

Mao, Zedong. (1965). *Quotations from Chairman Mao Tse-tung: "The Little Red Book"*. Beijing: People's Liberation Army General Political Daily.

Mao, Zedong. (2014). "On Correcting Mistaken Ideas in the Party. December 1929." *Selected Works*. Vol. 1. New York: Pergamon, 111–112.

Mirrlees, J. A. (1999). "The Theory of Moral Hazard and Unobservable Behavior: Part I." *The Review of Economic Studies*. Vol. 66, No. 1, 3–21.

Perkins, Dwight. (1991). "China's Economic Policy and Performance. Chapter 6 in Roderick MacFarquhar." In John K. Fairbank and Denis Twitchett (eds.). *The Cambridge History of China*. Vol. 15. London: Cambridge University Press.

Reinhart, Carmen and Kenneth Rogov. (2009). *This Time Is Different: Eight Centuries of Financial Folly*. Princeton: Princeton University Press.

Robinson, Joan. (1969). *The Cultural Revolution in China*. Harmondsworth: Penguin.

Rosefielde, Steven. (1980). *World Communism at the Crossroads: Military Ascendancy, Political Economy and Human Welfare*. Amsterdam: Martinus Nijhoff.

Rosefielde, Steven. (2010). *Red Holocaust*. London: Routledge.

Rosefielde, Steven and Henry Latane. (1980). "Decentralized Economic Control in the Soviet Union and Maoist China: One-Man Rule versus Collective Self-Management." In Steven Rosefielde (ed.). *World Communism at the Crossroads: Military Ascendancy, Political Economy, and Human Welfare*. Boston: Martinus Nijhoff, 260–273.

Rosefielde, Steven and Jonathan Leightner. (2017). *China's Market Communism: Challenges, Dilemmas, Solutions*. London: Routledge.

Rue, John. (1966). *Mao Tse-tung in Opposition, 1927–1935*. Palo Alto: Hoover Institution on War, Revolution, and Peace.

Sakwa, Richard. (1988). *Soviet Communists in Power: A Study of Moscow during the Civil War,* 1918–1921. New York: St. Martin's Press.

Sandel, Michael. (2010). *Justice: What's the Right Thing to Do?* New York: Farrar, Straus and Giroux.

Schuman, Michael. (2015). *Confucius: And the World He Created.* New York: Basic Books.

Teiwes, Frederick. (2010). "Mao and His Followers." In Timothy Check (ed.). *A Critical Introduction to Mao.* Cambridge: Cambridge University Press, 129–168.

Thurston, Anne. (1987). *Enemies of the People.* New York: Knopf.

Trotsky, Leon. (2010). *The Permanent Revolution and Results and Prospects.* Seattle: Red Letter Press.

Wang, Xian and Yin Chen. (2017). "A Model on the Contract Management Responsibility System in China." Unpublished manuscript. www.law.uchicago.edu/files/file/176._xian_wang_a_model_on_the_contract_management_responsibility.pdf

Wheelwright, E. L. and Bruce McFarlane. (1971). *The Chinese Road to Socialism: Economics of the Cultural Revolution.* New York: Monthly Review Press.

Wittgenstein, Ludwig. (1922). *Tractatus logico-philosophicus.* New York and London: Harcourt & Brace.

Yan, Jiaqi and Gao Gao. (1996). *Turbulent Decade: A History of the Cultural Revolution.* Honolulu: University of Hawaii Press.

10 Castroism

Fidel Castro's guerilla army defeated the military dictatorship of Cuban President Fulgencio Batista on December 31, 1958. He installed a Marxist–Leninist one-party socialist dictatorship (Republic of Cuba) the next day. He canceled capitalism, abolishing private property, criminalizing markets and entrepreneurship and compelling the able-bodied workforce to toil in state-owned enterprises or agricultural cooperatives. The economy was centrally planned command regime with wages and prices fixed by the state price committee. The Communist Party ruled as it thought best on behalf of the workers imposing appropriate economic, legal, political and social institutions. This mainly involved state price-fixing, a state foreign trade monopoly, central planning, state enterprise management, rationing, subsidized services, free universal education and criminalization of markets. Castro was committed to communist egalitarianism. He imposed income, status, ethnic, gender equality and suppressed class enemies.

The logic of egalitarianism drove Castro's revolutionary communist policies. See Chapter 20. He transferred assets confiscated from private owners to the state's account and provided basic housing, transport, medical, educational services, food and other necessities to the masses. He retrained, redeployed and expanded the labor force to meet revolutionary objectives. Castro exhorted women and minorities to work outside their homes, receiving equal pay for equal work. The Cuban Republic granted them equal access to education and occupational opportunities. All these confiscatory and redistributive actions benefited the workers and peasants, but had one deficiency. The Cuban Communist Party decided where people worked, occupations, terms of labor, the amount and assortment of goods produced and rationed. Castro compelled Cubans to work, and rationed jobs, higher educational opportunities and consumption. Workers and peasants had some small voice, but their leaders illiberally compelled them to obey. Although, Castro had been optimistic, disappointing results prompted him to consider other options.

He shunned Mikhail Gorbachev's radical economic, political and globalist reforms of 1987–1991 (perestroika, democratization and new thinking), but began liberalizing in 1994 after the Soviet Union dissolved, gravitating toward Deng Xiaoping's marketization strategy "crossing streams one step at a time"

DOI: 10.4324/9781003371571-13

(1980–1997). He permitted a small number of workers to operate as private entrepreneurs in the early 1990s and legalized small private business more broadly in 2016, but stopped short of Xi Jinping's leasehold entrepreneurial market communism. The private sector gradually grew during 1994–2021. Private enterprises today employ approximately a quarter of the labor force, nonetheless, results have been lackluster.

The behavior of Cuba's Soviet-style socialist economy of 1959–1994 from a systems standpoint should have closely resembled the Kremlin's Marxist–Leninist prototype. The performance of its mixed plan and market reform model after 1994 should have paralleled Deng Xiaoping's achievements, but both Cuban models underperformed. Cuba failed to industrialize its civilian and military machine-building sectors rapidly in the first period, and did not develop effective market transition institutions like Deng's "town-village-enterprises" (TVE) in the second mixed-economy phase (Naughton, 2007).[1]

Fidel Castro appears neither to have felt the need to mimic Soviet sectoral development policy, nor tinker with Marx–Leninist central planning methods and khozraschyot managerial bonus incentives (Zimbalist, 1989). He placed his faith primarily in revolutionary moral fervor and rationing rather than in planning and material incentives before 1994 and continued to do so afterward under the Cuban mixed plan-market regime. Although, Fidel and, later, Raul Castro[2] could have emulated the Chinese market communist mechanism, they chose to preserve Communist Party authority in the economic and social spheres, absolute political power before 1994 and a hybrid Maoist-NEP model thereafter (Cheng, 2007, 2012; Gonzalez-Corzo, 2012). See Chapters 5 and 9.

This preference relying on redness more than material incentives, expert planning and management distinguishes Cuba from Soviet communism. Lenin and Castro both employed redness (the criminalization of private property, markets and entrepreneurship, revolutionary zeal and terror) to construct their socialist orders, but Castro underweighted central planning (Courtois, Margolin et al., 1999).[3] The Soviets prioritized superpower, harnessing planning and khozaschyot to propel civilian and military industrial growth. Castro emphasized redness in the economic and social spheres at the expense of prosperity.

Official Cuban and Soviet GDP data are too unreliable to assess the comparative economic performance of the two Marxist–Leninist systems with precision. See Appendix 5. Both were economies of forced consumer substitution, shortage and spartan living standards behind a statistical façade of economic progress. Nonetheless, it appears that the Soviet Union successfully industrialized and became a military superpower, while Cuba did neither.

The subpar economic performance of Cuban Marxist-Leninism judged from its revolutionary promises and the Soviet-Chinese benchmarks is most likely attributable to Castro's prioritization of redness over expertness and liberalization. The Soviet and Cuban models both were straitjacket economies of shortage and rationing that allowed leaders to boast about ostensible ideological benefits of proletarian liberation, but the Soviet and later Xi Jinping variant delivered much more benefits (Naím and Francisco Toro, 2020).

Cuba's overdependence on redness, like similar revolutionary progressive promises today, was a trap. Castro's strategy for success was a wager on egalitarian politics and blind faith that the nationalization of wealth, equal income, status and opportunity would magically provide workers with a high quality of existence, when in practice his revolutionary egalitarian politics camouflaged inequities, depressed living standards and repressed personal freedom. Red revolutionary communist regimes sacrifice productive efficiency and ration supplies. Workers cannot improve themselves for personal benefit and cannot reserve their effort. They are disempowered and at the communist party's mercy. If officials abuse their authority, workers have no recourse against the one-party state.

Overdependence on redness is pernicious. Egalitarian paternalism depresses productive and distributive efficiency. It reduces living standards and fosters secular economic stagnation. It spawns abuses of power and corruption. It forces the proletariat to overwork. It straitjackets worker personal liberty and rubs salt into the wound by insisting that redness for its own sake assures a sublime life. There is no escape from revolutionary triumphalism.[4]

This reality is easily illustrated. Most Cubans cannot afford to purchase unsubsidized goods in state and private retail outlets. They subsist on approximately 200 US dollars per year.[5] The state owns the housing stock, but under-maintains it. Communist Party insiders receive the best apartments. Women hold seemingly prestigious positions in the medical profession, but receive the average state salary. Women have little influence in the Communist Party, holding only 7% of the powerful positions. Machismo is rampant, and racial discrimination is acute. Black women receive the lowest-paying jobs and have the highest rates of unemployment and the lowest education levels. They often live with the threat of gender violence.

The reality behind Cuba's rhetoric of red egalitarianism and social justice matches the Soviet experience. The communist party in both cases assumed the role of a new class that siphoned off the best of the systems' meager fruits to itself and guarded its power (Bulgakov, 1996).

Communists do not have a monopoly on authoritarianism. Any authoritarian state regardless of ideology that prioritizes obedience over efficiency is apt to exhibit the same pathologies. Cuba has imitators. None succeeded.

Notes

1 The reforms of 1978 changed TVEs, which became the most vibrant part of the Chinese economy as they experienced significant expansion in the 1980s and early 1990s. TVE employment grew from 28 million in 1978 to a peak of 135 million in 1996.

2 Raul Castro was First Secretary of the Communist Party of Cuba (2011–2021).

3 According to the "Black Book of Communism," death squads had shot at least 14,000 Cubans by 1970s; in all, more than 100,000 have died or been killed as a result of the revolution. In 1960, Cuba established its first GULAG-style concentration camps.

4 Torpor is a state of decreased physiological activity in an animal, usually by a reduced body temperature and metabolic rate. Torpor enables animals to survive periods of reduced food availability.
5 www.codepink.org/dividing_the_pie_cuba_s_ration_system_after_50_years

References

Bulgakov, Mikhail. (1996). *Master and the Margarita*. New York: Vintage.
Cheng, Yinghong. (2007). "Fidel Castro and "China's Lesson for Cuba": A Chinese Perspective." *The China Quarterly*. No. 189, 24–242.
Cheng, Yinghong. (2012). "The 'Socialist Other': Cuba in Chinese Ideological Debates since the 1990s." *The China Quarterly*. No. 209, 198–216.
Courtois, Stéphane, Jean-Louis Margolin, et al. (1999). *The Black Book of Communism: Crimes, Terror, Repression*. Cambridge: Harvard University Press.
González-Corzo, Mario. (2012). "Entrepreneurship in Transition Economies: Selected Characteristics and Relevant Lessons for the Future of Cuba." *Journal of Current Chinese Affairs*. Vol. 41, No. 1, 155–179.
Naím, Moisés and Francisco Toro. (2020). "Venezuela's Problem Isn't Socialism: Maduro's Mess Has Little to Do with Ideology, Carnegie Endowment." . https://carnegieendowm ent.org/2020/01/27/venezuela-s-problem-isn-t-socialism-pub-80909
Naughton, Barry. (2017). *The Chinese Economy: Transitions and Growth*. Cambridge: MIT Press.
Zimbalist, Andrew. (1989). "Incentives and Planning in Cuba." *Latin American Research Review*. Vol. 24, No. 1, 65–93.

11 Reform Communism

Perestroika, Yugoslavian worker self-governance, Mao's three-in-one revolutionary committees and Castro all tried to replace the core Marxist–Leninist command paradigm with better communist systems. The People's republics of Eastern Europe founded in the late 1940s took a different path.[1] They attempted to fine-tune Marxist–Leninist dogma and refine the authoritarian command paradigm to accommodate local conditions and enhance performance. These adjustments enabled Poland to slow the pace of agricultural collectivization during 1947–1956 and decollectivize in 1957 (McConnell Brooks, 1991). They allowed Czechoslovakia to enjoy Prague Spring in 1968,[2] and Hungary to introduce "Goulash Communism" (Kornai, 1996; Benczes, 2016)[3] with simulated market characteristics in 1966 (CIA, 1972; Hare, 1976; Csikos-Nagy, 1969; Belassa, 1983).[4]

Opposition to the strict Stalinist communist paradigm with an "inhuman face" also emerged independently in the Soviet Union. Nikita Khrushchev tried to soften Communist Party governance by reforming the command mechanism without overstepping the ideological divide separating planning and markets after Stalin died on March 5, 1953. He launched a de-Stalinization campaign in 1956 (Khrushchev, 1956), known as the "Khrushchev Thaw" (referencing Ilya Ehrenburg's 1954 novel) (Ehrenburg, 1955; Taubman, 2004),[5] and tried to give Bolshevism a "human face" by encouraging officials to make everyday communist life economically, socially and culturally bearable.[6] His reformed Marxist–Leninist brand of communism sought to raise living standards and other aspects of the quality of existence by giving the people more degrees of personal, cultural, spiritual and social freedom.

The Khrushchev Thaw and parallel East European experiments with sundry institutional, managerial, incentive and price reforms modestly improved economic efficiency, and made life less oppressive by tolerating limited freedom of thought, expression and independent action. The reforms constituted a second top-down command planning communist path, encouraging western intellectuals chastened by Stalin's Gulag communism to disregard Nadezhda Mandelshtam's *Hope Abandoned*, and retain their *Hope against Hope* that communism someday would prove its metal (Mandelshtam, 1981, 1999).

DOI: 10.4324/9781003371571-14

Cultural Reforms

The common cultural core of the Khrushchev Thaw and parallel Eastern European reforms was de-Stalinization (Barghoorn, 1956; Applebaum, 2003; Filtzer, 2002).[7] The Soviet Union and its satellites kept Marxist–Leninist ideology, political economy, avant-garde propaganda art,[8] socialist realism (James, 1973)[9] and anti-capitalist culture, (Reid, 1996) but strove to eradicate the abuses of Stalin's terror (Baberowski, 2017). This was the meaning of Alexander Dubček's slogan "socialism with a human face." De-Stalinization had the narrow objectives of curbing terror, downsizing gulag and civilizing intraparty governance. The Khrushchev Thaw and parallel Eastern European reforms neither rejected socialist values, nor embraced the democratic, rule of law and humanist ethos of anti-Soviet dissidents.[10] Eastern leaders neither attributed Stalin's crimes to the communist system nor called for the eradication of planning. Post-Stalinist Communist Party reformers only permitted constructive intraparty criticism and approved some western cultural, social and political values.

Tolerance and grudging approval for aspects of westernization had always been part of the Bolshevik landscape. Lenin praised the core French revolutionary principles of liberty, fraternity and equality, as well as the virtues of democracy (democratic centralism), the rule of law (obedience to Soviet administrative law) and humanism (socialist humanism) insofar as they could be reconciled with Bolshevik authoritarianism (Fromm, 1965; Lipset, 1960; Marcuse, 1964; Mises, 1951).[11] The thaw revitalized these sentiments among the East's intelligentsia, in some quarters of the Communist Party, and among many ordinary people, especially the desire for expanded liberty and democracy across the post-Stalinist space (Hejdánek and Brain, 1985; Rothschild, 1993). The ferment favored expanded personal liberties and "liberal democracy" over pervasive social controls and Communist Party "democratic centralism" (Locke, 1988),[12] giving "thaw" communism a western ambiance missing during the austere Stalinist period. Czechoslovakia's Prague Spring symbolized this new spirit best.

Resurgent trade unionism in the Fabian, revolutionary syndicalist and Soviet Workers' Opposition traditions was another of the thaw's manifestations (Daniels, 1960; Sorenson, 1969).[13] Poland's Solidarity (Solidarność) established itself as an independent worker organization in 1980 and briefly battled abusive state bureaucracy until the government repressed it in 1981. Solidarity resurfaced in the late 1980s, pressing vigorously for liberal democracy.[14] Although, communism in many respects during the Khrushchev Thaw outwardly differed little from daily life under Stalin, the Prague Spring, Goulash communism and Solidarność did modestly improve Soviet and Eastern European life quality and dampened internal anti-communist sentiment. Hungary often was referred to as the "the happiest barrack" in barracks communism.

Reform Communism with Market Characteristics

Solidarity's grievances with the Polish Communist Party, the Prague Spring and the discontent expressed in Hungary's Goulash Communism and later in Gorbachev's radical reforms pertained to all aspects of the quality of existence. Few called for rethinking the core tenants of command planning in favor of consumer sovereign market socialism, or capitalism. Nonetheless, from the outset of Khrushchev's Thaw, Soviet and East European leaders displayed a willingness to incorporate market-assisted elements into command planning if they did not infringe planner sovereignty. The communist parties of the East feared the counterrevolutionary potential of market forces, but they were willing to gamble that they could borrow some market management techniques without jeopardizing communist rule.

Soviet and East European leaders hoped that judiciously applied market methods would enhance the informational and coordinative efficiency of command planning in the factor, output and transfer spaces, fostering innovation-driven guns and butter GDP growth.[15]

Lange's "Simulated Competitive Market Socialist Solution"

Oskar Lange, a Polish economist working in England and Chicago in the mid-1930s,[16] and a seminal figure in debate over socialism's efficiency potential (Bergson, 1948, 1966, 1967; Rosefielde, 1973, 1986a, 1986b), originated the idea of embedding a market price mechanism in the Soviet Union's command planning mechanism in 1935 (Lange, 1935, 1936, 1937, 1938). He advised the Soviets to substitute simulated "competitive prices" generated from a state-orchestrated pricing algorithm, for Marxist-labor value prices fixed by the State Price Committee (Goskomtsen). Lange described his prices as socialist because the State Price Committee determined them in an intrastate auction choreographed at Gossnabsbyt (state wholesale agency) trading facilities. The free market played no role in the process (Bornstein, 1966).[17] The State Price Committee acting as Léon Walras' inventory auctioneer (see Appendix 4, Figure A4.5) called out prices, and buyers (intermediate input and retail purchasers) and sellers (wholesale departments) in Gossnabsbyt responded until the inventory market cleared (see Appendix 4, Figure A4.3).[18] This was the beginning, not the end of the process. Lange's inventory clearing prices had second-order ramifications in the factor and production spaces. Red directors in accordance with Lange's instructions, after inventories cleared, were supposed to adjust production until enterprise marginal cost (including intermediate inputs) equaled price, given state set wages and Marxist labor cost prices.[19] See Appendix 4, Figures A4.1, A4.2 and A4.3. Lange's marginal cost rule for determining supply was almost identical to Liberman's enterprise profit maximizing introduced by Khrushchev in 1956, later refined with multiproduct firm linear programming optimization. It could not have saved the day. See Chapter 6.

Planner, not consumer demand, governed wholesale market clearing. Lange's solution was Walrasian inventory clearing, not a competitive Marshallian production adjustment (see Appendix 4, Figure A4.1). The algorithm only applied obliquely to the retail market because in an economy of shortage, gluts at the retail level resolved themselves through forced substitution, and consumers could not alleviate deficits by bidding up prices. Households had consumer choice (they could only purchase products delivered to state retail stores), not consumer sovereignty (they could not obtain the products that they really desired).

Lange's Walrasian scheme did not extend to Marshallian quantity adjustments that would have enabled households to supervene planner preferences (see Appendix 4, Figure A4.6).[20] This limitation preserved Communist Party control over product supply.[21] See Appendix 4, Figures A4.1 and A4.3.[22] Lange claimed that the efficiency characteristics of his socialist equilibrium would closely approximate competitive general equilibrium, but he was mistaken.

Although, Lange personally discussed Soviet planning with Stalin in Moscow in 1944 and Yalta in 1945, the Soviets never adopted his "market socialist" inventory-clearing scheme. Perhaps, Stalin grasped that Lange's "competitive solution" could not significantly improve the efficiency of administrative command planning. The Soviets designed the command planning system to assure that aggregate state demand always exceeded supply (see Chapter 6). A Walrasian price adjustment algorithm in an economy of perpetual and pervasive inventory shortages would have been of little use in attuning micro supply to consumer or planner demand, and Stalin would never have discarded resource mobilization to obtain minor improvements in microeconomic efficiency.

Lange's competitive solution inspired a spirited intellectual conversation about the feasibility of mitigating plan efficiency losses, but his scheme had little practical significance.

Kornai's Two-Level Planning Algorithm

Janos Kornai was another important East European pioneer in the effort to improve the efficiency of communist top-down command planning by simulating competitive market behavior (Kornai, 2017). During the late 1950s, his research led him to conclude that the Hungarian planned economy underperformed because the system was overcentralized (Kornai, 1959), an insight developed later into a full-fledged theory of communist economies of shortage (Kornai, 1971, 1979, 1980a, 1980b, 1992; Kornai and Weibull, 1978; Gomulka, 1985; Maskin, 2000). Hungarian central planning was highly aggregated. Central plans only provided limited guidance about product assortments, leaving the task of efficiently allocating resources to best use to red directors and their administrative supervisors (family circle), who had to muddle through without the assistance of competitive prices and incentives. These shortcomings made Hungarian enterprises, like their Soviet twins endemically inefficient (see Appendix 4, Figure A4.1).

Oskar Lange tried to solve this resource misallocation problem with his inventory price adjustment algorithm, but failed. Kornai believed that he could do better with a more direct approach. Instead of simulating the Walrasian auctioneer in wholesale inventory clearing, Kornai proposed employing linear programming to estimate shadow prices (marginal costs) for use by factory managers to compute counterplans. The scheme simulated competitive markets by requiring factory managers to compute "optimal" enterprise production counterplans at estimated opportunity cost (Bergson, 1953; Rosefielde and Pfouts, 1995),[23] initiating a "two level" iterative dialogue that side stepped Marxist wage and price setting, culminating in a more economically efficient national plan (Kornai, 1967; Kornai and Liptak, 1965). See Appendix 4, Figure A4.1. Kornai's idea and similar programming experiments in the Soviet Union seemed promising but were never effective enough to alleviate Hungary or the USSR's economy of shortage. This should have surprised no one. "Computopia" was a mirage (Neuberger, 1966).

The composite good shadow prices computed as the "duals" to the central primal linear program for a few dozen products were meaningless to managers maximizing profits for millions of specific items subsumed under centrally planned composites. The Kornai-Liptak reform was an intriguing toy for cyberneticists, linear programmers and neoclassical theorists debating the comparative merit of capitalism and socialism (Hayek, 1940, 1948; Nove, 1991), but were too detached from institutional realities to be of any real service (Lavoie, 1981). At first, Kornai and others including Paul Samuelson were delighted by the mathematical equivalence they discovered between "perfect planning" and "perfect competition" implied by linear programming ("duality theorem") (Dorfman, Samuelson and Solow, 1958; Bergson, 1967). However, Kornai soon realized the sterility of the exercise, first turning against Samuelson's neoclassical theory (Kornai, 1971; Rosefielde, 1978) and then against the belief that reform communist planning could ever successfully rival competitive markets (Kornai, 1992; Stiglitz, 1996; Roemer, 1994). Kornai never looked back (Kornai, 1990, 1995, 1997, 2008, 2013; Kornai and Eggleston, 2001; Rosefielde, 1996).

Hungary's New Economic Mechanism

Lange and Kornai both approached simulated market communism from an Olympian perspective. They tried to devise a grand design that would make post-Stalinist command planning superior to capitalist rivals. Khrushchev had approached Soviet economic reform more pragmatically. He borrowed market management techniques including "profitability" (profits computed at state-fixed wage rates and product prices) and bonus incentives to improve enterprise rational choice (Kaser, 1965). Hungary's New Economic Mechanism (NEM) introduced in 1968 went a step further. It supplemented market incentives with restricted competitive market elements.

The NEM not only rewarded red directors for maximizing enterprise profits as Khrushchev had done, the government permitted red directors to produce and sell whatever they desired on a commercial basis with other state entities and cooperatives. This included new and improved export goods facilitating Hungarian participation in the global economy. Factory managers could purchase intermediate inputs directly from other firms, and wholesalers could buy imports from abroad. Enterprises could also modernize their plant and equipment to a limited extent without explicit state authorization.

The NEM socialist product pricing system introduced flexible elements. Some prices remained fixed but others were negotiable. Limited prices allowed red directors and wholesalers of staples to modify fixed prices within centrally determined bands. Red directors and state vendors also could negotiate prices without state restriction for "luxury" items. Consumers, however, only influenced limited and flexible prices derivatively. They could not bargain directly with suppliers.

The impact of limited and free prices on the competitive efficiency of Hungary's reformed top-down planning system was positive. The freedom enjoyed by Hungarian red directors and wholesalers was another plus.[24] Nonetheless, the sum and substance of Hungary's NEM experiment was small beans. Although Hungarian leaders were willing to transfer more autonomy to state agents than the Soviets, the payoffs failed to fulfill hopes, allowing anti-communist forces to carry the day in 1989. History's verdict on East European reform communism is clear. The Bolshevik paradigm, with selected market characteristics was inferior to competitive market.

Notes

1 The European states that became postwar people's republics were Albania (1946), Bulgaria (1946), Czechoslovakia, Hungary, Poland, Romania and Yugoslavia. In Asia, China became a people's republic following the Chinese Communist Revolution in 1949. North Korea became a people's republic in 1948.

2 The Prague Spring was a period of political liberalization and mass protest in Czechoslovakia. It began on January 5, 1968, when reformist Alexander Dubček became the First Secretary of the Communist Party of Czechoslovakia (KSČ). It continued until August 21, 1968, when the Soviet Union and other members of the Warsaw Pact invaded to suppress the reforms. The Prague Spring reforms loosened restrictions on the media, speech and travel.

3 Goulash Communism, also called Kadarism, or the Hungarian Thaw, refers communism in Hungary following the Hungarian Revolution of 1956. János Kádár and the Hungarian People's Republic imposed policies to create high-quality living standards for the people of Hungary coupled with economic reforms. These reforms fostered a sense of well-being and relative cultural freedom. Hungary had the reputation of being "the happiest barracks" of the Eastern Bloc during the 1960s to the 1970s. With elements of regulated market economics as well as an improved human rights record, it represented a quiet reform and deviation from the Stalinist principles applied in the previous decade.

4 The NEM decentralized decision making and made profit, rather than plan fulfillment, the enterprises' main goal. Instead of setting plan targets and allocating supplies, the government was to influence enterprise activity only through indirect financial, fiscal and price instruments known as "economic regulators." The NEM introduced a profit tax and allowed enterprises to make their own decisions concerning output, marketing and sales. It eliminated subsidies for most goods except basic raw

materials. The government decentralized allocation of capital and supply and partially decentralized foreign trade and investment decision making. The economy's focus moved away from heavy industry to light industry and modernization of the infrastructure. Finally, agricultural collectives gained the freedom to make investment decisions.

5   The Khrushchev Thaw refers to the period from the early 1950s to the early 1960s when repression and censorship in the Soviet Union were relaxed, with millions of Soviet political prisoners released from Gulag labor camps due to Nikita Khrushchev's policies of de-Stalinization and peaceful coexistence with other nations.

6   Socialism with a human face was a political program announced by Alexander Dubček at the Presidium of the Communist Party of Czechoslovakia in April 1968, after he became Party Chairman in January 1968. The first author of this slogan was Radovan Richta. It was a process of mild democratization and political liberalization that sought to build an advanced socialist society that valued democratic Czechoslovakian traditions.

7   De-Stalinization consisted of a series of political reforms in the Soviet Union after Stalin's death in 1953, and the ascension of Nikita Khrushchev to power. The reforms changed or removed key institutions supporting Stalin's hold power: the cult of personality that surrounded him, the Stalinist political system and the Gulag labor-camp system.

8   The Russian avant-garde was wave of radical modern art that flourished in the Russian Empire and the Soviet Union, approximately from 1890 to 1930 – although some have placed its beginning as early as 1850 and its end as late as 1960. The term covers many separate, but related art movements that flourished at the time, including Suprematism, Constructivism, Russian Futurism, Cubo-Futurism, Zaum and Neo-primitivism. Many of the artists were born, grew up or were active in what is now Belarus and Ukraine including Kazimir Malevich, Aleksandra Ekster, Vladimir Tatlin, Wassily Kandinsky, David Burliuk and Alexander Archipenko.

   The Russian avant-garde reached its creative and popular height in the period between the Russian Revolution of 1917 and 1932, at which point the ideas of the avant-garde clashed with the newly emerged state-sponsored direction of socialist realism.

9   Socialist realism is a style of idealized realistic art that was developed in the Soviet Union and was the official style in that country between 1932 and 1988, as well as in other socialist countries after World War II. Socialist realism glorified communist values.

10 Soviet dissidents were people who disagreed with certain features in the embodiment of Soviet ideology and who were willing to speak out against them. The term dissident referred to small groups of intellectuals. The West supported their modest challenges to the Soviet regime. Famous dissidents were Andrei Sakharov, Andrei Amalrik, Vladimir Bukovsky, Vyacheslav Chornovil, Zviad Gamsakhurdia, Alexander Ginzburg, Natalya Gorbanevskaya, Pyotr Grigorenko, Anatoly Shcharansky and Alexander Solzhenitsyn.

11 Marxist humanism is an international body of thought and political action rooted in an interpretation of the works of Karl Marx. The tendency was born in the 1940s and reached a degree of prominence in the 1950s and 1960s.

12 Liberal democracy is a liberal political ideology and a form of government in which representative democracy operates under the principles of classical liberalism. It features elections among multiple political parties, separation of powers into different branches

of government, the rule of law in everyday life as part of an open society, a market economy with private property and the equal protection of human rights, civil rights, civil liberties and political freedoms for all people. Democratic centralism purports to combine two opposing forms of party leadership: democracy, which allows free and open discussion, and central control, which ensures party unity and discipline.

13 The Workers' Opposition was a faction of the Russian Communist Party that emerged in 1920 as a response to the perceived over-bureaucratization that was occurring in Soviet Russia. It, like George Douglas Howard Cole, advocated the transfer of national economic management to trade unions. Alexander Shlyapnikov, Sergei Medvedev, Alexandra Kollontai and Yuri Lutovinov led the group. It existed until 1922, when it was defeated at the 11th Congress of the Russian Communist Party.

14 Solidarity began in September 1980. The Polish government suppressed it. The movement revived eight years later becoming first opposition movement to participate in free elections in a Soviet-bloc nation since the 1940s. Solidarity subsequently formed a coalition government with the United Workers' Party (PUWP), after which its leaders dominated the national government. Solidarity's membership peaked at 10 million in September 1981. Its leader Lech Wałęsa was awarded the Nobel Peace Prize in 1983.

15 See Appendix 4, Figures A4.1, A4.2 and A4.3.

16 Lange visited England in 1934 on a Rockefeller Foundation grant and emigrated to the United States in 1937. He became a professor at the University of Chicago in 1938 and a naturalized US citizen in 1943. Stalin offered him a position in the future Polish cabinet in 1944. Toward the end of World War II, Lange broke with the Polish government in exile and transferred his support to the Lublin Committee (PKWN) sponsored by the Soviet Union. Lange served as a go-between for Roosevelt and Stalin during the Yalta Conference discussions on postwar Poland. After the war ended in 1945, he returned to Poland. Lange then renounced his American citizenship and went back to the United States in the same year as the Polish People's Republic's first ambassador to the United States. In 1946, Lange also served as Poland's delegate to the United Nations Security Council. From 1947, he lived in Poland.

Lange worked for the Polish government while continuing his academic pursuits at the University of Warsaw and the Main School of Planning and Statistics. He was Deputy Chairman of the Polish Council of State in 1961–1965, and as such one of four acting Chairmen of the Council of State.

17 Soviet prices were computed as "sebestoimost'" (prime cost) [unit labor cost plus "dead labor", that is, labor cost unit cost capital] plus turnover taxes and a profit margin.

18 Figure A4.3 depicts the behavior of consumers A and Z. In the Lange case, A and Z are redefined as two competing state wholesale distributors.

19 This was accomplished in Lange's scheme in two steps. First, red directors would begin the price adjustment process by calculating marginal cost (conditional on average cost being less than marginal cost) and second, the State Price Committee would take over the task of second-order price adjustment. The scheme broke down, if marginal costs continuously declined, but this was only a minor technicality that could have resolved by treating the firm as a "natural monopoly."

20 Lange's analysis made it seem that red directors would fix prices at marginal cost, and that these marginal cost prices would be transmitted to the State Price Committee. This assignment, however, was superfluous, because the State Price Committee discovered the inventory price equilibrium directly through trial and error.

21 The adjustment only enhanced economic efficiency to the extent that derived wage-rental price ratios nudged production from point R, closer to point D.

22 Red director in Lange's scheme maximized enterprise profits for the state's coffers, not their own pocketbooks.

23 Abram Bergson's concept of adjusted ruble-factor cost pricing was an alternative approach to replacing Soviet Marxist labor value prices with estimated opportunity costs. The resulting GPD estimate measured "production potential," that is planner sovereign satisficing macro supply without demand side micro-suboptimizing. Official Soviet NMP failed to measure production potential because its labor value prices omitted capital services.

24 Soviet red directors also negotiated prices for new goods and special order products, and tolkachi (pushers) routinely bartered intermediate inputs on their enterprises' behalf.

References

Applebaum, Anne. (2003). *Gulag: A History*. New York: Doubleday.

Baberowski, Jörg. (2017). "Nikita Khrushchev and De-Stalinization in the Soviet Union 1953–1964." In N. Naimark, S. Pons and S. Quinn-Judge (eds.). *The Cambridge History of Communism*. Cambridge: Cambridge University Press, 113–138.

Barghoorn, Frederick. (1956). "De-Stalinization: Temporary Tactic or Long Term Trend?" *International Journal*. Vol. 12, No. 1, 24–33.

Belassa, Bela. (1983). "Reforming the New Economic Mechanism in Hungary." *Journal of Comparative Economics*. Vol. 7, No. 3, 253–276.

Benczes, István. (2016). "From Goulash Communism to Goulash Populism: The Unwanted Legacy of Hungarian Reform Socialism." *Post-Communist Economies*. Vol. 28, No. 2, 146–166.

Bergson, Abram. (1948). "Socialist Economics." In H. Ellis (ed.). *A Survey of Contemporary Economics*. Homewood: Richard D. Irwin, 412–448.

Bergson, Abram. (1953). *Soviet National Income and Product in 1937*. New York: Columbia University Press.

Bergson, Abram. (1966). "Socialist Calculation: A Further Word." In Collection of Bergson's articles, *Essays in Normative Economics*, 237–242.

Bergson, Abram. (1967). "Market Socialism Revisited." *Journal of Political Economy*. Vol, 75, No. 4, 655–673.

Bornstein, Morris. (1966). "Soviet Price Theory and Policy." *New Directions in the Soviet Economy: Studies, Parts 1–4*. Joint Economic Committee of Congress. By United States. Congress. Joint Economic Committee. Subcommittee on Foreign Economic Policy, Washington DC, 63–94.

CIA. (1972). "Hungary: First Test of the New Economic Mechanism." www.cia.gov/libr ary/readingroom/docs/CIA-RDP85T00875R001700030086-3.pdf

Csikos-Nagy, Bela. (1969). "The New Hungarian Price Mechanism." In Istvan Friss (ed.). *Reform of the Economic Mechanism in Hungary*. Budapest: Akademiai Kiado.

Daniels, Robert. (1960). *The Conscience of the Revolution: Communist Opposition in Soviet Russia*. Cambridge: Harvard University Press.

Dorfman, Robert, Paul Samuelson and Robert Solow. (1958). *Linear Programming and Economic Analysis*. New York: McGraw-Hill.

Ehrenburg, Ilya. (1955). *The Thaw*. London: Regnery.

Filtzer, Donald. (2002). *Soviet Workers and De-Stalinization: The Consolidation of the Modern System of Soviet Production Relations 1953—1964*. Cambridge: Cambridge University Press.

Fromm, Erich (ed.). (1965). *Socialist Humanism: An International Symposium*. Garden City: Doubleday.

Gomulka, Stanislaw. (1985). "Kornai's Soft Budget Constraint and the Shortage Phenomenon: A Criticism and Restatement." *Economics of Planning*. Vol. 19, No. 1, 1–11.

Hare, P. G. (1976). "Industrial Prices in Hungary. Part I: The New Economic Mechanism." *Soviet Studies*. Vol. 28, No. 2, 189–206.

Hayek, Frederick. (1940). "Socialist Calculation: The Competitive Solution." *Economica*. Vol. 7, No. 26, 125–149.

Hayek, Frederick. (1948). *The Meaning of Competition*. Reprinted in *Individualism and Economic Order*. Chicago: University of Chicago Press, 92–106.

Hejdánek, Ladislav and A. G. Brain. (1985). "Prospects for Democracy and Socialism in Eastern Europe." *International Journal of Politics*. Vol. 15, No. 3, 141–151.

James, C. Vaugh. (1973). *Soviet Socialist Realism: Origins and Theory*. New York: St. Martin's Press.

Kaser, Michael. (1965). "Kosygin, Liberman, and the Pace of Soviet Industrial Reform." *The World Today*. Vol. 21, No. 9, 375–388.

Khrushchev, Nikita. (1956). "Khrushchev's Secret Speech, 'On the Cult of Personality and Its Consequences,' Delivered at the Twentieth Party Congress of the Communist Party of the Soviet Union." http://digitalarchive.wilsoncenter.org/document/115995

Kornai, János. (1959). *Overcentralization in Economic Administration: A Critical Analysis Based on Experience in Hungarian Light Industry*. Oxford: Oxford University Press.

Kornai, János. (1967). *Mathematical Planning in Structural Decisions*. Amsterdam: North Holland.

Kornai, János. (1971). *Anti-Equilibrium: On Economic Systems Theory and the Tasks of Research*. New York: American Elsevier.

Kornai, János. (1979). "Resource-Constrained versus Demand-Constrained Systems." *Econometrica*. Vol. 47, No. 4, 801–819.

Kornai, János. (1980a). *Economics of Shortage*, Vol. I and II. Amsterdam: North Holland.

Kornai, János. (1980b). "The Dilemmas of a Socialist Economy: The Hungarian Experience." *Cambridge Journal of Economics*. Vol. 4, No. 2, 147–157.

Kornai, János. (1990). *The Road to a Free Economy: Shifting from a Socialist System: The Example of Hungary*. New York: W. W. Norton.

Kornai, János. (1992). *Socialist Economy: The Political Economy of Communism*. Princeton: Princeton University Press.

Kornai, János. (1995). *Highway and Byways*. Cambridge: MIT Press.

Kornai, János. (1996). "Paying the Bill for Goulash Communism: Hungarian Development and Macro Stabilization in a Political-Economy Perspective." *Social Research*. Vol. 63, No. 4, 943–1040.

Kornai, János. (1997). *Struggle and Hope*. New York: Edgar Elgar.

Kornai, János. (2008). *From Socialism to Capitalism*. Budapest: Central European University Press.

Kornai, János. (2013). *Dynamism, Rivalry and the Surplus Economy: Two Essays on the Nature of Capitalism*. Oxford: Oxford University Press.

Kornai, János. (2017). *By Force of Thought: An Intellectual Journey*. Cambridge: MIT Press.

Kornai, János and Jörgen W. Weibull. (1978). The Normal State of the Market in a Shortage Economy: A Queue Model. *The Scandinavian Journal of Economics*, Vol. 80, No. 4, 375–398.

Kornai, János and Karen Eggleston. (2001). *Welfare, Choice, and Solidarity in Transition.* Cambridge: Cambridge University Press.

Kornai, János and Tamás Lipták. (1965). "Two-Level Planning." *Econometrica*. Vol. 33, No. 1, 141–169.

Lange, Oskar. (1935). "Marxian Economics and Modern Economic Theory." *Review of Economic Studies*. Vol. 2, No. 3, 189–201.

Lange, Oskar. (1936). "On the Economic Theory of Socialism, Part One." *Review of Economic Studies*. Vol. 4, No. 1, 53–71.

Lange, Oskar. (1937). "On the Economic Theory of Socialism, Part Two." *Review of Economic Studies*. Vol. 4, No. 2, 123–142.

Lange, Oskar. (1938). *On the Economic Theory of Socialism.* Minneapolis: University of Minnesota Press.

Lavoie, Don. (1981). "A Critique of the Standard Account of the Socialist Calculation Debate." *The Journal of Libertarian Studies*. Vol. 5, No. 1, 41–87.

Lipset, Seymour. (1960). *Political Man: The Social Bases of Politics.* New York: Doubleday.

Locke, John. (1988). In Peter Laslett (ed.). *Second Treatise of Government, in Two Treatises of Government, (1690).* Cambridge: Cambridge University Press.

Mandelshtam, Nadezhda. (1981). *Hope Abandoned.* New York: Atheneum.

Mandelshtam, Nadezhda. (1999). *Hope against Hope.* New York: Modern Library.

Marcuse, Herbert. (1964). *One-Dimensional Man.* Boston: Beacon Press.

Maskin, Eric. (2000). *Planning Shortage and Transformation: Essays in Honor of Janos Kornai.* Cambridge: MIT Press.

McConnell Brooks, Karen. (1991). *Decollectivization and the Agricultural Transition in Eastern and Central Europe, Policy.* Research, and External Affairs working papers; no. WPS 793. Washington: World Bank.

Mises, Ludwig von. (1951). *Socialism: An Economic and Sociological Analysis.* New Haven: Yale University Press.

Neuberger, Egon. (1966). "Libermanism, Computopia, and Visible Hand: The Question of Informational Efficiency." *The American Economic Review*. Vol. 56, No. 1, 13–14.

Nove, Alec. (1991). *The Economics of Feasible Socialism Revisited.* London: Routledge.

Reid, Susan Emily. (1996). "De-Stalinization and the Remodernization of Soviet Art: The Search for a Contemporary Realism, 1953–1963." https://repository.upenn.edu/disser tations/AAI9627994

Roemer, John. (1994). *A Future for Socialism.* Cambridge: Harvard University Press.

Rosefielde, Steven. (1973). "Some Observations on the Concept of 'Socialism' in Contemporary Economic Theory." *Soviet Studies*, Vol. 25, No. 2, 229–243.

Rosefielde, Steven. (1978). "Anti-Systems." *Slavic Review*. Vol. 37, No. 2, 286–289.

Rosefielde, Steven. (1986a). "Competitive Market Socialism Revisited: Impediments to Efficient Price-Fixing." *Comparative Economic Studies*. Vol. 28, No. 3, 17–23.

Rosefielde, Steven. (1986b). "Regulated Market Socialism: The Semi-Competitive Soviet Solution." *Soviet Union/Union Sovietique*. Vol. 13, Part 1, 1–21.

Rosefielde, Steven. (1996). "Review of Highway and Byways: Studies on Reform and Postcommunist Transition, Janos Kornai." *Comparative Economic Studies*. Vol. 38, No. 1, .85–86.

Rosefielde, Steven and R. W. Pfouts. (1995). "Neoclassical Norms and the Valuation of National Product the Soviet Union and Its Post-communist Successor States." *Journal of Comparative Economics.* Vol. 21, No. 3, 375–380.

Rothschild, Joseph. (1993). *Return to Diversity: A Political History of East Central Europe.* Oxford: Oxford University Press.

Sorenson, Jay. (1969). *The Life and Death of Soviet Trade Unionism: 1917—1928.* New York: Atherton Press.

Stiglitz, Joseph. (1996). *Whither Socialism?* Cambridge: MIT Press.

Taubman, William. (2004). *Khrushchev: The Man and His Era.* London: Free Press.

12 World Communism

"Workers of the world, unite! You have nothing to lose but your chains!"
(Karl Marx and Friedrich Engels, *The Communist Manifesto*, 1848)

Class war precedes classless communism in Karl Marx's dialectical materialist theory. The class struggle unfolds unevenly because degrees of industrialization and levels of development vary across the globe. Marx expected the proletariat in advanced nations to expedite world communist revolution by capturing state power from the capitalists, and creating international associations of workingmen to assist laggard brethren. Marx and Engels contended that the communist revolution would be incomplete until the proletariat vanquished capitalism and workers everywhere were free. Their call to arms was "Workers of the world unite! You have nothing to lose but your chains!" (Marx and Engels, 188).

Many Marxists including Vladimir Lenin believed that workers in advanced nations have a duty to lead a movement for universal communist rule and that the success of communism in one country like Russia might be jeopardized if the world communist movement faltered (Lenin, 1918). Joseph Stalin famously took the opposite position in 1924. He contended that communism could flourish in a single country (Stalin, 1924).[1] Nonetheless, Stalin like Lenin felt that it was wise to foster communism everywhere to minimize the risk of foreign-led counterrevolution in the USSR and lay the foundations for a prosperous and harmonious global communist order. He used the Third Communist International (Comintern) founded by Lenin on March 2, 1919, for these purposes, or in Lenin's words to "struggle by all available means, including armed force, for the overthrow of the international bourgeoisie and the creation of an international Soviet republic as a transition stage to the complete abolition of the state" (Fisher, 1950).[2]

World Communism was Soviet Communism writ large first in its early insurrectionary phase, and then later in the framework of Stalin's USSR's top-down command central planning system. Once Stalin consolidated power as the General Secretary of the Communist Party in the late 1920s, he encouraged communist forces outside the Soviet Union to seize power, serve Soviet Bolshevism, support

DOI: 10.4324/9781003371571-15

Moscow's foreign policy and work toward the establishment of global centrally planned communism.

During the pre-Great Terror period of 1928–1935, Comintern adopted a militant ultraleft agenda to foster the collapse of capitalism by encouraging members to destroy moderate left parties (social fascists) that Moscow considered capitalist collaborators (Draper, 1969).[3] The Comintern opposed socialist collaboration with nationalist parties in the colonies and the Kuomintang in China, making exceptions for the Indian Swarajist and the Egyptian Wafd parties.

With the rise of the Nazi movement in Germany after 1930, this strategy became controversial. Comintern reversed itself at The Seventh Congress held mid-summer 1935. The Congress endorsed the popular front against fascism, including alliances with nonsocialist parties. Moscow maintained its popular front policy thereafter until Stalin dissolved Comintern on May 15, 1943, to placate Roosevelt and Churchill, both of whom viewed the Third Communist International as a hostile organization.

Comintern from start to finish was an instrument of Kremlin power. It never worked toward the establishment of a consensus world communist order of any type. The organization operated on the vanguard principle maintaining tight central control over members with little or no attention paid to workers themselves. The Soviet People's Commissariat for Internal Affairs (NKVD) had a pervasive presence including foreign intelligence operatives. One of its leaders, Mikhail Trilisser, using the pseudonym Mikhail Aleksandrovich Moskvin, was chief of the foreign department of the Soviet OGPU. At Stalin's orders, 133 out of 492 Comintern staff members were victims of the Great Purge. The leaders of the Indian (Virendranath Chattopadhyaya or Chatto), Korean, Mexican, Iranian and Turkish communist parties were executed. Out of 11 Mongolian Communist Party leaders, only Khorloogiin Choibalsan survived (Radzinski, 1997).

Following the June 1947 Paris Conference on Marshall Aid, Stalin gathered key European communist parties and set up the Cominform, or Communist Information Bureau, often seen as a substitute for Comintern. The network included the communist parties of Bulgaria, Czechoslovakia, France, Hungary, Italy, Poland, Romania, the Soviet Union and Yugoslavia (expelled in June 1948). The Politburo dissolved Cominform in 1956 immediately after Nikita Khrushchev's secret speech to the 20th Congress of the Communist Party of the Soviet Union denouncing Stalin's cult of personality.

This was the last attempt by the Bolsheviks to forge an international workers organization promoting Marxist–Leninist world communism but did not mark the abandonment of the idea of world communism, or the interim goal of constructing a transnational communist economic order among communist states. The Soviet Red Army conquered much of eastern and central Europe during World War II. Moscow soon transformed these occupied territories into autonomous centrally planned communist regimes ripe for economic integration. Stalin was not particularly interested in constructing a regional communist economic order as a stepping stone to world communism but stumbled in this direction after the West created the Committee of European Economic Cooperation in 1948 to accelerate European postwar economic recovery. Stalin countered the initiative by founding the Council for Mutual Economic Assistance (Comecon) in 1949.

Between 1949 and 1953, Comecon's activities were restricted chiefly to the registration of bilateral trade and credit agreements among member countries. After 1953, the Soviet Union and Comecon began promoting industrial specialization among the member countries to exploit the possibilities of integrating production and fixing socialist rules of exchange. Comecon sought conventional trade gains from a planned division of labor and comparative advantage, enhanced by organizational synergies. Marx believed that central planning enabled dispersed socialist communities to capture untapped efficiencies. Comecon provided a framework for realizing Marx's insight with varying degrees of sophistication. The emergence of Soviet linear programming in the 1960 offered intriguing possibilities, but Moscow chose to proceed from the achieved level (Nove, 1980). Members compiled the wish lists of import and exports from official trade statistics in consultation with their foreign trade organizations and wholesalers. The wish list included vent-for-surplus products wholesalers hoped to dump (Kurz, 1992), and goods generating high profits at established state prices, given fixed Comecon foreign exchange rates. Trade representatives would then haggle over the assortment of bartered goods, including the possibility of expanding investment in enterprises with desirable product lines. The entire operation was an exercise in custom union rationing rather than managed market exchange because prices were set by state price bureaus on a Marxist labor cost basis (sebestoimost), given fixed Comecon exchange rate. It allowed members to benefit using multiple criteria, but officials could only satisfice without direct consumer participation. The fixed price and exchange rate constraints precluded comprehensive optimization (Haase and Vale, 1976).[4]

Comecon was better than autarky. However, it also underscored the contradictions of planned communism. Comecon members could not determine whether intra-economic union trading was equitable at competitive domestic prices, giving rise to concerns that the Soviet Union was systematically exploiting its satellites (Mendershausen, 1962; Holzman, 1987; Rosefielde, 1973, 1977a, 1977b; Montias, 1963; Pryor, 1963). The Soviets sometimes believed that the Poles were exploiting them, and of course, all Comecon members thought that they would be better off trading with the West because exchanges at current world prices offered lucrative alternative opportunities.

The Soviets restricted satellite trade with the West until Gorbachev launched perestroika and granted members the right to negotiate trade treaties directly with the European Community. Comecon swiftly declined thereafter, dissolving itself on June 24, 1991 (Bideleux and Jeffries, 1998).

The experiment in intra-communist economic integration, which began with a bang, ended with a whimper for those who believed in the superiority of world communism.

Notes

1 After the defeat of proletarian revolutions in Germany and Hungary in 1919, Joseph Stalin wrote, "the proletariat can and must build the socialist society in one country."
2 Delegates from Russia, Germany, German Austria, Hungary, Poland, Finland, Ukraine, Latvia, Lithuania, Byelorussia, Estonia, Armenia, the Volga German region; the Swedish Social Democratic Left Party (the opposition), Balkan Revolutionary People's of Russia; Zimmerwald Left Wing of France; the Czech, Bulgarian, Yugoslav, British, French and Swiss Communist Groups; the Dutch Social-Democratic Group; Socialist Propaganda League and the Socialist Labor Party of America; Socialist Workers' Party of China; Korean Workers' Union, Turkestan, Turkish, Georgian, Azerbaijanian and Persian Sections of the Central Bureau of the Eastern People's and the Zimmerwald Commission attended the first Comintern congress.
3 Social fascism was a theory supported by the Communist International and affiliated communist parties in the early 1930s that held that social democracy was a variant of fascism because it stood in the way of a dictatorship of the proletariat.
4 Comecon compiled dollar prices of basic goods (world prices). Members bought and sold products from each other at these prices. Each member simultaneously converted world prices to domestic prices at their established dollar price exchange rates. This enabled members to judge the benefit of exchange by comparing the domestic price of a good with the foreign import equivalent derived from the Comecon dollar price list computed as period averages. These prices differed imports from other sources based on current dollar prices.

References

Bideleux, Robert and Ian Jeffries. (1998). *A History of Eastern Europe: Crisis and Change.* London: Routledge.

Draper, Theodore. (1969). "The Ghost of Social-Fascism." *Commentary.* www.commentarymagazine.com/articles/theodore-draper/the-ghost-of-social-fascism/

Fisher, Harold. (1950). *The Communist Revolution: An Outline of Strategy and Tactics.* Palo Alto: Stanford University Press.

Haase, Herwig and Michel Vale. (1976). The COMECON Foreign-Trade Price System. *Soviet and Eastern European Foreign Trade.* Vol. 12, No. 2, 81–108.

Holzman, Franklyn. (1987). *The Economics of Soviet Bloc Trade and Finance.* London: Routledge.

Kurz, Heinz. (1992). "Adam Smith on Foreign Trade: A Note on the 'Vent-for-Surplus' Argument." *Economica.* Vol. 59, 475–481.

Lenin, Vladimir (1918). *Lenin's Collected Works.* Moscow: Progress Publishers, 85–158.

Marx, Karl and Friedrich Engels. (1848). *The Communist Manifesto.* London: Deutsche Londoner Zeitung.

Mendershausen, Horst. (1962). *Mutual Price Discrimination in Soviet Bloc Trade.* Santa Monica: RAND Corporation.

Montias, John Michael. (1963). *Economic Development in Communist Rumania.* Cambridge: MIT Press.

Nove, Alec. (1980). "Does the Soviet Union Have a Planned Economy? A Comment." *Soviet Studies.* Vol. 32, No. 1, 135–137.

Pryor, Frederic. (1963). *The Communist Foreign Trade System.* Cambridge: The MIT Press.

Radzinski, Edvard. (1997). *Stalin: The First in-depth Biography Based on Explosive New Documents from Russia's Secret Archives.* New York: Anchor.

Rosefielde, Steven. (1973). *Soviet International Trade in Heckscher-Ohlin Perspective.* Lexington: Heath-Lexington.

Rosefielde, Steven. (1977a). *East-West Trade and Postwar Soviet Economic Growth: A Sectoral Production Approach.* Stanford Research Institute.

Rosefielde, Steven. (1977b). "International Trade Theory and Practice under Socialism (Review Article)." *Journal of Comparative Economics.* Vol. 1, No. 1, 99–104.

Stalin, Joseph. (1924). *The Foundations of Leninism*, Works. 6. Moscow: Foreign Languages Publishing House, 71–196.

13 Dystopian Socialist Fiction (1890–1950)

Socialism was mostly a fringe phenomenon and cocktail tall
mid-1880s when the industrial labor movement gained mor
parties emerged in England and across the continent. People
New Harmony and Icaria would flourish or fail, and deba
efficiency losses of anti-libertarian productive policies, without paying attention
to the possibility that socialism might be dystopic. Socialists and communists
vetted their spleens about the evils of dystopian capitalism and feudalism. They
touted revolutionary lifestyles, but novelists did not pen nightmare tales about
socialism run amok. Many works of fiction addressed gothic science (Shelley,
1818),[1] technocratic regimentation (Harbou, 1927) and authoritarianism (Shelley,
1826),[2] but few touched on cooperatives, syndicalism, anarcho-syndicalism,
democratic socialism, planned economy and communism. Dystopian novelists
ignored communism's surreal potential until the 1920s (Zamyatin, 1924). There
was a code of silence.

The paucity of dystopian socialist concerns reflected the zeitgeist. Novelists
could have easily compiled a list of utopian socialist promises made by Fourier,
Owen, Saint Simon, Marx, Cabet, Proudhon, Morris and Cole, and then
projected dystopian forebodings. Fourier's dystopia would have been Sodom
and Gomorrah. Owen's libertarian cooperatives would be rancorous and despotic. Saint-Simon's technocracy would be dehumanizing. Cabet's community of sharing and Marx's proletarian vanguard state would be totalitarian
hallucinations. Proudhon and Marx's anarcho-communism would be pande-
monium. Morris' Arts and Crafts communities would be villages of the damned,
and Cole's direct democracy bedlams of perpetual balloting. Leon Trotsky's permanent revolutions would enslave workers in a red labor army (Trotsky, 2010;
Orwell, 1945).[3]

There are only two exceptions to the code of silence. The German socialist
politician Eugen Richter's *Pictures of the Socialistic Future* (1891) explores the possibility that democratic socialist and revolutionary communist systems might prove
dystopic, and a cluster of novels written during 1915–1950 glimpses Stalinism's
malign potential.

DOI: 10.4324/9781003371571-16

Eugen Richter

Eugen Richter (1838–1906) was a German politician and journalist in Imperial Germany. He was one of the leading advocates of liberalism and critic of Otto von Bismarck's policies. He opposed the Anti-Socialist Laws of 1878 banning the Social Democratic Party.

Richter's *Pictures of the Socialistic Future* (1891) is a dystopian novel predicting the dire consequences of Germany embracing trade unionism or Marxist democratic socialism. It is an ambivalent 19th-century harbinger of George Orwell's *Nineteen Eighty-Four* showing that state ownership of the means of production and central planning might cause shortages instead of prosperity. Richter draws attention to the problem of devising incentives as surrogates for profit seeking and ponders political corruption, warning that economic illiberalism might foster political tyranny.

The narrative is a duet between a socialist revolutionary contemplating the perils of expropriation, blocked emigration, and forced labor, and a narrator reassuring him that paradise is just around the corner. The revolutionary muses: "What is freedom of the press if the government owns all the presses? What is freedom of religion if the government owns all the houses of worship?" highlighting the abuse of power possible when institutions are state owned. The novel then frets about how socialism might spawn an authoritarian martial police state (Richter, 1893).

Specter of Totalitarianism

The cluster of novels glimpsing Soviet communism's malign possibilities composed during 1915–1950 include Yevgeny Zamyatin's *We* (1920–1921), Franz Kafka, *The Trial* (1925),[4] Andrei Platonov, *The Foundation Pit* (1930), Ayn Rand, *Anthem* (1938), Vladimir Nabokov, *Invitation to a Beheading* (1938), Arthur Koestler, *Darkness at Noon* (1940) and George Orwell, *Nineteen Eighty-Four* (1949). These dystopian tracts transform Richter's misgivings into prophesies of totalitarian disaster on the premise that power corrupts and totalitarian power corrupts absolutely (Zamyatin, 1924; Kafka, 1925; Platonov, 2009; Rand, 2018; Nabokov, 1959; Koestler, 1984; Orwell, 1954).

Zamyatin, Kafka, Platonov, Rand, Nabokov, Koestler and Orwell were all acquainted with Bolshevism and grasped its totalitarian potential (Arendt, 1958; Friedrich and Brzezinski, 1956; Laqueur, 1987; Mises, 1944; Schapiro, 1972; Fitzpatrick and Geyer, 2008). Those among them briefly enthralled by Leninist propaganda quickly corrected themselves (Goldman, 1923). Totalitarianism's opponents condemned revolutionary communist economic and political despotism and libertine lifestyles.[5] They descried the illiberalism of the Soviet Union's criminalization of private property, markets and entrepreneurship on humanist grounds but did not fixate on mundane economic issues like employment, efficiency, wages and living standards. The USSR's dystopian evil, immorality, squalor, torments, injustices, regimentation, indoctrination, degradation and dehumanization dismayed them more than Maxim Gorky's empty promises of a sky blue material life (Gorky, 1964).

Franz Kafka

Franz Kafka (1883–1924) was a Bohemian novelist and short-story writer, widely regarded as one of the major figures of 20th-century literature. He was a socialist in his youth, influenced by Peter Kropotkin and the emerging Austrian Social Democratic Party.[6] His oeuvre features isolated protagonists facing surrealistic predicaments and incomprehensible socio-bureaucratic powers, hallmarks of the dystopian socialist literature, but a variety of personal factors shaped his outlook. Kafka began exploring these themes in a series of draft novellas written before November 7, 1917, published posthumously after 1924. Kafka's themes influenced Koestler and Orwell, but not Zamyatin and Platonov. Their dystopias were the products of personal encounters with Soviet reality.

The Trial is Kafka's iconic work, written in 1914–1915, and it may reflect the atmosphere of the First World War, but not the mayhem of Soviet War Communism. The novel tells Josef K's story, a man arrested and prosecuted by a remote, inaccessible authority, with the nature of his crime revealed neither to him nor to the reader. Josef K is ordered to appear at court without being told the exact time or room. He finds the court in the attic. He arouses the assembly's hostility after an impassioned tirade against the absurdity of the trial and the emptiness of the accusation. He later tries to confront the presiding judge over his case, but only finds an attendant's wife. She attempts to seduce him before a law student bursts into the room and takes the woman away, claiming her to be his mistress. Worried by the rumors about his nephew, the uncle introduces Joseph K to Herr Huld, a sickly and bedridden lawyer tended by a young nurse. She calls Josef K away and takes him to the next room for a sexual encounter. Afterward, he meets his angry uncle outside, who claims that his lack of respect for the trial has hurt his case. Upon arriving at Huld's office, Josef K meets downtrodden Rudi Block, a client who offers him some insight. Block's case has continued for five years. He is bankrupt and enslaved by his lawyer and the nurse. On the eve of Josef K's 31st birthday, two men arrive at his apartment to execute him. They lead him to a small quarry outside the city and kill him with a butcher's knife. His last words are chilling. He understands that humanity is marked for extermination. People will be slaughtered like dogs.

The story has no unique interpretation. Its dystopian significance lies in the prospect that unaccountable rulers in what purports to be utopia will victimize, torment and kill innocents without rhyme or reason.

Yevgeny Zamyatin

Yevgeny Ivanovich Zamyatin (1884–1937) was a Russian author of science fiction, philosophy, literary criticism and political satire. He was active in the Bolshevik Party's prerevolutionary underground, repeatedly arrested, imprisoned and exiled, but Soviet reality dashed his utopian expectations. Zamyatin started as a true believer, but after 1917 his writings became increasingly satirical and critical toward the Communist Party. He believed that independent speech and thought are necessary for any healthy society. Zamyatin opposed the Party's suppression of freedom of speech and the censorship of literature, the media and the arts. He was the USSR's first prominent dissident (Zamyatin, 1967).

Zamyatin's novel *We*, written between 1920 and 1921, is set many centuries in the future. D-503, a mathematician, lives in the One State, an urban nation constructed almost entirely of glass apartment buildings, which assist mass surveillance by the Bureau of Guardians. The structure of the One State is a Panopticon[7] and operates on Fredrick Taylor's efficiency principles.[8] People are uniformed, assigned numbers and march in unison. The society runs like clockwork.

As the novel opens, One State is preparing to visit foreign planets intent on forcing alien races to be happy by accepting the Benefactor's tyranny. The spaceship's chief engineer D-503 meets a woman named I-330. She illegally smokes cigarettes, drinks vodka and shamelessly flirts with D-503 instead of applying for a pink ticket sex visit. I-330 reveals to D-503 that she is a member of MEPHI, an organization of rebels against the One State. She takes D-503 through secret tunnels to the untamed wilderness outside the Green Wall, which surrounds the city-state. There, D-503 meets primitives covered with animal fur. He joins MEPHI and plots to topple One State, destroy the Green Wall and reunite the people of the city with the outside world. There is a general uprising leaving One State's survival in doubt, but there is no happy-ending for I-330 and D-503. Just as there can be no highest number, there can be no final revolution. One State is thoroughly vicious, but the higher crimes in dystopia are speaking truth and advocating libertarian justice.

Soviet authorities suppressed the book and persecuted Zamyatin until Stalin at Maxim Gorky's urging allowed him to emigrate in 1931. Zamyatin died impoverished six years later in Paris.

Andrei Platonov

Andrei Platonov (1899–1951) was the pen name of Andrei Platonovich Klimentov, a Soviet Russian writer, philosopher, playwright and poet. Although Platonov regarded himself as a communist, the Communist Party heavily censored and sometimes suppressed his works, especially stories displaying a skeptical attitude toward forced agricultural collectivization (1929–1940). Platonov produced two major works during the opening phase of the First Five-Year Plan (1928–1932): *Chevengur* (1928) and *The Foundation Pit* (1930). One chapter of *Chevengur* appeared in the 1920s. Soviet authorities published *The Foundation Pit* in 1987.

It is gloomily symbolic and semi-satirical, mingling peasant and Marxist jargon to create a sense of jibberish, punctuated by abrupt and fantastic plot twists. The novel concerns a group of workers living in the early Soviet Union. They attempt to excavate a huge foundation pit as a platform for the construction of a colossal proletarian dormitory, but become increasingly disoriented because the pit drains their physical and mental energy. Their plight symbolizes the conflict between the Soviet state and its workers in the late 1920s. The novel criticizes Stalin's domestic policies and questions the validity of the Bolshevik premise that happiness lies in submersing oneself in the collective.

The story begins with a boss berating the machinist Voschev for idling. Voschev defends himself by explaining that he is trying to find the meaning of life because it is the key to raising productivity. He is fired and searches for a new job. Voschev tries to protect a group of pioneer girls, but people scold him for being soft headed. If he had fought for the revolution, he would know better. Eventually Voschev joins a group of workers digging an enormous foundation pit. He works slowly, while Stakhanovites criticize management for not prodding them hard enough.[9]

Prushevsky feels that something is missing in his life. "People make use of me," he says to himself, "but no one is glad of me."

Chiklin discovers a gully that might facilitate the excavation. Safronov condemns him for his initiative asking whether he received "a special kiss in infancy" that makes him smarter than government experts.

Safronov asks Nastya about her family. She tells him that she waited a long time to be born in fear that her mother may belong to the bourgeoisie. "But now that Stalin's become," she adds, "I've become too!" Nastya urges comrades to liquidate the kulaks as a class.

An activist rounds up all of the peasants but is terrified to make a mistake. He has not received guidance and is worried about both underachieving and over-achieving, fearing that the peasants will use smaller animals like goats in order to prop up capitalism.

A few days later, the activist announces that the kulaks will be exterminated "as a class," and their "bodies" sent down river on a makeshift raft. Many peasants were expecting this to happen and stopped taking care of themselves long ago. One woman, for instance, is alive only to the pain she feels when stray dogs chew on her feet. Others rip their crops out of the ground, refusing to let their property be collectivized. The rest of the peasants spend the night vomiting.

Zhachev and Nastya visit the village, and Yelisey introduces them to the local blacksmith who touts a keen ability to sniff out and kill kulaks. He takes Nastya and Chiklin hunting for the kulaks. Before dying, one of their victims shouts out, "The only person who'll ever reach socialism is that one important man of yours." They send the last of the corpses down the river and set up speakers for music and dancing. Zhachev tells Chiklin that Marxism will resurrect Lenin one day.

The activist receives a letter from the Soviet government stating that peasants who seem too willing to have their property collectivized are likely to be under-cover agents.

Chiklin becomes suspicious of an activist's optimism and energy. He kills him with a sledgehammer. The activist's body floats down the river like the kulaks euphemistically liquidated only as a class.

Voschev returns to the worksite with all of the collectivize property, including its previous owners. He tells Chiklin that the peasants would like to enroll as regular workers. They realize this means that they must enlarge the foundation pit. Zhachev refuses to help. "Communism's something for kids." He leaves the worksite and never returns.

Platonov, like Richter before him, was double minded about the Soviet future. He astutely grasped Stalin's doublethink, and its pernicious consequences, but still held out hope against hope for a utopian outcome (Mandelstam, 1999, 2011).

Ayn Rand

Ayn Rand (1905–1982) was a Russian-American writer and philosopher,[10] known for her fiction and "Objectivism."[11] The Bolsheviks confiscated her father's business in 1917, and the family fled Saint Petersburg to the Crimean Peninsula. She returned with her family to Petrograd in 1921, living in difficult circumstances to study history at Petrograd State University, completing her degree in 1924. Rand visited family in the United States in 1926 and became an American citizen in 1931. She had firsthand experience with the Bolshevik Revolution, War Communism and the New Economic Policy (NEP), influencing her to oppose collectivism, statism and anarchism. Her writings have influenced libertarians and some conservatives.

Anthem is Rand's contribution to the dystopian socialist literature. The story is set in a new technologically advanced, anti-libertarian Dark Age. A young man known as Equality 7-2521 rebels by doing secret scientific research. He flees into the wilderness with the girl he loves and attempts to build a society devoted to individual human accomplishment.

Equality 7-2521, a 21-year-old man writing by candlelight in a tunnel under the earth, tells the story of his life using plural pronouns ("we," "our," "they"). He lived in the Home of Infants from birth until the age of five, then the Home of Students from five to fifteen. Equality 7-2521 excels at the Science of Things and dreams of becoming a Scholar, but when the Council of Vocations assigns his Life Mandate at 15, he is assigned to be a Street Sweeper.

Equality 7-2521 works with the handicapped Union 5-3992 and International 4-8818. He explores an underground tunnel near the City Theatre tent and finds metal tracks. Equality believes the tunnel is from the Unmentionable Times of the distant past. He begins sneaking away from his community at night to use the tunnel as a laboratory for scientific experiments. He steals paper from the Home of the Clerks to write his journal, using candles stolen from the larder at the Home of the Street Sweepers.

While cleaning a road at the edge of the City, Equality meets Liberty 5-3000, a 17-year-old peasant girl who works in the fields. He commits another transgression by thinking constantly of her, instead of waiting to be assigned a woman at the annual Time of Mating, in which men aged 20 and over and females of 18 and over, are assigned to each other solely for breeding. When he speaks to her, he discovers that she also thinks of him. He reveals his secret name for her (The Golden One), and Liberty tells Equality she has named him "The Unconquered."

Equality rediscovers electricity. In the ruins of the tunnel, he finds a glass box with wires that gives off light when he passes electricity through it. He presents his work to the World Council of Scholars. They assail him and threaten to destroy his discovery to avoid disrupting the plans of the Department of Candles. Equality seizes the box, cursing the council before fleeing into the Uncharted Forest that lies outside the City.

He enjoys his freedom. No one will pursue him into this forbidden place. Liberty follows him into the forest and vows to stay with him forever. They live together in the forest and try to express their love for one another, but they lack the words to speak of love as individuals.

They find a house from the Unmentionable Times in the mountains and decide to live in it. While reading books from the house's library, Equality discovers the word "I" and tells Liberty about it. Having rediscovered individuality, they give themselves new names from the books: Equality becomes "Prometheus" and Liberty becomes "Gaea." Months later, Gaea is pregnant with Prometheus' child. Prometheus wonders how men in the past could have given up their individuality; he plans a future in which they will regain it.

The fable is an ode to life-affirming, heroic, transfiguring individualism.[12]

Vladimir Nabokov

Vladimir Nabokov (1899–1977) was a Russian-American author famed for the novel *Lolita*[13] and an opponent of the Soviet government, tsarist autocracy and fascism. He was born in Saint Petersburg to a prominent aristocratic family that traced its roots to the 14th-century Tatar prince Nabok Murza. His wife was Ayn Rand's gymnasium classmate. After the October Revolution, the Nabokov family fled to Crimea. His father became a minister of justice in the Crimean Regional Government before emigration to Berlin in 1920. Nabokov went to England, joining his family in Germany after completing his studies at Cambridge University. He escaped Nazi Germany with his Jewish wife in 1937 and became an American citizen.

Invitation to a Beheading is Nabokov's dystopian masterpiece, published originally in the Russian émigré journal *Sovremennye zapiski* in 1935–1936. The story relates the final 20 days of Cincinnatus (Pagels, 1989),[14] a citizen of a fictitious country, imprisoned and sentenced to death for "gnostical turpitude" (treating Stalin as a lesser God).[15] Cincinnatus has a peculiarity that makes him impervious to the rays of others, producing a bizarre impression, as of a lone dark obstacle in this world of souls transparent to one another. Although he tries to hide his condition and feign translucence, people are uncomfortable with his existence and feel there is something wrong with him.

Cincinnatus searches for his true self (gnostic revelation) in his writing. He refuses to believe in either death or his executioners, and as the axe falls, the false existence dissolves around him and he joins the spirits of his fellow visionaries in reality.

Nabokov's tale is preternatural. The absurdity of Cincinnatus' dystopian socialist world is so extreme that it provides a pathway for grasping its inanity from a transcendental perspective. People delude themselves into acting as if they were translucent and that their lesser God is sublime, precluding their salvation. Revolutionary communism premises are false. This is why it is dystopic. Bolshevism is sound and fury signify nothings and cannot transform hell into heaven. No amount of tinkering can make Soviet totalitarianism sublime.

Other interpretations are possible.

Arthur Koestler

Arthur Koestler (1905–1983) was a Hungarian British author and journalist, born in Budapest and educated in Austria. In 1931, Koestler with Eva Striker's encouragement,[16] impressed by the achievements of the Soviet Union, supported Marxism-Leninism. He joined the German Communist Party convinced that it was the only bulwark against the rising Nazi tide, but resigned in 1938 disillusioned by Stalinism. Koestler's anti-socialist-totalitarian dystopian novel *Darkness at Noon*, published in 1940, received international acclaim (Orwell, 1970).[17]

It is an allegory of an Old Bolshevik arrested, imprisoned and tried for treason. The story is set in 1938 at the tail end of the Great Purge (1936–1938), which exterminated Stalin's Communist Party, military and professional rivals, but this is not explicit. Most of the novel recounts the prison recollections of Rubashov. The story has four parts: First, Second and Third Interrogations, and Grammatical Fiction.

The First Interrogation

The action begins with Rubashov's arrest by two secret policemen (NKVD). He ponders the Old Bolsheviks, Number One, and the Marxist interpretation of history. Throughout the novel Rubashov, Ivanov and Gletkin speculate about historical processes. Each hopes that history will vindicate their vile deeds. This makes the regime's abuses tolerable as they contemplate the suffering of millions weighed against the happiness of future generations. Rubashov reflects on his Party life. He commanded soldiers, won a commendation for bravery, volunteered for hazardous assignments, endured torture, denounced fellow communists who deviated from the Party line and proved his Party loyalty, but has doubts. Despite millions of executions, a socialist utopia does not seem at hand.

The Second Interrogation

The next section of the book begins with an entry in Rubashov's diary. He struggles to find his place and that of the other Old Bolsheviks within the Marxist interpretation of history. Ivanov and a junior examiner, Gletkin, discuss Rubashov's fate. Gletkin recommends forcing Rubashov to confess, while Ivanov suggests persuasion. Gletkin recalls that peasants could not be persuaded to surrender their individual crops until they were tortured (and later killed), inferring that his recommendation is logical and virtuous because it contributes to the building socialism. Ivanov cannot refute Gletkin's reasoning.

Rubashov learns that the authorities will execute Michael Bogrov, distinguished revolutionary naval commander and friend. Shocked at Bogrov's pathetic state, he despairingly cries out his name. Later Ivanov visits Rubashov telling him that Gletkin orchestrated every aspect of Bogrov's execution to weaken Rubashov's resolve, but that he (Ivanov) knows it will have the opposite effect. Ivanov tells him that he knows Rubashov will only confess if he resists his growing urge to sentimentality "for when you have thought the whole thing to a conclusion – then, and only then, will you capitulate."

The Third Interrogation and the Grammatical Fiction

Rubashov continues to write in his diary. He tells No. 402 that he intends to confess. They quarrel over the magnitude of the horrors of Soviet socialism. Rubashov signs a letter to the state authorities in which he pledges "utterly to renounce his oppositional attitude and to denounce his errors publicly."

Gletkin takes over Rubashov's interrogation forcing him to sit under a glaring lamp for hours. Later, Gletkin informs him of Ivanov's execution. Rubashov notices that he is impervious to news of Ivanov's fate, and capitulates.

As he confesses to the false charges, he thinks of the many times he betrayed agents in the past: Richard, the young German; Little Loewy in Belgium; and Orlova, his secretary-mistress. He recognizes that his own betrayals justify his punishment and abjectly confesses.

The final section of the novel begins with a four-line quotation ("Show us not the aim without the way ...") by the German socialist Ferdinand Lasalle.

The novel ends with Rubashov's execution.

George Orwell

George Orwell (1903–1950) was an English novelist, essayist, journalist and democratic socialist famous for his biting social criticism (Orwell, 1941) and opposition to totalitarianism. He wrote two influential allegorical dystopian novels exposing the horrors of fascism and communism: *Animal Farm* (1945) and *Nineteen Eighty-Four* (1949). The latter created an Orwellian lexicon of terms and concepts crystalizing Bolshevik totalitarianism's counter-reality and deceits like "Big Brother" (Stalin), "Thought Police" (NKVD), "Two Minutes Hate" (hate propaganda), "Room 101" (Ministry of Love torture chamber), "memory hole" (truth suppression), "Newspeak" (deceitful jargon), "doublethink" (approved contradictions), "unperson" (discredited authority), "thought crime" (contemplated deviance), "2 + 2 = 5" and "proles."

Nineteen Eighty-Four delves into the Soviet dystopian experience. The story takes place in 1984, at the time 35 years in the future, when much of the world has fallen prey to perpetual war, omnipresent government surveillance, atrocity denial and propaganda. Great Britain, known as Airstrip One, has become a province of totalitarian Oceania employing Thought Police to persecute libertarian individualism. Big Brother is the leader of the Party, sustained by a cult of personality even though he may not actually exist. The protagonist, Winston Smith, is a diligent and skillful rank-and-file worker and Outer Party member who secretly detests the Party and dreams of rebellion. He enters into a forbidden relationship with a colleague, Julia, and starts to remember what life was like before the Party assumed power.

In the year 1984, Oceania ruled by Big Brother under the banner of Ingsoc (a Newspeak contraction of "English Socialism") is one of the three totalitarian superstates. The Thought Police identify nonconformists through constant surveillance (two-way television) and brutally purge them. They become "unpersons," erased without a trace. Winston Smith, a member of the London Outer Party, works at the Ministry of Truth, altering historical records to conform to the state's ever-changing version of history. He revises past editions of The Times and discards the original documents down memory holes. He secretly opposes the Party, even though he recognizes that the Thought Police are likely to detect his transgression. While in a prole (proletarian) neighborhood, he meets Mr. Charrington, the owner of an antiques shop, and buys a diary. He records his criticisms of the Party and Big Brother and expresses the view that "if there is hope, it lies in the proles." He discovers to his dismay that proles are politically inert and suspects that Inner Party official O'Brien is part of the Brotherhood, an enigmatic underground resistance movement formed by Emmanuel Goldstein (Leon Trotsky). Julia, a suspicious coworker, secretly hands Winston a love note, and the two begin an illicit affair. Julia confides that she also loathes the Party. They later meet in a rented room above Mr. Charrington's shop. Weeks later, O'Brien invites Winston to his flat, where he introduces himself as a Brotherhood member and sends Winston a copy of The Theory and Practice of Oligarchical Collectivism by Goldstein. Meanwhile, during the nation's Hate Week, Oceania's enemy suddenly changes sides from Eurasia to Eastasia, a stunning volte-face that goes mostly unnoticed. The Ministry summons Winston to revise the records. Winston and Julia read parts of Goldstein's book, which explains how the Party maintains power, the true meanings of its slogans and the concept of perpetual war. It argues that the proles can overthrow the Party.

Mr. Charrington denounces Winston and Julia. They are imprisoned at the Ministry of Love. O'Brien arrives, also revealing himself as a Thought Police agent. O'Brien tells Winston that he will never know whether the Brotherhood exists, and that Emmanuel Goldstein's book was written collaboratively by O'Brien and other Party members. The police starve and torture Winston to "cure" his "insanity." O'Brien reveals that the (Communist) Party seeks power for its own sake. O'Brien then coerces Winston into betraying Julia.

O'Brien takes Winston to Room 101 for the final stage of reeducation, where each prisoner must face his worst fear. Confronted by frenzied rats, he wishes the same fate for Julia.

O'Brien releases Winston and he encounters Julia. She too has been tortured. Both reveal that they betrayed the other and deny feelings of remorse. A news alert celebrates Oceania's victory over Eurasian armies in Africa. Winston finally accepts his unconditional love for Big Brother.

Summary

The dystopian socialist literature is a collective cautionary tale. It does not prove that utopia is unattainable or that socialism is a primrose path to hell. It only exposes the naïve optimism of Fourier, Saint-Simon, Marx, Cabet, Proudhon, Sorel, Morris and Cole's socialist constructs and reveals that the importance of knowledge, reason, wisdom, virtue, compassion, self-discipline, self-defense and perseverance for achieving satisfactory existences and avoiding misery.

Hope may spring eternal in the human breast but requires tempering (Pope, 1733). Pretending that socialist institutions spontaneously generate virtuous harmony will not make it so. Pretending that socialist coercion transforms libertinism into proletarian bliss is nonsense. Socialist leaders are not supermen. They suffer from delusions of adequacy.

Notes

1 Frankenstein tells the story of Victor Frankenstein, a young scientist who creates a sapient creature in an unorthodox scientific experiment. The novel frets about how abused science might blight human futures.

2 Shelley also published a dystopian tale about how degenerate government might subvert Enlightenment ideals.

3 This possibility is the central them of George Orwell's *Animal Farm*. Farm animals' rebellion is futile.

4 *The Trial* was written 1914–1915.

5 Bolsheviks and other socialist revolutionaries linked libertinism to socialism because it was the antithesis of bourgeois morality, was concentrated within narrow revolutionary political circles, was compatible with placing revolutionary duty above family ties and the epitome of sophisticated taste.

6 Workers' Party of Austria (Sozialdemokratische Arbeiterpartei Österreichs, SDAPÖ) formed in 1889. At the start of the World War I, it was the strongest party in parliament. Karl Renner, the party leader, became Chancellor of the First Republic in 1918.

7 The panopticon is a type of institutional building and a system of control designed by the English philosopher and social theorist Jeremy Bentham in the 18th century. The manager or staff of the institution are able to watch the inmates from the center.

8 Frederick Winslow Taylor (1856–1915) was an American mechanical engineer. He was a leader of the Efficiency Movement in the Progressive Era (1890s–1920s).

9 The term Stakhanovite refers to Soviet workers who modeled themselves after Alexei Stakhanov. These workers took pride in their ability to produce more than was required, by working harder and more efficiently, thus strengthening the socialist state.

10 Ayn Rand was born Alisa Zinovyevna Rosenbaum. Ayn Rand was her pen name.

11 Objectivism as "the concept of man as a heroic being, with his own happiness as the moral purpose of his life, with productive achievement as his noblest activity, and reason as his only absolute."

12 *Anthem* sold more than 3.5 million copies after its belated publication in 1946.

13 Many authors consider it the greatest work of the 20th century. It has been included in several lists of best books, such as Time's List of the 100 Best Novels and Le Monde's 100 Books of the Century.

14 Lucius Quinctius Cincinnatus (c. 519–c. 430 BC) was a Roman patrician, statesman and military leader of the early Roman Republic who became a legendary figure of Roman virtue – particularly civic virtue – by the time of the late Republic.

15 Gnosticism is a collection of religious ideas and systems, which originated in the late 1st-century AD among Jewish and early Christian sects, emphasizing personal spiritual knowledge (gnosis) above the orthodox teachings, traditions and authority of the church. Gnostic cosmogony distinguishes a supreme, hidden God from a malevolent lesser divinity, sometimes associated with the Yahweh of the Old Testament who is responsible for creating the material universe. Gnostics considered the principal element of salvation to be direct knowledge of the supreme divinity in the form of mystical or esoteric insight. Many Gnostic texts deal not in concepts of sin and repentance, but with illusion and enlightenment. Turpitude is depravity. Gnostical turpitude is the depravity of denying Stalin's infallibility.

16 Eva Striker was Koestler's childhood friend. She was the artistic director of the Russian China and Glass Trust. The Soviets imprisoned her for 16 months in 1936 for allegedly plotting Stalin's assassination. Some of her prison experiences form the basis for *Darkness at Noon*.

17 In 1998, the Modern Library ranked *Darkness at Noon* number eight on its list of the 100 best English-language novels of the 20th century. George Orwell, who reviewed the book for the New Statesman in 1941, stated:

> Brilliant as this book is as a novel, and a piece of brilliant literature, it is probably most valuable as an interpretation of the Moscow "confessions" by someone with an inner knowledge of totalitarian methods. What was frightening about these trials was not the fact that they happened – for obviously such things are necessary in a totalitarian society – but the eagerness of Western intellectuals to justify them.

References

Arendt, Hannah. (1958). *The Origins of Totalitarianism*. New York: Schocken Books.

Fitzpatrick, Sheila and Michael Geyer (eds.). (2008). *Beyond Totalitarianism: Stalinism and Nazism Compared*. Cambridge: Cambridge University Press.

Friedrich, Carl and Z. K. Brzezinski. (1956). *Totalitarian Dictatorship and Autocracy*. Cambridge: Harvard University Press.

Goldman, Emma. (1923). *My Disillusionment in Russia*. New York: Doubleday, Page & Company.

Gorky, Maxim. (1964). *A Sky-Blue Life and Selected Stories*. New York: Signet.

Kafka, Franz. (1925). *The Trial*. Berlin: Verlag Die Schmiede.

Koestler, Arthur. (1984). *Darkness at Noon*. New York: Bantam.

Laqueur, Walter. (1987). *The Fate of the Revolution Interpretations of Soviet History from 1917 to the Present*. London: Collier Books.

Mandelstam, Nadezhda. (1999). *Hope against Hope: A Memoir*. New York: Modern Library.

Mandelstam, Nadezhda. (2011). *Hope Abandoned*. New York: Random House.

Nabokov, Vladimir. (1959). *Invitation to a Beheading*. New York: Vintage Books.

Orwell, George. (1941). *The Lion and the Unicorn: Socialism and the English Genius*. London: Penguin.

Orwell, George. (1945). *Animal Farm*. London: Secker and Warburg.

Orwell, George. (1954). *Nineteen Eighty-Four*. London: Penguin.

Orwell, George. (1970). *A Collection of Essays*. New York: Mariner.

Pagels, Elaine. (1989). *The Gnostic Gospels*. New York: Random House.

Platonov, Andrei. (2009). *The Foundation Pit. New York: New York Review of Books.*

Pope, Alexander. (1733). *An Essay on Man: Epistle II*. London: J. Wilford.

Rand, Ayn. (2018). *Anthem*. Orinda: Sea Wolf.

Richter, Eugen. (1893). *Pictures of the Socialist Future*. London: S. Sonnenschein & Company, Limited.

Schapiro, Leonard. (1972). *Totalitarianism*. London: The Pall Mall Press.

Shelley, Mary. (1818). *Frankenstein; or, The Modern Prometheus*. London: Lackington, Hughes, Harding, Mavor & Jones.

Shelley, Mary. (1826). *The Last Man*. London: Henry Colburn.

Trotsky, Leon. (2010). *Permanent Revolution and Results and Prospects*. Seattle: Red Letter Press.

von Harbou, Thea (1927). *Metropolis*. New York: Readers Library.

von Mises, Ludwig. (1944). *Omnipotent Government: The Rise of the Total State and Total War*. New Haven:Yale University Press.

Zamyatin, Yevgeny. (1924). *We*. New York: E. P. Dutton.

Zamyatin, Yevgeny. (1967). *The Dragon: Fifteen Stories*. Chicago: University of Chicago Press.

14 Crimes against Humanity

Marxist–Leninists make no bones about their intention to cancel capitalism. They are bloody, bold and resolute. The Soviets, East Europeans, Chinese, North Koreans, Vietnamese, Cambodians and Cubans repressed and killed their opponents during the initial phase of their insurrections, and again thereafter in campaigns to purge communist parties and win wars against economic backwardness. Their terror and repression eventually abated; nonetheless, there are ample grounds for indicting them for crimes against humanity including genocide and ethnic cleansing.[1] International law on crimes against humanity is not settled but clearly involves proscribed acts connected with political, class, social, religious and ethnic "cleansing" (Rosefielde, 2010; UN, 2022).[2]

Marxist–Leninist campaigns intended to "liquidate" the capitalist class (classicide) (Courtois, Werth, Panné, Paczkowski, Bartošek and Margolin, 1999), subjugate the peasantry, ethnic minorities (ethnicide) and purge communist parties (politicide) through violent means constitute clear grounds for considering their actions crimes against humanity under the Treaty of Rome. However, proving guilt to everyone's satisfaction is impossible because there is no consensus about how to assess intent, and mitigating circumstances like "justifiable extermination" (kto kovo?) (Clemens, 2018).[3] If Marxist–Leninists believed their enemies were outside the pale of humanity, then from their perspective Soviet dragon slaying was a virtuous blow for humanity, not a crime against it. Maurice Merleau-Ponty and Jean Paul Sartre broke over this "existentialist" issue (Merleau-Ponty, 1947, 1955).[4]

A staunch defense of ruthless violence against class, political, social, religious and ethnic enemies, supplemented by psychological, sociological, anthropological, philosophical and legal justifications does not preclude indictment (Suny, 2007; Getty, 2000). It is unnecessary to prove that revolutionary Marxist–Leninist repressive policies constituted unpardonable crimes against humanity (Neumayer, 2018; Tismaneanu, 2001).[5] It suffices to show that acts the Treaty of Rome defines as crimes against humanity were committed and may warrant conviction, unless judges find them pardonable on diverse grounds. Those who conclude that Marxist–Leninist actions were unpardonable must acknowledge that communist

DOI: 10.4324/9781003371571-17

avenging angels were unmerciful.[6] Others who feel that Stalin, Mao and Pol Pot justifiably rid the world of vermin are free to disagree (Rosefielde, 2010).

Insurrections

Insurrections are violent attempts to seize power from established authorities and repress counterattacks. Marxist–Leninists insist that they have a duty to liberate the oppressed, and bellow when opponents employ violent methods against them (Waldman, 1958). The double standard reflects the belief that they are righteous, and those who disagree vicious.[7] They write the rules of the game and absolve themselves, even when casualties run into the tens of millions as they did in the Soviet and Chinese cases. Impartial observers are not obliged to exonerate them. The Western literature seeking to decouple socialist ideals from revolutionary Marxist–Leninist praxis has been notably tolerant of communist excesses construing them as pardonable emergency measures forestalling crimes against the proletariat (Furet, 1999).

Warp Speed Industrialization

The same attitude applies to revolutionary Marxist–Leninist breakneck industrialization and forced collectivization against peasants who posed no immediate counterrevolutionary threat, carried out after leaders captured the state and consolidated their power. The Soviet, Chinese and Cambodian revolutionary Marxist–Leninists demanded that the peasantry submit to their control (Chen and Lan, 2007; Chen Yang, 2019; Dikötter, 2010; Li and Yang, 2005; Lin, 1990). The destruction of existing agrarian institutions and imposition of communist economic, political and social authority were nonnegotiable. Peasants had two choices: meekly submit or be beaten into submission.

Marxist–Leninists construe forced collectivization and high-speed industrialization differently. They treat breakneck industrialization as a matter of socialist survival indispensable for averting domestic and foreign anti-communist aggression, winking at the communist party's insistence on totalitarian control.

Stalin's industrial great leap forward during 1928–1937 provides a classic example of how Bolshevism's obsession with totalitarian institutional control over political, social, economic and ethnic affairs needlessly precipitated a humanitarian catastrophe.

The 1926 Soviet census estimated that the All Union population was 147,027,915. There were 26,314,114 urban dwellers and 120,713,801 rural inhabitants (Dubester, 1948). Soviet statisticians reported that 14.8 million citizens were workers and employees, 1.3 million people were collective farmers and 8.5 million were bourgeoisie, traders and kulaks (Narodnoe khoziaistvo za 60 let, 1977, 8). They all were employed by state-owned enterprises and controlled by government institutions. The lion's share of the Soviet population, perhaps as much as 100 million people, however, worked in agriculture on state-owned land without strict communist party supervision. The number of collective farmers doubled, and self-employed halved between 1924 and 1928. Industrial output in 1928 was 80% higher than in 1917 despite the war communist hyper-depression, implying an extraordinary post-recovery growth surge during 1926–1928. The industrial growth spurt included the producer and consumer subsectors and was in the high double-digits (Narodnoe khoziaistvo za 60 let, 1977, 9, 12, 167). If these trends persisted, Bolshevik New Economic Policy (NEP) socialism would have proven its mettle without forced collectivization and central planning.

Stalin, however, was unimpressed with official Soviet industrial growth statistics. He abhorred the idea that the peasantry was beyond the strict purview of Bolshevik power (Adorno, Frenkel-Brunswik, Levinson and Sanford, 1950; Costello, Bowes, Waldman, Tasimi, Stevens and Lilienfeld, 2020) and claimed to foresee economic disaster impending on the horizon if the Soviet mixed state command-market NEP experiment continued (Erlich,1960). Marxists and sympathetic Western analysts attribute Stalin's sense of imminent danger to two fairy tales: one concocted by Leon Trotsky called the "scissors crisis" and the other by Evgeny Preobrazhensky predicting the imminent collapse of Russia's industrial capital stock. Trotsky as head of the Red Army (People's Commissar for Military and Naval Affairs) devoted much of his time to requisitioning (commandeering) food and materials from the peasants. He was leery of the market aspect of Lenin's NEP warning that peasants would hoard foodstuff and frustrate industrialization if supply and demand determined prices. To support his view, Trotsky devised a cock and bull story purporting to explain price fluctuations during the chaotic period of 1917–1923 (Black, 2000),[8] blaming the peasants for hoarding and ignoring Lenin's policy of forced requisitioning and market repression.

Official Soviet statistics of 1921–1928, however, tell the opposite story. Agriculture was not a bottleneck to industrialization during NEP. Industry flourished regardless of fluctuations in agricultural production and marketing. The only legitimate basis for Stalin's apprehensions was that he might have difficulty exploiting the peasantry as much as he desired unless he waged a ruthless war against them.

Preobrazhensky was Trotsky's ally in urging Stalin to end NEP and adopt a planned version of War Communism. He was a Marxist political economist, serving on the Board of the People's Commissariat of Finance, 1924–1927, concerned with imposing taxes on the peasantry to finance industrialization. He had no grasp of microeconomics or engineering to back his claim that Russia's capital stock was on the brink of collapse, or that the peasantry's agrarian surplus had to be confiscated to fund a "primitive capital accumulation" indispensable for Soviet industrialization,[9] but these alarmist ideas provided Stalin's supporters with a pretext for forced agrarian collectivization (Preobrazhensky, 1965, 1973, 1980).[10]

Neither Marx's musings on primitive capital accumulation driven economic growth, nor politics compelled Stalin to exploit the peasantry. He could have persuaded the Politburo to adopt a moderate approach. Marx's *Das Kapital* and contemporary Soviet economic literature provided ample justification. Marx linked the speed of industrialization to the pace of new capital formation in Das Kapital without any agrarian constraint, and the Soviet literature on "teleological planning" proclaimed that synergies created by improved institutions and planning were sufficient to achieve warp speed industrialization (Strumilin, 1928; Fel'dman, 1964; Ellman, 1990; Ofer, 2008; Erlich, 1978; Domar, 1957; Kontorovich, 2013b).[11]

Neoclassical economic theory supports Marx's Das Kapital view of the sources of economic growth and recognizes the validity of synergies. Capital widening, deepening, planning, better labor training and other institutional improvements were sufficient in and of themselves to support rapid industrialization without any significant agricultural drag had the Soviets chosen to go that route (Carr and Robert Davies, 1969; Cheremukhin, Golosov, Guriev and Tsyvinski, 2017).

Vladimir Kontorovich contends that military modernization was the main motive of Stalin's industrialization drive (Kontorovich, 2013a, 2013b Samuelson, 2000).[12] Japanese designs on Primorie and Manchuria were clear by 1930, and Hitler quickly drove home the immanent German threat. Foreign threats did not require forced collectivization.

Forced Collectivization

The Treaty of Rome does not classify crash industrialization as a crime against humanity. Building new factories with better technologies did not starve the peasantry, or necessitate forced labor, terror, purges and political executions. Stalin's collectivization was primarily responsible for these proscribed acts connected with political, class, social and religious cleansing (Rosefielde, 2010).

Forced collectivization, gulag penal labor, terror, purges, mass executions and aspects of the Great Soviet Famine were discretionary political acts (Rozenas and Yuri Zhukov, 2019). Rapid industrialization merely provided an excuse for employing trademark Stalinist "emergency methods." Terror, repression, property confiscation, relocation, incarceration and extrajudicial killings all had been staples of revolutionary communist tactics from day one of the Bolshevik insurrection, widely employed during War Communism and thereafter by Mao Zedong and Pol Pot.

Forced collectivization was not inadvertent. The Bolsheviks had begun laying the groundwork in the mid-1920s against their erstwhile peasant allies as part of the Trotsky-Preobrazhensky-Stalin campaign to scrap NEP for a planned version of War Communist requisitioning and rationing (Lenin, 1920; Storella and Sokolov, 2013).[13] Anti-NEP activists were averse to relying on market incentives to stimulate the sale of peasant grain surpluses to USSR cities. They were opposed to, suspicious of and ignorant of competitive market mechanisms. In 1928, the Politburo – including Nikolai Bukharin voted to supplement normal trade with forced requisitioning. Although characterized as an extraordinary measure, the leadership treated it as a routine class-war political operation, triggering a vicious cycle. The peasants curtailed production, and the Politburo retaliated by intensifying forced requisitioning in the winter of 1929.

The Bolsheviks justified their political assault on the peasantry by insisting that exploiting the peasantry was essential for achieving rapid industrialization (primitive socialist accumulation). They portrayed rich kulaks as enemies of socialism, middle peasants as frenemies and poor peasants as village proletarian allies.[14] This agrarian class division was mostly fiction. Enterprising peasants prospered under NEP, but this did not mean that kulaks became rich by exploiting poor peasants. Official documents make clear that the poorer peasants, far from resenting the kulaks, generally regarded them as leaders and depended on them for help in times of adversity.

Stalin did not care (Service, 2006). He gave the signal to attack in September 1928. The speed and scope of collectivization quickly accelerated. The Five-Year Plan as approved in April–May 1929 envisaged 5 million peasant households collectivized by 1932–1933. The figure doubled by November, and doubled again in December 1930. Stalin decreed collectivization's completion in Ukraine by the autumn of 1930 and in the other main grain areas by the spring of 1931.[15] At the same time, the kulak's plight steadily worsened culminating in a decision to liquidate kulaks as a class (classicide) (Narodnoe khoziaistvo SSSR za 70 Let, 1987, 35).

The party claimed most peasants favored collectivization, and assured everyone that Stalin's strategy would increase agricultural production despite kulak opposition, but this was a false narrative. Activists from the cities (Twenty-Five Thousanders) and OGPU men forced peasants into collective farms (kolkhozy) with economically disastrous consequences (Viola, 1989).[16] Yefim Yevdokimov played a major role in organizing and supervising the arrest, incarceration in gulag (Scherer and Michael Jakobson, 1993) and mass executions of peasants.[17] He oversaw the confiscation of kulak and sub-kulak property and deported peasants wholesale. Seven million abandoned their households and fled to the cities. Two million died prematurely.

In mid-1929, only about 5 million peasants resided on collective farms. The number "spontaneously" increased to more than 70 million by March 1930. Peasant resistance to Stalin's aggression took various forms, including local insurrections and the mass slaughter of livestock. Official figures given in 1934 showed a loss of 26.6 million head of cattle (42.6% of the country's total) and 63.4 million sheep (65.1% of the total). On March 2, 1930, Stalin reversed field, blaming local officials for overzealousness (being "dizzy with success") (Stalin, 1930). Forty to 50 million peasants deserted kolkhozy shortly thereafter.

The remaining kolkhozy held the best land and most of the surviving livestock allowing Stalin to impose large grain quotas and crippling fines on them. Peasants who returned to their pre-collectivization villages enjoyed a short respite. Twenty-Five Thousanders and OGPU men soon forcibly resettled them anew on collective farms surrounded by barbed wire (Solzhenitsyn, 1975).

The Bolsheviks drove about one-quarter of a million Kazak nomad herders into permanent settlements. Some managed to escape over the Chinese border. One to two million Kazaks perished (Pianciola, 2001; Cameron, 2018; Ellman, 2007; Kindler 2018).

The immediate result of these measures was a catastrophic decline in agricultural output. The government responded by basing its obligatory kolkhoz grain deliveries not on actual production but on the estimated size of the crop in the fields (biological yield). This increased the peasant burden by 40%. The obligation was ruthlessly enforced. As a result, over the winter of 1932–1933, a major famine swept the grain-growing areas. Four to five million died in Ukraine (Rosefielde, 2021, 37–41; Naumenko, 2021; Applebaum 2017; Danilov, 2011; Ellman, 2007; Meslé, Vallin and Evgeny Andreev, 2013; Rudnytskyi, Levchuk, Wolowyna, Shevchuk and Kovbasiuk, 2015; Lewin, 1968), and another 2–3 million in the North Caucasus and the Lower Volga area (Cameron, 2018; Conquest, 1986; Davies and Wheatcroft, 2004; Wheatcroft, 2013; Wheatcroft and Garnaut, 2013).[18] Both the dekulakization terror of 1930–1932 and the terror-famine of 1932–1933 were particularly lethal in Ukraine and the Ukrainian-speaking area of the Kuban, accompanied by a series of repressive measures against the Ukrainian cultural, political and social leaderships. During this period about 1.7 million tons (1.5 million metric tons) of grain were exported, enough to have provided two pounds (one kilogram) a head to 15 million people over three months. There is no doubt that the Stalin leadership knew what was happening and used famine as a weapon against the peasantry (Ellman, 2007.

A census taken in January 1937, but only revealed in 1990, showed a population of 162 million. The Soviet demographers had forecast 177 million. The population deficit, including a decline in births, was thus 15 million. Reliable demographic data and estimates show that 11.6 million of this shortfall were excess deaths from all sources including collectivization, terror, execution, gulag and mass deportations. Some experts believe that premature deaths attributable to deportation and famine explain at least 10 million of these casualties (Rosefielde, 2010). Most Great Terror executions occurred in 1937 after the completion of the1937 Census, January 1937. Many of these excess deaths qualify for consideration as crimes against humanity under the Rome Statute. The exact number is open to dispute because of the dubious reliability of Soviet statistics, disagreement about Stalin's political intent, the pertinence of natural factors and the merit of various other mitigating circumstances. Smoke obscures the size of the fire, but does not nullify evidence of reckless endangerment,[19] and crimes against humanity (classicide, politicide, sociocide and ethnocide).

Great Terror

Marxist–Leninists are not squeamish about terror and sometimes openly advocate its use as a legitimate instrument of class struggle (Moore, 1954; Moore, Wolff and Marcuse, 1965; Trotsky, 2017). They are not anarchists seeking to spark spontaneous revolution (Yarmolinsky, 2016).[20] They carefully target victims for political purposes. They threaten opponents with demotion, dismissal, deprivation of civil liberties, interrogations, banishment, corporal punishment, incarceration, torture, starvation, executions and murder. They also may employ terror tactics to mobilize supervisory, managerial and labor effort in the Party's war against economic backwardness. Terror in all these senses was permissible and even imperative for Bolsheviks depending on the context. Protecting socialism was the highest good for revolutionary communists and many of their Western supporters. It justified extreme measures against opponents within the Communist Party (Moore, Wolff and Marcuse, 1965).

Marxist–Leninists did not want to believe party members could betray the revolution but were conscious of the possibility. They were sensitive to the risks of subversion, sabotage, wrecking, espionage, factionalism, military putsch and palace coup d'état opening the door for Stalin to use terror as an instrument for preserving his power. Most revolutionary communists and Western sympathizers supported terror measures to daunt and eradicate "counter-revolutionaries" within the Soviet Communist Party during the 1930s. They applauded Stalin's use of purges, judicial and extrajudicial killings and nonlethal terror to subdue adversaries within party ranks. There was no open vocal opposition to this terror within the USSR, but some foreign socialists abroad were critical. Leon Trotsky's supporters considered Trotsky's murder and Stalin's judicial mass executions of Old Bolsheviks crimes against the revolution tantamount to crimes against humanity (Trotsky, 1937; Levine, 1960).[21]

Stalin had always been a master of political trench warfare against his Communist Party rivals. He was not heir apparent when Lenin died in 1923 (Lih, 1991),[22] but outfoxed and subdued the Old Bolsheviks: Leon Trotsky, Nikolai Bukharin, Grigory Zinoviev, Lev Kamenev and Georgy Pyatakov to become the party's undisputed leader by 1928.

The assassination of Sergei Kirov, First Secretary of the Leningrad City Committee of the All-Union Communist Party by Leonid Nikolaev,[23] on December 1, 1934 served as a justification for repressing party dissidents with lethal means (Conquest, 1989; Figes, 2007). Stalin promptly had Vasilii Ulrikh secretly try Nikolayev. Ulrikh convicted and executed Nikolayev on December 1934 (Pietrow, 2012).[24] Stalin's role in Kirov's murder remains controversial (Yakovlev, 1991; Getty, 1993).[25]

Kirov's death served as a pretext for escalated political repression, the Moscow Trials and Great Terror. The Kremlin portrayed Nikolaev as a Zinovyevite terrorist. Stalin jailed Zinovyev, Kamenev and their followers for inciting Kirov's murder. Andrey Zhdanov repressed most of Kirov's supporters in Leningrad.

Over the ensuing four years, Stalin waged an intense campaign against secret enemies of the people.[26] In August 1936, the NKVD tried Zinovyev and Kamenev for terrorism (followed by two similar trials in 1937 and 1938). The court found them and 14 accomplices guilty and had them shot. Nikolai Yezhov (1895–1940) prosecuted a new terrorist group,[27] allegedly headed by Grigory Pyatakov in January 1937. He charged them with espionage, sabotage, treason and terrorism.

Stalin's old ally and Politburo colleague Sergo Ordzhonikidze committed suicide on February 18, 1937.[28] The February–March 1937 plenum of the Central Committee arrested of Bukharin and Rykov. The terror reached its climax during 1937–1938. Extralegal tribunals (NKVD troikas) sentenced hundreds of thousands of people to death in absentia. The mass graves of the victims remained secret until the late 1980s.

Stalin ruthlessly purged the Communist Party. He arrested 115 of the 139 full and candidate members of the Central Committee elected at the 17th Party Congress in 1934. He decimated the leadership of the Leningrad and Ukrainian Communist Parties and may have had more than a million party members executed.[29] Many of those treated less harshly died in gulag labor camps.

Stalin purged the industrial, engineering and economic cadres. The army suffered heavy losses. He had eight senior generals, including Marshal Mikhail Tukhachevsky arrested in May and June 11, 1937.[30] Over the next two years, almost all their senior colleagues were arrested, tried in secret and executed including 3 of the 5 marshals, 13 of the 15 army commanders, 50 of the 57 corps commanders and 6 of the 7 fleet admirals. The officer corps lost about half its members.

Stalin also arrested and executed academics and literary figures like Osip Mandelshtam (husband of Nadezhda Mandelshtam), Boris Pilnyak and Isaak Babel. Many died in gulag. More than 1.2 million people may have perished during the Yezhovshchina (Rosefielde, 2010; Kuromiya, 2007; Homkes, 2004).[31] Disputable estimates of gulag populations and concentration camp mortality rates obscure the death toll (Rosefielde, 2010).

Stalin indicted Bukharin, Rykov and the former police commissar Yagoda in the third Moscow Trial, March 1938. They confessed to several murders, including those of Kirov and the writer Maxim Gorky, as well as to treason, espionage and terrorism. Yezhov accused Bukharin of plotting Lenin's murder in 1918, but he did not confess. The only survivors of Lenin's last Politburo in 1939 were Stalin and Trotsky. Stalin had Trotsky killed the following year.

The Great Purge and Terror retarded economic growth during 1937–1940 (Katz, 1975)[32] and dislocated society. Stalin arrested Yezhov in 1939 and had him shot in 1940. Lavrenty Beria took on the NKVD/MVD leadership. He institutionalized purges thereafter at a sustainable rate of "classicide," "politicide," "sociocide" and "ethnocide" until Stalin's death and Beria's execution in 1953 (Knight, 1996).[33] Beria was responsible for the Katyn massacre (Ellman, 2002; Paul, 2010),[34] the infamous execution of 22,000 people in Soviet annexed Poland on March 5, 1940 (Brown, 2011, 140).[35]

The Great Terror, its harbingers and echoes claimed millions of lives. Executions more narrowly defined as NKVD shooting of "political" victims of Soviet repression are approximately 1 million.

Ethnic Cleansing

Ethnic cleansing is a euphemism that entered the English lexicon during the Balkan Wars of the 1990s to describe the repression, imprisonment, expulsion and killing of ethnic minorities. The term includes systematic forced deportation of ethnic, racial, political and religious groups from their homelands and the compulsory eradication of their language and culture. The Rome Statute classifies ethnic, political and religious deportation as crimes against humanity, aggravated by the destruction of property, rape, murder and genocide.

Soviet communists are indictable on many counts during 1930–1953. Stalin culturally repressed and deported peasant enemies of the workers (dekulakization) and entire nationalities (Soviet Koreans in 1937), replacing them with new settlers (Chang, 2018; Chong, 2002.[36] The deportations included citizens from other countries under Moscow's control. Forced migrations involved at least 6 million people (Rosefielde, 2010, 83; Ellman, 2002; Werth, 2004, 73). Stalin deported 1.8 million kulaks in 1930–1931, and 1 million peasants and ethnic minorities in 1932–1939. He resettled 3.5 million in 1940–1952 (Ellman, 2002, 1159).

Soviet archives document 390,000 kulak deportation deaths in the 1930s (Pohl, 1997, 58, 1999). They reveal 400,000 resettlement fatalities in the 1940s (Pohl, 1997, 148). Nicolas Werth puts total deaths at 1–1.5 million (Werth, 2004, 73). The Ukraine and the European Parliament recognize the deportation of the Crimean Tatars and Chechen and Ingush as genocides (Rosefielde, 2010, 84). Boris Yeltsin, passed the law in April 1991 "On the Rehabilitation of Repressed Peoples" denouncing all mass deportations as "Stalin's policy of defamation and genocide" (Perovic, 2018).

Stalin's Baltic States deportations killed 50,000, and the expulsion of Germans from Eastern Europe claimed another 300,000–360,000 lives. In 1944, Beria accused the Balkars, Karachays, Chechens, Ingush, Crimean Tatars, Kalmyks, Pontic Greeks and Volga Germans of anti-Sovietism. He deported them to Soviet Central Asia (Montefiore, 2014).

Stalin ethnically cleansed hapless minorities in 1928–1953. He deported and assailed the Poles (1939–1945), Kola Norwegians (1940–1942), Romanians (1941–1953), Estonians, Latvians and Lithuanians (1941–1949), Volga Germans (1941–1945), Ingrian Finns (1929–1939), Finns in Karelia (1940–1944), Crimean Tatars, Crimean Greeks (1944), Caucasus Greeks (1949–1950), Kalmyks, Balkars, Crimean Italians, Karachays, Meskhetian Turks, Karapapaks, Far East Koreans (1937) and Chechens and Ingush (1944).

Internments and Forced Labor

Many nations wrongfully incarcerated citizens and foreign captives in prisons and concentration camps and exploited their labor during the 20th century, claiming that forced labor expedited rehabilitation. The slogan at the Auschwitz gate read "Arbeit Macht Frei" (work will set you free). Bolsheviks and their Western supporters stoutly denied any wrongful Soviet incarceration and abusive forced labor. They rejected allegations that Moscow committed crimes against humanity and the proletariat (Berg, 1985). The record belies the denials.

Official, but suspect Soviet archival data report that authorities sent 18 million prisoners to state concentration camps (gulag) from 1930 to 1953.[37] One and a half to 1.7 million perished (Bacon, 1944; Healey, 2018; Wheatcroft, 1999; Rosefielde, 2010, 77).[38] The categories and numbers of people incarcerated and mistreated (excluding enemy prisoners of war) are extraordinary and indictable as crimes against humanity under the Rome Statute. Communists can claim mitigating political, economic and social circumstances, but cannot dismiss the colossal scale of incarcerations and excess deaths.

There is an enormous discrepancy between the selectively released Soviet archival gulag inmate data, the scale of repression indicated by the demographic data (20 million excess deaths 1929–1953) (Rosefielde, 2010)[39] and the testimonial literature that is unlikely to be resolved any time soon.

On the eve of World War II, Soviet archives indicate a combined camp and colony population upwards of 1.6 million in 1939 (Gulaga, 2004). Anne Applebaum estimates that 1.2 to 1.5 million people were in gulag system's prison camps and colonies when the war started (Applebaum, 2012; Rosefielde, 2007). The testimonial evidence puts the figure at 10 million (Rosefielde, 2010, 69).

After the German invasion of Poland that marked the start of World War II in Europe, the Soviet Union occupied and annexed eastern parts of the Second Polish Republic. In 1940 it occupied Estonia, Latvia, Lithuania, Bessarabia (now the Republic of Moldova) and Bukovina. According to some estimates, hundreds of thousands of Polish citizens and inhabitants from other annexed lands, regardless of their ethnic origin, were arrested and sent to the gulag camps (Proch, 1978, 146).

The USSR captured approximately 300,000 Polish prisoners of war during and after the "Polish Defensive War." Almost all of the captured officers and a large number of ordinary soldiers were murdered or sent to gulag (Chodakiewicz, 2004).

The gulag system expanded dramatically before World War II. Forced labor provided 46.5% of the nation's nickel, 76% of its tin, 40% of its cobalt, 40.5% of its chrome-iron ore, 60% of its gold and 25.3% of its timber (Mikhailovna Ivanova, 2000).

Gulag quickly switched to the production of arms and supplies for the army after WW II began. In 1940s, the NKVD focused most of its energy on railroad construction, using forced labor in remote corners of the Soviet space (Mikhailovna Ivanova, 2000).

After World War II, the number of inmates in prison camps and colonies excluding prisoners of war rose sharply, reaching approximately 2.5 million people by the early 1950s (about 1.7 million of whom were in camps) based on incomplete official statistics. The real figure including prisoners of war was many times higher, approximately 11 million. Some prisoners of war remained imprisoned in gulag until 1959.[40] CIA estimates based on "national technical means" put the figure between 2.5 and 4 million in the early 1960s.[41]

When the war in Europe ended in May 1945, the USSR repatriated approximately 2 million former Russian citizens. Stalin treated many surviving Red Army soldiers imprisoned by the Germans as traitors (Order No. 270) and sent them to gulag (Zemskov, 1990).

Eyewitness testimony and US Defense Intelligence Agency "national technical means" suggest that both the prisoner count and excess deaths are significantly underestimated. There is no reason to accept selectively vetted and reported former Soviet statistics from restricted Soviet archives, but those sympathetic with communist statistics insist on it.

At the behest of President Vladimir Putin, the Russian Supreme Court on December 29, 2021 ordered the dismantling of Memorial International, the primary institution documenting Stalin's atrocities.[42] The prospect for unearthing the full truth about gulag populations and killings from closed Kremlin sources is dim.

Reign of Terror, Treadmill of Reform and Market Communism

The feeding frenzy that gripped revolutionary Marxist–Leninists in a protracted Bolshevik Reign of Terror during 1917–1953, persecuting, imprisoning and killing anyone who stood in their way subsided soon after Stalin died ushering in the "Thaw" and treadmill of Soviet economic reform (Ehrenburg, 1954; Schroeder, 1979).[43] Some observers may be tempted to exonerate Marxist-Leninism, placing blame entirely on Stalin's shoulders for the crimes against humanity perpetrated under his watch, but the evidence is counterindicative. The Maoist and Pol Pot revolutionary Marxist–Leninist experiences point to the opposite inference. Revolutionary communists during the Great Famine of 1959–1962 and Cultural Revolution in China and the Killing Fields era in Cambodia committed the same crimes against humanity.

China: Liquidating Sun Yat-sen's Republican Order

Mao Zedong as the leader of the Communist Party of China (CPC) established the People's Republic of China (PRC) on September 21, 1949 after vanquishing Chiang Kaishek in a 22-year civil war. Unlike Lenin, he was not immediately plunged into an internecine military struggle. The Communists had won the civil war and seized control of the national government. Nonetheless, Mao quickly dismantled the social underpinning of Sun Yat-sen's republican order. He nationalized the means of production, expropriated large landholders and economically, politically, socially and religiously cleansed the system (classicide, politicide and sociocide). He subjugated Tibet and ethnically cleansed it (Choesan, 2015).[44] Although, Marxist–Leninist sympathizers contend that the early years of the PRC were constructive and benign, credible scholars take the opposite position. They describe the era as "calculated terror and systematic violence," marked by uprooting traditional social relations, mass indoctrination and "death quotas" that contributed to 5 million premature deaths between 1949 and 1958 (Dikötter, 2013; Li, 2006).[45] There were mass repression campaigns and public executions targeting Kuomintang remnants, businesspersons, ex-employees of Western companies, intellectuals and vestiges of the rural gentry (Mosher, 1992). The US State Department estimated that as many as 1.9 million people perished in land reform and anti-counterrevolutionary crackdowns (Shalom, 1984, 24). Mao himself boasted that 700,000 people were executed during 1949–1953 (Chang and Halliday, 2011, 337);[46] a figure estimated to be far higher by those taking account of obligations placed on every village to execute at least one landlord (MacFarquhar and John K. Fairbank, 1987). They put the death toll between 2 and 5 million (Courtois et al., 1999, 479; Rummel, 1994), excluding an additional 1.5 million laogai (gulag type) lethal forced labor excess deaths (Short, 1999; Wu, 1992, 99; Seymour and Anderson, 1998).[47] Mao acknowledged a significant portion of these mass homicides (Li, 2005), but rejected any allegation that they were crimes against humanity (Brown, 2004).

The People's Republic during this consolidation period was indictable under the Rome Treaty for Crimes against Humanity, but contemporary China specialists are disinclined to prosecute.

Mao's Great Famine

Mao began agitating for collectivization in 1953, preparing the way for the Great Leap Forward at the end of 1957 and the Great Famine of 1958–1962 (Dikötter, 2010). The strategy repeated Stalin's forced collectivization drive in 1928–1933 and crash industrialization program. He replaced local political, economic and social institutions with Communist Party governance, state ownership, cadre farm management and collective peasant labor.[48] The power shift was coercive. Peasants preferred indigenous local government (without large landowner domination). They wanted to retain private farms and family agrarian management. They disliked living communally with shared personal property. They opposed communist officials dictating crop, labor and income policy and resisted the suppression of their culture. Mao was determined to cleanse the peasantry's politics, economy and society and violently bent peasants to his will for the sake of Marxist–Leninist progress. He took the opportunity to purge the Communist Party at the same time (Dikötter, 2010).[49]

Chinese peasants, like their Soviet counterparts, had no voice in their fate. If they disobeyed, Mao beat them into submission and subservience. They were expendables in Mao's transformation of the countryside supporting crash industrialization. Mao flogged and starved the peasantry to augment Beijing's power, not for their own good as he claimed (Dikötter, 2010).

He did not need to do any of these things. Communist domination of the peasantry did not require collectivization. Agrarian prosperity did not depend on communalization. Rapid industrialization did not require food exports and mass peasant starvation. Mao's Great Famine and policies were crimes against humanity precisely because Chinese authorities placed their will to power above other people's basic human rights.

China's rural population in 1960 was 558 million people.[50] Hundreds of millions were victims of class, political and social cleansing during 1958–1962. There were innumerable atrocities, including the forced flight of the Dalai Lama from Lhasa. The excess death total captures the enormity of Mao's crimes against humanity. The lion's share is attributable to Mao's Great Famine (Meng, Qian and Yared, 2015; Dikötter, 2010),[51] but there were numerous other contributing factors including Communist Party purges and executions. Credible estimates range from 30 to 55 million (Rosefielde, 2010). Roderick Macfarquhar and Douglas Fairbanks prefer the lower bound (Macfarquhar and Fairbanks, 1987).

Jisheng Yang authoritatively asserts in *Tombstone (Mu Bei)* that 36 million died of hunger (Yang, 2012). Frank Dikötter rejects both estimates putting the figure at 45 million (Dikötter, 2010). Reliable data therefore substantiate that as much as half of China's population in 1958–1962 were victims of nonlethal crimes against humanity (cleansings) under the Rome Statute and between 5% and 8% of the rural population was killed, mostly by starvation.

Mao's Cultural Revolution

Mao Zedong's Great Proletarian Cultural Revolution of 1966–1976 was a complex historical event. It sought to revitalize Marxist–Leninist zeal for a communist pure land based on worker-party-PLA enterprise management (MacFarquhar and Schoenhals, 2006),[52] purged of capitalist self-seeking (capitalist roaders), while simultaneously eradicating anti-Mao elements in the Communist Party and state bureaucracy (Wheelwright and McFarlane, 1971; Wemheuer, Walder, Unger, Andreas and Wu, 2016). These goals were laudable from a Marxist–Leninist perspective, but their implementation caused indictable human rights crimes to Mao's opponents.

Red Guards in collaboration with the Maoist faction of the CPC confronted, harassed, intimidated, killed suspected capitalist roaders (Chong, 2002)[53] and had them exiled and interred in laogai and laojiao, reeducation labor camps (Wu, 1992; Thurston, 1987. Three-in-one committees organized struggle sessions to badger and bully opponents until they acknowledged their folly and embraced Mao's policies (Lipman and Harrell, 1990).[54]

The combination of militant leadership and terror made the Cultural Revolution doubly radical. Mao not only concluded that persuasion, compromise and consensus building were inadequate tools for building communism, he insisted that unrelenting class war and worker self-struggle were indispensable for saving socialism from capitalist roaders.[55] Perhaps, he was right. If so, however, it seems that it will take many more crimes against humanity for Marxist-Leninism to succeed.

Frank Dikötter estimates the total number of people killed during the Cultural Revolution of 1962–1976 as 1.5–2 million. Most fell victim to top-down purges in 1968–1971, after the Red Guard suppression (Dikötter, 2017; Walder, 2014).[56] Millions were sent to laogai or laojiao non-penal forced labor assignments in the countryside. There were millions of wrecked lives, but the death toll was mild compared to the Great Leap Forward because terror-starvation was unnecessary to fulfill the Cultural Revolution's mission. Beyond the homicides, a 5.1% fall in GDP during 1966–1968 blighted Chinese lives.

The revolutionary Marxist–Leninist–Stalinist mindset generated an enormous number of indictable crimes against humanity in the Soviet Union during 1917–1953 and China during 1949–1976. The unreliability and incompleteness of the data preclude precise comparisons. For example, there are no publicly available Chinese archival documents and demographic records verifying official secret police executions, laogai, laojiao and ethnic cleansing excess deaths. Estimates exist. Chang and Halliday surmise that 27 million people died in prisons and labor camps during Mao's rule (Chang and Halliday, 2011, 338).[57] Tibetan leaders claim that over 17% of Tibetans have been victims of Chinese genocide,[58] but the figure is disputable (Zavel, 2001).

Nonetheless, the evidence firmly demonstrates that Mao revolutionary communist policies claimed 35–50 million lives. Terror-starvation was the largest component, with executions (including nonjudicial shootings) and lethal forced labor accounting for significant shares of the carnage, followed by a smaller number of ethnic cleansing victims. Lesser crimes against humanity involving class, political, social, religious and ethnic cleansing run into the hundreds of millions.

Pol Pot's Killing Fields

Pol Pot (Saloth Sâr) was a leading member of Cambodia's communist movement, the Khmer Rouge, from 1963 until 1997. He was a revolutionary Marxist–Leninist and a Khmer nationalist, serving as the General Secretary of the Communist Party of Kampuchea from 1963 to 1981. Aided by the Việt Cộng militia and North Vietnamese troops, Pol Pot's Khmer Rouge forces controlled all of Cambodia by 1975. He governed Cambodia as General Secretary of the Communist Party of Kampuchea and Prime Minister of Democratic Kampuchea between 1975 and 1979. Pol Pot met Mao Zedong in the mid-1960s. The Great Leap Forward and Cultural Revolution inspired him. He began implementing Mao's ideas immediately upon becoming the Prime Minister on April 14, 1975, transforming Cambodia into a one-party state. His government forcibly relocated the urban population to the countryside to work on makeshift collective farms. It nationalized the means of production, criminalized business and entrepreneurship, repressed opponents, obliterated class and social distinctions, ordered rural Cambodia communalized, abolished money, preached complete egalitarianism and compelled citizens to wear the same black clothing, but neglected to timely erect essential supportive economic institutions.

Pol Pot terrorized the population into storming the future, compelling them to construct ill-conceived irrigation networks under slave-like conditions as a platform for Mao-style warp speed industrialization (Margolin, 1999). The boundless enthusiasm of the peasants, commune leaders and zealots guided by central planning (never constructed) would determine everything in Pol Pot's view, not the machinations of bureaucrats, technocrats and intellectuals (Margolin, 1999, 801).[59] The reality was mass starvation. Pol Pot compelled villagers to increase production to three tons of rice per hectare (Chandler, 1992), despite the fact that production levels had remained stable at around one ton since 1970. The size of rice fields in the rich northwest tripled by clearing massive tracts of land. Colossal irrigation projects attempted to make the new paddies cultivable in a country with a small population, abundant rainfall and an annual flood. The goal was to achieve three rice harvests a year. The workday was 11 hours, but during village competitions, 18-hour days became the norm.

The results were calamitous. In less than six months, the surface area farmed fell by 50%, and large parts of the countryside were desolate. Poor planning and execution turned the irrigation drive into a fiasco. Although some dikes, canals and dams continue in use today, many vanished in the first flood. Other projects caused the water to flow in the wrong direction or created ponds that silted up in a matter of months. Hydraulic engineers were powerless to stop the waste. Occasionally, the Khmer Rouge sought advice from their experts, but results more often than not were unsatisfactory. Authorities eliminated dikes dividing rice fields to make every field exactly one hectare, even when it impaired productivity.

These absurdities were just the tip of the iceberg. Pol Pot's dystopic economy was a travesty of productive science. Transferring industrial labor from urban factories to villages or Maoist agro-industrial communes had a devastating impact on both industrial and agricultural productivity. Quixotic public works projects subtracted value and forewent opportunities for alternative value-adding enterprise. Mass executions destroyed labor power and human capital. The model was catastrophic, culminating in a ghastly famine and lethal destitution. After three and a half years of revolutionary Marxist–Leninist–Maoism, Cambodia was prostrate.[60]

Mass killings (Killing Fields) of perceived government opponents (Pran and Kim DePaul, 1999; Ngor, 2003; Cook, 2005), coupled with inhumane labor conditions, malnutrition and poor medical care, killed between 1.5 and 2.1 million people (Chandler, 1992; Sliwinski, 1995; Maddison, 2003, 168),[61] approximately a quarter of Cambodia's population, a process later termed as the Cambodian Genocide. President Lon Nol put the Khmer Rouge holocaust at 2.5 million; Pen Sovan, the former secretary general of the People's Revolutionary Party of Kampuchea (PRPK), which assumed power on January 7, 1979 cited a figure of 3.1 million victims (echoing the Vietnamese official position) (Rosefielde, 2010, 118).[62] Marek Sliwinski found that 33.9% of men and 15.7% of women died prematurely during 1975–1979 (Sliwinski, 1995), suggesting that shooting and executions caused much of the killing. Thirty-four percent of young males aged 20–30, 40% of men aged 30–40 and 54% of people of both sexes over age 60 perished.

Quantitative studies also indicate that the resettlement of city dwellers in villages and agro-communes caused no more than 400,000 deaths. Executions account for roughly 500,000 murders. Henri Locard puts prison killings between 400,000 and 600,000 (Locard, 1996). Silwinski estimates 1 million executions and more than 900,000 terror-starvation deaths (Sliwinski, 1995, 82). After four years of purges and turmoil, Vietnam invaded Cambodia in December 1978, toppling Pol Pot and installing a rival Marxist-Leninist government in 1979.

The Khmer Rouge blame the Vietnamese for their crimes against humanity (Chandler, 1992, 171–172), not Marxist–Leninist–Maoism. The real explanation is self-evident and does not include a desire to rid the world of Cambodians.

Bolshevik, Maoist and Pol Pot revolutionary communists and lesser imitators in Eastern Europe and Cuba were bloody, bold and resolute.

Notes

1 Crimes against humanity have not yet been codified in a dedicated treaty of international law, unlike genocide and war crimes. The 1998 Rome Statute establishing the International Criminal Court (Rome Statute) is the document that reflects the latest consensus among the international community on this matter.

2 Rome Statute of the International Criminal Court. Article 7. Crimes against Humanity.

For the purpose of this Statute, "crime against humanity" means any of the following acts when committed as part of a systematic attack directed against any civilian population, with knowledge of the attack:

Murder;

Extermination;

Enslavement;

Deportation or forcible transfer of population;

Imprisonment or other severe deprivation of physical liberty in violation of international law;

Torture;

Rape, sexual slavery, enforced prostitution, forced pregnancy, enforced sterilization;

Persecution against any identifiable group on political, racial, national, ethnic, cultural, religious, gender;

Enforced disappearance of persons;

The crime of apartheid;

Other inhumane acts intentionally causing great suffering.

For the purpose of paragraph 1:

"Attack directed against any civilian population" means a course of conduct involving the multiple commission of acts against any civilian population;

Elements of the crime

According to Article 7 (1) of the Rome Statute, crimes against humanity do not need to be linked to an armed conflict and can occur in peacetime, similar to the crime of genocide. That same Article provides a definition of the crime that contains the following main elements:

A physical element, which includes the commission of "any of the following acts":

Murder;

Extermination;

Enslavement;

Deportation or forcible transfer of population;

Imprisonment;

Torture;

Grave forms of sexual violence;

Persecution;

Enforced disappearance of persons;

The crime of apartheid;

Other inhumane acts.

3 "Kto kovo? The term means "kill or be killed." Lenin claimed that the principle was the essence of politics.

4 Merleau-Ponty distanced himself from revolutionary Marxism and sharply criticized Sartre for "ultra-bolshevism."

5 The literature blurs "classicide" by equating condemnation of Marxist–Leninist violence with anti-communism, and by rejecting the suggestion that Nazism and Marxist-Leninism were filial totalitarian phenomena.

6 The Angels of Vengeance, or Avenging Angels, were the first angels created by God. Traditionally, there are 12 Avenging Angels, and they are sometimes associated with the role of punishing wrongdoers.

7 The instinct to demonize, denigrate and dehumanize other people is not a Marxist–Leninist monopoly.

8 The Scissors Crisis is the name for an incident in early 1923 Soviet history during the New Economic Policy when there was a widening gap ("price scissors") between industrial and agricultural prices, misinterpreted as peasant assault against Soviet authority.

9 Marx claimed that the capital needed to jump start capitalism was accumulated from the surplus labor value of colonials. Preobrazhensky contented without explanation that socialist industrialization likewise depended on confiscating property from nonsocialists. The claim is false. Technological progress is the principal source of economic growth.

10 Preobrazhensky argued that the government had to commandeer peasant grain beyond what subsistence norms to industrialize the Soviet Union. He called this the "agrarian surplus."

Stalin executed Preobrazhensky on July 13, 1937. Mikhail Gorbachev posthumously rehabilitated him in 1988.

11 Stanislav Strumilin, G. Pytatakov, Valerian Kuibyshev and Grigory Fel'dman were prominent members of the "teleological" planning school. Kuibyshev chaired the Supreme Council of the National Economy from 1926 to 1930, and he directed Gosplan, 1930–1934. Grigory Alexandrovich Fel'dman (1884–1958) was a Russian mathematician and economist. He was an electrical engineer and worked at Gosplan from 1923 to 1931.

12 Vitaly Shlykov concurs. Personal conversation with Shlykov and Samuelson in Stockholm.

13 Lenin advocated a worker and peasant alliance (smychka) during war communism. Bolshevism was for the toiling masses, worker and peasant alike. In his last writings, particularly, "On Cooperation" and "Better Fewer, But Better" he argued that the smychka meant gaining the peasants' trust by recognizing and meeting their needs.

14 There were a small class of rich peasants, who owned 60–80 acres (25–35 hectares) of land. They were liquidated by party detachments in 1918.

15 *Narodnoe khoziaistvo SSSR za 70 Let, Iubileinyi statisticheskii ezhegodnik*, Finansy I Statistika, Moscow 1987, p. 35.

16 Twenty-five-thousanders was a collective name for the frontline workers who "volunteered" to help improve kolkhoz performance in early 1930. The OGPU (Joint State Political Directorate) was the main Soviet secret police organization (1923–1934).

17 Yefim Georgievich Yevdokimov (1891–1939) was a Soviet politician and member of the Cheka and OGPU. He was a key figure in the Red Terror, the Great Purge and dekulakization that saw millions of people executed and deported. Stalin had him arrested on November 9, 1938 and executed in February 1940. Khrushchev rehabilitated him posthumously in 1956.

18 The 1933 Ukrainian famine killed as many as 2.6 million people out of a population of 32 million. Historians offer three main explanations: weather, economic policies and genocide. Available data do not support weather as the main explanation: 1931

and 1932 weather predicts harvest roughly equal to the 1924–1929 average; weather explains up to 8.1% of excess deaths. Collectivization of agriculture significantly increased famine mortality. It explains up to 52% of excess deaths.

19 The offense of recklessly engaging in conduct that creates a substantial risk of serious physical injury or death to another person.

20 On August 25–26, 1879, on the anniversary of his coronation, the 22-member Executive Committee of Narodnaya Volya resolved to assassinate Alexander II, hoping to precipitate a revolution.

21 On August 20, 1940, Trotsky was attacked with an ice-axe in his study by Spanish-born NKVD agent Ramón Mercader and died the following day. Mercader was convicted of the murder, spent the next 20 years in a Mexican prison and was released in 1960. Alexander Shelepin on Leonid Brezhnev behalf presented Mercader with the Order of Lenin, the Gold Star of the Hero, and the title of the Hero of the Soviet Union "for the special deed."

22 Lenin warned the party that Stalin was dangerous in his "Testament," a document he dictated in the final weeks of 1922 and the first week of 1923. The Kremlin published the document in 1956. In the testament, Lenin recommended removing Stalin from his position as General Secretary of the Russian Communist Party's Central Committee.

23 Nikolaev was a member of the Cheka and Chairman of the Military Collegium of the Supreme Court of the USSR (1926–1948).

24 Ulrikh sentenced Zinoviev, Kamenev, Bukharin, Tukhachevsky, Rodzaevsky and Yezhov. He attended the executions of many of these men, and occasionally performed executions himself. He personally executed Yan Karlovich Berzin, former head of Red Army Intelligence Directorate, later called GRU.

25 The Yakovlev Commission (1988) concluded that no materials objectively support Stalin's participation or NKVD participation in the organization and carrying out of Kirov's murder.

26 There had been show trials in early Soviet times, including that of the Socialist Revolutionaries in 1922 and the Shakhty case in 1928. During the early 1930s several more were mounted, notably the "Metro-Vic" case, involving British and Soviet engineers, in April 1933, following the "Menshevik Trial" in March 1931. Both cases were mainly concerned with sabotage.

27 Yezhov headed the NKVD during 1936–1938. Yezhov organized mass arrests, torture and executions during the Great Purge but fell from Stalin's favor. Stalin had him arrested. He confessed after torture to a range of anti-Soviet activity and executed in 1940.

28 Ordzhonikidze was Peoples' Commissar of Soviet Heavy Industry in 1932.

29 During the collectivization campaign and industrialization campaigns of the First Five-Year Plan from 1929 to 1933, party membership grew rapidly to approximately 3.5 million. There was a culling in 1933–1935. The culling and executions reduced membership to 1.9 million by 1939.

30 Mikhail Nikolayevich Tukhachevsky (1893–1937) was an eminent Soviet military officer and theoretician. He served as chief of staff of the Red Army from 1925 to 1928, as assistant in the People's Commissariat of Defense after 1934 and as commander of the Volga Military District in 1937. He achieved the rank of Marshal of the Soviet Union in 1935. Soviet authorities accused Tukhachevsky of treason and after confessing executed him in 1937.

31 The 1.2 million figure is uncertain.

32 Western sources supporting Katz's calculations put the GDP growth rate of 1937–1940 at 2%–3% per annum.

33 Beria became First Deputy Chairman of the Council of Ministers and head of the Ministry of Internal Affairs Nikita Khrushchev removed Beria from power in June 1953. He was tried for treason and other offenses, sentenced to death and executed on December 23, 1953.

34 Katyn Massacre was a mass execution of Polish military officers, policemen and civilian prisoners of war order by Soviet authorities on March 5, 1940. Michael Ellman reports that these statistics were excluded from NKVD data.

35 On March 5, 1940 Stalin, Vyacheslav Molotov, Lazar Kaganovich, Kliment Voroshilov, Anastas Mikoyan and Mikhail Kalinin signed an order to execute 25,700 Polish nationalists and counterrevolutionaries kept at camps and prisons in occupied western Ukraine and Belarus.

36 The Deportation of Koreans in the Soviet Union, originally conceived in 1926, initiated in 1930 and carried through in 1937, was the first mass transfer of an entire nationality in the Soviet Union. Almost the entire Soviet population of ethnic Koreans (171,781 persons) were forcefully moved from the Russian Far East to unpopulated areas of the Kazakh SSR and the Uzbek SSR in October 1937.

37 The Gulag is an acronym for chief administration of the camps. It was the government agency in charge of the Soviet network of forced labor camps set up by order of Vladimir Lenin, reaching its peak during Joseph Stalin's rule from the 1930s to the early 1950s. The word gulag may also refer to all forced-labor camps and the prisons housing convicts before transiting to the concentration camps.

38 The best archival-based estimate of Gulag excess deaths at present is 1.6 million from 1929 to 1953.

39 The 20 million excess death figure includes 9.7 million in 1928–1937 and 9 million in 1939–1953. The residual is attributable to war deaths misascribed to battle casualties. The Soviet sustained 8,806,453 million military fatalities during World War II, but claimed total population fatalities of 27 million. Excess deaths from the 1930s were buried in the World War II totals. This subject is heatedly debated by Russian scholars.

40 The last surviving Japanese prisoners of war returned to Maizuru in 1959.

41 The figures are from the unclassified portion of a confidential document. They are reliable. The author discussed the issue with the technicians.

42 www.themoscowtimes.com/2021/12/30/the-derailment-of-memorials-goals-for-now-a75955

43 The cultural "Thaw" that set in under Khrushchev transformed the intellectual environment. It molded a generation, even though Khrushchev reverted at times to repression. It was spurred by Ilya Ehrenburg's *Ottepel*, a short novel first published in the spring 1954 issue of Novy Mir. *Ottepel* inspired Khrushchev Thaw, the period of liberalization following the 1953 death of Stalin, marked a break from Ehrenburg's earlier purely pro-Soviet work and from previous ideas about socialist realism.

44 The Chinese communists contend that Tibet peacefully agreed to join PRC as an autonomous republic. The Tibetans counterclaim that they have been victims of ethnic cleansing and genocide.

Starting in 1949, Tibet was invaded by 35,000 Chinese troops who systematically raped, tortured and murdered an estimated 1.2 million Tibetans, one-fifth of the country's population. Since then over 6,000 monasteries have been destroyed, and thousands of Tibetans have been imprisoned. According to different sources, it is estimated that up to 260,000 people died in prisons and labor camps between 1950 and 1984.

45 In their Take-Over, the Communists relied heavily on quotas for violence. They managed by numbers: "Like steel production or grain output, death came with a quota mandated from above." Mao set a national ratio of killing one person in a thousand, but was willing to adjust it to the particular circumstances of each region. Perhaps 2 million were killed; several times that number were sent to labor camps or subjected to surveillance by local militia.

46 Mao claimed that the total number executed was 700,000, but this did not include those beaten or tortured to death in the post-1949 land reform, which would at the very least be as many again. Then there were suicides, which, based on several local inquiries, were very probably about equal to the number of those killed.

47 Laogai is an abbreviation for Laodong Gaizao. It means "reform through labor" and is a euphemism for prison labor and prison farms in the People's Republic of China (PRC). An estimated 50 million people were sent to Laogai camps. Laogai is distinct from Laojiao or reeducation through labor, nonpenal administrative detention. Laojiao detainees are lodged in facilities outside the Laogai prison system.

48 The people's commune was the highest of three administrative levels in rural areas of the People's Republic of China during the period from 1958 to 1983 when they were replaced by townships. Each commune was a combination of smaller farm collectives and consisted of 4,000–5,000 households. Larger communes could consist of up to 20,000 households. Private farming was prohibited, and those engaged in it were persecuted and labeled counterrevolutionaries.

49 Some 2–3 million of these were victims of political repression, beaten or tortured to death, or summarily executed for political reasons, often for the slightest infraction.

50 www.macrotrends.net/countries/CHN/china/rural-population

51 Dikötter supports an estimate of at least 45 million premature deaths in China during the famine years. He came to the conclusion that decisions coming from the top officials of the Chinese government in Beijing were the direct cause of the famine. Beijing government officials, including Mao Zedong and Zhou Enlai, increased the food procurement quota from the countryside to pay for international imports. Dikötter wrote: "In most cases the party knew very well that it was starving its own people to death." In 1959, Mao was quoted as saying in Shanghai "When there is not enough to eat people starve to death. It is better to let half of the people die so that the other half can eat their fill."

52 Revolutionary committees were tripartite bodies established during China's Cultural Revolution to facilitate government by three mass organizations – the people, the PLA and the Party.

53 Red Guards were a student-led paramilitary social movement mobilized and guided by Chairman Mao Zedong in 1966 and 1967, during the first phase of the Chinese Cultural Revolution. Mao made use of Red Guards to destroy symbols of China's pre-communist past, including ancient artifacts and gravesites of notable Chinese figures.

54 A struggle session is a form of public humiliation and torture used by the Communist Party of China during the Cultural Revolution to shape public opinion and humiliate, persecute or execute political rivals and those deemed class enemies.

55 Mao called for a mobilization of the people to cleanse the communist party of capitalist saboteurs at all levels, including the top (specifically Liu Shaoqi and Deng Xiaoping). University and middle school students responded to this call and formed groups of "Red Guards."

56 Walder estimates the total number of casualties based on a survey of local annals as having been 1.1–1.6 million people.
57 By the general estimate China's prison and labor camp population was roughly 10 million in any one year under Mao. Descriptions of camp life by inmates, which point to high mortality rates, indicate a probable annual death rate of at least 10 percent.
58 Consul B. John Zavrel (2001), "Tibet: Give Us Liberty and Peace." www.meaus.com/ Tibet_-_Give_Us_Liberty.html
59 Money had become worthless during the Soviet civil war, but Lenin and Asia's communist leaders refrained from abolishing it until Pol Pot decreed money illegal.
60 The Khmer Rouge acknowledge excesses, but downplay the atrocities.
61 David Chandler favors a figure between 800,000 and 1 million. Marek Sliwinski, using demographic data computes more than 2 million excess deaths (derived from census statistics for the late sixties and 1993). Maddison's report that Cambodia's population was 7.3 million in 1974 fell to 6.4 million in 1980, for a decline of 13%.
62 Vietnamese forces invaded Cambodia and captured Phnom Penh on January 7, 1979, but the Khmer Rouge did not vanish. Pol Pot continued waging guerilla war until his death in 1998.

References

Adorno, Theodor, Else Frenkel-Brunswik, Daniel Levinson and Nevitt Sanford. (1950). *The Authoritarian Personality*. New York: Harper and Brothers.
Applebaum, Anne. (2012). *Gulag: A History of the Soviet Camps*. London: Penguin Books Limited.
Applebaum, Anne. (2017). *Red Famine: Stalin's War on Ukraine*. Toronto: McClelland and Stewart.
Bacon, Edwin. (1994). *The Gulag at War: Stalin's Forced Labor System in the Light of the Archives*. New York: New York University Press.
Berg, Per Pieter van den. (1985). *The Soviet System of Justice: Figures and Policies*. Dordrecht: Marinus Nijhoff.
Black, Clayton. (2000). "Legitimacy, Succession, and the Concentration of Industry: Trotsky and the Crises of 1923 Re-examined." *Russian History*. Vol. 27, No. 4, 397–416.
Brown, Archie. (2011). *The Rise and Fall of Communism*. New York: HarperCollins.
Brown, Jeremy. (2004). "Terrible Honeymoon: Struggling with the Problem of Terror in Early 1950s China." https://ucsdmodernchinesehistory.wordpress. com/2010/05/01/1045/
Cameron, Sarah. (2018). *The Hungry Steppe: Famine, Violence, and the Making of Soviet Kazakhstan*. Ithaca: Cornell University Press.
Carr, Edward Hallett and Robert Davies. (1969). *Foundations of a Planned Economy, 1926– 1929*, Vols. 1–2. London: Macmillan.
Chandler, David. (1992). *Brother Number One: A Political Biography of Pol Pot*. Boulder: Westview Press.
Chang, Jon. (2018). *Burnt by the Sun: The Koreans of the Russian Far East*. Honolulu: University of Hawaii Press.
Chang, Jung and Jon Halliday. (2011). *Mao: The Unknown Story*. New York: Knoph Doubleday.
Chen, Shuo and Xiaohuan Lan. (2017). "There Will Be Killing: Collectivization and Death of Draft Animals." *American Economic Journal: Applied Economics*. Vol. 9, No. 4, 58–77.

Chen, Yuyu and David Yang. (2019). "Historical Traumas and the Roots of Political Distrust: Political Inference from the Great Chinese Famine." https://ssrn.com/abstract=2652587

Cheremukhin, Anton, Mikhail Golosov, Sergei Guriev and Aleh Tsyvinski. (2017). "The Industrialization and Economic Development of Russia through the Lens of a Neoclassical Growth Model." *Review of Economic Studies*. Vol. 84, No. 2, 613–649.

Chodakiewicz, Marek Jan. (2004). *Between Nazis and Soviets: Occupation Politics in Poland, 1939–1947.* Lexington: Lexington Books.

Choesan, Yeshe. (2015). "Genocide in the 20th Century: Massacres in Tibet: 1966–1976." *Tibet Post International.* www.thetibetpost.com/en/outlook/opinions-and-columns/4533-genocide-in-the-20th-century-massacres-in-tibet-1966-76

Chong, Woei Lien. (2002). *China's Great Proletarian Cultural Revolution: Master Narratives and Post-Mao Counter-narratives.* London: Rowman & Littlefield Publishers.

Clemens, Walter. (2018). "Kto Kovo? The Present Danger, as Seen from Moscow." www.cambridge.org/core/journals/worldview/article/abs/kto-kovo-the-present-danger-as-seen-from-moscow/5C27A4804998FD047F8355157F4BB160

Conquest, Robert. (1986). *The Harvest of Sorrow: Soviet Collectivization and the Terror-Famine.* London: Oxford University Press.

Conquest, Robert. (1989). *Stalin and the Kirov Murder.* New York: Oxford University Press.

Cook, Susan. (2005). *Genocide in Cambodia and Rwanda.* New Brunswick: Transaction.

Costello, Thomas, Shauna Bowes, Irwin Waldman, Arber Tasimi, Sean Stevens and Scott Lilienfeld. (2020). "Clarifying the Structure and Nature of Left-wing Authoritarianism." *Journal of Personality and Social Psychology.* Vol. 122, No. 1, 135–170.

Courtois, Stéphane, Nicolas Werth, Jean-Louis Panné, Andrzej Paczkowski, Karel Bartošek and Jean-Louis Margolin. (1999). *The Black Book of Communism: Crimes, Terror, Repression.* Cambridge: Harvard University Press.

Danilov, Viktor. (2011). *Istoriya krestyanstva Rossii v XX veke [The History of the Peasantry of Russia in the Twentieth Century].* Moscow: Rosspen.

Davies, Robert and Stephen Wheatcroft. (2004). *The Industrialization of Soviet Russia: The Years of Hunger: Soviet Agriculture, 1931–1933.* Basingstoke: Palgrave Macmillan.

Dikötter, Frank. (2010). *Mao's Great Famine: The History of China's Most Devastating Catastrophe, 1958–1962.* New York: Bloomsbury.

Dikötter, Frank. (2013). *The Tragedy of Liberation: A History of the Chinese Revolution, 1945–1957.* London: Bloomsbury Press.

Dikötter, Frank. (2017). *The Cultural Revolution: A People's History, 1962–1976.* New York: Bloomsbury Press.

Domar, Evsey. (1957). "A Soviet Model of Growth." In *Essays in the Theory of Economic Growth.* New York: Oxford University Press.

Dubester, Henry Joachim. (1948). *USSR: Census of 1926. National Censuses and Vital Statistics in Europe, 1918–1939: An Annotated Bibliography.* Detroit: Gale Research Company.

Ehrenburg, Ilya. (1954). *Ottepel (The Thaw).* Moscow: Novy Mir.

Ellman, Michael (1990). "Grigorii Alexandrovic Fel'dman." In John Eatwell, Murray Milgate and Peter Newman (eds.). *Problems of the Planned Economy.* New York: W. W. Norton.

Ellman, Michael (2002). "Soviet Repression Statistics: Some Comments." *Europe-Asia Studies.* Vol. 54, No. 7, 1154.

Ellman, Michael (2007). "Stalin and the Soviet Famine of 1932–1933 Revisited." *Europe-Asia Studies.* Vol. 59, No. 4, 663–693.

Erlich, Alexander. (1960). *The Soviet Industrialization Debate, 1924–1928.* Cambridge: Harvard University Press.

Erlich, Alexander. (1978). "Dobb and the Marx-Fel'dman Model: A Problem in Soviet Economic Strategy." *Cambridge Journal of Economics.* Vol. 2, 203–214.

Fel'dman, Grigory. (1964). "On the Theory of Growth Rates of National Income." In Nicolas Spulber (ed.). *Foundations of Soviet Strategy for Economic Growth.* Bloomington: Indiana University Press.

Figes, Orlando. (2007). *The Whisperers.* London: Allen Lane.

Furet, François. (1999). *The Passing of an Illusion: The Idea of Communism in the Twentieth Century.* Chicago: University of Chicago Press.

Getty, J. Arch. (1993). "The Politics of Repression Revisited." In J. Arch Getty and Roberta T. Manning (eds.). *Stalinist Terror New Perspectives.* New York: Cambridge University Press.

Getty, J. Arch. (2000). "The Future Did Not Work." *Atlantic.* Vol. 285, No. 3, 113–116.

Gulaga, Naselenie. (2004). "Sobranie dokumentov v 7 tomakh." In V. P. Kozlov et al. (eds.). *Istorija stalinskogo Gulaga: konec 1920-kh – pervaia polovina 1950-kh godov,* Vol. 4.. Moskva: ROSSPEN.

Healey, Dan. (2018). "Illness and Inhumanity in Stalin's Gulag." *The American Historical Review.* Vol. 123, No. 3, 1049–1051.

Homkes, Brett. (2004). "Certainty, Probability, and Stalin's Great Party Purge." *McNair Scholars Journal.* Vol. 8, No. 1. http://scholarworks.gvsu.edu/mcnair/vol8/iss1/3

Katz, Barbara. (1975). "Purges and Production: Soviet Economic Growth, 1928–1940." *Journal of Economic History.* Vol. 35, No. 3, 567–590.

Kindler, Robert. (2018). *Stalin's Nomads: Power and Famine in Kazakhstan.* Pittsburgh: Pittsburgh University Press.

Knight, Amy. (1996). *Beria: Stalin's First Lieutenant.* Princeton: Princeton University Press.

Kontorovich, Vladimir. (2013a). "The Military Origins of Soviet Industrialization." *Comparative Economic Studies.* Vol. 57, No. 4, 669–692.

Kontorovich, Vladimir. (2013b). "The Preobrazhenskii-Feldman Myth and the Soviet Industrialization." http://ssrn.com/abstract=2200184

Kuromiya, Hiroaki. (2007). *The Voices of the Dead: Stalin's Great Terror in the 1930s.* New Haven: Yale University Press.

Lenin, Vladimir. (1920). *The Proletarian Revolution and the Renegade K. Kautsky.* Ann Arbor: University of Michigan.

Levine, Isaac. (1960). *The Mind of an Assassin.* New York: New American Library.

Lewin, Moshe. (1968). *Russian Peasants and Soviet Power.* Evanston: Northwestern University Press.

Li, Changyu. (2005). "Mao's Killing Quotas." www.hrichina.org/sites/default/files/PDFs/CRF.4.2005/CRF-2005-4_Quota.pdf

Li, Hua-yu. (2006). *Mao and the Economic Stalinization of China, 1948–1953.* New York: Rowman & Littlefield Publishers.

Li, Wei and Tao Yang Dennis. (2005). "The Great Leap Forward: Anatomy of a Central Planning Disaster." *Journal of Political Economy.* Vol. 113, No. 4, 840–877.

Lih, Lars. (1991). "Political Testament of Lenin and Bukharin and the Meaning of NEP." *Slavic Review.* Vol. 50, No. 2, 241–252.

Lin, Justin Yifu. (1990). "Collectivization and China's Agricultural Crisis in 1959–1961." *Journal of Political Economy.* Vol. 98, No. 6, 1228–1252.

Lipman, Jonathan and Stevan Harrell (eds.). (1990). *Violence in China: Essays in Culture and Counterculture.* New York: SUNY Press, 154–157.

Locard, Henri. (1996). "Le goulag Khmer rouge." *Communisme.* No.47–48, 127–161.

MacFarquhar, Roderick and John K. Fairbank. (1987). *The Cambridge History of China*, Vol. 14. New York: Cambridge University Press.

MacFarquhar, Roderick and Michael Schoenhals. (2006). *Mao's Last Revolution*. Boston: Belknap Harvard.

Maddison, Angus. (2003). *The World Economy: Historical Statistics*. Paris: OECD.

Margolin, Jean-Louis. (1999). "Cambodia: The Country of Disconcerting Crimes." In Courtois et al. (eds.). *The Black Book of Communism*. Cambridge: Harvard University Press, 599, 626—627.

Meng, Xin, Nancy Qian and Pierre Yared. (2015). "The Institutional Causes of China's Great Famine, 1959–1961." *Review of Economic Studies*. Vol. 82, No. 4, 1568–1611.

Merleau-Ponty, Maurice. (1947). *Humanisme et terreur. Essai sur le problème communiste*. Paris: Gallimard.

Merleau-Ponty, Maurice. (1955). *Les aventures de la dialectique*. Paris: Gallimard.

Meslé, France, Jacques Vallin and Evgeny Andreev. (2013). "Demographic Consequences of the Great Famine: Then and Now." In Andrea Graziosi, Lubomyr A. Hajda and Halyna Hryn (eds.). *After the Holodomor: The Enduring Impact of the Great Famine on Ukraine*. Cambridge: Harvard University Press, 217–242.

Mikhailovna Ivanova, Galina.(2000). *Labor Camp Socialism: The Gulag in the Soviet Totalitarian System*. Armonk: Sharpe.

Montefiore, Simon. (2014). *Stalin: The Court of the Red Tsar*. New York: Knopf Doubleday.

Moore, Barrington. (1954). *Terror and Progress, USSR: Some Sources of Change and Stability in the Soviet Dictatorship*. Cambridge: Harvard University Press.

Moore, Barrington, Robert Paul Wolff and Herbert Marcuse. (1965). *A Critique of Pure Tolerance*. Boston: Beacon Press.

Mosher, Steven. (1992). *China Misperceived: American Illusions and Chinese Reality*. Lexington: Basic Books.

Narodnoe khoziaistvo SSSR za 70 Let, Iubileinyi statisticheskii ezhegodnik. (1987). Moscow: Finansy I Statistika.

Narodnoe khoziaistvo za 60 let, iubileinyi statisticheskii ezhegodnik. (1977). Moscow: Finansy I Statistika.

Naumenko, Natalya. (2021). "The Political Economy of Famine: The Ukrainian Famine of 1933." *The Journal of Economic History*. Vol. 81, No. 1, 156–197.

Neumayer, Laure. (2018). *The Criminalization of Communism in the European Political Space after the Cold War*. London: Routledge.

Ngor, Hing. (2003). *Survival in the Killing Fields*. New York: Basic Books.

Ofer, Gur. (2008). "Soviet Growth Record." In Steven N. Durlauf and Lawrence E. Blume (eds.). *The New Palgrave Dictionary of Economics*, Vol. 7. New York: Palgrave Macmillan.

Paul, Allen. (2010). *Katyń: Stalin's Massacre and the Triumph of Truth*. DeKalb: Northern Illinois University Press.

Perovic, Jeronim. (2018). *From Conquest to Deportation: The North Caucasus under Russian Rule*. London: Oxford University Press.

Pianciola, Niccolo. (2001). "The Collectivization Famine in Kazakhstan, 1931–1933." *Harvard Ukrainian Studies*. Vol. 25, No. 3, 237–251.

Pietrow, Nikita. (2012). *Psy Stalina*. Warszawa: Demart.

Pohl, Otto. (1997). *The Stalinist Penal System*. New York: McFarland.

Pohl, Otto. (1999). *Ethnic Cleansing in the USSR, 1937–1949*. Westport: Greenwood Press.

Pran, Dirth and Kim DePaul (eds.). (1999). *Children of Cambodia's Killing Fields: Memoirs by Survivors*. New Haven: Yale University Press.

Preobrazhensky, Evgeny. (1965). *The New Economics*. London: Oxford University Press.

Preobrazhensky, Evgeny. (1973). *From NEP to Socialism: A Glance into the Future of Russia and Europe.* London: New Park Publications.

Preobrazhensky, Evgeny. (1980). In Donald A. Filtzer (ed.). *The Crisis of Soviet Industrialization: Selected Essays.* London: Macmillan.

Proch, Franciszek. (1978). *Poland's Way of the Cross.* Brooklyn: Polstar Publishing Corp.

Rosefielde, Steven. (2007). *Soviet Economy from Lenin to Putin.* New York: Wiley.

Rosefielde, Steven. (2010). *Red Holocaust.* London: Routledge.

Rosefielde, Steven. (2021). "Communist Economy: The Verdict of History." In Vladimir Tismaneanu (ed.). *100 Years of Communism.* Prague: Central European University Press, 119–140.

Rozenas, Arturas and Yuri Zhukov. (2019). "Mass Repression and Political Loyalty: Evidence from Stalin's 'Terror by Hunger'." *American Political Science Review.* Vol. 113, No. 2, 569–583.

Rudnytskyi, Omelian, Nataliia Levchuk, Oleh Wolowyna, Pavlo Shevchuk and Alla Kovbasiuk. (2015). "Demography of a Man-Made Human Catastrophe: The Case of Massive Famine in Ukraine 1932–1933." *Canadian Studies in Population.* Vol. 42, No. 1, 53–80.

Rummel, Rudolf. (1994). "Power, Genocide and Mass Murder." *Journal of Peace Research.* Vol. 31, No. 1, 1–10.

Samuelson, Lennart. (2000). *Plans for Stalin's War Machine: Tukhachevskii and Military-Economic Planning, 1925–1940.* Basingstoke and London: Macmillan Press.

Scherer, John and Michael Jakobson. (1993). "The Collectivization of Agriculture and the Soviet Prison Camp System." *Europe-Asia Studies.* Vol. 45, No. 3, 533–546.

Schroeder, Gertrude. (1979). "The Soviet Economy on a Treadmill of Reforms." In *Soviet Economy in a Time of Change.* Washington: Joint Economic Committee of Congress, 312–366.

Service, Robert. (2006). *Stalin, a Biography.* Cambridge: Harvard University Press.

Seymour, James and Richard Anderson. (1998). *New Ghosts, Old Ghosts, Prison and Labor Reform Camps in China.* New York: M. E. Sharp.

Shalom, Stephen Rosskamm. (1984). *Deaths in China due to Communism.* Tempe: Arizona State University Press.

Short, Philip. (1999). *Mao: A Life.* London: Hodder and Stoughton.

Sliwinski, Marek. (1995). *Le genocide Khmer rouge: Une analyze demographique.* Paris: L'Harmattan.

Solzhenitsyn, Aleksandr. (1975). *Gulag Archipelago,* Vol. 1–3. Paris: YMCA Press.

Stalin, Joseph. (1930). "Dizzy with Success: Concerning Questions of the Collective-Farm Movement." *Pravda.* No. 60.

Storella, C. J. and A. K. Sokolov. (2013). *The Voice of the People.* New Haven: Yale University Press.

Strumilin, Stanislav. (1928). *Otcherkiy Sovetskoy Ekonomikiy (Essays on the Soviet Economy).*

Suny, Ronald. (2007). "Russian Terrorism and Revisionist Historiography." *Australian Journal of Politics and History.* Vol. 53, No. 1, 5–19.

Thurston, Anne. (1987). *Enemies of the People.* New York: Knopf.

Tismaneanu, Vladimir. (2001). "Communism and the Human Condition: Reflections on the Black Book of Communism." *Human Rights Review.* Vol. 2, No. 2, 125–134.

Trotsky, Leon. (1937). *The Revolution Betrayed.* New York: Doubleday, Doran & Co.

Trotsky, Leon. (2017). *Terrorism and Communism: A Reply to Karl Kautsky.* New York: Penguin.

United Nations, Office of Genocide Prevention and the Responsibility to Protect. (2022). www.un.org/en/genocideprevention/office-methodology.shtml

Viola, Lynne. (1989). *The Best Sons of the Fatherland: Workers in the Vanguard of Soviet Collectivization*. New York: Oxford University Press.

Walder, Andrew G. (2014). "Rebellion and Repression in China, 1966–1971." *Social Science History*. Vol. 38, No. 4, 513–539.

Waldman, Eric. (1958). "The Spartacist Uprising of 1919." https://epublications.marque tte.edu/cgi/viewcontent.cgi?article=1022&context=mupress-book

Wemheuer, Felix, Andrew Walder, Jonathan Unger, Joel Andreas and Yiching Wu. (2016). "Grassroots Factionalism in China's Cultural Revolution: Rethinking the Paradigm." *H-Asia: H-PRC*. https://networks.h-net.org/node/3544/discussions/141257/transcript-grassroots-factionalism-china%E2%80%99s-cultural-revolution

Werth, Nicholas. (2004). "Strategies of Violence in the Stalinist USSR." In Henry Rousso and Richard Golsan (eds.). *Stalinism and Nazism: History and Memory Compared*. Omaha: University of Nebraska Press.

Wheatcroft, Stephen. (1999). "Victims of Stalinism and the Soviet Secret Police: The Comparability and Reliability of the Archival Data. Not the Last Word." *Europe-Asia Studies*. Vol. 51, No. 2, 315–345.

Wheatcroft, Stephen. (2013). "Indicators of Demographic Crisis in the Soviet Famine." *Golod v SSSR, 1929–1933*, Vol 3. Moscow. www.melgrosh.unimelb.edu.au/famine.php

Wheatcroft, Stephen and A. Garnaut. (2013). "Losses of Population in Separate Regions of USSR (1929–1934): Statistics, Maps and Comparative Analysis (with Special Reference to Ukraine)." *Famine 1933 Ukraine: Collection of Scientific Papers*. Kiev: Priority, 376–391.

Wheelwright, E. L. and Bruce McFarlane. (1971). *The Chinese Road to Socialism: Economics of the Cultural Revolution*. New York: Monthly Review Press.

Wu, Harry. (1996). *Troublemaker*. New York: Crown.

Wu, Hongda Harry. (1992). *Laogai – The Chinese Gulag*. Boulder: Westview Press.

Yakovlev, Alexander. (1991). "O dekabr'skoi tragedii 1934." *Pravda*.

Yang, Jisheng. (2012). *Tombstone: The Great Chinese Famine, 1958–1962*. New York: Farrar, Straus and Giroux.

Yarmolinsky, Avrahm. (2016). *Road to Revolution: A Century of Russian Radicalism*. Princeton: Princeton University Press.

Zavrel, Consul B. John. (2001). "Tibet: Give Us Liberty and Peace." www.meaus.com/Tibet_-_Give_Us_Liberty.html

Zemskov, V. N. (1990). "On Repatriation of Soviet Citizens 1944–1951." *Istoriya SSSR*.

15 Oblivion

Marxist–Leninists perceive communism as the best response to workers' primal scream for social justice. They believe that half-measures are self-defeating, and communist vanguard-led revolutions are the only viable path from misery to utopia. They are bellicose. Their attitude brooks no dissent, precluding dry-eyed assessment because it presumes that any blemishes that might occur during the course of communist construction are of no enduring consequence. If communists misbehave in the heat of battle, Marxists insist that the damage will be ultimately undone and recompensed. They dismiss naysayers who contend that Marxist–Leninism will always remain "dizzy with success" (Stalin, 1930).

The record belies the promise that all will end well in the fullness of time. It reveals that although the vanguard of the proletariat held power for 73 years in the Soviet Union, Marxist-Leninism neither empowered workers, nor provided them with the high quality of existence Marx prophesized, leaving behind a legacy of ravaged lives and shattered dreams (Tismaneanu and Luber, 2021). Soviet and East European communism was swept into the dustbin of history, not private property, markets and entrepreneurship. North Korean Marxist–Leninist–Stalinism has managed to survive longer than the USSR, but its performance inspires no one (Koen and Beom, 2020). China and Vietnam abandoned Marxist–Leninist–Stalinism (criminalization of private property, markets and entrepreneurship) and rapidly modernized in the new millennium, but worker empowerment and egalitarian prosperity remain little more than a mirage on the bright shining horizon (Breslauer, 2021). The Marxist–Leninist dream is fading into oblivion.

The harm done by Soviet, Chinese, Vietnamese and Cambodian communism was monumental (Rosefielde, 2010), lasting and unredeemed. Yeltsin and Putin belatedly have acknowledged the crimes of Stalin's past, but there has been no comprehensive restorative justice. Nikita Khrushchev's First Secretary of the Soviet Communist Party secret speech to the 20th Congress of Communist Party of the Soviet Union, February 1956, revealed the disparity between the Party's promises and the realities of communist oppression (Khrushchev, 1956). Lenin and Stalin needlessly inflicted enormous suffering on the Soviet people that was never justified by compensatory achievements (Nove, 1990).[1] The Bolsheviks broke tens of millions of eggs to make an unpalatable omelet.[2]

DOI: 10.4324/9781003371571-18

The original sin of Soviet Marxist-Leninism was its double think despotic seizure of state power from the democratically elected Constituent Assembly in the name of a proletariat that it subsequently and steadfastly refused to empower. An enlightened and compassionate working class compatible with Marx and Engels musings in the *Economic and Philosophical Manuscripts of 1844* would have held fast to libertarianism and democracy (Wolfe, 1961; Luxembourg, 1970). It would have mapped a transition path that maximized the quality of people's exist-ence as the workers themselves perceived it, guided by the advice of communist leaders, compassion, tolerance and desire for social reconciliation and harmony. It would have treated Mensheviks, Social Revolutionaries, Kadets,[3] industrialists, businesspersons, kustars, aristocrats and the deposed tsar mercifully, reforming and integrating them gradually into the new order. It would have initially limited nationalization of the means of production to the commanding heights and provided modest compensation to former owners as circumstances warranted. It would have protected people's basic political, civil, property, entrepreneurial and labor rights taking account of communist vanguard counsel and Marx's own early libertarian outlook (1844). It would have raised the people's consciousness and assisted them to continuously learn and adapt to enhance the quality of worker existence.

The late-20th- and early 21st-century democratic socialist experience in England and the Nordic corporatist states (Denmark, Finland, Iceland, Norway and Sweden) illuminate the possibilities. Both prove that the workers lot and the causes of social justice and democracy were improvable without signifi-cant loss of human lives and liberties (Cohen, 1980).[4] Corporatist Nordic states delivered prosperity and social justice; none of the Marxist–Leninist regimes did. Instead of pursuing a path of compassion, tolerance, social reconciliation, adaptive learning and harmony, revolutionary communist governments chose class war, street justice, tyranny, dogmatism and repression. Bolshevism was a blunder, but Marxist–Leninists refuse to admit it, still certain that while they make mistakes, they are never wrong. Acknowledging fundamental error is apostasy.

No Remorse, No Contrition

Marxist–Leninists seldom display remorse for revolutionary communism and are seldom contrite. If they could, they would correct tactical errors, but Bolsheviks would never have voluntarily subordinated themselves to the majority rule of the All Russian Constituent Assembly. Marxist–Leninists, even those advocating democratic socialism, cannot acknowledge ideological fallibility and simultan-eously sustain their claim to exclusive political legitimacy. This condemns them to repeating mistakes and perpetually replicating past failures with no exit because dogma precludes learning and constructive adaptation. There is no authorita-tive Marxist–Leninist treatise explaining why its infallible prophesies failed, or offering plausible timetables for fulfilling broken promises.

Wilderness of Mirrors

False statistics and double think narratives obscure matters further. Aeschylus (525/524–456/455 BC) famously suggested that the first casualty of war is truth.[5] Revolutionary Marxism is a self-proclaimed, no holds barred state of perpetual war against capitalism (Sombart 1896, 1898; Schumpeter, 1942).[6] Economic statistics that give aid and comfort to the enemy betray the revolution. Soviet statisticians from an ideological perspective had a duty to the proletariat to demonstrate Bolshevism's superiority on paper. The official statistical performance of the USSR's economy in 1921–1928 ostensibly confirmed the wisdom of Lenin's New Economic Policy (NEP) (Narodnoe Khoziaistvo, 1977, 9, 12, 167). Official data showed even better results under Stalin's five-year plans (Zaleski, 1980, 2011). Postwar economic growth was superlative during 1950–1968, and although growth slowed thereafter, it always exceeded the American standard until 1989 on Goskomstat numbers, yet these paper successes were insufficient to deter Gorbachev from dissolving the Soviet Union. No one conversant with revolutionary Marxist ethics should be astonished that the Bolsheviks cosmetically enhanced official statistics (Rosefielde, 2003b, 2005b, 2007).

Did Gorbachev throw in the towel on Soviet power blinded by the light of the sun,[7] or were Soviet statistics the first casualties of revolutionary Marxist war against capitalism? (Aslund, 1988). Admirers of revolutionary Marxist–Leninist ideals still believe the official statistics (Dobb, 1948).[8] They use them without qualification or embarrassment concocting fictitious histories justifying a repeat performance of Marxist–Leninist–Stalinist successes (Davies, 2010). The American Central Intelligence Agency half-believed official Soviet statistics (Rosefielde, 1987b; CIA, 1991; Berkowitz, Berliner, Gregory, Linz and Millar, 1993; Treml and Hardt, 1972), and only a handful of specialists spoke truth to power (Nutter, Borenstein and Kaufman, 1962).

The conundrum of Marxist–Leninist statistics is complex. See Appendix 5 for a conceptual overview. The problem lies in the paradox of righteousness and expedience. Marxist–Leninists assert a double duty to tell the truth and an obligation to prevaricate in the war against capitalism. The Soviets insisted their data were reliable (but only in public),[9] that the data supported system directors' rational choice and that published civilian and defense performance statistics were accurate. Gorbachev's admission in 1989 that the official defense budgetary expenditures omitted weapons did not give pause to most analysts who continue treating Soviet and Chinese communist defense budgetary statistics as reliable (Rosefielde, 2012). Analysts likewise looked past Gorbachev's acknowledgment that hidden inflation warped Soviet civilian figures (Aganbegyan, 1988).

Impartial experts concerned with assessing the economic performance of Marxist–Leninist systems cannot have it both ways. They cannot admit the false statistics, and simultaneously downplay their relevance as Alec Nove did in the wake of communism's collapse in the USSR and Eastern Europe (Nove, 1961; Rosefielde, Shabad and Yanov, 1982; Harrison, 2010; Markevichi and Harrison.

(2011).[10] No Marxist–Leninist saw the Soviet Union's demise coming because the data provided no basis for assuming anything other than bright tomorrows. Only Andrei Amalrik, a prominent Soviet dissident, prophesized the end of days (Amalrik, 1970).

The second layer of complexity stems from Karl Marx's labor theory of value (Becker, 1968, 1970; Bergson, 1972). Marx contended in *Das Kapital* that labor was the sole source of value added. He denied that demand determined prices, attributed capitalist profits to labor exploitation (surplus value) and asserted that socialist prices had to be based on unit wage cost of production (computed at state fixed wage rates) (Bornstein, 1978). Product prices employed to compute GDP in market and planned economies consequently were incompatible. The Soviets set output prices on an embodied unit factor cost basis. Western markets set them as joint effects of supply and demand. Soviet prices reflected unit labor cost without regard to purchaser demand; Western prices took account of consumer preferences. Soviet GDP measured the fiat labor cost of output detached from consumer demand for quantities and qualities of goods and services. Western GDP measured the consumer utility of the quantities and qualities of competitive purchases.

Value conventions East and West were antithetic (Bergson, 1966a). Marxist labor valuation encouraged producing goods and services in micro assortments and quantities that few other than the Ministry of Defense wanted.[11] Consequently, the correlation between rapid Soviet GDP growth and the growth of Soviet consumer utility was weak. More Soviet physical output might generate more utility, or might not. This means that even if official Soviet economic production statistics reporting superior GDP performance were true (which they were not), this did not necessarily imply that Soviet consumer utility growth (and the quality of existence) was outperforming the West. Faster Soviet physical output growth did not guarantee better performance, but Marxist–Leninists and the CIA needed no encouragement to assume that the utilitarian benefits of growth as reported in GDP statistics East and West were similar (CIA, 1991; Bergson, 1966b).[12]

The third layer of complexity involved adjusting Soviet labor value prices to improve their correspondence with competitive prices. Abram Bergson using Soviet price setting rules added a capital charge to Marxist prime labor cost (sebestoimost') to establish a uniform East-West standard of comparison (Bergson, 1950, 1953, 1954, 1961, 1963b). He subtracted turnover taxes and added capital charges to large aggregate composite goods. The relative ruble price of capital-intensive goods increased. The adjustments affected GDP size and rates of growth. Bergson argued that his factor cost adjustments would be especially revealing if Soviet production functions were Cobb-Douglas because changes in estimated marginal rates of technical substitution would have limited impact on activity levels (Bergson, 1961; Rosefielde and Pfouts, 1995, 1998).

Bergson acknowledged that his adjusted factor costs adjustments did not improve the correspondence between implied utility and the estimated value of production (the demand side of the problem) (Rosefielde, 2003a), nonetheless, he insisted that it did provide a better impression of Soviet "production potential" (supply side output possibilities on production feasibility frontiers, also sometimes called "technical efficiency"). Soviet economic statistics, it seemed to him, were reliable enough on this basis to justify the surmise that the supply of Soviet goods had grown rapidly enabling the USSR to become a major industrial power (Bergson, 1953b) whether or not anyone including Soviet leaders wanted the output produced. He buttressed his judgment by recomputing Soviet GDP growth with adjusted factor cost prices that purportedly measured production potential free from distortions caused by turnover taxes, subsidies and omitted capital services (Bergson, 1961, 1963b). Although, there was an interesting index number relativity phenomenon in 1928—1940) (Bergson, 1975), adjusted factor cost per se had little effect on GDP growth estimates in 1950–1991 (Bergson and Levine, 1989). Soviet economic performance as Bergson measured it on an adjusted factor cost basis was slower, but nonetheless consonant with the Marxist–Leninist view. Although, Soviet GDP growth decelerated and appeared headed toward secular stagnation (Hansen, 1939), it outperformed the West in 1950–1990 (Bergson, 1963a, 1963b; Rosefielde and Lovell, 1977). Bergson in the 1970s began counseling that the Kremlin should expect growth retardation and economic turbulence due to low incremental factor productivity, tight labor supplies and a low elasticity of capital-labor substitution (Bergson, 1978b, 1979, 1987, 1989, 1991; Bergson and Levine, 1989), but this did not preclude the possibility of a reversal of fortune. His pessimistic assessment of Soviet economic prospects in the 1980s was prescient. Soviet science and technological progress and sustainable economic growth proved deficient no matter whether computed with official Soviet data, adjusted factor cost statistics or CIA hidden inflation corrected statistics. Table 15.1 illuminates the link between deficient Soviet technological progress and deepening Soviet secular economic stagnation.

$$TFP = \dot{Y} / \left[\alpha \dot{K} + (1 - \alpha) \dot{L} \right]$$

where $\dot{Y}$, $\dot{K}$ and $\dot{L}$ are output, capital and labor growth, and α and $(1-\alpha)$ are the output elasticities of these factors measured in 1955 rubles (GNP) and 1959 rubles (industry). Capital weights are net of depreciation.

Many Western economic experts agreed with Bergson's growth retardation prognosis (Desai, 1986; Trachtenberg, 2018, Rosefielde and Kuboniwa, 2003; Ofer, 1987), but not always for the technical reasons he adduced. His interpretation of the production potential standard was inadequate. The composite goods rates of marginal factor substitution he computed were for large aggregates, not the weighted average of 27.5 million individual marginal rates of factor substitution. His adjusted factor cost prices did not reflect either prevailing or ideal micro opportunity costs (Rosefielde, 1994a).[13] The only thing that Bergson's calculations proved was that if Goskomstat physical output and quality improvement statistics were accurate, Soviet physical output grew rapidly during 1950–1968,

Table 15.1 Soviet Factor Productivity Growth of 1965–1985 (Official Industrial Output Series) Percent

	1965–1970	*1970–1975*	*1975–1980*	*1980–1985*	*1965–1985*
GNP	6.2	4.3	3.1	2.8	4.1
Combined inputs	3.8	3.8	3.1	2.5	3.3
Workhours	2.0	1.7	1.2	0.7	1.4
Capital	7.4	8.0	6.9	6.3	7.1
TFP	2.4	0.5	0	0.3	0.8

TFP is total factor productivity.
Sources: Allocation of Resources in the Soviet Union and China – 1985, Joint Economic Committee of Congress, March 19, 1986, Table 4, p. 80 and Table 5, p. 81; Rosefielde, *Economic Foundations of Soviet National Security Strategy*, unpublished manuscript 1987, Tables 9.4 and 9.14; Abram Bergson, *Productivity and the Social Systems*, Harvard University Press, Cambridge, 1978, Appendix Table 11, p. 236. *Measures of Soviet Gross National Product in 1982 Prices*, Joint Economic Committee of Congress, November 1990, Table A.1, pp. 54–57.

Method: The Factors are combined, following Bergson, according to the Cobb-Douglas specification (See Bergson, 1978, pp. 159–160 note 8). The income elasticities (shares) imputed to capital (.328 GNP, .217 industry) are provided in (Bergson 1978), Appendix Table 11. Labor is .672 GNP, and .683 industry. Cf. Appendix Table 22, p. 245. The factor data are taken from CIA sources: the industrial component of the CIA's GNP is the official Goskomstat series. Total factor productivity growth for aggregate output and industry are computed with the following function:

$$TFP = \dot{Y}/\left[\alpha\dot{K} + (1-\alpha)\dot{L}\right]$$

where $\dot{Y}$, $\dot{K}$ and $\dot{L}$ are output, capital, and labor growth, and α and (1-α) are the output elasticities of these factors measured in 1955 rubles (GNP), and 1959 rubles (industry). Capital weights are net of depreciation.

decelerating markedly thereafter regardless of the prices used for valuing growth indices. His adjusted factor cost statistics did not prove that physical output and quality improvements were reliable, or that there was a strong positive correlation between the growth of output and consumer utility.

The fourth layer of complexity is an artifact of product quality and new goods. Marx's labor cost theory of value rejects the commonsense view that utility determines value. From a Marxist perspective, the quality of goods should not matter. The unit labor cost of production determines the value of quality, not utilitarian demand. Marx was wrong and his error had consequences. The Soviet State Price Committee was compelled to reduce the prices of improved goods making them appear less "valuable," if better designs cut unit labor cost. Conversely, if design changes diminished product quality, but increased unit labor cost, inferior goods would become more "valuable." Soviet leaders gradually recognized that Marxist labor-value theory failed to provide them with a sensible demand-based criterion for pricing new and improved goods; that Marx's theoretical error was impeding high-quality economic modernization (Berliner, 1976).

They grudgingly persuaded themselves that labor-value prices needed hedonic adjustment to spur production of new and superior quality goods, but could not do the job well (Berliner, 1976). First, Goskomtsen (Soviet Price Committee) was unable to judge the consumer utility of new and improved products accurately. Second, bureaucratic rules incentivizing enterprise managers to improve quality and expand new goods production led to hidden inflation. Managers seeking to increase bonuses padded the labor cost of new and improved goods that they submitted to state price setters. This enabled them to raise prices and pour old wine into new bottles, adding stars to bottle labels misleadingly suggesting that star-studded bottles contained better wine (with justifiably higher prices). Goskomstat mistakenly presuming that padded unit costs represented better quality treated price increases in national income accounts as value added instead of inflation. Economists call the phenomenon "hidden inflation." Goskomstat should have reported fake quality improvements (padded costs) as open inflation, but instead reported them as real economic growth (Harrison, 2000; Rosefielde, 1994b, 2003b, 2004, Kontorovich, 1989).

The deceit was win-win. Enterprise managers received lucrative bonuses for "spurious innovation," and the government benefited from the illusion of progress. It could brag about the rapidity of Soviet economic growth. The Communist Party based on its own falsified evidence was able to prove the superiority of revolutionary Marxist-Leninism. It even convinced the CIA that Soviet consumer goods were growing rapidly (Schroeder and Elizabeth Denton, 1982; Chapman, 2013), even though shelves in Moscow retail stores were bare.

The fifth layer of complexity is a corollary of the fourth. If the government winked at deceptive new and improved product pricing, why scruple about physical production statistics. Bergson and many others argued that overreporting output would wreak havoc with planning,[14] but the suggestion conflates optimal planning with muddling through. Efficiency necessitates accurate statistics. Satisficing does not. There is no compelling reason to believe that Soviet leaders would have shunned a propaganda victory because they felt a duty to scrupulous public accounting.[15]

Peace and Internal Security

Soviet Marxist–Leninists also tampered with data and obscured the scale of their efforts in other important ways. They manipulated military and internal security statistics for external consumption to deter, suppress and defeat international political and class adversaries (disinformation warfare). Military statistics and data on the repression of internal enemies were secret, even though defending and expanding socialism were core Marxist–Leninist missions. The Soviets published a single defense budgetary expenditure statistic annually in *Narodnoe Khoziaistvo SSSR*. The figure was approximately 2.5% of net material product (NMP)[16] and declined one-tenth of a percent annually. It was a third to half of America's defense burden (defense spending as a share of GDP). Moscow and peace activists used the Soviet defense budget statistic to pressure Washington into curbing American military activities (Becker, 1977). The CIA fell for the bait (CIA, 1976). It assumed that the official Soviet budgetary defense figure was right, but incomplete and tried estimating omissions it conjectured the Kremlin hid in other budget categories. The agency was able to add another 2.5% of NMP to the defense total,[17] but learned much later that this was an underestimate. The KGB had outsmarted America's best and brightest. Those like CIA Melvin Goodman who believed that Washington exaggerated the Soviet military threat supported the official Soviet and CIA ruble defense spending estimates (Goodman, 2008, 2021), apparently unaware of the Agency's improper learning curve adjustments which reduced estimated Soviet weapons growth 1960–1987 to zero! (Firth and Noren, 1998; Rosefielde, 1986, 2005a).

The CIA's statistical profile of Soviet military activities was not all dovish. Its dollar estimates trebled the Soviet ruble defense burden, mostly by valuing the services of the USSR's multimillion soldiers at America dollar wages (CIA, 1979).[18] The American Defense Intelligence Agency buttressed the formidable impression of Soviet military power provided by the CIA's dollar cost estimates with satellite photo intelligence-based weapons production data. The Soviet Union on this evidence incontestably was a military superpower (Rosefielde, 1987a, 2005a). The Kremlin leadership concurred, but did not have to boast. They let the Americans tell the world not to trifle with peace-loving Soviet Marxist–Leninists, while the official Soviet defense budget statistic showed the Kremlin spending peanuts on its armed forces.

Moscow deftly played a similar game with its gulag and domestic repression statistics. The Soviet Ministry of Justice published data on prisoners and rehabilitation (Rosefielde, 2010). The statistics and narratives suggested that Soviet prisoners were overwhelmingly criminals humanely rehabilitated through productive gulag labor. See Chapter 14. Marxist–Leninist–Stalinists canceled class enemies of 1928–1953 with few telltale signs of mass incarceration and killing, other than the show trials of 1936–1938.[19] This enabled Soviet leaders to present a benign face to the West, while simultaneously terrorizing anyone who opposed Bolshevik authority at home and abroad (Service, 2010).[20] The same principle held for excess deaths. Stalin ordered demographers to redo the 1937 census to conceal a shocking 7 million excess deaths, including victims of "Holodomor."[21] He had offending demographers purged and a new census taken in 1939 with "better" results (Rosefielde, 2010). Later Stalin "buried" millions demographically "missing" in the 1930 as victims of Nazi aggression during World War II (Rosefielde, 1987b, 1988, 1996, 1997, 2010).[22]

Soviet Marxist-Leninism was two-faced. It was angelic when spreading the communist gospel, but the USSR was as an authoritarian martial police state whenever expedience dictated.

Illusion of Redeeming Virtues

Most Marxist–Leninists and others sympathetic with the Soviet experiment aware that workers and peasants had solid grounds for concluding that Bolshevism had blighted their lives were unperturbed. They continued to insist that the Soviet quality of life was catching up with and would soon surpass the capitalist West (Allen, 2003).[23] When Godot failed to arrive, they switched metrics (Beckett, 1956. Yes, there were few private Soviet automobiles, but there was Moscow's metropolitan subway system. Yes, restaurants and basic retail outlets were scarce, but essentials were available in factory canteens and shops. Yes, recreation facilities for the masses were primitive, but workers could work overtime without pay (subbotnik).[24] Yes, birth control was almost nonexistent, but abortions were available on demand (Popov, 1990; Avdeev, Blum and Troitskaya, 1995).[25] Yes, the quality of Soviet housing was wretched, but there was a lot of it. Yes, medical care was deficient, but it was adequate for routine ailments (Rowland and Telyukov, 1991; Feshbach, 1984; Eberstadt, 2006). Yes, Soviet education was mostly training and indoctrination, but it served the communist mission (Balzer, 2019; Reilly, 1996). Yes, travel was severely restricted, but people journeyed on assignment (kommandirovka). Yes, access to Western literature was available only on a need to know basis, but everyone could read the collected works of Marx, Lenin and Stalin. Yes, promises of women's equality were broken,[26] but Marxist feminism was better than bourgeois women's liberation (Lokaneeta, 2001).[27] Yes, the Bolshevik upper crust lived lavishly, but workers enjoyed subsistence level equality (McAuley,1971; Alexeev and Gaddy, 1993, Bulgakov, 1967; Bergson, 1984).Yes, the Soviets ravaged the environment, but they built the Belomor Canal (Feshbach and Friendly, 1984; Feshbach, 1995; Blakemore, 2019; Solzhenitsyn, 2007). Yes, workers lived dreary lives, but appreciated that their misery was for a glorious cause.

Triumph of Hope over Experience

The Soviet Marxist–Leninist debacle was foreseeable long before 1917, and its failings were readily discernible throughout its 73-year history, despite the miasma of misleading statistics. The "red scare" in the West during 1917–1920 called public attention to the issue. Emma Goldman and Rosa Luxemburg denounced Lenin's dictatorship (Goldman, 1923; Luxemburg, 1970). Leon Trotsky and his supporters assailed Stalin (Trotsky, 1932, 1937, 1946). Boris Nicholaevsky and David Dallin exposed the realities of gulag (1947, Bergson, 1948).[28] Alexander Solzhenitsyn and Evgenia Ginsburg validated Nicholaevsky and Dallin's narrative (Solzhenitsyn, 2007; Ginzburg, 1967, 1982). Robert Conquest exposed the Great Terror and Holodomor (Conquest, 1987, 2007). Distinguished emigres like Wassily Leontief,[29] Leonid Schapiro (Schapiro, 1970, 1984)[30] and Alec Nove had firsthand knowledge of Bolshevism and voiced their reservations (Nove, 1990).[31] Abram Bergson (Samuelson, 2004),[32] John Maynard Keynes (Sicsú, 2020)[33] and Maurice Dobbs[34] all visited the USSR during the mid-1930s and disclosed various deficiencies. Richard Pipes debunked official Soviet narratives,[35] and Hannah Arendt raised awareness of totalitarianism (Stanley, 1987; Schapiro, 1972). The rise of the Polish Solidarity labor movement signaled deep worker discontent.[36] Nonetheless, many Western intellectuals habituated to revolutionary Marxist–Leninist sentiment refused to see the reality in plain sight (Aron, 2001).

Revolutionary communists everywhere were unable to fulfill their promises. The Soviet, East European, Yugoslav, Chinese, Cambodian, Vietnamese and North Korean dictatorships of the proletariat neither realized Marx's utopian dreams nor outperformed the West. They neither morphed into democratic socialism nor converged to a common East-West social democratic economic system (Tinbergen, 1956; 1960, 1964)

The left blew smoke in the public's eyes for more than a century to avoid confronting this harsh verdict. It seldom displayed any doubt that the workers cause justified whatever actions Marxist–Leninists took and dismissed most criticism as anti-communist distemper. Bolsheviks criminalized private property, markets and repressed their enemies as Marxist-Leninism required to no avail. Communist leaders had no one to blame except themselves for history discrediting Marxist–Leninist theory. Communism ruled the Soviet Union for 73 year. Marxist-Leninism lasted 45 year in Eastern Europe and more than 75 years in North Korea without generating prosperity or harmonious worker self-management. Marxist-Leninism was bunk (Fischer, Gide, Koestler, Silone, Spender and Wright, 1949; Đjilas, 1957; Wiles, 1965).

Communists and their sympathizers, abetted by four fundamental statistical misassumptions,[37] won the Cold War on paper. The Soviet, East European, Yugoslavian, Chinese, Cambodian, Vietnamese and North Korean economies outperformed their peers according to official statistics (even during the Killing Fields of 1975–1979 in Cambodia) and appeared better than normal to them in all regard. They reported rapidly improving living standards, and successfully hid the magnitude of their military activities, forced labor and suppression of proletarian democracy well enough that having succumbed to a grand illusion, most Marxist–Leninists were surprised the Soviet Union collapsed. Marxist–Leninist embers persist in the Third World, but there are no proven pathways for advance.

Marxist–Leninist Growth Theory

The allure of revolutionary Marxist-Leninism persists despite its failures partly because many conceive planning as the antidote to the anarchy of capitalist markets.[38] They hope that Marxist–Leninist socialism offers the Third World a fast track to rapid economic growth, development and modernization, even though Xi Jinping insists that markets are more efficient than plans.

Is there merit to the idea that Marxist–Leninist growth theory is superior and valid in its own right despite the shortcomings of Soviet central planning? Was Soviet breakneck industrialization and forced collectivization of 1928–1936 indispensable for winning the war against economic backwardness?

Great Leap Forward in 1928–1937

Stalin industrialized the USSR by rapidly constructing new factories. He prioritized new capital formation embodying best locally available technologies and staffed them with peasants fleeing forced collectivization. Consistent with Marx's analysis in *Das Kapital*, Stalin believed that the sustainable rate of GDP growth depended on increased new capital formation. The larger the capital stock, the greater production potential and the greater the possibilities for growth accelerating scientific and technological progress. Stalin prioritized industrial over agrarian investment because following Marx he believed that machines producing more machines drove economic growth. Industrial investment increased the economy's ability to enlarge the capital stock; agricultural investment only generated increased food, raw materials and other intermediate input supplies.

Marxist–Leninists, based on this reasoning contended that socialism was an inherently superior engine of economic growth and development because it was unconstrained by short-term capitalist consumer demand. The Soviet Union could catch up with and overtake the West by mobilizing resources, channeling agricultural output to industrial processors, and concentrating new capital formation in industry at the expense of current consumption. Belt tightening today, combined with an industry first strategy of new capital formation, resource mobilization and forced labor would serve as a turnpike to prosperous tomorrows (Dorfman, Samuelson and Solow, 1958; McKenzie, 1976; Marrewijk and Jos Verbeek, 1993).[39]

The Marxist–Leninist–Stalinist disequilibrium growth strategy violates the neoclassical competitive ideal because it ignores consumer demand and time preference[40]; nonetheless, it suited Stalin. The turnpike maximized his priorities, enabling the USSR to industrialize at breakneck speed (Millar, 1974)[41] and accumulate a powerful military arsenal (Samuelson, 2000).

The East Europeans and Mao Zedong emulated the Marxist–Leninist–Stalinist growth model with similar results. They industrialized and their GDP grew rapidly on paper. The utilitarian benefits for workers were sparse. The goods and services transported on Marxist–Leninist–Stalinist turnpikes seldom reached consumers (economy of consumer goods shortage) and what little arrived was undesirable and shoddy. Building machines to build more machines that ultimately provided little consumer utility created an illusion of progress and proved to be a treadmill to oblivion.

Moreover, cluttering the landscape with factories (capital widening) without paying adequate attention to competitive scientific and technological progress (capital deepening) led inexorably to growth retardation. Economic growth rates in the Marxist–Leninist USSR and Eastern Europe stagnated after 1968 and began converging asymptotically to zero.

Marxist–Leninist disequilibrium socialist growth thus was a bust in two senses. Central planning failed to satisfy consumer demand, and growth slowed to a crawl (Bergson, 1963a, 1978b, 1979, 1987; Bergson and Levine, 1989). The failure of Marxist-Leninism was comprehensive. The collateral human cost of Stalin's growth strategy compounded the failure of central planning. Rapid Marxist–Leninist disequilibrium growth did not provide enduring compensation for the people's pain and suffering. See Appendix 3 for a discussion of other inadequacies of Marxist economic theory.

Notes

1 Alec Nove suggests, however, that if Stalin had not pressed forced industrialization, Hitler would have defeated the Soviet Union in World War II.
2 This expression is attributed to Robespierre and Lenin.
3 The Constitutional Democratic Party was a centrist, liberal political party in the Russian Empire that promoted Western constitutional monarchy (like England) – among other policies – and attracted a base ranging from moderate conservatives to mild socialists.
4 These successes, however, only demonstrate possibilities, not necessities because the German, Italian, Japanese, Austrian and Spanish democratic socialism stumbled during the fascist period. Although, non-Marxist–Leninist–Stalinist scholars broadly accept the plausibility of a democratic communist transition, post-tsarist Russian democracy might have degenerated into Muscovite authoritarianism.
5 "God is not averse to deceit in a just cause."
6 The war is directed against all types of capitalism including Werner Sombart and Joseph Schumpeter's concepts.
7 Burnt by the Sun is a 1994 film by Russian director and screenwriter Nikita Mikhalkov and Azerbaijani screenwriter Rustam Ibragimbekov.
8 Maurice Dobb, an economics professor at Trinity College, Cambridge University, joined the Communist Party in 1920 and in the 1930s was central to the burgeoning Communist movement at the university. One recruit was Kim Philby, who later became a Soviet high-placed mole in British intelligence.
9 Emil Ershov, head of the audit division of Goskomstat, spent days regaling me with details of Soviet statistical fraud.
10 See Nove's discussion of the "law of equal cheating."
11 The Ministry of Defense fixed the engineering characteristics of weapons and determined production volumes and assortments.
12 The weak link between Soviet output and utility growth includes the issue of value subtracted. The Japanese refused to purchase Soviet processed wooden products. They preferred raw timber, contending that Soviet processing reduced rather than added value. This illustrates how Soviet output statistics might overstate utility. However, it does not mean that the growth of low value-added products does not increase consumer utility. The value-subtracted concept is an opportunity cost issue.
13 Bergson could have saved the day by assuming that aggregation did not matter because the production functions of each of the 27.5 million products manufactured in the USSR were identical and Cobb-Douglas. The claim would be silly, but consistent with the sort of simplifying assumptions used to justify the notion of community indifference curves.
14 Bergson and others believed that the leadership would lose disciplinary control if enterprises and Goskomstat cosmetically enhanced their statistics. He mused that authorities would have to maintain two sets of book if they wanted to maintain command control and exaggerate Soviet economic performance, and then persuaded himself that this was impractical, ignoring the ad hoc character of the Soviet command control system.
15 Albina Tretyakova disclosed to the Office of Net Assessment that input-output table accountants did not have access to weapons production data. Vitaly Shlykov, Co-Chairman of Yeltsin's Russian Defense Council, chuckled at the claim made by Western experts such as Abraham Becker that the military industrial complex fully

and accurately disclosed weapons data. Private conversation. Emile Ershov detailed widespread chicanery in production statistics to the author.

16 NMP is like GDP, but excludes consumer services because they are considered as nonproductive.

17 NMP is roughly GDP less services.

18 The Soviets themselves only acknowledged around 1 million men in arms. CIA estimates of Soviet military manpower ran as high as 6 million.

19 The Moscow Trials were a series of show trials held in the Soviet Union at Joseph Stalin's instigation between 1936 and 1938 against Trotskyists and members of Right Opposition of the Communist Party of the Soviet Union.

20 On August 20, 1940, Ramón Mercader, Spanish-born NKVD agent, murdered Leon Trotsky. Stalin denied any Soviet complicity.

21 The Holodomor, Terror-Famine was a famine in Soviet Ukraine from 1932 to 1933 that killed millions of Ukrainians.

22 The 20 million excess death figure includes 9.7 million in 1928–1937 and 9 million in 1939–1953. The residual is attributable to war deaths misascribed to battle casualties. The Soviet sustained 8,806,453 million military fatalities during World War II, but claimed total population fatalities of 27 million. Excess deaths from the 1930s were buried in the World War II totals.

23 Allen argues that the USSR was one of the most successful developing economies of the 20th century. He reaches this conclusion by recalculating national consumption and using economic, demographic and computer simulation models to address the "what if" questions central to Soviet history.

24 Subbotnik is a day of unpaid labor, usually on a Saturday. It promoted the idea of socialism through labor. "War is peace. Freedom is slavery. Ignorance is strength" (Orwell, 1949).

25 In 1920, the Russian Soviet Republic under Lenin became the first country in the world in the modern era to allow abortion in all circumstances, but over the course of the 20th century, the legality of abortion changed more than once, with a ban on unconditional abortions enacted again from 1936 to 1955.

26 Gender wage disparity was greater in the USSR than in America. Soviet men and women received equal pay but women's work was concentrated in low-wage occupations.

27 Marxist feminism is a philosophical variant of feminism that incorporates and extends Marxist theory. It analyzes the ways in which capitalism exploits women. According to Marxist feminists, women's liberation is only achievable by dismantling the capitalist systems in which they contend much of women's labor is uncompensated. Marxist feminists extend traditional Marxist analysis by applying it to unpaid domestic labor and sex relations.

28 Nicholaevsky was a Menshevik and head of the Marx-Engels Institute in Moscow. The Soviets deported him in 1922. His extensive collection of revolutionary documents is stored at the Hoover Institution Archives in Palo Alto, California. Dallin and Nicolaevsky's 1947 *Forced Labor in Soviet Russia* had been a pioneering study of the Soviet labor camp system, well received in the academic world at the time, but retroactively discredited in the 1960s due to its use of defector testimony and Dallin's Menshevik origins. Bergson cautioned about the reliability of Dallin and Nicholaevsky's sources.

29 Wassily Leontief, born on August 5, 1906, St. Petersburg, Russia, called the father of input-output analysis, won the Nobel Prize for Economics in 1973. He entered

University of Leningrad in 1921 and graduated in 1925. He was detained three times by the Cheka (secret police) for supporting libertarianism but was permitted to emigrate in 1925.

30 Leonard Schapiro (1908–1983) was a British scholar of Russian politics. He taught for many years at the London School of Economics, where he was a Professor of Political Science with Special Reference to Russian Studies.

Born in Glasgow, he was taken to Russia and spent some of his childhood in Riga (his father having taken over the family timber business) and St. Petersburg, when his father took a position in railway administration. He joined the General Staff at the War Office from 1945 to 1946.

31 Alexander Nove (1915–1994) was a Professor of Economics at the University of Glasgow and a noted authority on Russian and Soviet economic history. Born in Petrograd, he moved to Britain with his father in the early 1920s. His experience in the Board of Trade alerted him to the inherent weaknesses of state planning.

32 Bergson visited the USSR in 1936 and understood the dark reality of Stalin's show trials. Personal conversation. He was the chief of the Russian Economic subdivision of the Office of Strategic Services during World War II.

33 John Maynard Keynes (1883–1946) visited Russia three times between 1925 and 1936. His wife Lydia Lopokova was a Russian ballerina. He knew Russia, the country's economy and its political regime very well. He praised Stalin's planned economy. Keynes believed that state planning was necessary. Keynes spoke to the Soviet politburo on September 14, 1925. Leon Trotsky attended, as he was the chairman of the technical and scientific board of industry. Trotsky identified Keynes as a socialist: "Even the more progressive economist, Mr. Keynes told us only the other day that the salvaging of the English economy lies in Malthusianism! For England, too, the road of overcoming the contradictions between city and country leads through socialism." https://mises.org/wire/keynes-called-himself-socialist-he-was-right Keynes grew increasingly close to Sidney and Beatrice Webb in the mid-1920s. He was chairman of Britain's leading socialist newspaper, *the New Statesman*.

34 Maurice Herbert Dobb (1900–1976) was an English economist at Cambridge University and a Fellow of Trinity College, Cambridge. He was one of the preeminent Marxist economists of the 20th century.

Dobb joined the Communist Party in 1920 and in the 1930s was central to the burgeoning Communist movement at the university. One recruit was Kim Philby, who later became a high-placed Soviet mole within British intelligence. It has been suggested that Dobb was a "talent-spotter" for Comintern. Dobb was a highly placed communist revolutionary in Britain at the time. He was politically very active and spent much time organizing rallies and presenting lectures on a consistent basis. As an economist, he was commonly focused on vulnerability to economic crisis and pointed to the United States as a case of capitalist money assisting military agendas instead of public works.

35 Richard Pipes (1923–2018) was an American academic who specialized in Russian and Soviet history. He published several books critical of communist regimes throughout his career. In 1976, he headed Team B, a team of analysts organized by the Central Intelligence Agency who analyzed the strategic capacities and goals of the Soviet military and political leadership. Pipes was born in Cieszyn, Poland. He fled to the United States in 1940 and became a naturalized citizen in 1943. He was the director of Harvard's Russian Research Center from 1968 to 1973 and later Baird Professor Emeritus of History at Harvard University. Pipes contended that the Bolshevik

Revolution was a coup foisted upon the majority of the Russian population by a tiny segment of the population driven by a select group of intellectuals who subsequently established a one-party dictatorship that was intolerant and repressive from the start.

36 Lech Wałęsa and others formed a broad anti-Soviet social movement ranging from people associated with the Catholic Church to members of the anti-Soviet left. Polish nationalism, together with pro-American liberalism, played an important part in the development of Solidarity in the 1980s.

37 The author discussed these issues on numerous occasions with Bergson. He was certain that the official defense budgetary statistic contained weapons in accordance with study of Soviet defense accounting practice during the Stalin era. Gorbachev revealed that Bergson was mistaken in 1989. His error affected to calculation of the structure of Soviet GDP activities, giving the false impression that the USSR was a "normal" country. Bergson insisted that Soviet GDP data were "reliable." Boris Ershov and Vitaly Shlykov contend that he was wrong. Bergson was aware of the hidden inflation controversy, but considered it subsidiary. He was skeptical of Dallin and Nicholaevsky's account of Soviet forced labor and did not take it into account in his national income studies. Alex Nove and most other experts on the Soviet economy shared Bergson's views on defense, gulag, Holodomor and the reliability of Soviet statistics. Nove and his British colleagues, however, were unimpressed by Bergson's adjusted factor costing.

38 Competitive markets are not "anarchic," but they are occasionally subject to bubbles. Planned economies are vulnerable to the same "teleological" excesses. The teleological school in the USSR was represented by major economists such as S. Strumilin, G. L. Pytatakov, V. V. Kuibyshev and P. A. Fel'dman. They urged aspirational planning unrestricted by prior achieved levels.

39 "The best intermediate capital configuration is one which will grow most rapidly, even if it is not the most desired one, it is temporarily optimal" (Dorfman, Samuelson, Solow, 1958, 331).

40 People can choose between consuming today or investing to enjoy an augmented future stream of consumption tomorrow. This option is called time preference.

41 Millar misconstrues the turnpike argument. He concentrates on the Marxist concept of agricultural surplus, which is only tangential to the turnpike concept.

References

Aganbegyan, Abel. (1988). *The Economic Challenge of Perestroika*. Bloomington: Indiana University Press.

Alexeev, Michael and Clifford Gaddy. (1993). "Income Distribution in the U.S.S.R. in the 1980s." *Review of Income and Wealth Series*. Vol. 39, No. 1, 23–36.

Allen, Robert. (2003). *Farm to Factory: A Reinterpretation of the Soviet Industrial Revolution*. Princeton: Princeton University Press.

Amalrik, Andrei. (1970). *Will the Soviet Union Survive until 1984?* New York: Harper & Row.

Aron, Raymond. (2001). *Opium of the Intellectuals*. New Brunswick: Transaction.

Aslund, Anders. (1988). "How Small Is Soviet National Income?" In Henry Rowen and Charles Wolf, Jr. (eds.). The *Impoverished Superpower: Perestroika and the Soviet Military Burden*. San Francisco: ICS Press, 13–62.

Avdeev, Alexandre, Alain Blum and Irina Troitskaya. (1995). "The History of Abortion Statistics in Russia and the USSR from 1900 to 1991." *Population*. Vol. 7, 39–66.

Balzer, Harley. (2019). *Soviet Science on the Edge of Reform*. New York: Routledge.

Becker, Abraham. (1968). *Soviet National Income: 1958–1964, National Income Accounts of the USSR in the Seven Year Plan Period*. Berkeley: University of California Press.

Becker, Abraham. (1970). *National Income Accounting in the USSR*. Santa Monica: Rand Corporation.

Becker, Abraham. (1977). *Military Expenditure Limitation for Arms Control: Problems and Prospects*. Cambridge: Ballinger.

Beckett, Samuel. (1956. *Waiting for Godot*. London: Faber and Faber.

Bergson, Abram. (1948). "Review of David Dallin and Boris Nicholaevsky, *Forced Labor in Soviet Russia*." *The Journal of Economic History*. Vol. 8, No. 2, 234–237.

Bergson, Abram. (1950). "Soviet National Income and Product in 1937, Parts I and II." *Quarterly Journal of Economics*. Vol. 64, Nos. 2, 3, 208–241, 408–441.

Bergson, Abram. (1953a). "Reliability and Usability of Soviet Statistics: A Summary Appraisal." *American Statistician*. Vol. 7, No. 3, 13–16.

Bergson, Abram. (1953b). *Soviet National Income and Product in 1937*. New York: Columbia University Press.

Bergson, Abram. (1954). *Soviet National Income and Product, 1940–1948*. New York: Columbia University Press.

Bergson, Abram. (1961). *The Real National Income of Soviet Russia since 1928*. Cambridge: Harvard University Press.

Bergson, Abram. (1963a). "The Great Economic Race." *Challenge Magazine*. Vol. 11, No. 6, 4–46.

Bergson, Abram. (1963b). "National Income." In Abram Bergson and Simon Kuznets (eds).. *Economic Trends in the Soviet Union*. Cambridge: Harvard University Press, 1–37.

Bergson, Abram. (1966a). "Socialist Calculation: A Further Word." In Abram Bergson (ed.). *Essays in Normative Economics*. Cambridge: Harvard University Press, 237–242.

Bergson, Abram. (1966b). "Soviet Economics." The *New York Review of Books*. Vol. 5, No. 12, 37–38.

Bergson, Abram. (1972). "Soviet National Income Statistics." In V. Treml and J. Hardt (eds.). *Soviet Economic Statistics*. Durham: Duke University Press, 148–152.

Bergson, Abram. (1975). "Index Numbers and the Computation of Factor Productivity." *Review of Income and Wealth*. Vol. 4, No. 3, 259–278.

Bergson, Abram. (1978). "The Soviet Economic Slowdown." *Challenge Magazine*. Vol. 20, No. 6, 22–33.

Bergson, Abram. (1979). "Notes on the Production Function in Soviet Post-War Industrial Growth." *Journal of Comparative Economics*. Vol. 3, No. 2, 116–126.

Bergson, Abram. (1984). "Income Inequality under Soviet Socialism." *Journal of Economic Literature*. Vol. 22, No. 3, 1052–1099.

Bergson, Abram. (1987). "Comparative Productivity: The USSR, Eastern Europe and the West. *American Economic Review*. Vol. 77, No. 3, 342–357.

Bergson, Abram. (1991). "The USSR before the Fall: How Poor and Why?" *Journal of Economic Perspectives*. No. 5, 29–44.

Bergson, Abram and Herbert Levine (eds.). (1991). *Planning and Performance in Socialist Economies*. New York: Unwin and Hyman.

Berkowitz, Daniel, Joseph Berliner, Paul Gregory, Susan Linz and James Millar. (1993). "An Evaluation of the CIA's Analysis of Soviet Economic Performance, 1970–1990." *Comparative Economic Studies*. Vol. 35, No. 2, 33–48.

Berliner, Joseph. (1976). *The Innovation Decision in Soviet Industry*. Cambridge: MIT Press.

Blakemore, Erin. (2019). "The Accident at a Nuclear Power Plant in Ukraine Shocked the World, Permanently Altered a Region, and Leaves Many Questions Unanswered." *National Geographic.*

Bornstein, Morris. (1978). "The Administration of the Soviet Price System." *Soviet Studies.* Vol. 30, No. 4, 466–490.

Breslauer, George. (2021). *The Rise and Demise of World Communism.* New York: Oxford University Press.

Bulgakov, Mikhail (1967). *Master and the Margarita.* New York: YMCA Press.

Chapman, Janet. (2013). "Consumption.: In Janet Chapman (ed.). *Economic Trends in the Soviet Union.* Cambridge: Harvard University Press.

CIA. (1976). *Estimate Soviet Defense Spending in Rubles, 1970–1975.* SR 76-10121U.

CIA. (1979). *A Dollar Cost Comparison of Soviet and U.S. Defense Activities, 1968–1978.* SR-79-10004.

CIA. (1991). *Measures of Soviet Gross National Product in 1982 Prices.* Washington: Joint Economic Committee of Congress.

Cohen, Stephen. (1980). *Bukharin and the Bolshevik Revolution: A Political Biography, 1888–1938.* New York: Oxford University Press.

Conquest, Robert. (1987). *Harvest of Sorrow.* London: Oxford University Press.

Conquest, Robert. (2007). *The Great Terror.* London: Oxford University Press.

Dallin, David and Boris Nicholaevsky. (1947). *Forced Labor in Soviet Russia.* New Haven: Yale University Press

Davies, Robert. (2010). "The Economic History of the Soviet Union Reconsidered." *Kritika: Explorations in Russian and Eurasian History.* Vol. 11, No. 1, 145–159.

Desai, Padma. (1966). "Soviet Growth Retardation." *The American Economic Review.* Vol. 76, No. 2, 175–180.

Djilas, Milovan. (1957). *The New Class: An Analysis of the Communist System.* New York: Harcourt Brace Jovanovich.

Dobb, Maurice. (1948). *Soviet Economic Development Since 1917.* London: Routledge.

Dorfman, Robert, Paul Samuelson and Robert Solow. (1958). *Linear Programming and Economic Analysis.* New York: McGraw-Hill Book Company.

Eberstadt, Nick. (2006). "The Health Crisis in the USSR." *International Journal of Epidemiology.* Vol. 35, No. 6, 1384–1394.

Feshbach, Murray. (1984). "Soviet Health Problems." *Proceedings of the Academy of Political Science.* Vol. 35, No. 3, 81–97.

Feshbach, Murray. (1995). *Ecological Disaster: Cleaning up the Hidden Legacy of the Soviet Regime.* New York: Twentieth Century Fund Press.

Feshbach, Murray and Alfred Friendly. (1984). *Ecocide in the USSR: Health and Nature under Siege.* New York: Basic Books.

Firth, Noel and James Noren. (1998). *Soviet Defense Spending: A History of CIA Estimates 1950–1990.* College State: Texas A&M University.

Fischer, Louis, André Gide, Arthur Koestler, Ignazio Silone, Stephen Spender and Richard Wright. (1949). *The God that Failed.* New York: Harper and Brothers.

Ginzburg, Evgenia. (1967). *Journey into the Whirlwind.* New York: Harvest Book.

Ginzburg, Evgenia. (1982). *Within the Whirlwind.* New York: Harvest Book.

Goldman, Emma. (1923). *My Disillusionment in Russia.* New York: Doubleday and Page.

Goodman, Melvin. (2008). *Failure of Intelligence: The Decline and Fall of the CIA.* New York: Rowman & Littlefield Publishers.

Goodman, Melvin. (2021). "The Dangerous Exaggeration of the Threat." *Counterpunch.* .

Hansen, Alvin. (1939). "Economic Progress and Declining Population Growth." *The American Economic Review*. Vol. 29, No. 1, 1–15.

Harrison, Mark. (2000). "Soviet Industrial Production, 1928 to 1955: Real Growth and Hidden Inflation." *Journal of Comparative Economics*. Vol. 28, No. 1, 134–155.

Harrison, Mark. (2010). "Forging Success: Soviet Managers and Accounting Fraud, 1943 to 1962." Unpublished draft. https://warwick.ac.uk/fac/soc/economics/staff/mharrison/public/jce2011postprint.pdf

Khrushchev, Nikita. (1956). "Crimes of the Stalin Era." *Special Report to the 20th Congress of the Communist Party of the Soviet Union*.

Koen, Vincent and Jinwoan Beom. (2020). *North Korea: The Last Transition Economy? Economics Department Working Papers No.1607*. Paris: OECD.

Kontorovich, Vladimir. (1989). "Inflation in the Soviet Investment and Capital Stock." *Soviet Studies*. Vol. 41, No. 2, 318–329.

Lokaneeta, Jinee. (2001). "Alexandra Kollontai and Marxist Feminism." *Economic and Political Weekly*. Vol. 36, No. 17, 1405–1412.

Luxemburg, Rosa. (1970). *The Russian revolution and Leninism or Marxism?* Ann Arbor: University of Michigan Press.

Markevich, Andrei and Mark Harrison. (2011). "Great War, Civil War, and Recovery: Russia's National Income, 1913 to 1928." *Journal of Economic History*. Vol. 71, No. 3, 672–703.

Marrewijk, Charles van and Jos Verbeek. (1993). "Disequilibrium Growth Theory in an International Perspective." *Oxford Economic Papers*. Vol. 45, No. 2, 311–331.

McAuley, Alistair. (1971). *Economic Welfare in the Soviet Union: Poverty, Living Standards and Inequality*. Hemel Hempstead: George Allen & Unwin, Ltd.

McKenzie, Lionel. (1976). "Turnpike Theory." *Econometrica*. Vol. 44, No. 5, 841–865.

Millar, James. (1974). "Mass Collectivization and the Contribution of Soviet Agriculture to the First Five-Year Plan: A Review Article." *Slavic Review*. Vol. 33, No. 4, 750–766.

Narodnoe khoziaistvo za 60 let, iubileinyi statisticheskii ezhegodnik. (1977). Moscow: Finansy I Statistika.

Nove, Alec. (1961). *The Soviet Economy*. London: George Allen and Unwin Ltd.

Nove, Alec. (1990). *An Economic History of the U.S.S.R.*. London: Penguin.

Nutter, G. Warren, Israel Borenstein and Adam Kaufman. (1962). *Growth of Industrial Production in the Soviet Union*. Princeton: Princeton University Press.

Ofer, Gur. (1987). "Soviet Economic Growth: 1928–1985." *Journal of Economic Literature*. Vol. 25, No. 4, 1767–1833.

Orwell, George (1949). *Nineteen Eighty-Four*. London: Secker & Warburg.

Popov, A. A. (1990). "Family Planning in the USSR. Sky-High Abortion Rates Reflect Dire Lack of Choice." *Entre Nous Cph Den*. Vol. 16, 5–7.

Reilly, David. (1996). "Lessons from Soviet Education: The Need for an Educational System with Responsibility, Authority, and Courage." *The Journal of Educational Thought*. Vol. 30, No. 3, 239–261.

Rosefielde, Steven. (1986). "The Underestimation of Soviet Weapons Prices: Learning Curve Bias." *Osteuropa Wirtschaft*. Vol. 31, 53–63.

Rosefielde, Steven. (1987a). *False Science: Underestimating the Soviet Arms Buildup*. New Brunswick: Transaction.

Rosefielde, Steven. (1987b). "Incriminating Evidence: Excess Deaths and Forced Labor under Stalin." *Soviet Studies*. Vol. 39, No. 2, 292–313.

Rosefielde, Steven. (1988). "Excess Deaths and Industrialization: A Realist Theory of Stalinist Economic Development in the Thirties." *Journal of Contemporary History*. Vol. 23, 277–289.

Rosefielde, Steven. (1994a). "The Absurdity of Soviet Value Statistics: Comment on Abram Bergson's Real National Income in Soviet Perspective." *Economic Statistics for Economies in Transition: Eastern Europe in the 1990s.* U.S. Bureau of Labor Statistics and Eurostat, 117–126.

Rosefielde, Steven. (1994b). "The Meaning and Measurement of Hidden Inflation in Demand Insensitive Economic Systems: A Comment on H. Stephen Gardner's Paper 'Product Quality and Price Inflation in Transitional Economies.'" *Economic Statistics for Economies in Transition: Eastern Europe in the 1990s.* U.S. Bureau of Labor Statistics and Eurostat, U. S. Department of Labor, 192–200.

Rosefielde, Steven. (1996). "Stalinism in Postcommunist Perspective: New Evidence on Killings, Forced Labor and Economic Development in the Thirties." *Europe-Asia Studies.* Vol. 48, No. 6, 959–987.

Rosefielde, Steven. (1997). "Documented Homicides and Excess Deaths: New Insights into the Scale of Killings in the USSR During the 1930s." *Communist and Post Communist Studies.* Vol. 30, No. 3, 321–331.

Rosefielde, Steven. (2003a). "Comparative Production Potential in the USSR and the West: Pre-Transition Assessments." In Steven Rosefielde (ed.). *Efficiency and Russia's Economic Recovery Potential to the Year 2000 and Beyond.* Aldershot: Ashgate, 101–135.

Rosefielde, Steven. (2003b). "The Riddle of Postwar Russian Economic Growth: Statistics Lied and Were Misconstrued." *Europe-Asia Studies.* Vol. 55, No. 3, 469–481.

Rosefielde, Steven. (2004). "Postwar Russian Economic Growth: Not a Riddle – A Reply." *Europe-Asia Studies.* Vol. 56, No. 3, 463–466.

Rosefielde, Steven. (2005a). *Russia in the 21st Century: The Prodigal Superpower.* Cambridge: Cambridge University Press.

Rosefielde, Steven. (2005b). "Tea Leaves and Productivity: Bergsonian Norms for Gauging the Soviet Future." *Comparative Economic Studies.* Vol. 47, No. 2, 259–273.

Rosefielde, Steven. (2007). *Russian Economy from Lenin to Putin.* New York: Wiley.

Rosefielde, Steven. (2010). *Red Holocaust.* London: Routledge.

Rosefielde, Steven. (2012). "Economics of the Military Industrial Complex." Chapter 18, In Michael Alexeev and Shlomo Weber (eds.). *The Oxford Handbook of Russian Economy.* Oxford: Oxford University Press.

Rosefielde, Steven and Knox Lovell. (1977). "The Impact of Adjusted Factor Cost Valuation on the CES Interpretation of Postwar Soviet Economic Growth." *Economica*, Vol. 44, 381–392.

Rosefielde, Steven and Masaaki Kuboniwa. (2003). "Russian Growth Retardation Then and Now." *Eurasian Geography and Economics.* Vol. 44, No. 2, 87–101.

Rosefielde, Steven and R. W. Pfouts. (1995). "Neoclassical Norms and the Valuation of National Product the Soviet Union and Its Post-communist Successor States." *Journal of Comparative Economics.* Vol. 21, No. 3, 375–380.

Rosefielde, Steven and R.W. Pfouts. (1998). "The Mis-specification of Soviet Production Potential: Adjusted Factor Costing and Bergson's Efficiency Standard." In Steven Rosefielde(ed.). *Efficiency and Russia's Economic Recovery Potential to the Year 2000 and Beyond.* Aldershot: Ashgate, 11–31.

Rosefielde, Steven, Theodore Shabad and Alexander Yanov. (1982). "Letters." *Slavic Review.* Vol. 41, No. 4, 766–775.

Rowland, Diane and Alexandre Telyukov. (1991). "Soviet Health Care from Two Perspectives." *Health Affairs.* Vol. 10, No. 3, 71–86.

Samuelson, Lennart. (2000). *Plans for Stalin's War Machine: Tukhachevskii and Military-Economic Planning, 1925–1941*. London: Palgrave Macmillan.

Samuelson, Paul. (2004). "Abram Bergson April 21, 1914–April 23, 2003." *Biographical Memoirs*, Vol. 84. Washington: National Academies Press. www.nap.edu/read/10992/chapter/3

Schapiro, Leonard. (1970). *The Communist Party of the Soviet Union*. New York: Random House Publishers.

Schapiro, Leonard. (1972). *Totalitarianism: Key Concepts in Political Science*. Ann Arbor: The University of Michigan.

Schapiro, Leonard. (1984). *The Russian Revolutions of 1917: The Origins of Modern Communism*. New York: Basic Books.

Schroeder, Gertrude and Elizabeth Denton. (1982). "An Index of Consumption in the USSR." *USSR: Measures of Economic Growth and Development*. Washington: Joint Economic Committee of Congress, 317–401.

Schumpeter, Joseph. (1942). *Capitalism, Socialism and Democracy*. Floyd: Impact Books.

Service, Robert. (2010). *Trotsky: A Biography*. New York: Macmillan Publishers.

Sicsú, João. (2020). *Keynes's State Planning: From Bolshevism to the General Theory*. Instituto de Economia, Universidade Federal do Rio de Janeiro, Discussion Paper 024. www.ie.ufrj.br/publicacoes-j/textos-para-discussao.html

Solzhenitsyn, Alexander. (2007). *The Gulag Archipelago, 1918–1956: An Experiment in Literary Investigation*, Vol. 1,2, 3. New York: Harper Perennial Modern Classics.

Sombart, Werner. (1896). *Sozialismus und soziale Bewegung*. Jena: Verlag von Gustav Fischer.

Sombart, Werner. (1898). *Socialism and the Social Movement in the 19th Century*. New York: G.P. Putnam's Sons.

Stalin, Joseph. (1930). "K voprósam kolkhóznogo dvizhéniya (On the Question of the kolkoz movement)." *Pravda*.

Stanley, John. (1987). "Is Totalitarianism a New Phenomenon? Reflections on Hannah Arendt's Origins of Totalitarianism." *The Review of Politics*. Vol. 49, No. 2, 177–207.

Tinbergen, Jan. (1959). *The Theory of the Optimum Regime*. Amsterdam: North Holland.

Tinbergen, Jan. (1960). "Do Communist and Free Economies Show a Converging Pattern?" *Soviet Studies*. Vol. 12, No. 4, 333–341.

Tinbergen, Jan. (1964). *Central Planning*. New Haven: Yale University Press.

Tismaneanu, Vladimir and Jordan Luber (eds.) (2021). *One Hundred Years of Communist Experiments*. Budapest–New York: CEU press.

Trachtenberg, Marc. (2018). "Assessing Soviet Economic Performance during the Cold War: A Failure of Intelligence?" *The Scholar*. Vol. 1, No. 2. https://doi.org/10.15781/T2QV3CM4W

Treml, Vladimir and John Hardt (eds.). (1972). *Soviet Economic Statistics*. Durham: Duke University Press, 148–152.

Trotsky, Leon. (1932). *The Stalin School of Falsification*. New York: Pioneer Publishers.

Trotsky, Leon. (1937). *The Revolution Betrayed: What Is the Soviet Union and Where Is It Going?* New York: Doubleday, Doran and Co.

Trotsky, Leon. (1946). *Stalin: An Appraisal of the Man and His Influence*. New York: Harper and Brothers.

Wiles, Peter. (1965). "Rationalizing the Russians." *New York Review of Books.*

Wolfe, Bertram. (1961). "Rosa Luxemburg and V. I. Lenin: The Opposite Poles of Revolutionary Socialism." *The Antioch Review.* Vol. 21, No. 2, 209–226.

Zaleski, Eugène. (1980). *Stalinist Planning for Economic Growth, 1933–1952.* Chapel Hill: The University of North Carolina Press.

Zaleski, Eugène. (2011). *Planning for Economic Growth in the Soviet Union, 1918—1932.* Chapel Hill: University of North Carolina Press.

Part III

Post Command Planning

16 Chinese Market Communism

The communist parties of the USSR, Eastern Europe, China, North Korea, Vietnam and Cuba before 1992 perceived themselves as the people's guardians tasked to rule on the proletariat's behalf until the working class came of age in accordance with fundamentals set forth in Marx's *Economic and Philosophical Manuscripts of 1844* and the *Communist Manifesto*. These principles include people's ownership of the means of production, criminalization of markets, and entrepreneurship, cooperative worker self-management, shared consumption according to need and eventually full abundance and perpetual harmony. Marxist–Leninists contended that private ownership, markets and entrepreneurship are tools enabling self-seekers to exploit others (Dahrendorf, 1959).They inure inegalitarianism and preclude harmonious cooperation.

From 1917 until 1991, orthodox Marxist–Leninists considered "market communism" heresy. They believed that markets were engines of labor exploitation and therefore incompatible with socialism and full communism. A few heterodox Marxist–Leninist disagreed, suggesting that market communism might be acceptable if efficiency gains for workers outweighed costs of labor exploitation. Nikolai Bukharin (Bukharin, 1982; Cohen, 1980; Bergmann and Lewin, 2017; Smith, 1979; Clarke, 1982, nd),[1] Oscar Lange (Lange, 1938)[2] and various Yugoslav theorists debated the possibility of integrating markets into communist systems of 1924–1991 from neoclassical and political economic perspectives. Their proposals received mixed reviews. Neoclassical and Austrian theorists were skeptical of Lange's "competitive solution" (MacKenzie, 2006; Roberts, 1971; Rosefielde, 1973; Miller, 1990). See Chapter 11. Orthodox Marxist–Leninist political economic theorists dismissed market socialism in any form including democratic socialism, social democracy and evolutionary socialism as naïve or perfidious, fearing counterrevolution (Clarke, 1994). See Chapter 17. Nonetheless, Yugoslavia began introducing market elements into its communist system in the mid-1950s. See Chapter 8. The Hungarians quietly followed suit (Antal, 1979; Bauer, 1982; Berend, 1990; Kornai, 1983, 1986; Samuely, 1978, 1984; Hare, Radice, and Swain, 1981; Révész, 1990; Miller, 1987, 1990). See Chapter 11. The Chinese began shifting to market communism under Deng Xiaoping in the early 1980s on the assumption that if the state retained freehold ownership rights over the

DOI: 10.4324/9781003371571-20

entire means of production, markets could improve socialist economic efficiency without unduly harming the working class.

"White Cat" Market Communism

Deng used folk maxims to justify his position. He asserted that "It doesn't matter if a cat is black or white; as long as it catches mice, it's a good cat" to make the point that markets can be employed if they benefit the Party and the people, without citing Marx chapter and verse.[3] His revisionist declaration was metaphorical, but the message was clear (Di, 2016). China on Deng's authority would permit some competitive market processes, shifting priority from suppressing labor exploitation to the four modernizations (agriculture, industry, science and technology and the military), while remaining loyal to communism's ultimate goal of communal self-management and egalitarian sharing. China's Communist Party would discover how to capture the benefits of markets at an acceptable price by "touching stones to cross the river" until China was ready for full communism (Nolan, 1994).

The problem with Deng's white cat/black cat metaphor lay in its social costs. Markets spawn inequality by allowing some to prosper, leaving the rest behind even under perfect competition. When markets are imperfect, the strong exploit the weak more intensely (Stiglitz, 2019). Would the rich who prosper from market activities share their wealth with the poor? Would the CPC as freehold owner of the means of production and state protector defend vulnerable workers during the transition to full market-free communism?

Deng brushed these objections aside presuming that the CPC would solve the dilemma by retaining state freehold ownership of the means of production and claiming that China's leadership would use its monopoly of state power to foster communitarian cooperation (fairness and sharing) and market competition.[4] The CPC as custodian of the people's freehold property would lease its assets to various state and private profit-seeking managers and set leasehold terms to protect the workers from abuse. It would inculcate labor with communist values preparing the way for full communal self-management. China during the transition period would produce goods "from each according to ability" and provide for special needs. Plans and competition would be complements instead of substitutes, jointly applied to maximize the quality of socialist existence.

The notion that competition and planning are complements is not an oxymoron. Although, economists and political economists are inclined to draw a sharp dichotomy between markets and plans (capitalism and socialism), competition and state economic management are compatible with a wide variety of political economic systems, given appropriate assumptions about rational choice optimizing and the quality of existence (Rosefielde, 2022). Deng's "white cat" market communism does not elaborate how private utility seekers and state administrators comanage, but the concept seemed plausible enough to justify his market communist experiment.

Deng's revision of Marxist-Leninism has two aspects. First, managers and entrepreneurs cannot own freehold property.[5] They may only lease property from the state. They cannot be freeholders of public property (land, factories, commercial, financial and service facilities). The state alone has this right and uses it to assign leases supporting the CPC's "four modernizations" program.

Second, the Communist Party can obligate enterprise managers, entrepreneurs and communal institutions to operate on a team basis (Marschak and Radner, 1972; Boswell, 1994; Etzioni, 1988; Eecke, 1996; Avineri and de-Shalit, 1992),[6] taking explicit account of utilitarian benefits from communitarian cooperation and solidarity. Leaseholders, workers and consumers can maximize their personal utility as a platform for improving society's quality of existence in Deng Xiaoping's white cat universe.

During the market communist transition period, the CPC integrates supervisory and competitive aspects of the economy (vertical communism). After the proletariat reaches maturity, workers themselves will manage the system (nonmarket horizontal communism) (McCloskey, 2019).

Deng never said that white cat market communism would be optimal. He merely suggested that outcomes would be better than black cat market capitalism, top-down command planning and Mao's "red cat" anti-market Cultural Revolution. See Chapter 9. The weight of Western expert opinion in the 1990s was against Deng's vision (Kornai, 1990, 2003);[7] however, the Middle Kingdom's economic performance of 1980–2022 has challenged this consensus. China has not only survived, it developed, modernized, grew rapidly and integrated into the global economy. Deng's white cat scheme worked. The only outstanding issue is its comparative merit (Nolan, 1994).

Xi's Market Communism

Xi Jinping's market communist economy follows Deng's "white cat" script and resembles the libertarian leasehold ideal, expanded to include a theory of teams. The differences between Taiwan's "black cat" Confucian free enterprise (capitalists versus workers) and Xi's "white cat" market communism (state entrepreneurial managers versus workers) are largely imperceptible to the untrained eye. "White and black cat" workers have job choice and negotiate wages in both systems. "White cat" Chinese communist companies lease offices, factories and land from the state just as their capitalist counterparts can in Taiwan. "White cat" communist managers and entrepreneurs compete for factors and sales and strive to make profits domestically and abroad. Xi's communist and Taiwan's capitalist companies both endeavor to construct extended family-related business networks founded on exchanges of favors and economies of trust (guanxi) (Gold, Guthrie and Wank, 2002).[8] Banks make competitive business and personal loans on the mainland and in Taiwan. "White cat" communists and "black cat" free enterprise Taiwanese trade securities, bonds and derivatives on the Shanghai and Taipei stock exchanges. They purchase and sell securities in other countries. Foreigners directly invest in special economic zones and in China's heartland. Companies can franchise, merge and conglomerate. Entrepreneurs can start new businesses. Citizens can travel at home and across the globe. They can shop until they drop in stores or become comatose on the internet. China and Taiwan both employ standard macroeconomic tools to regulate aggregate economic activity, and their currencies are exchangeable across the globe. Beijing and Taipei both stress the importance of cooperation and communal harmony. The only things conspicuously distinguishing China's white cat market communism from Taiwan's democratic free enterprise are the CPC's state monopoly on freehold property (means of production); its role in directing and regulating the economy, political governance, civil liberties, ethical priorities, restrictions on democracy and civil liberties.

The CPC is China's sovereign. Xi Jinping is the CEO of China Incorporated and market communism's master puppeteer. The state monopoly on freehold property enables the CPC's right hand to determine who leases the nation's enterprises and the scope of delegated authority and obligation. The CPC's left hand (the executive, legislative, judicial branches of government) grants leaseholders and the people considerable freedom to choose rationally in the marketplace, but also commands obedience.

Managerial and entrepreneurial leaseholders are tenants with limited rights. They have no legal basis for claiming unrestricted control over enterprise management and revenues. The state as the freehold lease grantor has authority to stipulate enterprise use, merger, acquisition, spinoff, finance and compensation (including the distribution of profits). State authorities in the West can do these things too (e.g., by setting a minimum wage), but only through legislation, executive mandates and bureaucratic regulation. The CPC as freehold lease grantor does not have to bother with democratically negotiating the details. It simply compels leaseholders to comply with the terms it stipulates in the leasing agreement. The CPC also is the arbiter of lease disputes because it controls the courts. It can abrogate leases at its discretion and transfer leases from one company to another when they expire. Managerial and entrepreneurial leaseholders, regardless of how they perceive themselves, and despite expanded managerial authority and perquisites, essentially remain state-appointed factory directors. The communist party at its discretion can allow companies to clone the behavior of its "black cat" twins in Taiwan. It can compel leaseholders to hew a communist path, or coax them with ancillary tax, subsidy and regulatory instruments. The CPC monopoly of state power allows it to take a communist pro-worker, or capitalist road, or flit back and forth at its discretion. Taiwan's government and its "black cat" markets by contrast are democratic and consumer sovereign.

CPC Turnpike

Xi Jinping has chosen to use CPC market communist power to transition from Stalin and Mao's top-down planning turnpike to modern industrial communism. The goals of the 14th Five-Year Plan period (2021-2025) are to prepare a foundation for Marxist full communism by building a prosperous secular nation that defends workers from capitalist and imperialist exploitation, advances equality, entitlement, affirmative action and social justice, and acculturates the masses to harmonious self-governing communitarian cooperation (Koleski, 2017; Zhang, 2021).[9] This communism with Chinese characteristics requires maintaining the CPC monopoly on political power, military might and repressing the people's enemies at home and abroad as it did under Mao, but with differences. Xi no longer forbids markets and entrepreneurship or insists on a Spartan proletarian lifestyle. He has made markets, entrepreneurship and imperial opulence the engine of the "white cat" socialist revolution designed to increase productivity and efficiency, transfer technology from abroad, spur domestic innovation and worker effort ("Everyone is an entrepreneur, creativity of the masses"). The plan calls for China to:

1 Move up the value chain by abandoning old heavy industry and building up bases of modern information-intensive infrastructure.
2 Achieve significant results in innovation-driven development; bridge the welfare gaps between countryside and cities by distributing and managing resources more efficiently.
3 Achieve an overall improvement in the quality of the environment and ecosystems.
4 Encourage the people of China to share the fruits of economic growth to bridge existing welfare gaps.
5 Implement universal health care proposed in 2020 Health Action Plan.
6 Finish building a moderately prosperous society in all respects.
7 Deepen participation in supranational power structures and expand international cooperation.

These goals embody "Xi Jinping's thought,"[10] lauded as the centenary culmination of the Chinese Communist success story (Zhang, 2021). They differ little superficially from Taiwan's "black cat" indicative national plan of 2017–2020 (Four-Year National Development Plan, 2017). However, the invisible fine print of China's Five-Year Plan determines its real character. If it obliges the CPC master puppeteer to protect the masses, then China's goals are "pink cat" communist ("white" efficiency mixed with "red cat" worker security). Alternatively, if instead the CPC intends to rule over the proletariat for its own benefit, then the system is a "white cat" anti-worker order. The invisible fine print matters.

Market Communism with Chinese Characteristics

China's status as a Marxist–Leninist regime shepherding workers to full communism today lies more in its promises, than its substance. The CPC promises to assign and set leasing terms on a case-by-case basis in a fashion compatible with egalitarian communism, including wages, conditions of labor, participatory management and benefits, but there is no evidence that it does so. Leasing is a black box. The CPC does not explain its choices or substantiate its professed concern for fostering harmonious intra- and interenterprise worker solidarity. It only provides information on the framework and structures of state leases.

The framework is the classification of leasehold property into various forms of CPC freehold granted state, provincial, municipal and private leaseholds based on ownership shares. The CPC grants, or permits state entities, provinces, municipalities and individuals to purchase shares in company leaseholds, wholly freehold owned by the state (CPC, provinces and municipalities)[11] on a fixed-term basis.[12] It classifies leasehold companies as state enterprises (SOE) if the state is the majority lease shareholder.[13] If the state is a minority lease shareholder in any degree, the CPC classifies leaseholds as provincial, municipal or private depending on whether provinces, municipalities or nongovernmental investors are the majority shareholder. The CPC sets the rules of private leaseholds, even if the leases are 100% privately owned.

This classification scheme (State-Owned Enterprises, Provincial Enterprises, Municipal Enterprises and Private Enterprises) does not negate CPC freehold ownership of provincial, municipal and private businesses. It only establishes the degree to which the CPC oversees and supervises different types of companies. There are currently 97 centrally owned mega-conglomerate leasehold companies (SASAC, 2021), subject to regulatory supervision by the State-owned Assets Supervision and Administration Commission (SASAC), which account for 39% of China's GDP (Zhang, 2019). There are more than 150,000 other SOE business leaseholds controlled by the central, provincial and municipal governments, some operating in protected (closed) sectors including defense, but the numbers are shrinking gradually due to mergers and acquisitions. The trend holds for all categories of SOE leaseholds including Red Chips (CITC, COSCO, China Resources, Beijing Enterprise, etc.) traded abroad on the Hong Kong stock exchange, which constitute the Chinese economy's "commanding heights." The CPC has additional stakes in foreign joint ventures like Alcatel, Motorola and Volkswagen subject to Chinese leasehold laws.

CPC political control buttresses its leasehold dominance. It issues government procurement contracts to centrally owned mega-conglomerates, other SOEs, municipalities and "private" leaseholds (corporations with minority state ownership stakes) providing household and public services. It imposes tariffs, grants subsidies and sets taxes. It regulates business and labor organizations effecting profits, income distribution, communal cooperation and social safety nets. It has the power to rescind the majority shareholder status of "private" companies and bar foreign leasehold participation (variable interest entity [VIE]) (Barfield, 2021)[14]. There are no civil institutions independently defending worker or shareholder rights against the CPC.[15]

This concentration of power suggests that lease holding serves as vehicle for the enrichment and empowerment of high CPC officials and their circles, subject to what appears to be the lax regulatory supervision by the SASAC.

The evidence indicates that if the CPC ever intends to foster egalitarianism and harmonious intra- and interenterprise egalitarian communitarianism, it is being notably tolerant of inequities, injustices and worker disempowerment, although

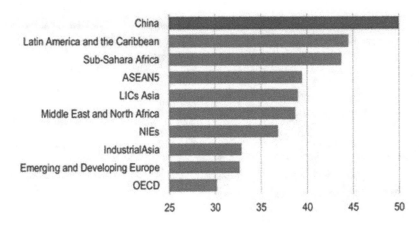

Figure 16.1 Regional Comparison of Income Inequality Levels

Sources: SWIID Version 5.1; IMF, and IMF staff calculations.

Note: ASEAN = Association of Southeast Asian nations; LIC = low-income county; NIE = newly industrialized economy; OECD = Organization for Economic Cooperation and Development

it has recently curbed some entrepreneurial malpractices.[16] China today has the second largest number of billionaires in the world (Dhiraj, 2019),[17] a statistic that must surely make Marxist–Leninists uncomfortable, and it has a weak record on basic entitlements, affirmative action and restorative and social justice. Critics consider the 996 labor regime compelling workers to toil from 9 am to 9 pm six day per week in many factories modern wage slavery.[18]

World Bank data further illuminate China's market communism inegalitarianism (Jain-Chandra, 2018; Jain-Chandra, Khor, Mano, Schauer, Wingender and Zhuang, 2008). Figures 16.1 and 16.2 show that China has moved from being moderately unequal in 1990 to being one of the world's most unequal countries, based on the widely used Gini statistic measure of income inequality.[19] China's Gini coefficient has risen by 15 points since 1990 to 50 (a reading of zero would indicate that everyone has the same income, while a reading of 100 would mean that the richest person gets all the income) (Jain-Chandra, Khor, Mano, Schauer, Wingender and Zhuang, 2008; Chen and Lin, 2012).

Taiwan's Gini coefficient by contrast is 33.7, placing it in the neighborhood of the OECD (Statista, 2021) (Figure 16.1). Chinese market communism not only is less egalitarian than Mao's top-down command communism, it is far more unequal than Taiwan's market capitalism. See Chapter 20 for an analysis of the costs and benefits of egalitarianism. Taiwan's competitiveness keeps a lid on its Gini coefficient. The anticompetitiveness of China's Communist Party managed commanding heights has the opposite effect.

China's high Gini coefficient does not mean that workers are being immiserated. Given the stability of its Gini coefficient, worker per capita income

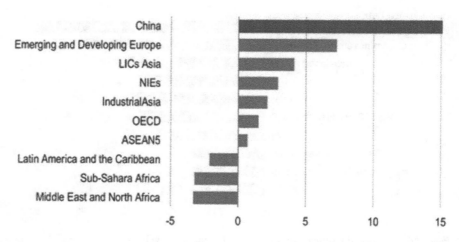

Figure 16.2 Regional Comparison of Income Inequality Trends

Sources: SWIID Version 5.1; IMF, and IMF staff calculations.

Note: ASEAN = Association of Southeast Asian nations; LIC = low-income county; NIE = newly industrialized economy; OECD = Organization for Economic Cooperation and Development

in the new millennium probably rose in proportion with the national mean (Jain-Chandra, Khor, Mano, Schauer, Wingender and Zhuang, 2008), at a faster rate than it would have under an egalitarian modernization strategy. See Chapters 9 and 20. The CPC has not abandoned the underclass. It has only been unconcerned about social inequities, worker participation (Chen and Lin, 2012; Chen and Cao, 2013; Xu, Lu and Xu, Qianqian and Guangjian, 2020; Wan, Lu and Chen, 2005; Xu, Lu and Xu, 2020) and communitarianism (Opinions of the CPC, 2020).[20] The same inference applies to social services. China provides mass, low-cost elementary education and moderate-cost secondary education without regard to social status. This benefits the nation. However, access to higher education is solely based on the university entrance exam (Gao Kao) score, a criterion that severely disadvantages poor rural and urban students attending inferior schools with no supplementary opportunities. China does not prioritize affirmative action for the disadvantaged or restorative justice for its oppressed (Uighurs and Tibetan) (Roberts, 2020).[21] Beijing's primary concern is harnessing meritocratic competition to meet state requirements and spur national productivity. This is practical, but also insensitive to special needs, a point suggested by the plateauing of China literacy rate during the past two decades (World Bank, 2019) (Figure 16.3).

Public housing and transportation have the same characteristics. The CPC has neither neglected underclasses entirely, nor displayed concern for eradicating the privileges of the burgeoning professional classes (disparaged by Mao Zedong as capitalist road experts). Low-income housing is in acute shortage,

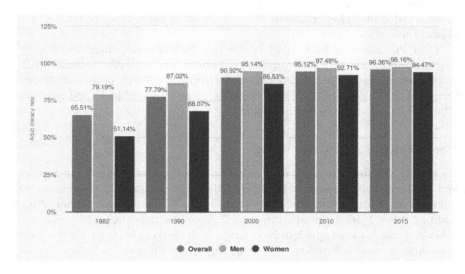

Figure 16.3 Adult Literacy Rate in China from 1982 to 2015

Source: World Bank, ©Statista 2019.

while the demands of the affluent are satisfied, amid skyrocketing private land and apartment prices (Huang, 2012; Poon, 2019; Man, 2001).[22] The rural and urban underclass receive no-frills housing entitlements, and little else. There is no restorative housing justice for Tibetans and Uighurs. The CPC privileges emerging professional and military elites (Popov, 2021) in its quest to become a military superpower (Office of the Secretary of Defense, 2020).

Empowerment

The primary stated purpose of Deng Xiaoping's experiment in market socialism was improving China's economic performance by tapping the people's competitive entrepreneurial energies and individual desires for self-betterment. His experiment succeeded. China's household and public sectors (including public–private partnerships) (Chan, Yeung, Yu, Wang and Ke, 2011) have enhanced productivity, propelled growth and supplied consumers with goods they desired, rather than the inferior products Mao's system foisted on them. China's cityscapes, transportation and infrastructure have modernized and cultural amenities improved, enabling China to catch up with Thailand. This is a significant accomplishment, but does not make China a Marxist–Leninist paragon.

Entrepreneurial empowerment also has had an important unintended consequence. It increased the utility people derive from nonpecuniary relations and activities. Chinese entrepreneurs and professionals enjoy expanded personal freedom. They have learned how to improve their philosophical and spiritual understanding in the process of enhancing their educational, entrepreneurial and professional skills. They gradually became aware of the virtues of intellectual, political and cultural pluralism.

The CPC, however, has limited the size and scope of these benefits by clinging to its monopoly on political power, imperial ambitions (Doshi, 2021; Blumenthal, 2021) and repressing behavior that might jeopardize Party power. Although Deng's liberalization agenda has softened the repressiveness of Marxist-Leninism, China's communitarian benefits are scant.[23]

Communist or Anti-Communist?

Xi Jinping promises to eradicate inequality, install proletarian self-governance and empower communitarianism after 2049, the hundredth anniversary of China's communist revolution. This is his dream (Central Party School, 2013; Kuhn, 2013).[24] Market communism with Chinese characteristics as he sees it will usher in a communalist epoch in 2049 where each worker cooperatively produces according to his ability and receives according to his vast needs as Marx foresaw in his *Critique of the Gotha Program* (1875) (Marx, 1938).

This gives the CPC a quarter century to continue its great power modernization agenda, paying limited attention to the people's quality of existence, coddling professionals and the high-strata Communist Party elite before Deng Xiaoping's socialist promises become testable. Until then, the only thing that seems proven is that clever mandarins can harness markets successfully for their own purposes for decades without having to deliver on their egalitarian, worker empowering promises.[25] They have constructed a new post Mao hierarchy that marginalizes workers, rewards the CPC elite and modifies the Marxist–Leninist concept of proletarian class struggle. Will the CPC stop here or complete Deng's mission? Will China ever become democratic? Will China clone Nordic corporatism (Olson, 1965)?[26] Will China become a social democracy (welfare state with multiple classes)? Will China degenerate into predatory capitalism? Will Chinese workers ever rule themselves?

The fate of China's communist experiment depends on its substance, not semblances. "True" communism, as Marx envisioned it, is a worker self-governing system providing members with the high quality of existence they desire across the spectrum of productive, political and social relations. It is not a Mandarin regency or transition vehicle. It is a dream that Marxist–Leninist believe can be realized, if not ideally, then within the parameters of bounded rationality. If the goal forever goes unrealized, the fault Marxist–Leninists believe lies in tactical errors and the machinations of class enemies.

Notes

1 Bukharin was General Secretary of the Executive Committee of the Communist International (1926–1929) and Full Member of the Soviet Politburo (1924–1929). He was executed by Stalin as an enemy of the people on March 15, 1938.
2 Influential Polish Marxist–Leninist economist.

3   The black cat represents a market economy with private ownership of the means of production. The white cat (Communist China) represents a market economy with state ownership of the means of production. Red cats represent Marxist–Leninist–Stalinist command planning systems or Mao's Cultural Revolution economic regime.

4   Key Communist Party documents describe the economy as one in which public ownership, planning and "socialist" values were central to socioeconomic life.

5   Freehold property is a form of ownership permitting proprietors to possess, use, lease, sell or bequeath assets without legal restraint. Freehold businesses maximize profits as they think best without restrictions imposed by state and/or stakeholder comanagement. Leasehold property by contrast restricts leaseholder possession, use and disposition of leased assets in accordance with terms imposed by the freehold owner, including freeholder rights to comanage leased property. Leasehold property is inheritable if it is included in the lease.

6   A team is an organization in which individual members have common goals, for example, in allocating scarce resources, but are endowed with different information (structures). Goal-setting in a team is approached in a normative fashion by assuming that a team is maximizing its expected net payoff.

7   Kornai (1990) wrote

> … the basic idea of market socialism simply fizzled out. Yugoslavia, Hungary, China, the Soviet Union, and Poland bear witness to its fiasco. The time has come to look this fact in the face and abandon the principle of market socialism.

8   Guanxi is the fundamental dynamic in personalized social networks of power and is a crucial system of Confucian-based beliefs in Chinese culture.

9   The 14th Five-Year Plan period (2021-2025) is ushering in a new stage of achieving socialist modernization and building a great modern socialist country that is prosperous, strong, democratic, culturally advanced, harmocratic, culturally advanced, harmonious, and beautiful. Industrial and supply chains should be made safer, more stable, and more competitive. China should improve institutional design to stimulate and expand social financing. optimize the business environment to make it market-oriented, rule-based, and international; upgrade government services; and strive for excellence by aiming to provide a top-flight business environment.

10 Xi Jinping Thought on Socialism with Chinese Characteristics for a New Era is a set of policies and ideas derived from the writings and speeches of Chinese Communist Party General Secretary Xi Jinping. The 19th National Congress of the Chinese Communist Party in 2017 first mentioned Xi's Thought. The First Session of the 13th National People's Congress on March 11, 2018 amended the Constitution of the People's Republic of China to include Xi Jinping's Thought.

11 The CPC permits provinces and municipalities to act as freeholder at its discretion. The CPC can reverse itself.

12 When leases expire, business assets revert to the state. The maximum lease is 40 years.

13 A business is a for-profit activity. Businesses in China require CPC approval to operate. The CPC can determine the value of its approval and other contributions (land, factories, offices, services) on any basis it desires, allowing it to fix "ownership" shares. The state's ownership share entitles the CPC to receive a proportionate share of operational control and profits. The state also taxes profits distributed to non-state actors separately to finance state spending.

14 Under Chinese law, foreigners cannot own shares in most domestic sectors, so a quasi-legal mechanism known as a variable interest entity (VIE) was created to allow foreign

investment in Chinese companies via offshore entities. According to one estimate, almost 80% of foreign investment in Chinese companies occurs through VIEs, located largely in offshore holding companies in the Cayman Islands. Chinese leaders plan to dramatically restrict the VIE route in order to rein in foreign influence on future technologies.

15 The All-China Federation of Trade Unions is the nationalized organization federation of the People's Republic of China. It is the largest trade union in the world with 302 million members in 1,713,000 primary trade union organizations. There has been dispute over whether ACFTU is an independent trade union or even a trade union at all.

16 "China Bans For-Profit School Tutoring in Sweeping Overhaul," *Bloomberg*, July 24, 2021.   www.bloomberg.com/news/articles/2021-07-24/china-bans-school-curriculum-tutoring-firms-from-going-public

17 The United States has the most billionaires in the world, with 420 more than the next closest country, China, according to Wealth-X's 2019 Billionaire Census report. There are 705 billionaires in the United States, 285 in China, 146 in Germany, 102 in Russia and 97 in the United Kingdom.

18 996 was ruled illegal by China's Supreme People's Court on August 27, 2021, but other abusive variations persist.

19 What accounts for the jump? Differences in education are one important driver of inequality, according to a recent IMF working paper. Rapid technological change and industrialization have boosted demand, and therefore incomes, for highly skilled workers. Differences in incomes between urban and rural areas is another major factor. Educational attainment is lower in rural areas, and China's hukou system of household registration limits migration to urban areas where wages are higher.

20 In 2020, the *Opinions of the CPC Central Committee and the State Council on Improving the Systems and Mechanisms for Market-based Allocation of Factors of Production* promised to establish and improve a unified urban and rural construction land market, actively promote land reform and optimize resource allocation.

21 The Uighurs are Turkic Muslims. There are 12.8 million Uighurs living in China, mostly in Xinjiang.

22

When rural migrants flock to "first-tier" cities like Shanghai looking for jobs, their lack of permanent residency, or hukou, push them to China's informal housing market. Most migrants live on the outskirts, some clustering in "urban villages" and others living in storage basements and converted bomb shelters, even in sewers.

Joyce Yanyun Man, "Affordable Housing in China", Peking University – Lincoln Institute Center for Urban Development and Land Policy, 2011. www.lincolninst. edu/publications/articles/affordable-housing-china.

23 https://freedomhouse.org/country/china/freedom-world/2020

24 The dream seeks to realize the "Two 100s": a "moderately well-off society" by 2021, and full national development by 2049, the 100th anniversary of the founding of the People's Republic.

25 A mandarin (guān) was a high government official in imperial China, Korea and Vietnam.
    The term is generally applied to the officials appointed through the imperial examination system; it sometimes includes and sometimes excludes the eunuchs also involved in the governance of the two realms.

26 Corporatism is a political ideology that advocates the organization of society by corporate groups, such as agricultural, labor, military, scientific or guild associations based on their common interests. The term is derived from the Latin corpus, or "human body." Corporatist ideas are compatible with some forms of socialism, but also authoritarianism, absolutism, fascism and liberalism.

References

Antal, László. (1979). "Development – with Some Digression: The Hungarian Economic Mechanism in the Seventies." *Acta Oeconomica*. Vol. 23, No. 3, 257–273.

Avineri, Shlomo and Avner de-Shalit. (1992). *Communitarianism and Individualism*. Oxford: Oxford University Press.

Barfield, Claude. (2021). "Investment Deglobalization: How Far Will It Go? *AEI*. www.aei.org/technology-and-innovation/investment-deglobalization-how-far-will-it-go/

Bauer, Tamas. (1982). "The Hungarian Alternative to Soviet-Type Planning." *Journal of Comparative Economics*. Vol. 56, No. 3, 304–316.

Berend, Ivan. (1990). *The Hungarian Economic Reform*. New York: Cambridge University Press.

Bergmann, Theodor and Moshe Lewin (eds.). (2017). *Bukharin in Retrospect*. London: Routledge.

Blumenthal, Dan. (2021). "Beijing's Grand Strategy." *National Review*. July 15. www.nationalreview.com/magazine/2021/08/02/beijings-grand-strategy/

Boswell, Jonathan. (1994). *Community and the Economy: The Theory of Public Co-operation*. London: Routledge.

Bukharin, Nikolai. (1982). *Selected Writings on the State and the Transition to Socialism*. Boston: M. E. Sharpe.

Central Party School/Central Committee of the Communist Party of China, (2013). "The Chinese Dream Infuses Socialism with Chinese Characteristics with New Energy." *Qiushi*. https://chinacopyrightandmedia.wordpress.com/2013/05/06/the-chinese-dream-infuses-socialism-with-chinese-characteristics-with-new-energy/

Chan, Albert, John Yeung, Calvin Yu, Shou Qing Wang and Yongjian Ke. (July 2011). "Empirical Study of Risk Assessment and Allocation of Public-Private Partnership Projects in China." *Journal of Management in Engineering*, 136–148.

Chen, Binkai and Cao, Wenju. (2013). "From Opportunity Equity to Income Equality: Income Distribution Dynamics in China Comparative." *Economic & Social Systems*. Vol. 6, 44–59.

Chen, Binkai and Lin Yifu (2012). "Financial Inhibition, Industrial Structure and Income Distribution." *The Journal of World Economy*. Vol. 35, 3–23.

Clarke, Simon. (nd). "Marx and the Market." https://homepages.warwick.ac.uk/~syrbe/pubs/LAMARKW.pdf

Clarke, Simon. (1982). *Marx, Marginalism and Modern Sociology*. London: Macmillan.

Cohen, Stephen. (1980). *Bukharin and the Bolshevik Revolution: A Political Biography, 1888–1938*. London: Oxford University Press.

Dahrendorf, Ralf. (1959). *Class and Class Conflict in Industrial Society*. Palo Alto: Stanford University Press.

Dhiraj, Amarendra Bhushan. (2019). "The Top 15 Countries with the Most Billionaires, Ranked." *CEO World Magazine*. www.businessinsider.com/countries-with-the-most-billionaires-2019-5

Di, Fan. (2016). "Reflecting on Deng Xiaoping's 'Cat Theory' of Economic Reform." *Epoch Times*. www.theepochtimes.com/reflecting-on-deng-xiaopings-cat-theory-of-economic-reform_2173740.htmlClarke, Simon. (1994). *Marx's Theory of Crisis*. New York: Macmillan, Basingstoke and St Martins.

Doshi, Rush. (2021). *The Long Game: China's Grand Strategy to Displace American Order (Bridging the Gap)*. New York: Oxford University Press.

Eecke, Wilfried Ver. (1996). "The Limits of Both Socialist and Capitalist Economies." *Institute for Reformational Studies*. Vol. 348, 1–12.

Etzioni, Amitai. (1988). *The Moral Dimension: Toward a New Economics*. New York: Free Press.

Four-Year National Development Plan (2017–2020) and Plan for National Development in 2017. (2017). https://ws.ndc.gov.tw/Download.ashx?u=LzAwMS9hZG1pbmlzdHJhdG 9yLzExL3JlbGGZpbGUvMC8xMDI1Ny9mNTJmYTUzYi0wODljLTQ4NjAtYjI5Y S0xYzU5YTRiNWEyNjYucGRm&n=TmF0aW9uYWxfRGV2ZWxvcG1lbnRfUG xhbi0wMzA3KG5ldykxMDYwMzA3LnBkZg%3d%3d&icon=..pdf

Gold, Thomas, Douglas Guthrie and David Wank. (2002). *Social Connections in China: Institutions, Culture and the Changing Nature of Guanxi*. Cambridge: Cambridge University Press.

Hare, Paul, Hugo Radice and Nigel Swain (eds.). (1981). *Hungary: A Decade of Economic Reform*. London and Boston: Allen and Unwin.

Huang, Youqin. (2012). "Low-Income Housing in Chinese Cities: Policies and Practices." *The China Quarterly*. No. 212, 941–964.

Jain-Chandra, Sonali. (2018). "Chart of the Week: Inequality in China." https://blogs. imf.org/2018/09/20/chart-of-the-week-inequality-in-china/

Jain-Chandra, Sonali, Niny Khor, Rui Mano, Johanna Schauer, Philippe Wingender and Juzhong Zhuang. (2008). "Inequality in China – Trends, Drivers and Policy Remedies." *IMF Working Paper, WP/18/127*. www.google.com/search?cli ent=firefox-b-1-d&q=Sonali+Jain-Chandra%2C+Niny+Khor%2C+Rui+Man o%2C+Johanna+Schauer%2C+Philippe+Wingender%2C+and+Juzhong+Zhu ang%2C+%E2%80%9CInequality+in+China+%E2%80%93+Trends%2C+Driv ers+and+Policy+Remedies%E2%80%9D%2C+IMF+Working+Paper%2C+WP%2F1 8%2F127%2C+June+2008

Koleski, Katherine, (2017). "The 13th Five-Year Plan." *U.S.-China Economic and Security Review Commission*. www.uscc.gov/sites/default/files/Research/The%2013th%20F ive-Year%20Plan_Final_2.14.17_Updated%20(002).pdf

Kornai, János. (1983). "Comments on the Present State and Prospects of the Hungarian Economic Reform." *Journal of Comparative Economics*. Vol. 23, No. 3, 257–273.

Kornai, János. (1986). "The Hungarian Reform Process: Visions, Hopes and Reality." *Journal of Economic Literature*. Vol. 24, No. 4, 1687–1737.

Kornai, János. (1990). *The Road to a Free Economy: Shifting from a Socialist System – The Example of Hungary*. New York: W.W. Norton.

Kornai, János. (2003). "Ten Years after the Road to a Free Economy: The Author's Self-evaluation of Privatization." In Y. Kalyuzhnova and W. Andreff (eds.). *Privatization and Structural Change in Transition Economies*. New York: Palgrave Macmillan, 13–28.

Kuhn, Robert. (2013). "Xi Jinping's Chinese Dream." *New York Times*. www.nyti mes.com/2013/06/05/opinion/global/xi-jinpings-chinese-dream.html?pagewan ted=all&_r=0

Lange, Oskar. (1938). "On the Economic Theory of Socialism." In Benjamin E. Lippincott (ed.). *On the Economic Theory of Socialism*. Minneapolis: University of Minnesota Press.

MacKenzie, D. W. (2006). "Oscar Lange and the Impossibility of Economic Calculation." *Studia Ekonomiczne* (Economic Studies). Vol. 2, No. 1, 105–121.

Man, Joyce Yanyun. (2001). "Affordable Housing in China." Peking University – Lincoln Institute Center for Urban Development and Land Policy. www.lincolninst.edu/publi cations/articles/affordable-housing-china

Marschak Jacob and Roy Radner. (1972). *Economic Theory of Teams*. New Haven and London: Yale University Press.

Marx, Karl. (1938). *Critique of the Gotha Programme*. Moscow: International Publishers.

McCloskey, Deirdre. (2019). *Why Liberalism Works: How True Liberal Values Produce a Freer, More Equal, Prosperous World for All*. New Haven: Yale University Press.

Miller, David. (1987). "Marx, Communism, and Markets." *Political Theory*. Vol. 15, No. 2, 182–204.

Miller, David. (1990). *Market, State, and Community: Theoretical Foundations of Market Socialism*. London: Oxford University Press.

Nolan, Peter. (1994). "The China Puzzle: 'Touching Stones to Cross the River.'" *Challenge*. Vol. 37, No. 1, 25–33.

Office of the Secretary of Defense. (2002). *Annual Report to Congress: Military and Security Developments Involving the People's Republic of China 2020*. https://media.defense. gov/2020/Sep/01/2002488689/-1/-1/1/2020-DOD-CHINA-MILITARY-POWER-REPORT-FINAL.PDF

Olson, Mancur. (1965). *The Logic of Collective Action: Public Goods and the Theory of Groups*. Cambridge: Harvard University Press.

Poon, Linda. (2019). "When Affordable Housing in Shanghai Is a Bed in the Kitchen." *CityLab*. www.citylab.com/equity/2019/07/china-affordable-housing-migrant-work ers-shanghai/593461/

Popov, Vladimir. (2021). "Why Europe Looks So Much Like China: Big Government and Low Income Inequalities." *Munich Personal RePEc Archive*. https://mpra.ub.uni-muenc hen.de/106326/

Révész, Gabor. (1990). *Perestroika in Eastern Europe: Hungary's Economic Transformation, 1945–1988*. Boulder: Westview Press.

Roberts, Paul Craig. (1971). "Oskar Lange's Theory of Socialist Planning." *Journal of Political Economy*. Vol. 79, No. 3, 562–577.

Roberts, Sean. (2020). *The War on the Uyghurs: China's Internal Campaign against a Muslim Minority*. Princeton: Princeton University Press.

Rosefielde, Steven. (1973). "Some Observations on the Concept of 'Socialism' in Contemporary Economic Theory." *Soviet Studies*. Vol. 25, No. 2, 229–243.

Rosefielde, Steven. (2022). "Economic Systems: Nature, Performance, Prospects." In Bruno Dallago (ed.). *Handbook of Comparative Economic Systems*. London: Routledge, 69–80.

Samuely, Laszlo. (1978). "The First Wave of the Mechanism Debate in Hungary (1954–1957)." *Acta Oeconomica*. Vol. 29. No. 1, 1–24.

Samuely, Laszlo. (1984). "The Second Wave of the Economic Mechanism Debate and the 1968 Reform in Hungary." *Acta Oeconomica*. Vol. 33, No. 1, 43–67.

SASAC. (2021). https://en.wikipedia.org/wiki/State-owned_Assets_Supervision_and_ Administration_Commission#Central_SOEs

Smith, Keith. (1979). "Introduction to Bukharin: Economic Theory and the Closure of the Soviet Industrialization Debate." *Economy and Society*. Vol. 8, No. 4, 446–472.

Statista. (2021). "Gini's Concentration Coefficient in Taiwan from 2008 to 2017." www. statista.com/statistics/922574/taiwan-gini-index/

Stiglitz, Joseph. (2019). *People, Power, and Profits: Progressive Capitalism for an Age of Discontent.* New York: W. W. Norton & Company.

Wan, Guanghua, Ming Lu and Zhao Chen. (2005). "Globalization and Regional Inequality: Chinese Evidence." *Social Sciences in China.* 17–26. www.gov.cn/zhen gce/2020-04/09/content_5500622.htm

World Bank, Statista. (2019). www.google.com/search?q=chinese+illiteracy+rate&cli ent=firefox-b-1-d&tbm=isch&source=iu&ictx=1&fir=mP0QDOTSpFv JeM%253A%252CfBgwHdRSnhUHQM%252C_&vet=1&usg=AI4_-kSz7_49RmV GLadJ5bgZ_AnYyvdz1w&sa=X&ved=2ahUKEwiT0MbL9-7lAhWOc98KHVy2A14 Q9QEwAHoECAUQAw#imgrc=mP0QDOTSpFvJeM

Xu, Kun, Lu Qianqian and Xu Guangjian. (2020). "Land Finance, Real Estate Price and Gap of Property Income." *Journal of Shanxi University of Finance and Economics.* Vol. 42,1–16.

Zhang, Chunlin. (2019). "How Much Do State-Owned Enterprises Contribute to China's GDP and Employment?" *World Bank*, July 15. http://documents.worldbank.org/cura ted/en/449701565248091726/pdf/How-Much-Do-State-Owned-Enterprises-Contrib ute-to-China-s-GDP-and-Employment.pdf

Zhang, Zhanbin. (2021). "The Centenary of the Communist Party of China: Creating, Economic Miracles and Embarking upon a New Journey." *China Economic Transition.* Vol. 4, No. 3. https://journal.hep.com.cn/cet/EN/article/downloadArticleFile.do?att achType=PDF&id=30756

17 Democratic Socialism

Democratic socialism is the paring of democracy with socialist economy. The term implies substantial state ownership of the means of production, strong state economic regulation and a robust social safety net, but can encompass more libertarian arrangements. Circa 1840 socialist democracy referred to economic decision-making rules governing cooperatives and communes, not national politics. See Chapter 2. Robert Owen was the gold standard for direct democracy. Others shared Owen's sentiment, although Cabet inclined toward authoritarian-democratic economic management. Saint-Simonians tipped hats toward democracy, but were more concerned with business organization and entrepreneurship. Democracy was superfluous in Marx's communist utopia (1844–1848) because he believed that naturally harmoniously workers would be mutually accommodating. Fourier concurred for the opposite reason. He assumed responsibility for choreographing communal activity. Democratic socialist economy before 1870 meant self-regulating cooperative and communal production and distribution solely for members' collective benefit. It accounted for a small fraction of global economic activity. Economic production and distribution outside the socialist sphere operated on laissez-faire or other nonsocialist principles.

Democratic socialists after 1870 strove to improve workers' well-being in two disparate ways. First, the emergence of socialist political parties across the globe during 1870–1914 raised the possibility that workers might enlist state public policy to protect and promote their welfare. Second, associations, cooperatives and communes devised direct democratic methods for the same purpose.

George Douglas Howard Cole was the apostle of direct democracy. Democratic socialism for him meant managing industrial syndicates (Guild Socialism) on a majority rule balloting basis, leaving other public policy matters to republican parliaments. Democratic socialist economy as he saw it was the guild system, not parliamentary state economic control. Cole was a traditional libertarian. He sought to maximize individual worker liberty within the guild framework, together with everyone else's liberty through competitive parliamentary participation under the rule of law. Democratic socialism from Cole's perspective did not require society to provide workers with lavish entitlements.

DOI: 10.4324/9781003371571-21

British labor unions, the Labor Party and many Fabians in the 1920s saw matters differently. They were not wedded to Cole's direct democracy and sought political power as a vehicle for compelling the affluent to finance their social policies and eradicate aristocratic privilege. Democracy as the Labor Party perceived it in 1918 was a vehicle for nonviolently acquiring working-class power, including the nationalization of industry and leveling class status. British democrat socialists were more attracted to the Marxist–Leninist state-owned and controlled economy than to Cole's direct-democracy syndicalism. They were prepared to shred the Lockean social contract (Magna Carta) once in power and repress capitalists and aristocrats,[1] but less ruthlessly than the Bolsheviks.[2] They took a more patient approach toward liquidating capitalists "as a class" and eradicating social stratification, including the constitutional monarchy.[3] Continental democratic socialist parties likewise were more concerned with political power than direct worker self-management.

The political mayhem of the interwar period and the Great Depression fostered right-wing (fascist) and left-wing illiberalism (suppression of personal freedom, enemies and shredding liberal social contracts). Democratic socialism in the interwar period was as much about bashing capitalists and aristocratic privilege as it was devising institutions, methods and policies for protecting labor and enhancing social welfare. Class war was a central theme for democratic socialists, Marxist–Leninists and revolutionary syndicalists.

Politicians, however, did not have to be socialists or communists to attract electoral support with public spending and job programs. Franklin Roosevelt and progressive reformers elsewhere during the 1930s and throughout the post World War II era succeeded in advancing their parties at the ballot box by spending generously on the welfare state.[4] Marxist–Leninists call Roosevelt's class inclusive approach to democratic coalition building revisionist "social democracy" and consider it anti-socialist. They view Eduard Bernstein's "evolutionary" socialism the same way (Bernstein, 1961; Engels, 2004; Steger, 1997),[5] but others believe that British social democracy will evolve into democratic socialism for the working class (Gay, 1970).

Politicians and journalists today bandy the terms democratic socialism, social democracy, welfare state and Nordic model. Anti-market Marxists define democratic socialism in terms of state ownership and/or social control of the means of production. This institutionalist supply side approach clarifies little. Anti-market democratic socialism, market-based democratic socialism, welfare states and the Nordic model all socially regulate production, transfers and distribution. The rival systems are distinguishable in only two respects: (1) worker priority and (2) worker control.

The highest priority for anti-market and pro-market democratic socialists is worker well-being, sometimes judged from the vanguard and other times from the workers' own perspective. The Nordic model protects labor interests less vigorously. Workers in today's welfare states are becoming "invisible people." Welfare state politicians are more concerned about other constituencies. Attitudes toward full employment deficit spending vary more with circumstances than system.

Welfare states and the Nordic model appear superficially socialist if one supposes that the interests of the working class and the rest of society coincide. Improving society's lot on this supposition enhances worker welfare. The inference, however, is misleading because the interest of nonworkers predominates in welfare states and strongly influences economic and social outcomes in the Nordic model. Contemporary welfare states in many cases are anti-socialist.

This means that the prospects for democratic socialism, the Nordic model and welfare states are independent. The three systems are competitors, not variants of democratic socialism even though all reject 19th-century laissez-faire (free enterprise), apply microeconomic tools to alter the distribution of income and wealth and macroeconomic instruments to achieve full employment and bolster economic growth (Olson, 1965).

Harold Hotelilng, Abram Bergson and James Meade pioneered the microeconomic tools needed to serve the working class in the 1930s (Hotelling, 1938; Bergson, 1938, 1954; Meade, 1993).They devised analytic and statistical techniques for setting prices in imperfectly competitive environments, rationing and "lump sum" transfers essential for protecting workers from market power. The British and American governments put these techniques to practical use during World War II. John Kenneth Galbraith, a non-Marxist democratic socialist, was deputy head of the Office of Price Administration (OPA) during 1941–1943 (Galbraith, 1952, 1966).

John Maynard Keynes revolutionized attitudes toward managing economic crises in 1936 by showing how deficit spending on investment could stimulate aggregate economic activity and spur full employment in a neoclassical framework (Keynes, 1936), setting the stage for governments to expand state programs of all sorts and deficit spend, justified as employment and growth stimulants.[6] These advances created a dual economic order blending competitive economic efficiency and big state public spending that replaced 19th-century libertarian laissez-faire with democratic socialist, welfare state and Nordic corporatist systems by the mid-1960s.

Democratic socialists in the post World War II era mostly favor the working class, managed enterprise and generous state support for the needy. Marxist democratic socialists continue to oppose traditional libertarian free enterprise, but support big government spending on working-class social programs and public ownership of essential industries. Welfare states (of the neoliberal type) and Nordic corporatist systems marry supply side market competition with the cradle-to-grave "nanny state."[7] All four systems are wedded to big government in ways unimaginable in 1840. Non-Marxist democratic socialists, welfare states and Nordic regimes are pro-competitive. Only Marxist democratic socialists prefer state ownership and comprehensive control to market competition.

Nordic Model

The political, economic and social governance of the Nordic States reflect individualist values of the Renaissance, Enlightenment and French Revolution, expressed in the "Declaration of the Rights of Man," on August 26, 1789.[8] These rights are liberty, private property, security and democracy. They empower individuals politically, economically and socially, prioritizing personal liberty over conformism, but also are compatible with worker-focused socialism, when most individuals share the same pro-worker values. The Nordic reality in these regard is mixed. Scandinavians, Norwegians, Danes, Icelanders and Finns do broadly support workers, degrees of egalitarianism, collective entitlements and progressive values, but this does not deter them as individuals from defending their personal rights and interests. Their behavior often conflicts with their socialist professions.

Denmark, Norway and Sweden are all monarchies. Finland and Iceland were monarchies but became republics in the 20th century. Monarchial socialism is an oxymoron if monarchs are sovereign authorities.

The Nordic States also are multiparty parliamentary democracies, governing often behind closed doors to advance the interests of competing constituencies. Parliaments operate as social democracies, meaning opposing parties abide by a Lockean social contract protecting the interests of diverse groups. They restrict their ambitions including laissez-faire objectives to promote social harmony by protecting private property and social status, while simultaneously providing the nation with social mobility, entitlements and progressive affirmative action programs. Entitlements include public housing, education, universal health care, pensions and comprehensive workplace regulations and rights spanning parental maternity leaves to labor retraining and relocation assistance. Nordic affirmative action promotes economic and social equality, radical feminism, homosexuality, bisexuality, transgender-hood, cohabitation (Cohabitation, 2020),[9] minority advancement, multicultural immigration and some restorative justice causes. Workers benefit from state support for trade unions, cooperatives and other labor institutions and generous entitlements financed by high flat income and payroll (in the vicinity of 45%), wealth and value-added consumption taxes (VAT is 25%). Everyone (workers and shirkers; rich and poor) pays extremely high taxes. Nordic Gini coefficients (after taxes and transfer) computed by the OECD indicate that these entitlements and uncapped flat taxes have made the Nordic system significantly more egalitarian than the United Kingdom, United States, India and China,[10] although Nordic Gini coefficients have risen steadily in recent decades (Aaberge et al., 2018). Nonetheless, despite this inequitable trend, poverty in the Nordic States remains low due to the effects of transfers. Poverty rates in 2011, before taking into account of transfers, were 24.7% in Denmark, 31.9% in Finland, 21.6% in Iceland, 25.6% in Norway and 26.5% in Sweden. After accounting for transfers, poverty rates fall to 6%, 7.5%, 5.7%, 7.7% and 9.7%, respectively (Aaberge et al., 2018).

Neither these low poverty rates nor the high concentration of jobs in the government sector have impoverished the Nordic States (Sauter, 2018). The Central Intelligence Agency reports that in 2017 Norway enjoyed 20.6% higher per capita GDP (purchasing power parity basis) than America, while living standards in the other Nordic nations were below the US benchmark. The shortfalls, respectively, were Iceland (12.7%), Sweden (14.4%), Denmark (16.2%) and Finland (26.4%)

(CIA, 2022). As of 2019, all of the Nordic countries rank highly on the inequality-adjusted Human Development Index (HDI) and the Global Peace Index. They ranked among the top ten in the World Happiness Report (Happiness, 2020). All are imperfect, but sensible indicators.

The Nordic countries are corporatist in a 21st-century sense (Happiness, 2020), with Bismarck characteristics (Gregory and Stuart, 2003, 207).[11] They strive to mitigate labor-management conflict by encouraging government-mediated dispute resolution and bargaining between employer federations and trade unions at the national level and support cooperatives marketing agricultural products, operating hundreds of retail stores, and manufacture light bulbs, tires, cash registers, rayon, fertilizers and other products. Norway, Finland and Iceland also have strong cooperative associations (Strand and Freeman, 2015).

Proponents insist that the corporatist Nordic system is not anti-capitalist, and that entitlements, affirmative action, unionization (OECD, 2013)[12] and stout labor protection, although restrictive in various senses (Wearing, 2014),[13] do not stifle business competitiveness, contrary to experience elsewhere (Mathur, 2020). Nordic nations are vigorous competitors in the international marketplace as befit small, seafaring economies. Corruption is low (Transparency, 2018). Nordic corporatist laws make it relatively easy for employers to hire and shed workers or introduce labor-saving technology, having learned hard lessons about the consequences of an anticompetitive mindset in the 1970s (Bergh, 2017). Employment rates are high, despite generous entitlements and high taxation (Aaberge et al. 2018). There is little product regulation. Supporters view pro-competitive Nordic laws as quid-pro-quos for generous social welfare programs, job retraining and relocation services that dampen labor management conflicts.

The Nordic model differs from welfare state schemes elsewhere in terms of its priorities. The Nordics emphasize labor force participation, gender equality (Gender Equality, 2018),[14] lifestyle tolerance and egalitarianism more than most other welfare states.[15] They do not belittle productivity and competitiveness and in this important sense are opposed to American anti-meritocratic radical progressivism (Sandel, 2020; Young, 1958, 2006, 73–77).[16]

America has been moving selectively in the Nordic direction for decades including ethnic hybridization, but Washington is less concerned about economic competitiveness, technological progress, GDP growth, social amity, government efficiency, permanent dependencies and negative aspects of restorative justice and political correctness.

The Nordic system has a socialist patina (worker protection and income support), combining solicitude for the working class missing in America for nearly a half century, with a progressive agenda focused on social and economic egalitarianism, radical feminism, sexual liberation, personal liberty, multiculturalism and ethnic hybridization.

The Nordic States are neither Bismarckian collectivist shams nor worker sovereign socialist regimes. They are democratic, socially pluralist, systems stressing private freehold ownership and business competition rather than stultifying business overregulation. They balance traditional and progressive libertarianism. Some find them appealing, others repellent depending on their values and judgments.[17] Marxist–Leninist–Stalinists will never consider the Nordic States socialist, but non-Marxist democratic socialists may judge them socialist enough to be included in the fold. American conservatives classified the Nordic States as democratic socialist during the 1970s and condemned them when their economies were failing, but are less disparaging today (Pethokoukis, 2020a, 2020b).

Transferability

The Nordic States' successes have attracted self-described socialist advocates like Bernie Sanders, who recommends that America adopt the spirit, but not the letter of Nordic corporatism (Pethokoukis, 2020a).They want to separate the wheat from the chaff, preserving prosperity, entitlements, progressivism and social harmony, while eliminating monarchical residues and other features that smack of Bismarck corporatism or Bolshevism. Is the Nordic model transferrable?

The answer is no and yes.

Scandinavian monarchy, natural resource wealth, Lutheran cultural moral self-discipline, geography, working class sympathies and Bismarck-style collectivism are not transferrable. They are endowments and historical artefacts.

Nonetheless, the Nordic model's core might be transferrable if imitators find surrogates for missing prerequisites (Gerschenkron, 1962, 1968). John Kenneth Galbraith, considered a socialist by many (Reynolds, 2019), tried to foster a progressive American corporatist ethos on behalf of the "Great Society" a half century ago by urging worker, business and government technocratic cooperation (Galbraith, 1966). His *New Industrial State* advocated Nordic-type worker institutions together with active state-mediated worker-business conflict resolution mechanisms and collaboration. Galbraith's vision was widely acclaimed, but soon lost traction as Washington's concern for the working class diminished to the vanishing point, and radical politics and social activism became steadily more confrontational.

The growing distain for America's Enlightenment heritage, Constitution and white males, together with internecine progressive power struggles make the creation of an American surrogate for Nordic collectivism unthinkable (Rosefielde and Mills, 2020). Similar obstacles preclude the transfer of Nordic collectivism to the United Kingdom and other welfare states that prioritize political struggle over social cooperation and harmony.

Spectrum of Worker Sovereign Systems

All worker sovereign systems of, for and by workers are socialist. Marxist–Leninist systems qualify if one accepts that the vanguard of the proletariat represents the workers' will. Workers' sovereignty in Marxist and non-Marxist democratic socialist regimes can be restricted to the workplace or can include political rule. Workers can choose the scope of their sovereignty. Workers' sovereign systems determine the degrees of freedom permitted to nonworkers of all descriptions.

Democratic socialism is a spectrum of possible institutional and political systems. It is not singular.

Contemporary democratic socialists, both Marxist and non-Marxist, support state ownership of the means of production in varying degrees, as well as some forms of cooperative labor activity. They distinguish themselves from Nordic corporatism and welfare states by advocating a greater presence of labor-controlled economic institutions, a larger role for worker-friendly state management policies and greater political influence. Podemos (Spanish "We Can" Party)[18] and The Coalition of the Radical Left – Progressive Alliance (SYRIZA) are Marxist democratic socialist parties.[19] The left faction of the British Labor Party shares much of the Marxist outlook. They are more like Bolsheviks than market communists, and it is unclear whether they would defend the Lockean social contract if they garnered sufficient political power.

The left faction of the British Labor Party (Crossland, 1956),[20] Podermos and SYRIZA could transform themselves into non-Marxist democratic socialists if they desired, but political realities preclude the option. They would blur their political identify, and they would have difficulty forging a distinctive moderate program competitive with ordoliberal welfare states (Massimiliano, 2010)[21] and the Nordic model. This poses a serious dilemma. If the left faction of the British Labor Party, Podermos and SYRIZA reveal their weak commitment to political democracy, they will lose the support of fellow travelers. If they embrace pluralist democracy, they will lose their Marxist–Leninist base. If they play the nationalist card following Hitler or Mussolini, the reverberations are apt to be negative. There should be a viable democratic socialist solution, but contemporary democratic socialist parties have not discovered it (Steger, 1997; Gay, 1970). The economic performance of Marxist and non-Marxist democratic socialist influenced national economies in the new millennium has been unimpressive.

Notes

1 Magna Carta Libertatum (Great Charter of Freedoms) is a royal charter of rights agreed to by King John of England at Runnymede, near Windsor, on June 15, 1215. The Magna Carta recognized the principle of the rule of law and the Petition of Right on 1628.
2 Harold Joseph Laski (1893–1950) emphasized the need for a workers' revolution, which he hinted might be violent. He admired Joseph Stalin's Soviet Union.
3 The Glorious Revolution of 1688 led to a constitutional monarchy restricted by laws such as the Bill of Rights 1689 and the Act of Settlement 1701.
4 Clement Attlee, the head of the Labor Government announced in 1945 that he would introduce the Welfare State outlined in the 1942 Beveridge Report. This included the establishment of a National Health Service in 1948 with taxpayer funded medical treatment for all. A national system of benefits provided "social security" to protect the population from the "cradle to the grave."
5 Bernstein favored a peaceful evolutionary democratic path to socialism. Engels condemned him.

  6 Walter Heller altered Keynes' "multiplier" by urging government deficit consumption spending as a component of Lyndon Johnson's war on poverty.
  7 Nanny state is a term of British origin ridiculing big government for being overprotective.
  8 https://avalon.law.yale.edu/18th_century/rightsof.asp
  9 Cohabitation is a heterosexual or homosexual living arrangement subject to various state-imposed legal obligations, especially involving child support and joint property. The proportion of people living in a cohabiting couple is almost 20% in Sweden.
 10 Denmark   0.263
     Sweden   0.282
     Norway   0.272
     Finland   0.259
     Iceland   0.246
     United Kingdom   0.351
     United States   0.391
     India   0.495
     China   0.514

     These OECD Gini coefficients are after tax and transfers statistics. Pretax Gini coefficients are much higher.
 11 German Prime Minister Otto von Bismarck pioneered welfare state entitlements in the 1883 to co-opt the working class and suppress socialism. State Socialism was a set of social programs implemented in Germany that were initiated by Otto von Bismarck in 1883 as remedial measures to appease the working class and detract support from socialism and the Social Democratic Party of Germany following earlier attempts to achieve the same objective through Bismarck's anti-socialist laws.
 12 In 2013, labor union density was 88% in Iceland, 69% in Denmark, 67% in Sweden, 66% in Finland and 51% in Norway. In comparison, labor union density was 18% in Germany, 11% in the United States and 8% in France.
 13 The Nordic countries received the highest ranking for protecting workers' rights on the International Trade Union Confederation's 2014 Global Rights Index, with Denmark being the only nation to receive a perfect score.
 14 The Nordic countries have one of the smallest gaps in gender employment inequality of all OECD countries.
 15 Despite the common values, the Nordic countries take different approaches to the practical administration of the welfare state. Denmark features a high degree of private sector provision of public services and welfare, alongside an assimilation immigration policy. Iceland's welfare model is based on a "welfare-to-work." Norway relies most extensively on public provision of welfare.
 16 Anti-meritocracy has three antithetic senses. Some use the term to mean that public programs should benefit idlers or those who cannot compete. Some use it to deny that productive people have a right to superior rewards. Others insist that those claiming to be meritorious are villains. Michael Young is in the last camp and paints a dystopian picture of the consequences.
 17 Some advocates of Karl Popper's open society, neoliberals and conservatives consider the Nordic States viciously socialist, claiming that their entitlement and cooperative aspects hamper productivity, privilege the undeserving and diminish the quality of existence.
 18 After the November 2019 Spanish general election, in which the party and its allies won 12.8% of the vote and 35 seats in the Congress of Deputies, Podemos entered

a coalition government with the PSOE, the first multiparty cabinet in the current Spanish democratic era.

19 SYRIZA is the second largest party in the Hellenic Parliament. Party chairman Alexis Tsipras served as Prime Minister of Greece from January 26, 2015 to August 20, 2015 and from September 21, 2015 to July 8, 2019.

20 The British Labor party today is "center left" working within the established systems to improve social justice. The Labor Party only gained a socialist commitment with the original party constitution of 1918, Clause IV establishing nationalization of the means of production as a party goal. About a third of British industry was nationalized after World War II, remaining so until the 1980s. Anthony Crosland (1956) prodded Labor to rethink its position. Tony Blair amended and toned down Clause IV in 1995. The Party accommodated itself to privatization thereafter. The party favors government intervention in the economy, the redistribution of wealth, increased rights for workers and a welfare state including publicly funded health care. While affirming a commitment to democratic socialism, the new version of Clause IV no longer commits the party to public ownership of industry.

21 Ordoliberalism is the German variant of economic liberalism that emphasizes the need for the state to ensure that the free market produces results close to its theoretical potential. The term "ordoliberalism" was coined in 1950 by Hero Moeller.

References

Aaberge, Rolf, Christophe André, Anne Boschini, Lars Calmfors, Kristin Gunnarsson, Mikkel Hermansen, Audun Langørgen, Petter Lindgren, Causa Orsetta, Jon Pareliussen, P. O. Robling, Jesper Roine and Jakob Egholt Søgaar. (2018). "Increasing Income Inequality in the Nordics." *Nordic Economic Policy Review.* https://norden.diva-portal. org/smash/get/diva2:1198429/FULLTEXT01.pdf

Bergh, Andreas. (2017). "Triumph of Social Democracy – Or Serendipity?" *Milken Review.* www.milkenreview.org/articles/the-swedish-economy-triumph-of-social-democracy-or-serendipity

Bergson, Abram. (1938). "A Reformulation of Certain Aspects of Welfare Economics." *Quarterly Journal of Economic.* Vol. 52, No. 1, 310–334.

Bergson, Abram. (1954). "The Concept of Social Welfare." *Quarterly Journal of Economics.* Vol. 68, No. 2, 233–252.

Bernstein, Eduard. (1961). *Evolutionary Socialism.* New York: Knopf Doubleday.

CIA. (2022). www.cia.gov/library/publications/the-world-factbook/geos/us.html

Cohabitation. (2020). www.oecd.org/els/family/SF_3-3-Cohabitation-forms-partnership.pdf

Crossland, Anthony. (1956). *The Future of Socialism.* London: Jonathan Cape.

Declaration of the Rights of Man. (1789). https://avalon.law.yale.edu/18th_century/rightsof.asp

Engels, Friedrich. (2004). *Collected Works,* Vol. 50. New York: International Publishers.

Galbraith, John Kenneth. (1952). *American Capitalism: The Concept of Countervailing Power.* New York: Houghton Mifflin.

Galbraith, John Kenneth. (1966). *New Industrial State.* New York: Houghton Mifflin.

Gay, Peter. (1970). *The Dilemma of Democratic Socialism: Eduard Bernstein's Challenge to Marx.* New York: Collier.

Gender Equality. (2018). "Nordic Council of Ministers." www.oecd.org/els/emp/ last-mile-longest-gender-nordic-countries-brief.pdf

Gerschenkron, Alexander. (1962). *Economic Backwardness in Historical Perspective.* Cambridge: Belknap Press of Harvard University Press.

Gerschenkron, Alexander. (1968). *Continuity in History, and Other Essays.* Cambridge: Belknap Press of Harvard University Press.

Gregory, Paul and Robert Stuart. (2003). *Comparing Economic Systems in the Twenty-First Century.* Mason: South-Western Publishers.

Happiness. (2020). www.commondreams.org/news/2019/03/20/social-democratic-nati ons-rank-happiest-global-index-again-us-ranking-falls-again

Hotelling, Harold. (1938). "The General Welfare in Relation to Problems of Taxation and of Railway and Utility Rates." *Econometrica.* Vol. 6, No. 3, 242–269.

Keynes, John Maynard. (1936). *The General Theory of Employment, Interest and Money.* London: Palgrave Macmillan.

Massimiliano, Vatiero. (2010). "The Ordoliberal Notion of Market Power: An Institutionalist Reassessment." *European Competition Journal.* Vol. 6, No. 3, 689–707.

Mathur, Aparna. (2020). "Paid Leave and Labor Force Participation: What Do We Know?" *Forbes.*

Meade, James. (1993). *Liberty, Equality and Efficiency: Apologia pro Agathotopia Mea.* London: Palgrave Macmillan.

OECD. (2013). "Trade Union Density." *OECD StatExtracts.*

Olson, Mancur (1965). *The Logic of Collective Action: Public Goods and the Theory of Groups.* Cambridge: Harvard University Press.

Pethokoukis, James. (2020a). "Has Bernie Sanders Learned Anything over the Past 50 Years?" *AEI.* www.aei.org/articles/has-bernie-sanders-learned-anything-over-th e-past-50-years/?mkt_tok=eyJpIjoiWWpVeVptTmlPR1k1T0dKbCIsInQiOiJcL3k0 STAwcHdzR25Fako4MDZYTW9rS0puVlN4MEthQk1YQzRNQUJmc0hUREZ ZQ1wvcFpkZHBtQmlMUUlUNjF0dG5pSGJRaWJWdWxiOWJEbTAyQnNvMD MzUDBYZXhoQU5HZStFQjFjSkZQbmlueU1UQnZGSHl0cmZoS0ltRDFpSVBv In0%3D

Pethokoukis, James. (2020b). "Let's Stop Pretending That Bernie Sanders Wants to Duplicate Scandinavia." *AEI.* www.aei.org/economics/lets-stop-pretending-that-ber nie-sanders-wants-to-duplicate-scandinavia/

Reynolds, Alan. (2019). "1973: The Year John Kenneth Galbraith Made Socialism Mainstream." *Cato Institute.* www.cato.org/blog/1973-year-john-kenneth-galbra ith-made-socialism-mainstream

Rosefielde, Steven and Quinn Mills. (2020). *Populists and Progressives: New Forces in American Politics.* Singapore: World Scientific Publishers.

Sandel, Michael. (2020). *The Tyranny of Merit: What's Become of the Common Good?* New York: Farrar, Straus and Giroux.

Sauter, Michael. (2018). "Public Sector Jobs: States Where the Most People Work for the Government." *USA Today.* June 1.

Steger, Manfred. (1997). *The Quest for Evolutionary Socialism: Eduard Bernstein and Social Democracy.* Cambridge: Cambridge University Press.

Strand, Robert and R. Edward Freeman. (2015). "Scandinavian Cooperative Advantage: The Theory and Practice of Stakeholder Engagement in Scandinavia." *Journal of Business Ethics.* Vol. 127, 65–85.

Transparency. (2018). www.transparency.org/cpi2018

Wearing, David. (2014). "Where's the Worst Place to Be a Worker? Most of the World." *The Guardian*.

Young, Michael. (1958). *The Rise of the Meritocracy 1870–2033: An Essay on Education and Society*. London: Thames and Hudson.

Young, Michael. (2006). "Looking Back on Meritocracy." In G. Dench (ed.). *The Rise and Rise of Meritocracy*. Oxford: Blackwell, 73–77.

18 Anarcho-Socialism

Marxist–Leninist systems are socialist because leaders claim to rule for the workers' benefit. None has prospered. Anarcho-communists like Prince Peter Kropotkin (1842–1921) predicted Marxist-Leninism would fail at the First International (1864–1876). They argued that nationalizing the means of production, criminalizing markets and privileging unions would harm most workers. Kropotkin contended that there was only one true path to socialism (Kropotkin, 1899, 1906, 2009).[1] First, peasants and workers must learn the virtues of cooperation, mutual assistance and collectivism, which he called anarcho-communism (Shanin, 1972). Second, revolutionaries must educate cooperators about the necessity of collectivizing the means of production directly without state intermediation. Third, anarcho-communists must spark the anti-imperial and anti-capitalist revolution by propaganda of the deed (Abidor, 2016), that is, "dynamite anarchy," including bombing and assassinations against the established order (Cahm, 1989).[2] Anarcho-syndicalists like the Industrial Workers of the World (Wobblies) held similar views,[3] but stressed the importance of trade union struggle in sparking the revolution (Sorel, 1970).[4] Anarcho-socialists who advocated cooperatives, worker ownership and management without strong ties to communal living (shared personal property including children) and trade unions shunned dynamite activism.

Kropotkin believed that once people saw the light, a single deed would suffice to establish anarcho-communist order (free association of self-governing communes) without a proletarian dictatorship (Bakunin, 1987). Dynamite anarchy would free toilers and transform them into cooperators. Revolutionary communist anarchy would be self-ordering, not chaotic and would eradicate private business, markets and the repressive state. As in modern mathematical chaos theory (Mandelbrot, 1982),[5] there would be order in anarchy. Kropotkin argued that freedom and cooperation were inherent in the natural order and would spontaneously prevail after the revolution incinerated state governance.

The assassination of Tsar Alexander II on March 13, 1881 was supposed to be the dynamite showcase and harbinger of the worldwide anarcho-socialist future. The attack was planned by Narodnaya Volya (People's Will), a splinter terrorist faction of Zemlya i Volya (Land and Freedom) founded by Mark Natanson (1851–1919) in 1876. Natanson's revolutionary organization drew inspiration from

DOI: 10.4324/9781003371571-22

Slavophiles including Aleksey Khomyakov (1804–1860), Ivan Kireyevsky (1806–1856), Konstantin Aksakov (1817–1860), Alexander Herzen (1812–1870), Pyotr Lavrov (1823–1900), Mikhail Bakunin (1814–1876) and socialist study circles (kruzhki) in St. Petersburg, Moscow, Kiev and Odessa. Efforts to propagandize revolutionary and socialist ideas among factory workers and peasants prompted state repression, with the tsarist secret police (Okhrana) identifying, arresting and jailing agitators, driving activities underground.

Narodnaya Volya emerged as a distinct terrorist faction in 1879 after a failed attempt by Alexandr Soloviev (1846–1879) to kill Alexander II in the Palace Square St. Petersburg. Its mission was to try again. The "narodnovoltsy" (approximately 500 members strong) believed that regicide would break the government and end all vestiges of the tsarist regime in Russia. They perceived the government as weak and tottering, and chances for revolutionary overthrow promising. The Executive Committee of Narodnaya Volya sentenced the tsar to death on August 25, 1879, on the heels of the execution of former Zemlevolets Solomon Wittenberg, who had attempted to build a mine to sink a ship carrying the tsar into Odessa harbor the previous year. The chief architect of assassination was Andrei Zhelyabov. Nikolai Rysakov threw a bomb damaging the carriage, prompting the tsar to dismount, and Ignacy Hryniewiecki hurled a second bomb that fatally wounded Tsar Alexander II on March 13, 1881.

Hryniewiecki died shortly after the assassination. A Special Tribunal of the Senate convicted Zhelyabov, Sofia Perovskaya, Nikolai Kibalchich, Hesya Helfman, Timofey Mikhailov and Nikolai Rysakov. They hanged on April 15, 1881. Lenin's elder brother, Alexander Ulyanov attempted to assassinate Tsar Alexander III in 1886. His execution likewise failed to spark anarcho-socialism (Pomper, 2009).

Propaganda of the deed never ignited a dynamite anarcho-communist revolution. George Sorel's French anarcho-syndicalist movement (Sorel, 1929, 1970, 1972; Sombart, 2011; Lagardelle,1908, 1911; Lagardelle, 1908; Gray, 1968; Ridley, 1970),[6] and its counterparts elsewhere, which cast trade unions as the foundation of working-class governance fared no better (Berthe, 1908; Ascher, 1994).[7] George Douglas Howard Cole's nonviolent democratic guild socialist version of Sorel's anarcho-syndicalism was a passing fancy (Cole, 1944, 1951).

Anarcho-communist and anarcho-syndicalist revolution proved to be figments of anarchist imagination. The conviction that liberated masses would transform themselves into harmonious cooperators or worker supermen on a national or worldwide scale was similarly childish (Sorel, 1970; Horowitz, 1968; Ridley, 1970; Kamenka, 1970).[8] Trade unions and nonunion workers rarely responded to anarcho-communist and anarcho-syndicalist calls to arms,[9] and when they occasionally heeded the summons, the momentum was unstainable. Anarcho-socialism enjoyed some evanescent successes in Makhnovia (1918–1921),[10] most of Aragon, parts of the Levante and Andalusia as well as in the stronghold of anarchist Catalonia in 1936–1939 during the Spanish civil war, without significant lasting impact.

Anarcho-socialist revolutionary sentiment resurfaced during the 1970s and could revive in the new millennium (Wolff, Barrington Moore Jr. and Marcuse, 1965; Chomsky, 2005),[11] but prospects for ultimate success are slight (Rothbard, 1970). The fizzled attempt by the "The Capitol Hill Occupied Protest Solidarity Committee" to create a revolutionary insurrectionary autonomous zone in downtown Seattle on June 8, 2020 as a response to the killing of George Floyd is indicative (Toropin, 2020)·

Despite more than a century and a half of anarcho-socialist agitation in all its various manifestations, there is no evidence that workers prefer labor self-management, worker ownership and sharing to communist central planning or democratic market socialism. Only a small minority of workers finds the attractions of "small is beautiful" (Schumacher, 1973), member-owned, market free, cloistered and egalitarian cooperative enclaves sufficient compensation for the lifestyle sacrifices entailed. Kropotkin's anti-state, anti-commercial, anti-individualist, pro-sharing communes and artisan cooperatives are anachronistic.

Nonetheless, new more flexible worker managed and anarcho-socialist schemes have had some limited success and could blossom further. Neo-anarcho-worker self-management proponents accept the state and reject dynamite insurrection. They embrace capitalist relationships and shun barracks communalism.[12] They act as intranational autonomous entities and participate in local and global markets on a for-profit basis. They favor cooperative individualism, sharing and amicable community-state relations within an otherwise capitalist environment (Pérotin, 2012).

Worker cooperatives in Mondragon Spain and Israeli kibbutzim exemplify these weakly anarchist post-Kropotkin possibilities. They are worker-owned and managed organizations that oppose individualism and stress obligation and benefit sharing. They spurn private enterprise (but not profits) and are willing to coexist with supportive state structures (Pries, 1999; Webb, 1921).

Mondragon

The world's largest worker-owned and managed cooperative group is the Mondragon Cooperative Corporation in the Spanish Basque Country. It is a cost- and benefit-sharing anarcho-socialist institution employing some 81,000 people (67,000 in the Basque region) (Mondragon Corporation, 2019), operating on a for-profit basis in four areas: finance,[13] industry,[14] retail[15] and knowledge.[16] In 2013, the corporation posted a total revenue of over €12 billion and employed 74,061 workers, making it Spain's fourth-largest industrial and tenth-largest financial group.

It began globalizing operations after Spain joined the European Union (EU) in 1986 while retaining an anarcho-socialist lifestyle (cooperation and solidarity), humanist cooperative business culture and relative autonomy from central authorities.[17] Executive compensation on average exceeds the minimum wage by a factor of five, a disparity far less than the standard in private enterprises. Spain's progressive tax rate further reduces any difference in pay.

Neo-anarcho-socialist cooperatives like Mondragron do not claim to be more profitable, innovative or entrepreneurial than their private competitors (Fakhfakh, Pérotin and Gago, 2012). They do not pay superior wages or executive compensation. Nor do they provide higher welfare state benefits. Spanish and EU statute govern Mondragon's disability and retirement security. Mondragon's main attraction is philosophical. It emphasizes the desirability of non-predatory market-oriented communitarian cooperation. Neo-anarcho-socialist communities (as distinct from socialist states) prioritize the quality of group existence and fair treatment of their clientele. They stress mutual support, solidarity, harmony and a high quality of existence derived from democratic participation, consciousness raising, enlightenment, caring, environmental sensibility, and social responsibility over productivity, high material compensation and personal mobility. These communitarian benefits appeal to its members and customers, but are not yet attractive enough for most workers who prefer their current lifestyles and the perceived higher benefits provided by private and state employers. Mondragon is a niche option for workers temperamentally disposed toward cooperation. It does not appear to promote radical feminist and other revolutionary progressive causes like open immigration (Hacker and Elcorobairutia, 1987) and is not every worker's cup of tea.

Kibbutzim

The evolution of Israeli kibbutzim confirms this assessment. A kibbutz is a cooperative collectivist community in Israel that once was, but no longer is, rooted in agriculture. The first kibbutz (Degania1909) was a utopian anarcho-communist settlement seeking to reestablish a Jewish nation in the biblical homeland (Zion) after the destruction of the Second Temple in Jerusalem in 70 AD. It served as symbol of return and the desire to construct a new Eden (socialist utopia).

The anarcho-communism of most Israeli kibbutzim reflected late 19th-century iconoclastic attitudes toward individualism, communalism, private property, markets, business, entrepreneurship, religion, family, women, sex, sharing and mutual aid. Many kibbutz pioneers were hostile toward individualist self-seeking, business, commerce, finance, capitalism, wage labor, religious Judaism, traditional female role assignments, sexual inhibitions and nuclear families. Many staunchly advocated women's liberation, democratic participation, egalitarianism, special assistance to the needy and burden sharing. Many preferred communal living arrangements (dormitories, communal kitchens and childcare), and all bristled at external government opposition to their designs for living. The "barracks" communism of many kibbutzim resembled Sergei Nechayev's paradigm more closely (Pomper, 1979)[18] than Karl Marx's and Friedrich Engel's harmonious vision limned in the *Economic and Philosophical Manuscripts of 1844* and the *Communist Manifesto* of 1848.[19] Many kibbutzniks opposed Marxist-Leninism, but some were admirers.

Kibbutz anarchism reflected a nihilistic desire to escape a European social, political and economic order that ostracized and oppressed them for a brighter future based on communalist principles in a modern Jewish nation. The mission was more important for most kibbutzniks than material well-being and personal accomplishment. Although most kibbutzniks prized independence from outside meddling, they were also double-thinking pillars of the Israeli state.[20]

In recent decades, kibbutzim adjusted to changing times. Few conform to late-19th-century anarcho-communist archetypes. Some kibbutzim have privatized and cooperative communal lifestyles have evolved. There are approximately 270 kibbutzim with 120,000 members (1.2% of Israel's population) today.[21] The average kibbutz size is 444 persons (Abramitzky, 2011). The vast majority of kibbutzim are secular ("monasteries without God"). Their factories and farms account for 9% of Israel's industrial output, worth US$8 billion, and 40% of agricultural output, worth over $1.7 billion.

These successes, however, have come at the expense of traditional anarcho-communist principle. Individualism, materialism and flexible personal lifestyles are replacing orthodox anarcho-communist ethics (Abramitzky, Ben-Porath, Lahad, Lavy and Palgi, 2022). Many are more attracted to radical progressivism than socialism.

The problem is rooted in the static assumptions of the late-19th-century anarcho-socialist covenant. Pioneers failed to appreciate that their socialist idealism was unsustainable (Drezon-Tepler, 1990). "Leaning-by-doing" revealed that anarcho-socialism is plural. It is a set of implicit or explicit cooperative and communalist contracts governing member entry and exit, qualifications, participation, duties, beliefs, attitudes, sharing, mutual support, egalitarianism, special needs, collective property rights,[22] compensation, cooperative decision making, culture and external politics.

Implicit and explicit contracts are subject to continuous collective renegotiation that alters the character of kibbutz anarcho-socialist regimes and confronts disgruntled members with choices between compliance and exit. A gradual disenchantment with the barracks communist doctrinal conformity,[23] egalitarian inequities[24] and restraints on self-actualization has steadily shifted Kibbutz values away from collective obligations, relationships and distributive benefits toward individual self-fulfillment (Shapira, 2001).[25] Some kibbutzniks prefer their own apartments, families, home cooking and privacy. They dislike living and dining together in a common space as a communal family perpetually under group surveillance and see virtue in private property (personalty, realty and other assets) and wealth, an attitude congruent with the gradual privatization of all aspects of the Israeli economy. They desire to educate themselves and their children as they think best,[26] and many privately hold views disapproved by the kibbutz majority. They want to distribute and bequeath their personal assets as they choose, and to withdraw from kibbutzim with their accumulated net contributions to enhance quality of their existence whenever they desire.

Kibbutzniks often share the commune's net income equally and refrain from hiring external wage labor.[27] Some, however, tie compensation to value added and employ nonmember wageworkers violating founding anarcho-socialist principle.

They reward members for the value of their marginal products to prevent parasitism but in so doing transition toward capitalist joint-partnerships.

Revised kibbutz covenants while accommodating grievances and bolstering consensus, frequently dilute anarcho-socialist principle. The kibbutz ideal has morphed from a shared commitment to Zionist communalism into a cooperative group marriage of convenience (Spiro, 1963)[28] with protean rules governing member exit, retirement and death.[29] This adaptability is consistent with anarchy and may be compatible with communism, but only if at the end of the day members abridge individualism in the interest of the working members. Anarcho-socialism easily dissolves into free enterprise.[30] Some still believe that anarcho-socialism can be more efficient than capitalist laissez-faire (Fakhfakh, Pérotin and Gago, 2012); however, even if they are correct, the evidence suggests that labor ownership, management and cooperative commitment have limited appeal for most workers.

Notes

1 Anarcho-communism is a political philosophy advocating the abolition of the state, capitalism, wage labor, social hierarchies and private property in favor of common ownership of the means of production and direct democracy. Most anarcho-communists view anarcho-communism as a way of reconciling the opposition between the individual and society.

2 Caroline Cahm, *Kropotkin: And the Rise of Revolutionary Anarchism*, 1872–1886, Cambridge: Cambridge University Press, 1989.

3 The Industrial Workers of the World (IWW) is an international labor union founded in 1905 in Chicago. Wobblies advocate socialist revolution and organizing strikes as a prelude to a general worldwide strike among the working class.

4 Anarcho-syndicalism is a school of thought that views revolutionary industrial unionism or syndicalism as a method for workers in capitalist society to gain control of an economy and influence society. The end goal of syndicalism is to abolish the wage system. The basic principles of anarcho-syndicalism are solidarity, direct action (action undertaken without the intervention of third parties such as politicians, bureaucrats and arbitrators) and direct democracy, or workers' self-management.

5 Chaos theory is an interdisciplinary scientific theory and branch of mathematics focused on underlying patterns and deterministic laws highly sensitive to initial conditions in dynamical systems thought to have completely random states of disorder and irregularities.

6 Georges Eugène Sorel (1847–1922) was a French social thinker, political theorist, historian and journalist. His notion of the power of myth in collective agency inspired socialists, anarchists, Marxists and Fascists. Sorel elaborated a Marxism rejecting economic and historical determinism and seeing itself not as social science but as a historically situated ideology. He urged radical trade union violence as the antidote for collaborationist welfare-oriented unionism and the catalyst for the construction of a proletarian order. Syndicalism sprung from two sources: the workers movement and the intelligentsia. Emile Pouget, editor of La Voix du Peuple and Victor Griffuelhes of the confédération générale du travail. Other important syndicalists were Hubert Lagardelle and Edouard Berth.

7   The revolutionary syndicalist movement was active in Italy, Russia, Germany, America and England. Some historians contend that the 1905 revolution carried out in part by worker soviets (councils) was a revolutionary syndicalist uprising that set the stage for the 1917 Russian Revolution. They describe it as "The Great Dress Rehearsal."

8   Sorel contended that artisan-workers were creators, desiring to surpass everything previously achieved. They possessed supreme integrity and the spirit of glory.

9   One hundred and twenty years ago, the French labor movement was dominated by four distinct institutions: local craft unions, local labor exchanges (Bourses du Travail), national federations of bourses, craft and industrial unions and national federations of Syndicates under the aegis of the Confédération Générale du Travail (C.G.T.).

10 Nestor Makhno's Revolutionary Insurrectionary Army supported soviets and libertarian communes in the Ukraine during the civil war in Russia. Peasants who lived in Makhnovia organized farming communes with land held in common. They dined in communal kitchens and worked from each according to his ability, to each according to his need. Railroad workers in Aleksandrovsk formed a committee charged with organizing the railway network of the region, establishing a detailed plan for the movement of trains, the transport of passengers. Soviets coordinated factories and other enterprises across Ukraine. The economy of Free Ukraine was a mixture of anarcho-communism and market socialism, with factories, farms and railways becoming cooperatives and many moneyless communities.

11 Wolff recommended studying tolerance "by means of an analysis of the theory and practice of democratic pluralism." Marcuse echoed the advice: "the realization of the objective of tolerance" requires "intolerance toward prevailing policies, attitudes, opinions, and the extension of tolerance to policies, attitudes, and opinions which are outlawed or suppressed." He makes the case for "liberating tolerance," which would consist of intolerance to right-wing movements and toleration of left-wing movements.

12 The term barracks communism was coined by Karl Marx in a critique against Sergei Nechayev.

13 Finance includes the banking business of Laboral Kutxa, the insurance company Seguros Lagun Aro, and the Voluntary Social Welfare Body Lagun Aro. The yield obtained from this fund is used to cover long-term retirement, widowhood and disability benefits.

14 The corporation's companies manufacture consumer goods, capital goods, industrial components, products, and systems for construction, and services.

15 Mondragon runs Eroski, one of the leading retail groups all over Spain and in southern France, and maintains close contacts with the French group Les Mousquetaires and the German retailer Edeka.

16 This area has a dual focus: education-training and innovation.

17 Mondragon cooperatives embrace a humanist concept of business, a philosophy of participation and solidarity and a shared business culture. The culture is rooted in a shared mission and a number of principles, corporate values and business policies derived from the ten Basic Co-operative Principles: open admission, democratic organization, sovereignty of labor, subordination of capital, participatory management, payment solidarity, inter-cooperation, social transformation, universality and education.

18 Sergei Nechayev (1847–1882) was a Russian revolutionary figure associated with the Nihilist movement. He advocated cooperators living in disciplined artels where members could choose between work or death.

19 Karl Marx coined the term barracks socialism as a barb ridiculing Nechayev's concept. Marx and Engel's concept also had its shortcomings. It presumed a natural harmony entirely of their own imagining where desires were reciprocal. If A loved B, then B automatically loved A. This assumption obviated human conflict on paper, but not in reality.

20 Kibbutzim played an outsize role in Israel's defense. In the 1950s and 1960s, many kibbutzim were in fact founded by an Israel Defense Forces group called Nahal.

21 Kibbutzim grew and flourished in the 1930s and 1940s. In 1922, there were 700 people living on kibbutzim in Palestine. By 1927, the number had risen to 2,000. When World War II erupted, 24,105 people were living on 79 kibbutzim, comprising 5% of the Jewish population of Mandate Palestine. In 1950, the figures went up to 65,000, accounting for 7.5% of the population. In 1989, the kibbutz population peaked at 129,000. By 2010, the number decreased to about 100,000; the number of kibbutzim in Israel was 270.

22 Members could not possess individual items, like teakettles, and everything was strictly communal. Starting around the 1950s and 1960s, people were entitled to individual property, like teakettles, books, radios, etc.

23 Since kibbutzniks had no individual bank accounts, any purchase not made at the kibbutz canteen had to be approved by a committee, a potentially humiliating and time-wasting experience.

24 Kibbutzim also had members who were malingers, or who abused common property. They were viewed as parasites.

25 Artzi kibbutzim were also more devoted to gender equality than other kibbutzim. The children slept in children's houses and visited their parents only a few hours a day.

26 Kibbutzim created the communal children's houses, where the children would spend most of their time in learning, playing and sleeping. Parents spent three to four hours a day in the afternoon with their children after work and before dinner. Collective child-rearing some believed would uproot the patriarchy. The second generation of women who were born on the kibbutz eventually got rid of the children's houses and the Societies of Children. Most found that although they had a positive experience growing up in the children's house, they wanted their own children at home with them. Today, most women do not participate in the economic and industrial sectors of the kibbutz. They even embraced traditional marriage.

27 Many kibbutzim hired Mizrahi Jews (descendants of the Middle Eastern Jewish communities from Western Asia and North Africa) as laborers but were less inclined to grant them membership.

28 The principle of equality was sacred until the 1970s. Kibbutzniks did not individually own tools or even clothing. Gifts and income received from outside were turned over to the common treasury. If a member received a gift in services – like a visit to a relative or a trip abroad paid for by a parent – there could be arguments at members' meetings about the propriety of accepting such a gift. Up until recently, members ate meals together in the communal dining hall.

29 There are now three kibbutz compensation models: (1) the traditional collective kibbutz/kibbutz shitufi, egalitarian rationing; (2) the mixed model kibbutz/kibbutz meshulav, salary plus egalitarian dividend; and (3) the renewing kibbutz/kibbutz mithadesh, salary.

30 Among the communities that officially ceased being kibbutzim are Megiddo in the Jezreel Valley, Hag Goshrim in the Upper Galilee and Beyt Nir in the Negev.

References

Abidor, Mitchell. (2016). *Death to Bourgeois Society: The Propagandists of the Deed*. San Francisco: PM Press.

Abramitzky, Ran. (2011). "Lessons from the Kibbutz on the Equality – Incentives Trade-off." *Journal of Economic Perspectives*. Vol. 25, No. 1, 185–208.

Abramitzky, Ran, Netanel Ben-Porath, Shahar Lahad, Victor Lavy and Michal Palgi. (2022). "The Effect of Labor Market Liberalization on Political Behavior and Free Market Norms." NBER working paper 30186. www.nber.org/papers/w30186

Ascher, Abraham. (1994). *The Revolution of 1905: Russia in Disarray*. Palo Alto: Stanford University Press.

Bakunin, Mikhail. (1987). *Statism and Anarchy*. Cambridge: Cambridge University Press.

Berth, Edouard. (1908). *Le Nouveaux Aspects du Socialisme*. Paris: M. Riviere.

Cahm, Caroline. (1989). *Kropotkin: And the Rise of Revolutionary Anarchism, 1872–1886*. Cambridge: Cambridge University Press.

Chomsky, Noam. (2005). *On Anarchism*. Chico: AK Press.

Cole, George Douglas Howard. (1944). *A Century of Co-operation*. Oxford: George Allen & Unwin Ltd.

Cole, George Douglas Howard. (1951). *The British Co-operative Movement in a Socialist Society*. London: Routledge.

Drezon-Tepler, Marcia. (1990). *Interest Groups and Political Change in Israel*. Albany: State University of New York Press.

Fakhfakh, Fathi, Virginie Pérotin and MÓnica Gago. (2012). "Productivity, Capital, and Labor in Labor-Managed and Conventional Firms: An Investigation on French Data." *Industrial and Labor Relations Review*. Vol. 65, 847–879.

Gray, Alexander. (1968). *The Socialist Tradition*. New York: Harper Torchbooks.

Hacker, Sally and Clara Elcorobairutia. (1987). "Women Workers in the Mondragon System of Industrial Cooperatives." *Gender and Society*. Vol. 1, No. 4, 358–379.

Horowitz, Irving. (1968). *Radicalism and the Revolt against Reason*. Carbondale: Southern Illinois University Press.

Kamenka, Eugene. (1970). *Marxism and Ethics*. New York: St. Martin's.

Kropotkin, Peter. (1899). *Fields, Factories and Workshops*. https://theanarchistlibrary.org/library/petr-kropotkin-fields-factories-and-workshops-or-industry-combined-with-agriculture-and-brain-w

Kropotkin, Peter. (1906). *The Conquest of Bread*. London: Chapman and Hall.

Kropotkin, Peter. (2009). *Mutual Aid: A Factor of Evolution*. London: Freedom Press.

Lagardelle, Hubert. (1908). *Syndicalisme et Socialisme*. Paris: M. Rivière.

Lagardelle, Hubert. (1911). *Le Socialisme Ouvrier*. Paris: Ciard et Briere.

Mandelbrot, Benoit. (1982). *The Fractal Geometry of Nature*. New York: W. H. Freeman and Co.

Mondragon Corporation. (2019). Annual Report 2019 (PDF).

Pérotin, Virginie. (2012). "The Performance of Workers' Cooperatives." In P. Battilani and H. Schroeter (eds.). *The Cooperative Business Movement, 1950 to the Present*. Cambridge: Cambridge University Press, 195–221.

Pomper, Philip. (1979). *Sergei Nechaev*. New Brunswick: Rutgers University Press.

Pomper, Philip. (2009). *Lenin's Brother: The Origins of the October Revolution*. New York: W.W. Norton.

Pries, Anne. (1999). "The Cooperative Movement in Russia," Brill. https://brill.com/view/package/9789004197213?language=en

Ridley, Frederick. (1970). *Revolutionary Syndicalism in France.* Cambridge: Cambridge University Press.

Rothbard, Murray. (1970). "The Death Wish of the Anarcho-Communists." *The Libertarian Forum.* https://mises.org/library/death-wish-anarcho-communists

Schumacher, Ernst. (1973). *Small Is Beautiful: A Study of Economics As If People Mattered.* London: Blond & Briggs.

Shanin, Teodor. (1972). *The Awkward Class: Political Sociology of Peasantry in a Developing Society, Russia 1910–1925.* Oxford: The Clarendon Press.

Shapira, Reuven. (2001). "Communal Decline: The Vanishing of High-Moral Leaders and the Decay of Democratic, High-Trust Kibbutz Cultures." *Sociological Inquiry.* Vol. 71, No. 1, 13–38.

Sombart, Werner. (2011). *Socialism and the Socialist Movement.* New York: Gutenberg.

Sorel, George. (1929). *L'Avenir socialiste des syndicats.* Paris: M. Riviere.

Sorel, George. (1970). *Reflections on Violence.* London: Collier-Macmillan.

Sorel, George. (1972). *Illusion of Progress.* Berkeley: University of California Press. https://ia600504.us.archive.org/19/items/IllusionsofProgress/BookTitle.pdf

Spiro, Melford. (1963). *Kibbutz Venture in Utopia.* New York: Schocken.

Toropin, Konstantin. (2020). "Leader of Seattle's 'Autonomous Zone' Says Many Protesters Are Leaving." *CNN.* www.cnn.com/2020/06/24/us/seattle-autonomous-zone-protesters-leaving/index.html

Walton, John. (1997). "Co-operative movement." In John Cannon (ed.). *The Oxford Companion to British History.* London: Oxford University Press.

Webb, Sidney and Beatrice Webb. (1921). *The Consumers' Co-operative Movement.* London: Cooperative Union. London: Longmans.

Wolff, Robert, Paul Barrington Moore Jr. and Herbert Marcuse. (1965). *Critique of Pure Tolerance.* Boston: Beacon Press.

19 New Age Planning

Soviet planners began applying computers and cybernetic optimal control at the national and enterprise levels in the early 1960s. They thought that input–output, linear programming and the automatic system of planning and management (ASUP) would revolutionize Soviet economic performance. They believed that computers would vastly enhance planners' ability to acquire, store, process data and calculate the best use of economic resources (Neuberger, 1966), but the political leadership was disappointed to discover computerization and cybernetics failed to accelerate GDP growth or enhance consumer satisfaction, setting the stage for Gorbachev's rejection of central planning.

The ability of artificially intelligent machines to aid decision makers and solve complex problems today vastly exceeds 20th-century possibilities. Soviet cyberneticists instructed machines what to do and told them how to do it. They did not ask machines for advice or grant them discretionary authority. Contemporary planners can now permit artificially intelligent devices more degrees of freedom in solving complex problems (Poole, Mackworth and Goebel, 1998; Poole and Mackworth, 2017).[1] In the 1960s, linear programmers could optimize freight transportation under normal conditions. Their counterparts today, armed with artificially intelligent devices, can automatically and continuously monitor changing conditions and adjust. Could socialists soon tell Heuristically programmed ALgorithmic computer (HAL) what they want to accomplish and then confidently leave the details to artificial intelligence?[2]

The answer is not yet (McCorduck, 2004).[3] Even though HAL has the heuristic capacity to generate superior outcomes, socialists will want to judge the comparative merit themselves. Consider the Soviet case. Suppose that central planners with HAL's assistance were able to monitor consumer satisfaction through facial imaging, ascertain interaction effects in real time and instantaneously adjust production to maximize social utility given constraints on inegalitarianism and national security. Would Marxist–Leninists passively defer to HAL's judgments? They could, but only would if results were satisfactory.

Suppose that central planners with HAL's assistance were able to monitor consumer satisfaction and ascertain interaction effects in real time, and instantaneously adjust production to maximize social utility given HAL's preferences

DOI: 10.4324/9781003371571-23

(Chalmers, 1995).[4] Would consumers object, would they willingly defer to HAL? Not likely (Anderson and Anderson, 2010; Wallach, 2010). HAL may be able to understand human speech (Russell and Norvig, 2009) and beat humans in computable games like chess; however, this does not obligate them to abide by the decisions of artificially intelligent machines.

Artificial intelligence also can facilitate compliance. Authorities can task HAL to discover effective ways of prodding party members, managers, workers and consumers to obey, accept and even relish (brainwash) outcomes with potentially adverse behavioral ramifications (Rubin, 2003). In the best cases, facilitating plan implementation, acceptance and appreciation could increase the socialist merit (quality of existence) from the vanguard or workers' perspective. In the worst case, HAL could become an omnipotent and capricious tyrant.[5]

Artificial intelligence is a double-edged sword. It could make Marxist–Leninist planned economy a superior socialist alternative to laissez-faire market systems, or destroy socialism by deferring to HAL anti-socialist judgments.

Neither extreme is realistic. Artificial intelligence has advanced at an astonishing pace in the new millennium, without discernibly improving aggregate productivity and accelerating GDP growth. The global economy has been moribund for over a decade. Artificial intelligence facilitated a switch to online employment during the Covid-19 crisis, but did not prevent policy-makers from mismanaging the pandemic. It is an important scientific development, but not a panacea that vindicates Marxist–Leninist faith in the superiority of planning over markets.

Artificial intelligence likewise does not resolve two fundamental socialist issues: motivation and personal freedom. The vanguard of the proletariat (Communist Party) may prioritize power and ideological orthodoxy (labor theory of value) over the working class' welfare. The Central Executive Committee could limit the application of artificial intelligence to tasks compatible with the leadership's doctrinal agenda. Workers similarly might prefer regulated markets, private ownership, entrepreneurship and freedom to state planning and communist behavioral control. There was more to the dissolution of Soviet socialism than the mechanical deficiencies of Gosplan and khozraschyot. The Communist Party was unwilling to sacrifice its sacred cows for the people's benefit. Democratic socialists and anarcho-syndicalists could be similarly un-deferential (Berryhill, Heang, Clogher and McBride, 2019).

Finally, one may muse about how Marxist-Leninism might adapt if artificially intelligent sentient machines of disparate classes acquired human rights. Would worker robots become the new proletariat? Would the Communist Party feel obligated to repress artificially intelligent entrepreneurs and compel humans to work against their will? Sci-fi is likely to proliferate the contradictions of socialism rather than eradicate them (McCorduck, 2004; Russell and Norvig, 2009).

Notes

1 "Intelligent agents" are devices that perceive the environment and take actions that maximize its chance of successfully achieving goals.

2 HAL 9000 is a fictional artificial intelligence character and the main antagonist in Arthur C. Clarke's Space Odyssey series. First appearing in the 1968 film 2001: A Space Odyssey, Heuristically programmed ALgorithmic computer (HAL) is a sentient artificial general intelligence computer that controls the systems of the Discovery One spacecraft and interacts with the ship's astronaut crew.

3 There are three philosophical questions related to artificial intelligence:

1 Whether artificial general intelligence is possible; whether a machine can solve any problem that a human being can solve using intelligence, or if there are hard limits to what a machine can accomplish.

2 Whether intelligent machines are dangerous; how humans can ensure that machines behave ethically and that they are used ethically.

3 Whether a machine can have a mind, consciousness and mental states in the same sense that human beings do; if a machine can be sentient, and thus deserve certain rights − and if a machine can intentionally cause harm.

4 David Chalmers identified two problems in understanding the mind, which he named the "hard" and "easy" problems of consciousness. The easy problem is understanding how the brain processes signals, makes plans and controls behavior. The hard problem is explaining how this feels or why it should feel like anything at all. Human information processing is easy to explain; however, human subjective experience is difficult to explain.

5 Artificial biological intelligence (ABI) attempsts to emulate "natural."

References

Anderson, Michael and Susan Leigh Anderson. (2010). *Machine Ethics*. New York: Cambridge University Press.

Berryhill, Janie, Kevin Heang, Rob Clogher and Keegan McBride. (2019). *Hello, World: Artificial Intelligence and Its Use in the Public Sector*. Paris: OECD Observatory of Public Sector Innovation.

Chalmers, David. (1995). "Facing up to the Problem of Consciousness." *Journal of Consciousness Studies*. Vol. 2, No. 3, 200–219.

McCorduck, Pamela. (2004). *Machines Who Think*. Natick: A. K. Peters, Ltd.

Neuberger, Egon. (1966). "Libermanism, Computopia, and Visible Hand: The Question of Informational Efficiency." *The American Economic Review*. Vol. 56, No. 1, 131—144.

Poole, David and Alan Mackworth. (2017). *Artificial Intelligence: Foundations of Computational Agents*. 2nd ed. Cambridge: Cambridge University Press.

Poole, David, Alan Mackworth and Randy Goebel. (1998). *Computational Intelligence: A Logical Approach*. New York: Oxford University Press.

Rubin, Charles. (2003). "Artificial Intelligence and Human Nature." *The New Atlantis*. Vol.1, 88–100.

Russell, Stuart and Peter Norvig. (2009). *Artificial Intelligence: A Modern Approach*. Upper Saddle River: Prentice Hall.

Wallach, Wendell. (2010). *Moral Machines*. London: Oxford University Press.

20 Egalitarian Socialism

Socialism's primary task is protecting and improving the lives of productive workers. Libertarian socialists assign the job to workers themselves, and their elected representatives with a social romantic "all for one, and one for all" ethos.[1] They are prepared to accept broad dispersions of income, wealth, privileges and fulfillment if society protects workers.

Others feel that allowing workers to decide the best way of maximizing the quality of their existence is not good enough. Some Illiberal socialists claim that they have a duty to assure workers make correct choices in accordance with progressive socialist principles. Many of them contend that egalitarianism is a sine-qua-non, that socialism requires complete egalitarian distribution of wealth and income, together with eradication of social privilege. They reject gender, physical, intellectual, psychological, emotional and sexual distinctions. Egalitarians insist that anything less is "unfair." The rich, famous and upwardly mobile do not have the right to refuse. Fairness is egalitarians' sine-qua-non. Other ethical principles are subsidiary (Frankfurt, 2000; Hare, 1981). Egalitarianism for them is the essence of socialism. Without it, systems claiming to be socialist are fake.

Egalitarians prefer collective income satisficing to individual utility maximizing, even if this entails sacrificing efficiency, living standards and affluence, although some proclaim perfect planning or communist harmony assure efficiency and full abundance in the post-liberal era. If pressed, they concede that income equality (from wages and the competitive rental value of collectively owned productive assets) is more important to them than prosperity.

The sentiment rests on the ethical notion that people are equally worthy regardless of differences in competitively earned income and wealth, and that this worthiness is more important to community well-being than the economic deadweight loss of mandatory income leveling. People's equal worthiness is intrinsic, not a matter of age, gender, race, ethnicity, talent, virtue, rank or success (Anderson, 1999). Egalitarians feel that no one deserves to live better or worse than the average. Unequal wealth and income distribution is immoral (unfair) (Blake, 2001; Knight and Stemplowska, 2011). Distributive justice from this point of view necessitates universal equality of income and wealth, and insofar as

DOI: 10.4324/9781003371571-24

possible rank, talent, virtue, success and respect (Roemer, 1998, 2008). Refusing to share is anti-socialist.

Many egalitarians accepting these premises go a step further, contending that people should enjoy the same quality of existence (complete equality of utilitarian outcomes). Even if everyone receives the same average income, some may experience more utility from wages and nonmarket activities, or enjoy life less because they are physically, intellectually, morally and/or psychologically impaired. Some individuals may have privileged access to nonmarket assets (accomplished parents) and opportunities. Others may be unusually appreciative or derive pleasure from their self-perceived virtue. Differences in taste also may allow some to obtain greater utility from their purchases, and the handicapped or disadvantaged may have special needs that require supplementary assistance to attain the average quality of existence.

Egalitarians who prioritize earned income may be willing to compensate members with special needs out of the national wage fund before computing the community-wide average worker remuneration. This is not sufficient for egalitarians who claim that the quality of existence must be the same for everyone. If consumption and other aspects of the quality of existence are considered, achieving full egalitarianism is a two-step procedure. First, level income. Second, adjust for differences in sensibility and nonmarket utilities with tax transfers (Neumann and Morgenstern, 1944; Musikanski, 2017).[2]

Universal equality of both income and utility is thinkable,[3] even though sundry practical problems including moral hazard and the difficulty of measuring interpersonal utility may be nettlesome. Does it follow from "think-ability" that egalitarian socialism is likely to be a wise choice; that the deadweight utilitarian loss and sundry other nonmarket distortions from fixing worker remuneration do not outweigh the disputable ethical benefit of "fairness"? Do those who argue for equality of outcomes appreciate that the goal negates equality of opportunity?

Let us consider the issue in the simple case where egalitarianism only requires that everyone receive equal remuneration, with competitive nonwage income earned on collectively owned assets distributed equally across the labor force.[4]

Labor and Nonlabor Reservation

A simple mathematical example vivifies the adverse effect of egalitarian remuneration.

Assume a strictly concave production function for each activity (firm). Thus for the ith firm we write

$$x_i = f_i\left(x_{1i}, \ldots, x_{i-1,i}, x_{i+1,i}, \ldots, x_{ni}, y_i\right). \qquad \forall_{i=1}^m \tag{20.1}$$

Here x indicates goods and services including all productive factors except labor. Thus, x_{ji} indicates the quantity of good j used in the production of i while y_i indicates the amount of labor used in firm i.

The profit before labor payments, the pie divided among the workers, is

$$\pi_i = p_i x_i - \sum_{k \neq i} p_k x_{ki} - F_i. \qquad \forall_{i=1}^m$$

Where the p are prices and F is fixed cost. The dividend per worker before inter-firm transfers is

$$P_i = \frac{\pi_i}{y_i}, \qquad \forall i \tag{20.2}$$

And, the post-transfer egalitarian wage paid all workers regardless of place of employment is the average dividend per worker,

$$\bar{P} = \frac{\sum_{i=1}^m P_i \, y_i}{\sum_{i=1}^m y_i} = \frac{\sum_i \pi_i}{\sum_i y_i} \tag{20.3}$$

For later reference, we also record the equilibrium conditions for an egalitarian labor-managed firm (ELMF) that maximizes dividend per worker (Rosefielde and Pfouts, 1986).

$$p_i \frac{\partial x_i}{\partial x_{ki}} = p_k, \qquad \forall_{i=1, \, k \neq i}^m \tag{20.4}$$

$$p_i \frac{\partial x_i}{\partial y_i} = P_i. \tag{20.5}$$

Now consider certain problems that can arise under an egalitarian regime. First it may be noted from (20.3) that it is necessary that $\sum \pi_i > 0$ for a reasonable outcome. Usually, one would expect that this would be the case, but there is nothing assuring the desired outcome.

Even if $\sum \pi_i$ is sufficiently large, there are still serious problems. How should the firms that earn larger than average dividends behave? Should they try to maximize dividends per worker even though this will only benefit of those who are less productive? Surely, they would do this only if they were committed to egalitarianism. History, however, suggests that unreserved altruism is rare and seldom universal.

Egalitarianism cannot escape the problem. The payment per worker must be the arithmetic mean since this is the only numerical value for which the positive deviations and negative deviations are equal in absolute amount. The productive must give up part of their earnings to support the less productive. Are the productive willing to face a lifetime of this?

If we assume that the workers are utility maximizers and that altruism plays a limited role in their utility functions, then they will lack motivation to earn beyond the overall average. Consequently, we use the following behavioral rule: (i) **Firms whose dividend per worker is larger than the overall average in time period τ will reduce their dividends per worker in period τ + 1. Firms where the dividend per worker is equal to or less than the overall average will maintain the same dividend per worker in the next period.**

The second part of (i) may well impute more altruism to less productive firms than would actually be warranted. However, as will be seen, it is not necessary to impose a stronger condition.

Assume further that: (ii) **Efficient markets or the state fix product and nonlabor factor prices remain unchanged during all periods covered by the discussion.** This postulate serves as a simplifying device. It highlights the broad applicability of the approach (Figure 20.1).

COMMENT: The above mean income in firm A is transferred to the below mean income in firm B in each round until a community-wide egalitarian dividend is achieved.

An examination of (i) and (ii) clearly shows that they lead to a degenerate situation. Firms with per worker dividends above average have considerable latitude to reduce their effort. Since they cannot, or at least, may not be able to, judge the overall average of the next period, the size of their dividend reductions can only be guessed. Consequently, the overall mean might change either rapidly or

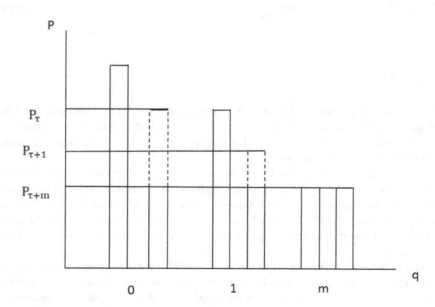

Figure 20.1 Egalitarian Convergence to the Output Minimum: The Two Firm Case

slowly, perhaps taking a large number of periods to change appreciably. There is no basis for judging the dividend per worker of each firm in any given period, or the movements of the system as a whole.

This complication is reducible by modifying (i) slightly with a lagged adjustment rule (I'): Firms whose dividends per worker are larger than the overall average will reduce their dividend per worker in the next period so that it equals the overall average of the current period. Those whose dividends are equal to or less than the overall average will maintain the same dividend per worker in the next period. Thus if a firm has an above-average dividend per worker in period τ, its dividend per worker in time period A+1 must equal the overall average per worker in τ. Or, in obvious notation

$$P_i(\tau+1) = \overline{P}(\tau), \qquad \forall_{i=1}^{\psi} \tag{20.6}$$

Where ψ is the number of firms that are above the average.

Consideration of the equilibration process can start in any period in which the system is in disequilibrium. At such a time, firms that are above $\overline{P}(\tau)$ will reduce their dividends per worker so that in period $\tau+1$ they will equal $\overline{P}(\tau)$, that is, (20.6) will hold. These adjustments will reduce this overall average or $\overline{P}(\tau+1) < \overline{P}(\tau)$. They may cause some of the firms where per worker dividends were lower than $\overline{P}(\tau)$ to be greater than $\overline{P}(\tau+1)$ and they, together with other above-average firms, will have to reduce their per worker dividend in $\tau+2$ so that it equals $\overline{P}(\tau+1)$. The process will continuously reduce $\overline{P}(\tau+q)$, but there is (are) some firm or firms where the dividend per worker is the lowest. As the overall average falls, it will approach this lower bound. It can never go below the minimum dividend per workers. Clearly, $\overline{P}(\tau+q) \to \min_{i \in m} P_i(\tau+q)$ as q increases.

Thus (i') and (ii) imply that the firms will equilibrate at a dividend per worker equal to the lowest dividend per worker.

These outcomes, of course, hold if (i') and (ii) apply. Clearly other axioms could be developed that would give somewhat different, possibly slightly more favorable results. Nonetheless, egalitarianism implies using a mean value so that the taxes levied on the more productive firms will provide a sufficient subsidy for the less productive firms. If the more productive firms choose their level of output, they will be motivated to regress toward the mean and the result will invariably be a diminished national product.

The process of serial contraction is analyzable further if a rule for organizing production can be suggested. Maximizing per worker dividend may be vague for firms curtailing their activities to levels generating last period's community-wide per worker dividend.

Suppose these firms decide instead to minimize nonlabor costs. They need a logical framework to organize production and minimizing nonlabor costs gives them a feasible basis. It is difficult to visualize any other basis because they are in a process of reducing workers' dividends, which precludes the usual optimization goal, and dividend maximization. Minimizing nonlabor cost provides a defensible alternative because it conserves society's resources. Thus if the firms minimize nonlabor costs while generating a dividend equal to the overall dividend of the last period, the Lagrangian using a time index, is

$$L_i(\tau) = \sum_{k \neq i} P_k\, x_{ki}(\tau) - F_i - \mu_i$$
$$(\tau)\left[\frac{P_i\, x_i(\tau) - \sum_{k \neq i} P_k\, x_{ki}(\tau) - F_i}{y_i(\tau)} - \overline{P}(\tau - 1)\right]. \qquad \forall_{i=1}^m$$

The relevant first-order conditions are

$$\frac{\partial L_i(\tau)}{\partial x_{ki}(\tau)} = P_k - \mu_i(\tau)\left[\frac{P_i \dfrac{\partial x_i(\tau)}{\partial x_{ki}(\tau)} - P_k}{y_i(\tau)}\right] = 0$$

or

$$P_k\left(1 + \frac{y_i(\tau)}{\mu_i(\tau)}\right) = P_i\, \frac{x_i(\tau)}{x_{ki}(\tau)}, \qquad \forall_{i=1, k \neq i}^m \qquad (20.7)$$

and

$$\frac{\partial L_i(\tau)}{\partial y_i(\tau)} = -\mu_i(\tau)\left(\frac{P_i \dfrac{x_i(\tau)}{x_{ki}(\tau)}}{y_i(\tau)} - \frac{P_i\, x_i(\tau) - \sum_{k \neq i} P_k\, x_{ki}(\tau) - F_i}{y_i(\tau)^2}\right) \qquad (20.7)$$

$$P_i \frac{\partial x_i(\tau)}{\partial y_i(\tau)} = P_i(\tau) \qquad (20.8)$$

The quantities in the parentheses in (20.7) are positive, and hence comparing (20.7) and (20.4) reveals that contracting firms will reduce their nonlabor factors, while employment rises, according to (20.8) because $P_i(\tau) < P_i(\tau - 1)$.

Can this excess labor demand be satisfied? Not likely. Workers have no incentive to change because their dividends are the same regardless of their employer. Labor is immobile. The authorities could compel workers to move from low- to high-productivity firms in order to generate a stable pan-commonwealth egalitarian per worker dividend above the unconstrained minimum, but any attempt of this sort undoubtedly would encounter formidable locational and practical difficulties.

Of course, if there were a pool of unemployed labor, then workers would be available, but this is incompatible with perfect competition and Marxist–Leninist antiparasitic policies. There is no escape. Worker egalitarian income sharing is intrinsically inefficient and productivity must decline because workers in more productive enterprises cannot minimize nonlabor factor costs, at the same time all workers reserve effort compared with the general competitive benchmark. Under these conditions (20.7) would hold and (20.8) would be impossible. Nonlabor factors usage must decrease and the relative scarcity of nonlabor factors must force workers to reserve their effort further.

These results apply with reduced force if socialists choose to tolerate some degree of inequality. The lower the transfer tax levied on high productive workers, the weaker the labor reservation effect (Rosefielde and Pfouts, 1998).

Moreover, if socialist leaders decide to expand the egalitarian mandate to worker dependents, community members outside the work force, and the proletariat across the globe as some non-Marxist–Leninists advocate, the resulting transfer tax increase would intensify the labor reservation effect. If everyone in and outside the global labor force receives the same income regardless of whether he and she works or plays, living standards will plummet everywhere because no one has the power to improve personal income by increasing productive effort, and everyone can increase utility by reserving labor and substituting leisure. If egalitarian morality prevents people from improving their lot because this offends neighbors, then everyone must bear the pain of a lower standard of living.

Some might counterargue that egalitarian socialism will actually increase per capita GDP because above-average incomes are attributable to oligopoly and monopoly power. However, the surmise is incorrect. As long as (20.7) holds, it does not matter if oligopoly and monopoly rents cause above-average earnings, because even though egalitarianism will eliminate oligopoly and monopoly, it remains intrinsically anticompetitive and will serially reduce productivity of below-average productive workers too. There is no escape. Egalitarian socialism must shrink national income if workers rationally maximize their constrained utility.

This perverse result may seem counterintuitive, but it is not. It is axiomatic in the neoclassical general competitive framework that if any anticompetitive action reduces labor effort and nonlabor input supplies, and prevents factor allocation to best competitive use, production will occur on a production feasibility frontier below the production possibilities curve, that is, per capita GDP must decline. See Appendix 4. Egalitarian socialists can level the income distribution, but workers must pay the price.

Although, egalitarian socialists neither condemn utility seeking nor take vows of poverty, they nonetheless repress private initiative, and tolerate subpar incomes without judiciously assessing whether the benefit is sufficiently large from an ethical standpoint to justify the material cost. Instead of treating socialist welfare as a constrained utility optimization problem, egalitarian socialists make the constraint the optimand, conflating quality of existence with egalitarianism,[5] perhaps fancifully assuming that burdens are borne mostly by above-average income recipients. They also casually suppose that abolishing wealth and income inequities significantly mitigates or eradicates class privilege and other gender, physical, intellectual, psychological, emotional and sexual distinctions and moral prejudices. Presumptions of these sorts are false. The tail of egalitarian socialism in all ways wags the dog of prosperity and life quality.

Egalitarian socialists can take countermeasures to mitigate labor reservation and the voluntary undersupply of nonlabor factors.[6] The Marxist–Leninist antidote for egalitarian leveling and wage repression in the Soviet Union and Mao's China during the Great Proletarian Cultural Revolution was exhorting worker zeal for the socialist cause. Antiparasite laws compelled everyone to work. Toilers were encouraged to set aside utilitarian self-interest and punished for malingering. Resource mobilization campaigns, stern discipline, terror and fear of forced labor mitigated the effort depressing effects of wage leveling, but did not save the Soviet Union and Mao's China from being economies of shortage (Birman, 1983). One way or another, egalitarian socialism must take its toll on the workers' standard of living unless superior workers altruistically and harmoniously exert themselves for others as Marx and Engels imagined they would under full communism. Short of fairy-tale communism, if workers desire egalitarianism, they must give to get.

Affirmative Action and Restorative Justice

The egalitarian socialist parable has two interesting corollaries. The first pertains to affirmative actions that provide some workers with positions above their competitive grade to overcome glass-ceiling barriers to entry or gratuitously elevate their status.[7] The effect of either action will affect productivity in all firms, both those above and below the egalitarian average wage. Equation (20.7) will continue as in the pre-affirmative action case to determine the egalitarian wage, but the exact wage after affirmative action will depend on whether the "hand up" is pro- or anticompetitive. If affirmative action reduces anticompetitive barriers to entry, the equilibrium egalitarian wage will rise (higher labor productivity). If barriers to entry are exacerbated, the equilibrium egalitarian wage will fall.

The second corollary pertains to restorative justice, where victims receive lump-sum income transfers from workers receiving the egalitarian average wage. Workers whose after tax income falls will reserve their effort. Beneficiaries will do likewise. The effects reinforce each other, necessarily depressing the egalitarian wage in the post-restorative justice order. This, of course, does not mean that restorative justice payments are unwarranted, but like all anticompetitive transfer, they impair competitive national productivity.

Growth Retardation, Soft Budgets and Moral Hazard

Foregone economic growth and sluggish modernization compound the steady-state utility losses imposed by egalitarian socialism. Utility maximizers can trade with the future by investing some of enterprise revenue (pre-dividend) in repair, maintenance and new capital formation. The new capital formation augments the steady-state stream of future revenues, allowing members to enjoy a larger stream of income by trading with the future (Fisher, 1930). If workers have a high time preference (strong demand for current consumption), they will invest little, preferring current to augmented future consumption. Conversely, workers with low time preference (strong demand for future consumption) can consume little today and enjoy more tomorrow from the fruits of their investment. Entrepreneurial firms moreover will energetically innovate, while timid egalitarians avoid change. Economic growth and modernization in a generally competitive setting, therefore, depend on member utility maximizing, attitudes toward innovation, time preference and risk. There is a general equilibrium best for every set of consumer demands today and tomorrow, given technologies, the fixed capital stock and the efficient allocation of variable factors of production. It is unattainable in "Egalitaria."

A general intertemporal equilibrium is unachievable in an egalitarian society because entrepreneurs and investors are obligated to divide accrued income above the steady-state norm equally among all community members. Innovative firms and high saving enterprises can only benefit to the extent that growth and innovation increase the average dividend across firms. Entrepreneurs and investors in both superior and inferior productive firms will reserve their innovative and growth-generating efforts according to the steady-state behavioral axioms (20.1)–(20.8). Firms with superior innovation and investment will reduce entrepreneurial and high investor effort after discovering that the fruits of their effort are confiscated.[8] Other things equal, innovation and growth in Egalitaria must be subpar compared to the general competitive utility maximizing norm.

Moral hazard is apt to compound these deadweight losses further. Although superior innovators and investors operating in Egalitaria's low reward environment have relatively little to gain from entrepreneurship and prudent investing, they can guilefully augment their consumption without having to share the gain with other community members by fraudulently "padding" nonlabor input and investment costs (reducing net revenue) to create the illusion of subpar net income. These improper accounting charges can be fictive (freely concocted) or represent intermediate inputs diverted to personal worker consumption. These ruses allow members to avoid sharing the fruits of their superior productivity with the rest of the community.

Entrepreneurs and investors also can double down by borrowing for disguised consumption and defaulting with little potential consequence in a transfer system that automatically underwrites subpar performance. These ploys illustrate the vulnerability of egalitarian regimes eschewing the competitive discipline of Adam Smith's invisible hand, and placing their trust instead in worker solidarity and weak judicial sanctions. Egalitarian socialists delude themselves when they suppose that they can have it all: utility maximizing and anticompetitive egalitarian remuneration.

Egalitarian socialism breeds corruption because it thwarts the normal ambitions of entrepreneurs and other high productive personnel and is prone to fraudulent accounting that allows superior workers to claw back income from less productive firms. Wily entrepreneurs and investors can even turn the egalitarian game upside down by reducing per worker income below the community average, gulling low productivity workers into transferring income from the poor to the rich. Instead of eradicating inequality, inegalitarianism may merely take new forms in an impoverished egalitarian socialist environment.

The danger of perverse outcomes increases if egalitarian socialists feel that satisfying special needs from post-transfer national income and distributing residual net income on an equal per member basis is not good enough, insisting that workers and nonworkers alike enjoy the same quality of existence (adjusted for differences in sensibility). This ambitious goal need not change the core model. The community can continue requiring interenterprise income transfers that equalize remuneration for everyone, subject to a second round of post-dividend transfers that compensate for difference in utilities generated by other activities and relationships. Some individuals may be happier than average for a wide variety of reasons other than those addressed from the collective budget on a post-dividend basis to compensate special physical and mental needs (the handicapped). Comprehensive egalitarian socialism requires taxing happier people and transferring revenues to the morose (Musikanski, 2017). Happiness is subjective and difficult to measure because there are no competitive prices to reflect utilities outside the marketplace, and hedonic estimates are weak interpersonally nonadditive proxies (Neumann and Oskar Morgenstern, 1944; Alchian, 1953; Baumol, 1958; Chipman 1960; Colander, 2007; Kahneman, Diener and Schwarz, 1999; Blackorby, Bossert and Donaldson, 2002).[9] Nonetheless, egalitarian socialists can try,[10] even though prospects for improving upon the core egalitarian income redistribution model are dim because high productivity firms, entrepreneurs and investors are apt to be more disgruntled than ever. They may reasonably suspect that ambiguities of measurement, spurious claims of unhappiness and the serendipity of monetizing subjective utilities for tax transfer purposes create more inequity than it alleviates. Above-average productive workers are likely to feel that they are being unjustly double taxed, first to achieve income equality and then again to placate people who feel they never have enough, prompting superior workers to further reduce their effort and increase their wily ways by pretending to be less happy than the community average.

Game over. Socialist "Egalitaria" cannot provide workers with the same quality of existence because disparate subjective states across heterogeneous workers are inadequately quantifiable. Chasing rainbows at the expense of living standards and growth is folly.

Egalitarian socialists cannot create a satisfactory egalitarian and just society, even in a universe without moral hazard because the simplifying homogeneity assumptions (identical ability, preference and supply functions) needed to obviate the problem are false, and if heterogeneity is acknowledged, technocrats cannot accurately measure interpersonally additive utility. Like Marx and Engels, contemporary socialists can appeal to natural proletarian harmony. Alternatively, they can switch ground by simply admitting that they prefer the optics of leveling income, and ameliorating special needs, acknowledging that universal utilitarian equality is an impossible dream. There is no satisfactory exit for egalitarian socialist utopianism (Dworkin, 2000).

The threat that egalitarian socialism poses to the community's living standard does not apply to other socialist goals. The elimination of prejudice in Egalitaria is positive, even though some workers may have to forgo anticompetitive advantages. Suppressing labor income inequality is an entirely different story. The gain from illiberal state-imposed egalitarianism (not workers' voluntary rational choice) comes at the expense of income losses borne by the entire population. Mandatory egalitarian socialism is Pareto inferior unless every worker prefers full egalitarianism to prosperity.

Notes

1 One for all, all for one (Unus pro omnibus, omnes pro uno) is the motto of Alexander Dumas' Three Musketeers and the traditional motto of Switzerland.

2 Utility is subjective. Utilitarian experiences may be the consequence of ethically astute rational choice, but often are not. The merit of subjective utilitarian experiences therefore varies across individuals. The subjective intensity of utilitarian experiences likewise varies from person to person. Nonmarket utilities are expressible in monetary terms in some circumstances with controlled behavioral experiments; nonetheless, even if these techniques are reliable, the solution would still be of little value because ethical worth and sensory intensities vary widely across populations. Egalitarians might not care. If their utilitarian calculus indicated that transfers made everyone equally happy, this might suffice.

3 Universal equality is thinkable, but only in never-never-land where egalitarians assume that everyone is the same; that all worthy individuals are mentally and physically identical (labor and consumer homogeneity). Neoclassical theory teaches that in a perfect socialist competitive multifactor and multiproduct world with public ownership of nonlabor factors, every clone will receive precisely the value of its marginal product, plus the per worker rental share of variable and fixed capital (workers collectively own the means of production). The utility they derive from egalitarian rations and nonpecuniary activities likewise will be identical for all if everyone shares the same utility function. This may make "Egalitaria" seem plausible to those who ignore the implausibility of assuming that everyone is the same. Heterogeneity shatters the delusion. It is the villain of the piece. If workers possess different talents, skills and physical attributes, quality of workers' existence must vary among individuals in the socialist marketplace and leisure experiences. Power necessarily increases disparities. Socialists can eradicate pecuniary inequities by taxing high productive workers and transferring the proceeds until workers enjoy the same average personal disposable income, but cannot rectify inequities attributable to heterogeneous physical characteristics, sensibilities, conditions of labor, consumer taste, appreciativeness and power.

4 Nonlabor income also could be distributed to the entire population without significantly altering outcomes.

5   Some egalitarians may mistakenly believe that exploitation rather than differences in skill is the sole cause of income and wealth disparities.

6   Marx and Engels famously coined the precept "from each according to ability, to each according to need" to alert comrades to the danger that unscrupulous workers might acquire more utility than they deserve by reserving their effort. The slogan, however, is a toothless commandment. It does not provide a lucid explanation of how socialists can combat moral hazards like parasitic free loading and free riding (unrationed free services).

7   The glass ceiling is a metaphor referring to an invisible barrier that prevents women and minorities from promotion to managerial- and executive-level positions within an organization.

8   Average remuneration will fall in the next period, causing some previously subpar performers into the affluent category, prompting them to reduce their effort too in subsequent rounds.

9   Jeremy Bentham (1748–1832) claimed that utility is cardinal and interpersonally additive, but his supposition is empirically unverified. For purposes of rational individual choice, all that counts is that we can assign numbers to entities or conditions, which a person can strive to realize. Then we say the individual seeks to maximize some function of those numbers. However, this is not enough to calibrate the quality of existence of heterogeneous people with variable sensibilities, precisely.

10 Technocrats can only guess workers' subjective inequalities and the magnitudes of monetary transfers necessary to make the quality of existence the same for everyone.

References

Alchian, Armen. (1953). "The Meaning of Utility Measurement." *American Economic Review.* Vol. 43, No. 1, 26–50.

Anderson, Elizabeth. (1999). "What Is the Point of Equality?" *Ethics.* Vol. 109, 287–337.

Baumol, William. (1958). "The Cardinal Utility Which Is Ordinal." *Economic Journal.* Vol. 68. No. 272, 665–672.

Birman, Igor. (1983). Экономика недостач *(Economy of Shortage).* New York: Chalidze Publications.

Blackorby, Charles, Walter Bossert and David Donaldson. (2002). "Utilitarianism and the Theory of Justice." In Kenneth Arrow, Amartya Sen and Kotaru Suzumura (eds.). *Handbook of Social Choice and Welfare.* Amsterdam: Elsevier, 597–633.

Blake, Michael. (2001). "Distributive Justice, State Coercion, and Autonomy." *Philosophy and Public Affairs.* Vol. 30, 257–296.

Chipman, John. (1960). "The Foundations of Utility." *Econometrica.* Vol. 28, No. 2, 215–216.

Colander, David. (2007). "Retrospectives: Edgeworth's Hedonimeter and the Quest to Measure Utility." *Journal of Economic Perspectives.* Vol. 21, No. 2, 215–226.

Dworkin, Ronald. (2000). *Sovereign Virtue: Equality in Theory and Practice.* Cambridge: Harvard University Press.

Fisher, Irving. (1930). *The Theory of Interest.* New York: Macmillan.

Frankfurt, Harry. (2000). "The Moral Irrelevance of Equality." *Public Affairs Quarterly.* Vol. 14, 87–103.

Hare, Romano. (1981). *Moral Thinking: Its Levels, Method, and Point.* Oxford: Clarendon Press.

Kahneman, Daniel, Ed Diener and Norbert Schwarz (eds.). (1999). *Well-Being: Foundations of Hedonic Psychology.* New York: Russell Sage Foundation.

Knight, Carl and Zofia Stemplowska. (2011). *Responsibility and Distributive Justice.* Oxford and New York: Oxford University Press.

Musikanski, Laura. (2017). "Happiness Index Methodology." *Journal of Social Change.* Vol. 9, No. 1, 4–31.

Neumann, John Von and Oskar Morgenstern. (1944). *The Theory of Games and Economic Behavior.* Princeton: Princeton University Press.

Roemer, John. (1998). *Theories of Distributive Justice.* Cambridge: Harvard University Press.

Roemer, John. (2008). "Socialism vs Social Democracy as Income–Equalizing Institutions." *Eastern Economic Journal.* Vol. 34, No. 1, 14–26.

Rosefielde, Steven and Ralph Pfouts. (1986). "The Firm in Illyria: Market Syndicalism Revisited." *Journal of Comparative Economics.* Vol. 10, No. 2, 160–170.

Rosefielde, Steven and Ralph Pfouts. (1998). "Egalitarianism and Production Potential in Postcommunist Russia." In Steven Rosefielde (ed.). *Efficiency and the Economic Recovery Potential of Russia.* London: Ashgate, 245–268.

21 Japanese Communalist-Socialism

The boundary line dividing Western concepts of socialism nurturing and protecting workers from hostile social forces through vanguard, democratic, cooperative and communal institutions and societies employing non-Western cultural surrogates to accomplish the same purposes is thin. Westerners tend to view traditional Eastern economic systems as non-socialist, even though some do excellent jobs nurturing and protecting productive workers. This is an ethnocentric blind spot. The presumption that workers have little economic influence are passive and vulnerable like counterparts in the West is false. Japan provides an instructive example of how an Asian communalist shame culture can nurture and protect workers in a socialist spirit at least as well as communist, democratic, anarcho-syndicalist and Fabian socialism. It is a matter of taste whether Japanese communalism is includable in the socialist spectrum, but the similarity of Japan's endgame with core Western socialist purposes deserves recognition.

Japanese Communalism with Socialist Characteristics

Japanese consider their system a welfare state with communalist characteristics supported by workers, businesspersons, professionals (bourgeoisie), aristocrats and the emperor. The government provides basic support for everyone, with special consideration given to the needy. Japan, like all EU welfare states and Nordic corporatist states, has a national pension system and health care system. It offers paid maternity leaves for women[1] and free public schooling up through junior high school.[2] It assists single mothers (Japanese Welfare, 2019)[3] and the elderly. It provides unemployment insurance and public works programs that build high-speed Shinkansen train lines, museums, art galleries, schools and Olympic stadiums. Japan's progressive income and inheritance taxes (Kaneko, 2009),[4] together with communalist fair wages contribute to the country's low Gini coefficient (29.9) (CIA World Factbook).[5] Tokyo supports and underwrites most of Japan's farmers.

The Japanese welfare state differs from the EU archetype. Unemployment benefits are smaller.[6] Consensus determines government programs with little partisan acrimony. Japanese culture discourages self-seeking at the community's

DOI: 10.4324/9781003371571-25

expense and encourages productive employment. All able-bodied adults including retirees strive to be self-reliant. Seventy percent of the nation's firms offer employment for life eliminating the need for large state-funded labor support. Politicians and the community prioritize public spending programs that consider everyone's needs not just powerful interests, an attitude that reflects the Japanese self-perception as the people of the great harmony (Carr, 1992).[7]

Communalism

Japanese do not consider the country's welfare state socialist because programs reflect the desires of multiple constituencies, the influence of socialist and communist parties are weak (Fukuda, 2019),[8] and people perceive the government as serving the common good. State programs seek to improve Japan's lot more than promoting blue-collar working class and progressive agendas. Japan's emperor is integral to the polity's notion of national welfare, but the preservation of Emperor Naruhito's rule (Reiwa era) is less important than promoting the people's quality of existence. Japan's welfare system is for the benefit of the Japanese people, not just the emperor, poor, those with special needs, elite or deserving groups. The only authority who saw the Japanese people as a community of productive workers was Tsuneaki Sato (1925–2014) (Ichimura and Sato, 2009).[9] He considered Japan socialist.

He might be right. The consensus classification of Japan as an EU-style welfare state might be a case of not seeing the forest for the trees. Socialism is an intrinsic aspect of Japan's communalist institutions that treat everyone regardless of position as productive workers for the community's benefit. The Japanese do not idealize idlers and misfits (anti-meritocracy). Communalism is not for the emperor, aristocracy, capitalists or collectivists. It is for productive people working cooperatively in teams for the national good. Productive Japanese are sovereign.

Communalism is a way of life for the productive community rooted in Yamato culture (people of the great harmony), influenced by Japanese Buddhism (Shingon, Tendai, Amida, Nichiren, Rinzai, Soto, Obaku and Soka Gakkai) to manage attachments, passions and suffering wisely, compassionately and harmoniously until samsara is complete. Communalism, like socialism, is not reducible to a laundry list of utilitarian ends. It is an institutional tool for managing conflict and exogenous shocks.

Japan communalist culture has endured for more than 2,000 years (Rosefielde, 2013).[10] Buddhism has been an important influence for 15 centuries. Group attitudes and managing human conflict rather than personal motives dominate individual behavior. The group influencing Japanese most is the community (family, neighbors, schools and workplaces). People participate in other groups: political, civic and social organizations, and the nation. All matter. Nonetheless, local concerns are salient. They inform a consensus-building dialogue that permeates the entire system in a way that makes the nation a unified community. Hence, the term communalism.

Japan is a hierarchically structured, ethnically homogeneous, communitarian nation with horizontal self-regulating autonomy, founded on the principle of considerate cooperation. People cooperate not only because it is good for them or even because it improves group well-being. They cooperate because every individual has an obligation to accommodate the needs of others. Japanese communalism fosters cooperativeness to mitigate the abusive proclivities of the strong.

The Japanese are cooperative because maximizing autonomous personal utility is not their raison d'être. They operate with interdependent utility functions that make their total utility partly depend on the effect their actions have on others (Becker, 1974).[11] The interdependency is cybernetic and culminates via consensus-building dialogues in mutually accommodative satisficing equilibria within and across groups (Bolton and Ockenfels, 2000; Fehr and Schmidt, 1999). This considerateness has been an aspect of the Yamato way of life since the 8th-century AD.[12] The Japanese inculcate it in their children generation after generation, and Yamato shame culture reinforces it.

Shame cultures subordinate individual choice to group obligation (Benedict, 1946; Creighton, 1990). Group attitudes guide personal behavior more than the universal ethical principles governing choice in Jewish, Christian and Islamic cultures. This simultaneously makes individuals in Japan less autonomous than people who use Kantian categorical imperatives to manage their personal conduct. Japanese are unusually deferential to group preferences. People in shame cultures conform with little friction, and in Japan given Yamato values; this means that they are empathetic and cooperative.

The Japanese easily subordinate their own to the group's utility preferences. They treat one another courteously, mutually support each other and unselfishly exert themselves. They cultivate team spirit, promote equity over efficiency and court outsiders in order to enhance the quality of group existence. These behaviors, which override the individualist axioms of neoclassical economic theory and partisan democracy, are congruent with idealist socialist goals. Japan's socialist characteristics are broader and deeper than welfare state entitlement.

Japanese Corporate Governance

The principle of considerate cooperation permeates Japanese corporate governance curtailing the scope of libertarian choice and neoclassical economic efficiency. Seventy percent of Japanese firms hire employees for life, precluding managers from adjusting employment to minimize marginal cost and maximize profits. Japanese overwork. They labor 33% more person-hours annually than Americans without overtime pay (bonuses, however, provide supplementary compensation). Although, lifetime employment is under pressure today (Murakami, 2019), interenterprise labor and variable capital remain weakly mobile. Intraenterprise wage and salary differentials are narrow. Requesting or paying workers and managers the value of their marginal products is inconsiderate because success is a team, not an individual endeavor, an ethical concept that flouts neoclassical optimization theory (Baker, Bivens and Schieder, 2019).

Variable factor allocation also is inefficient, raising costs and lowering profits. Japanese shareholder dividends, new capital formation and innovation are all constrained by group obligation, a problem compounded by an aversion to entrepreneurship. The Japanese dislike "creative destruction" because it destabilizes the workplace (Schumpeter, 1942). They shun technologies that threaten job security wherever possible, especially employment reducing innovations. Japanese corporations, moreover, price their products fairly to avoid injuring rivals because this would harm the community. Keiretsu cross-shareholding reinforces these anticompetitive shame culture proclivities (Aoki and Patrick, 1994; Miwa and Ramseyer, 2001). Japanese firms hold shares in affiliated companies to promote mutual assistance (Koyama, 2010) and discourage predatory behavior. If corporations treat affiliates as adversaries, they jeopardize each other's financial viability.

Economists appreciate that Japanese communalism is pervasively inefficient from a competitive perspective. Nonetheless, many insist that what Masahiko Aoki called economies of trust outweigh efficiency losses (Aoki, 1990). Aoki claimed that distrustful workers and managers in individualist guilt cultures reserve their effort and conspire to benefit personally at the group's expense. They deceive and abuse customers and the community, despite Adam Smith's ethical admonitions (Smith, 1761). Although, communalism diminishes productivity, growth and distributional efficiency, Aoki asserted that on balance economies of trust that obviate worker and customer wariness enable Japan to enjoy higher per capita GDP, faster sustainable growth, better customer satisfaction, superior environmental protection and full employment. Instead of underperforming, he contended Japan enjoyed stellar growth in 1954–1990 and should always excel despite its anticompetitive shortcomings (Patrick and Rosovsky, 1973; Johnson, 1982; Pack, Birdsall, Sabor, Kim, Stiglitz, MacDonald, Campos, Page and Cordon, 1993).

These successes, however, are only half the story. Communalism provides Japanese with a host of extra-market utilitarian benefits that do not count as value added in gross domestic product and income accounts (GDP and GDI). GDP is the annual monetary value of finished goods and services. The concept excludes non-commercial utilities generated from learning, self-discovery, self-improvement and self-therapy; gratifying family, community, social and political interpersonal relationships, and spiritual insights (nurture, security, romance, adventure and enlightenment).

There are two broad types of extra-market utilities: (1) pleasure generated from unpaid income and (2) satisfaction derived from living in congenial political, social, cultural, natural and spiritual surroundings. Equality, social justice, cooperativeness, mutual accommodation, amity, harmony, tranquility, security and enlightenment are outcomes of constructive communalist interpersonal behavior that enhance individual utility without contributing to GDP.

Japanese communalism promotes a wide variety of unpaid income ranging from self-help activities to mutual support and charitable assistance. The ichiban imperative (perfectionism) encourages Japanese to improve their intellectual, aesthetic, emotional and spiritual abilities through lifetime self-learning. One visible manifestation is the high quality of Japanese products, higher than justified by perfectly competitive profit maximizing.[13] Shame culture obligates group members at work and play to support one another providing a wide variety of unpaid insurance benefits. Lifetime employment does not count in GDP as value added, nonetheless it increases utility by reducing worker anxiety. If team members are ill, or, otherwise indisposed, coworkers fill the breech without compensation. When natural disasters strike, the community voluntarily aids the needy. When things are lost, shame culture obligates finders to bring valuables to the "koban man" (police station), who returns them to their rightful owner without pilfering. Many feel that egalitarianism, democracy, consensus building, solidarity, amity, belonging, communal memory, harmony and the shared spirituality of Buddhism and Shintoism intrinsic to Japanese communalist system provide extra-market utilities that improve the quality of existence.

Figure 21.1 illustrates these extra-market utilities in the X segment of Japan's vertical quality of existence bar. See Appendix 4, Figure A4.4. The diagram suggests, but does not prove, that although Japanese per capita income (H + P) is lower than the neoclassical competitive ideal, extra-market utilities (X) outweigh the loss. Insofar as these supplementary utilities have a socialist character, Japan may provide workers with a higher quality of existence than Western communism, democratic socialism, anarcho-syndicalism, Fabianism, welfare state entitlement and Nordic States corporatism.

This demonstration would not surprise utopian socialists, including Karl Marx in his youth when he lauded the extra-market benefits of communalism (Marx, 1988),[14] or even Marxist–Leninists who still accept the notion that the state ultimately will vanish under full communism. Nonetheless, many who consider themselves socialists of other stripes may find it disconcerting that a simple principle

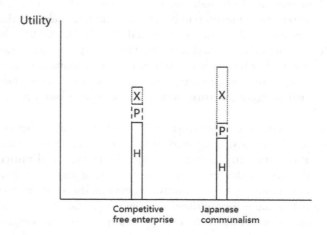

Figure 21.1 Japan: Quality of Existence

like considerate cooperation could be a more potent tool for achieving socialist ends than revolutionary politics. If they ponder the possibility, Marxist–Leninists and Marxist democratic socialist will discover that Japanese behavior today is more socialist in spirit than Marxist democratic socialism and Nordic social democracy.

This rosy picture of Japan's comprehensive communitarian success may be dated. Japan failed to sustain its stellar postwar economic performance of 1954–1990 as Aoki mistakenly supposed. Its "bubble" economy burst in 1991 (Rickards, 2016),[15] followed by three "lost decades" of dyspeptic economic growth (1.1% per annum).[16] Japan is no longer Asia's poster child. It was the regional leader in 1870–1990 (Akamatsu, 1962; Terry, 2002; Koyama, 2015),[17] but lost ground thereafter when it appears to have experienced a climacteric, succumbing to an era of secular stagnation (Hansen,1954).[18] Tokyo will not be able to restore its regional economic luster if it fails to revitalize its economy, and the Japanese themselves may be tempted to relinquish some extra-market utilities in the X space to enjoy higher per capita income as the opportunity costs of communalism mount. Japan may reconcile itself to slow growth to preserve national harmony, but other Asian powers like China are less likely to embrace communalist priorities.

Notes

1 Guaranteed maternity leave in Japan covers a period of 6 weeks prior to the expected birth date to 8 weeks after giving birth. If the employee desires to return to work earlier than 8 weeks, it is possible, but requires submitting an approval by a medical doctor. http://japan-payroll.com/japan-maternity-leave/

2 The central government finances half of teachers' salaries and construction costs of public schools. Municipalities finance the other 50%. Parents pay for textbooks.

3 Many Japanese experts consider the support provided to single mothers inadequate, amounting to less than 500 dollars per month covering the costs of two children.

4 Inheritance tax (sōzokuzei) in Japan is a tax paid by someone who inherits money or property from someone who has died. In Japan, it is paid as a national tax (between 10% and 55% after an exemption of ¥30 million + ¥6 million per heir is deducted from the estate). The 55% rate applies to distributions in excess of 5.5 million US dollars. Inheritance taxes in America are levied on the estates, with an exemption of 11.7 million dollars. Taxation of an individual's income in Japan is progressive. The tax rate for an individual in 2015 is between 5% and—45%.

5 https://knoema.com/atlas/Japan/topics/Poverty/Income-Inequality/GINI-index

6 Public unemployment spending, OECD. https://data.oecd.org/socialexp/public-unemployment-spending.htm

7 Nihon Shoki and Kojiki. Japanese scribes coined the name Nihon or Nippon 日本 circa 608–645 and replaced Wa 倭 with a more flattering Wa 和 "harmony; peace" around 756–757 CE (Carr, 1992, 6–7). The linguistic change is recorded in two official Tang histories.

8 The Society for the Study of Socialism was founded in October 1896. It was reorganized in 1901 into Japan's first socialist political party, the Social Democratic Party of Japan in 1901. The government outlawed the new party two days after its formation.

The Japan Socialist Party was founded on January 28, 1906 as a coalition representing a wide spectrum of socialist beliefs. Its many factions were suppressed under the Peace Preservation Laws. Various socialist parties emerged in postwar Japan. They had ups and downs and currently are insignificant. Japan's Communist Party founded in 1922 as an underground branch of Comintern. On July 15, 1927, the Comintern demanded that the party strive for an immediate two-stage revolution to overthrow the Japanese government. The Japanese communist movement virtually ceased to exist after 1935 with the arrest of its leadership and dissolution of supporting organizations. It reestablished after the war. It receives about 8% of the vote for parliament. The Social Democratic Party receives approximately 2% of the vote.

9 Professor Sato (Yokohama City University and then Nihon University) was one of the most famous researchers on socialism in the USSR and Eastern Europe. He wrote extensively on the economic reforms in the former Soviet and Eastern European Countries and then systemic transformation in these countries.

10 Steven Rosefielde, *Asian Economic Systems*, Singapore: World Scientific Publishers, 2013.

11 Interdependent utility assumes that the subjective well-being of an individual depends in some measure on the well-being of other individuals.

12 The Yamato period refers to the Kofun (c. 250–538) and Asuka era (538–710) when the Japanese Imperial court ruled from modern-day Nara Prefecture, then known as Yamato Province. Kofun period (c. 250–538) and the Asuka period (538–710).

13 Cars in Japan cease being legally "roadworthy" after 10 years. Car ownership is discouraged after five years by high, escalating roadworthiness taxes. Profit maximizing firms should design Japanese cars to match the national roadworthiness standard, but the ichiban ethic compels automakers to spend extra funds needed to assure longer service lives.

14 Marx's manuscript cover a wide range of topics, including material on private property and communism, money and alienation. His cure for capitalism and its discontents boils down to considerate cooperation.

15 The lost decade included more than just stock market losses. Japan also saw crashing property values, falling interest rates, rising unemployment, declining and stagnant GDP and the worst demographic profile of any major economy.

16 https://data.worldbank.org/indicator/NY.GDP.MKTP.KD?locations=JP

17 Kaname Akamatsu contended that Japan's technological prowess made it Asia's natural leader. His flying geese metaphor suggested, among other things, that latecomers to Asian economic development would always follow Japan's lead because Japan would stay technologically ahead of the flock. South Korea, Taiwan, Singapore and even China today rival Japan technologically, raising the prospect that Japan will not always be the leader of Asia's flying geese.

18 Secular stagnation is a condition when there is negligible or no economic growth in a market-based economy.

References

Akamatsu, Kaname. (1962). "A Historical Pattern of Economic Growth in Developing Countries." *Journal of Developing Economies*. Vol. 1, No. 1, 3–25.

Aoki, Masahiko. (1990). "Toward an Economic Model of the Japanese Firm." *Journal of Economic Literature*. Vol. 28, No. 1, 1–27.

Aoki, Masahiko and Hugh Patrick. (1994). *The Japanese Main Bank System*. London: Oxford University Press.

Baker, Dean, Josh Bivens and Jessica Schieder. (2019). "Reining in CEO Compensation and Curbing the Rise of Inequality." *Economic Policy Institute*. www.epi.org/publication/reining-in-ceo-compensation-and-curbing-the-rise-of-inequality/

Becker, Gary. (1974). "A Theory of Social Interactions." *Journal of Political Economy*. Vol. 82, No. 6, 1063–1093.

Benedict, Ruth. (1946). *The Chrysanthemum and the Sword*. New York: Houghton, Mifflin and Harcourt.

Bolton, Gary and Axel Ockenfels. "ERC: A Theory of Equity, Reciprocity and Competition." *American Economic Review*. Vol. 90, No. 1, 166–193.

Carr, Michael. (1992). "Wa 倭 Wa 和 Lexicography." *International Journal of Lexicography*. Vol. 5., No. 1, 1–30.

CIA World Factbook, Japan. "Japan's Current Gini Coefficient Is 29.9." https://knoema.com/atlas/Japan/topics/Poverty/Income-Inequality/GINI-index

Creighton, Millie. (1990). "Revisiting Shame and Guilt Cultures: A Forty-Year Pilgrimage." *Ethos*. Vol. 18, No. 3, 279–307.

Fehr, Ernest and Klaus Schmidt. (1999). "A Theory of Fairness, Competition and Cooperation." *Quarterly Journal of Economics*. Vol. 114, 309–320.

Fukada, Masahiko. (2019). "How Socialism and the Left Wing Failed in Japan." *Japan Times*. www.japantimes.co.jp/news/2019/12/30/national/politics-diplomacy/socialism-japan/#.XjbbWSNOk2w

Hansen, Alvin. (1954). "Growth or Stagnation in the American Economy." *Review of Economics and Statistics*. Vol. 36, 409–414.

Ichimura, Shinichi and Tsuneaki Sato (eds.). (2009). *Transition from Socialist to Market Economies: Comparison of European and Asian Experiences*. New York: Palgrave Macmillan.

Japan. "Public Unemployment Spending." *OECD*. https://data.oecd.org/socialexp/public-unemployment-spending.htm

Japan Gini. https://knoema.com/atlas/Japan/topics/Poverty/Income-Inequality/GINI-index

Japan, Growth. World Bank. https://data.worldbank.org/indicator/NY.GDP.MKTP.KD?locations=JP

Japanese Welfare. (2019). "Depending on Locale, Single Moms in Japan Can Depend on Social Support." *Japan Today*. https://japantoday.com/category/features/kuchikomi/depending-on-locale-single-moms-in-japan-can-depend-on-social-support

Johnson, Chalmers. (1982). *MITI and the Japanese Miracle: The Growth of Industrial Policy, 1925–1975*. Stanford: Stanford University Press.

Kaneko, Hiroshi. (2009). "The Japanese Income Tax System and the Disparity of Income and Wealth among People in Japan." Sho Sato Conference. www.law.berkeley.edu/files/sho_sato_tax_conf_web_paper--kaneko.pdf

Koyama, Yoji. (2010). "An Issue of Corporate Governance in Japan: For Whom Companies Exist?" *Romanian Economic and Business Review*. Vol. 5, No. 4, 99–113.

Koyama, Yoji. (2015). "Flying Geese Pattern and Central and East European Countries." *Journal of US-China Public Administration*. Vol. 12, No. 6, 440—453.

Marx, Karl. (1988). *The Economic and Philosophical Manuscripts of 1844*. New York: Prometheus Press.

Miwa, Yoshiro and Mark Ramseyer. (2001). "The Fable of the Keiretsu." *Journal of Economics & Management Strategy*. Vol. 11, No. 2,169–224.

Murakami, Yumiko. (2019). "End of Heisei Era and Lifetime Employment." *Japan Times*. www.japantimes.co.jp/opinion/2019/05/02/commentary/japan-commentary/end-heisei-era-lifetime-employment/#.Xk0sR0pOmK8

OECD. "Public Unemployment Spending." https://data.oecd.org/socialexp/public-unemployment-spending.htm

Pack, Howard, Nancy Birdsall, Richard Sabor, Chang-Shik Kim, Joseph Stiglitz, Lawrence MacDonald (ed.), Jose Campos, John Page and Max Cordon. (1993). *The East Asian Miracle: Economic Growth and Public Policy.* Washington: World Bank. http://documents.worldbank.org/curated/en/975081468244550798/Main-report

Patrick, Hugh and Henry Rosovsky. (1973). *Asia's New Giant: How the Japanese Economy Works.* Washington: Brookings Institution.

Rickards, Jim. (2016). "Japan's in the Middle of Its 3rd 'Lost Decade' and a Recovery Is Nowhere in Sight." *Business Insider.*

Rosefielde, Steven. (2013). *Asian Economic Systems.* Singapore: World Scientific Publishers.

Schumpeter, Joseph. (1942). *Capitalism, Socialism and Democracy.* New York: Harper & Brothers.

Smith, Adam. (1761). *Theory of Moral Sentiments.* Glasgow: Strand & Edinburgh.

Terry, Edith. (2002). *How Asia Got Rich – Japan, China, and the Asian Miracle.* Armonk: M.E. Sharp Publishing.

22 21st-Century Socialism

Robert Owen and Karl Marx conceived socialism as an economic system to assist productive people displaced by the industrial revolution from 18th-century agrarian, village and urban occupations. Peasants and villagers lost their tenancies and trades, compelling them to work for meager industrial day wages without rainy day reserves. Landless workers were poor, demoralized and lacked opportunities for vocational advancement. Owen offered them a hand up and Marx (after 1871) violent revolution.

Peasant and urban workers who inspired Owen and Marx no longer exist in the developed world. Free universal education and accessible vocational training opportunities are widely available. Governments protect worker job rights and assist them with social safety nets that include unemployment insurance, food, shelter, medical care, child support, education and retirement income. They set minimum wages and promote equal employment opportunity. Contraceptives give workers greater control over family size. The digital revolution increased worker communication and information technology skills to degrees unimaginable in the 19th century. Social power persists, but no longer depends primarily on pedigree.

Most people today work in the service sector. Some receive wages, others salaries. Disparities in labor remuneration are large, but graduated income taxes and affirmative action narrow the gap. Entrepreneurship, investment, speculation and inheritance are the main sources of income and wealth inequalities.

The working class is indisputably better off than it was two and a half centuries ago. Nonetheless, life remains difficult for workers and retirees exploited by corporations, politicians and frenemy activists. The powerful give with one hand and take with the other. Gainfully employed productive people with limited savings remain insecure. They are vulnerable to deteriorating job quality, diminishing benefits, indoctrination, wage-compression, circumscribed civil liberties, affirmative discrimination, canceling, overtaxation (including compulsory health insurance) and open and hidden inflation.

The main task of 21st-century socialism is ameliorating modern problems by democratically empowering workers and prioritizing their needs over the counterclaims of other motivated groups (Harrington, 1989). Socialists must

DOI: 10.4324/9781003371571-26

persuade contemporary polities that they have a moral duty to accommodate workers.

Owen was a libertarian humanist and democrat who valued personal freedom for everyone and believed that people would discover how to construct high-quality material, humane and spiritual existences. He believed workers would learn what was best for them through trial and error. If circumstances changed, institutions and policies would adjust. Self-perceived needs would drive action, not politics. Twenty-first-century socialism from Owen's perspective should be democratically responsive to workers' requirements (Nove, 1983).[1]

The model does not require nationalization of the means of production, trade unions, cooperatives, guilds, egalitarianism or 19th-century democratic socialist, revolutionary Marxist or syndicalist parties. Socialists can harness these institutions, but only insofar as the workers democratically decide appropriate solutions after consensus-building conversations with other motivated groups.

Twenty-first-century socialism may adopt various aspects of the progressive agenda, but is not obliged to do so. It is not utopian. Workers can decide for themselves when questing for the best becomes the enemy of the good. Ideals may shape but do not supervene labor utility maximizing. Workers who constitute the vast majority in developed economies may voluntarily agree to support the goals of others outside the labor context in diverse ways, but need not do so to be socialist. Workers, not progressives, intellectuals, capitalists or politicians are the final judge of what is in their best interest, vanguard claims to the contrary notwithstanding (Sajó, Uitz and Holmes, 2022).

Productive workers are the majority in much of the world. They outnumber businesspersons, landowners, politicians, journalists, entrepreneurs, professionals, intellectuals, the idle rich and free riders by a wide margin. They have the power via the ballot box to create modern socialist democracies with Lockean social contracts protecting minority rights including property ownership, sensitive to workers' special needs. Revolutionary violence is superfluous. Workers can simply shift their electoral allegiances from established political parties dominated by nonworking-class priorities to new worker-centric parties that defend productive labor against those championing rival interests. Anti-worker activists have captured established political parties falsely claiming to prioritize worker welfare.

Twenty-first-century socialism clarifies the boundary between core worker concerns and a vast array of social, political, religious, gender, defense and foreign policy issues on which the entire community is free to express diverse opinions. Workers are not obligated to take inflexible ideological positions on any of these matters. They can adjust their outlook to changing circumstances. New worker-centric parties are not hostage to trade union agendas. Established political parties cater to unions because they can deliver votes. They try to convey the impression that solicitude for unions is tantamount to serving all workers, but do very little to protect the nonunionized majority. Only 10% of American workers are union members. All worker voices would count in a modern worker centric party.

Advocates of diverse causes tangentially associated with labor have striven to define and hijack socialism since the early 19th century. Fourier pretended that bacchanals were the solution to everyone's plight. Saint-Simon conflated his technocratic infatuation with worker self-empowerment. Marx paid no serious attention to workers' desire for individual self-improvement. Radical feminists insisted that socialism and their agenda were synonymous. Pacifists equated socialism with universal disarmament when Hitler and Stalin were arming to the teeth. The substance of socialist politics for Marxist–Leninists in 1917–1991 was accommodating the Soviet communist party line. Twenty-first-century socialism cannot succeed if it relies on wolves in sheep's clothing.

Socialist workers in Owen's tradition determine their ends and means themselves. No one can authoritatively speak for them. Libertarian workers must shape the possibilities of 21st-century socialism. They receive part of their livelihood from wages and salaries, but may also own assets and participate in business and entrepreneurial activities. Worker libertarianism can accommodate the coexistence of state, cooperative and private ownership of the means of production together with markets and plans. It can democratically manage the risks of abusive private power arising from oligopoly and monopoly, as well as labor cliques.

Twenty-first-century libertarian socialism insofar as it is consistent requires every factor receive the competitive value of its marginal product within the limits imposed by bounded rationality before making egalitarian adjustments through tax transfers. The principle applies to government officials, experts, intellectuals and politicians. Twenty-first-century socialism should prohibit state and regulatory authorities from using their positions to prosper at the workers' expense. Politicians often manipulate the public to enrich themselves. The abuses are incompatible with 21st-century socialism. Politicians and state officials must be civil servants for the working class, and other interest groups mediated through a democratic process reflecting the majority status of productive workers.

Notes

1 The literature suggests a variety of themes socialists might choose as guides to discovering and constructing systems that maximize diverse notions of the quality of socialist existence. There are eight notable possibilities.

  1 Policing capitalist activities
  2 Defending the realm
  3 Fostering prosperity
  4 Creating comprehensive entitlements
  5 Eradicating inequality
  6 Eradicating injustice
  7 Cultivating human potential
  8 Promoting amity and harmony

Cf. Alec Nove, *The Economics of Feasible Socialism Revisited*, London: Harper Collins, 1983.

References

Harrington, Michael. (1989). *Socialism: Past and Future*. New York: Penguin.
Nove, Alec. (1983). *The Economics of Feasible Socialism Revisited*. London: Harper Collins.
Sajó, András, Renáta Uitz and Stephen Holmes. (2022). *Routledge Handbook of Illiberalism*. London: Routledge.

Conclusion

The word socialism entered the global lexicon in the late 1840s. It meant systems designed for esteeming, protecting and benefiting productive men and women including cooperative labor and communal living schemes for the burgeoning industrial age. The concept subsequently expanded first to include precapitalist forerunners and second worker-focused political movements that radically altered national and global economic and political institutions. These politically motivated extensions were powerful historical catalysts for economic, political and social change in 1870–1991, but blurred socialism's principal economic mission: ameliorating the plight of productive workers in an era of rapid economic, social and political transformation.

On one hand, journalists, public intellectuals, politicians and revolutionary activists imposed extraneous agendas on workers seeking tangible improvements in their life quality (Gregor, 2005). On the other, they conflated worker betterment with the political goal of canceling capitalism rather than scientifically constructing well-functioning worker beneficent systems. Both revisions made the best the enemy of the good. They forced workers needlessly to jump through revolutionary dreamers' hoops and prejudiced many against private property, markets and entrepreneurship. Revolutionary socialists enthusiastically embraced these mandates and constraints after 1848, providing a living laboratory for testing the merit of socialist schemes interpreted through the lenses of neoclassical economic theory and statistics. The experiment has taught many useful lessons.

We now know that while some 19th-century utopian communities briefly flourished, all eventually perished.

We now know that while revolutionary syndicalism has sometimes briefly seized state power, it never ruled effectively.

We now know that while guild socialism (direct economic democracy) seemed promising circa 1918, Bolshevism swiftly overshadowed it. Direct democracy never regained its former luster.

We now know that while some forms of communalism like the Mondragon federation of worker-cooperatives have flourished, their appeal is circumscribed.

DOI: 10.4324/9781003371571-27

We now know that while diverse socialist parties sometimes win democratic elections, none has transformed victory into durable democratic socialist rule.

We now know that while Marxist-Leninism reigned in Russia for 73 years, and continues to rule in North Korea, it failed to deliver the "full communism" prophesized in the *Communist Manifesto*, and has lost much of its appeal.

We now know that while Yugoslavian worker self-management inspired a legion of admirers in 1960–1989, the idea today is moribund.

We now know that libertarian cooperatives and anarcho-communalism are viable, but are not most workers' cup of tea.

We now know that egalitarianism is not a panacea and may have severely adverse side effects.

We now know that while illiberal Marxist democratic socialism is feasible, it has difficulty competing with liberal free enterprise, welfare states and Nordic corporatism. Democratic socialism no longer appears destiny's darling.

We now know that while numerous alternative socialist schemes were tested, most have proven passing fancies.

We now know with considerable confidence that illiberal Marxist-Leninism (including Stalin's command planning, Tito's labor self-management and Fidel Castro's revolutionary communist Cuban subcase), Sorel's revolutionary syndicalism, George Douglas Howard Cole's libertarian Fabian and William Morris' Guild socialisms are news to nowhere. They no longer are part of serious socialist conversation.

We now know that while varieties of contemporary socialism have been treading water, the West's blue-collar working class, once predicted by Marx to become the vast majority, has dwindled into a small minority, prompting politicians and activists to favor other constituencies.

We now know that New Age computopia is apt to be inferior to warts-and-all laissez-faire.

We now know that while the left continues to doff its hat to organized labor, politicians and activists today care little about ordinary workers. Trade unions are no longer dominant social forces or radically chic. The left has shifted its allegiance to other causes. The right and left are both squeezing socialism.

We now know that illiberal proletarian vanguard systems like Xi Jinping's China using markets, leaseholds and entrepreneurship are compatible with worker welfare improving economic growth. China's communist party, unlike most socialist parties in the West, has the political power to construct a worker sovereign socialist regime as the leadership promises, but it is doubtful that its efforts will culminate in self-governing communes of the sort described in Marx's *Communist Manifesto*.

We now know that prospects for world socialism ("workers of the world unite") are no better than those of revolutionary Marxist-Leninism, New Age planning, Marxist democratic socialism, Fabianism, Guild socialism, revolutionary syndicalism, anarcho-communalism, Saint-Simonian socialism, Cabet's socialism, Fourier's "Amour-topia," Mao's cultural revolution and Xi Jinping's full communism.

We now know that socialists everywhere shun scientific net assessments of socialism's failures and prospects. Faith is their solace. Many Western Sovietologists in the same vein pretend that official data underpinning benign assessments of Marxist–Leninist performance are reliable. Scholars in other disciplines, socialist politicians and activists continue to act as if communism contains meta-historical truths that somehow assure happy-endings. They are not always right, but never wrong.

We now know that intellectuals, activists and politicians are fickle. Progressivism today is displacing socialism as the left's ideological mantra. It promotes radical activism for nonworking class ends. If the trend persists, socialism will vanish into the dustpan of history.

We now know that despite two centuries of experience, socialist political rhetoric remains more about late-19th-century social romanticism and hostility toward private property, markets, privilege and inequity than rigorous designs for better living. There is no ethical consensus on the optimal configuration of socialist ends, institutionalist agreement about how to construct efficient socialist systems or definitive standards for assessing comparative merit.

We now know that while contemporary socialism faces an uphill battle, returning to basics might resuscitate its fortunes. If socialism means libertarian democracy prioritizing worker betterment, the goal is achievable because most Westerners are white- and blue-collar members of the working class. They are not class conscious and a potent social force today, but can be educated.

The situation is not hopeless, even for socialists who acknowledge past failures. Well-functioning 21st-century democratic socialist economic systems focused on protecting, and nurturing productive men and women without illiberal universal entitlements are easily constructed. They are compatible with multiple institutions. If socialism is to succeed, socialists must concentrate on contemporary working-class essentials, and build cultural and political movements transforming dreams into realities.

Abram Bergson laid out the mathematical foundations for worker sovereign socialist solutions in 1938 (Appendix 1). The working class majority and its supporters merely have to agree that workers should democratically decide the economic rights, institutions and altruistic public purposes that maximize the quality of their existence under the limitations imposed by bounded rationality. Workers across the occupational spectrum in developed nations today are the majority. If their democracies want libertarian socialism, workers can have it for as long as they wish. They do not have to entangle themselves with the contradictions of French Revolutionary social romanticism. They must merely accept Robert Owen's foundational concern for warts-and-all worker well-being, undistorted by wily worldly philosophers, starry-eyed revolutionaries and scoundrels.

Will the Zeitgeist be propitious? Will socialism come to fruition? Will the intelligentsia distain it if workers reject radical chic?

"You can never tell with bees, I always say" (Winnie the Pooh).

Reference

Gregor, Anthony. (2005). *Mussolini's Intellectuals: Fascist Social and Political Thought*. Princeton, NJ: Princeton University Press.

Appendix 1

Bergson's Systems Function

Abram Bergson was the first theorist to formulate the abstract characteristics and properties of diverse systems rigorously. He devised a social welfare function W, which included an economic sub-function E for this purpose in 1938 (Bergson, 1938, 1954). The W function encompasses all forms of discretionary individual and collective utility seeking (including non-GDP consumption and external economies), and the systemic variables constraining unfettered free choice (the system). The E sub-function differs from W solely because it excludes non-commercial activities and relations (including leisure) and externalities.[1]

Bergson's W function is:

$$W = W(x_1, y_1, a_1^x, b_1^x, a_1^y, b_1^y, \ldots, x_n, y_n, a_n^x, b_n^x, a_n^y, b_n^y, C^x, D^x, C^y, D^y, r, s, t, \ldots) \quad (1.1)$$

C^x and D^x are the amounts of nonlabor factors C and D employed in producing the consumer good x.

C^y and D^y are the amounts of nonlabor factors employed in producing the consumer good y.

x_i and y_i are the amounts of x and y consumed by the ith individual and a_1^x, b_1^x, a_1^y and b_1^y are the amounts of each kind of work performed by him/her during the given period of time.

The symbols r, s, t, ... denote elements other than the amounts of commodities, the amounts of work of each type and the amounts of the nonlabor factors in each of the production units, affecting the welfare of each individual and the community.[2] They can include institutions (cooperatives, communes, command planning regimes), political and social rights, arrangements (democracy, consensus) and relations (egalitarianism).

His E sub-function is:

$$E = E\left(x_1, y_1, a_1^x, b_1^x, a_1^y, b_1^y, \ldots, x_n, y_n, a_n^x, b_n^x, a_n^y, b_n^y, C^x, D^x, C^y, D^y\right) \quad (1.2)$$

It is obtained by taking r, s, t in (1.1) as given.

The "inclusive" function W and sub-function E both implicitly contain sets of systems with distinctive purposes, property rights regimes, institutions, mechanisms and rules of conduct (the economic system). The invisible fine print includes isoquants (elements of production functions), iso-utility curves (elements of individual and community utility functions) and counterpart micro supply side aspects of property rights, institutions and codes of conduct.

The E sub-function, assuming the existence of continuous production and utility functions, can generate Pareto optional outcomes in the factor, production, distribution and transfer spaces for each configuration of r, s and t (Bergson, 1938).[3]

Bergson notes that Pareto efficient systems can be capitalist or socialist and are achievable with both perfect markets and perfect plans (Dorfman, Samuelson and Solow, 1958).[4] The E sub-function determines the potential of efficient Pareto systems. Pareto efficient systems provide a theory normed benchmark for assessing the merit of all imperfectly competitive and anticompetitive E-type systems. They are defined for states of r, s and t, but do not take explicit account of nonpecuniary utility generating activities and relations and externalities disregarded in GDP statistics. W system functions include both utilities from GDP generated and other consumption. E system functions only measure GDP-generated utilities from consumption.

The production functions in the E equation reflect embodied technological potential. If systems are efficient, the potential will be realized. Otherwise, the system with satisfice. Embodied fixed capital and labor productivity potential is affected by science and technological progress. Bergson's W and E functions can be expanded to encompass economic growth and time preference. He interpreted them from an optimal perspective assuming perfect information. Stochastic and bounded rational assumptions provide analogous results.

Bergson recognized that the perfectly competitive market-type Pareto individual utility maximizing system (including democratically determined income transfers), which treats r, s and t as givens, is not society's only rational choice. Sovereigns may prefer alternatives on various grounds. Nonetheless, he ventured the opinion that the perfectly competitive democratic free enterprise Pareto standard provides an attractive and convenient starting point for conversations about "what should be done."

The contemporary discipline of comparative economics encompasses all non-Pareto, imperfectly competitive and Pareto ideal systems (capitalist, socialist, Nordic corporatist, progressive, etc.) contained in Bergson's W function and E sub-function. It imitates Isaac Newton's hard science mathematical approach to discovering the universal laws of economic motion, premised on the dubious supposition that human behavior, like gravity, is invariant.[5]

E sub-function outcomes are expressed as output values (GDP). Competitive market prices are used to value physical output in the perfectly competitive democratic free enterprise case given r, s, t in (1.1). They reflect purchaser marginal utilities. The same principle holds for each configuration of r, s, t including income transfers. This means that there is no unique best Pareto efficient GDP for market or perfectly planned economies, only a set of competitively efficient GDPs for each set of r, s, t.

Each efficient GDP can be transformed into utility with hedonic transformation functions. This is impossible, however, in practice because comprehensive real-time individual utility functions cannot be reliably estimated, and even if they could, utility is neither intertemporally cardinal nor interpersonally (internationally) commensurable, disregarding the further problems of mood, interdependent utilities and their transitory essence (Bentham 1948; Neumann and Morgenstern, 1948).[6] Theorists try to sidestep the issue by assuming that people share a common utility function (Scitovsky community indifference curve), but this is done for narrative convenience (Graaff, 1957; Samuelson, 1956; Scitovsky, 1941). Many do not appreciate the convention and erroneously imagine that disparate individual utility functions are uniquely additive to reflect shared preferences. They are not. However, the prices individuals pay for the products they purchase in Pareto efficient economies reflect their marginal value, making GDP expressed in monetary terms a cardinal utility measure for each individual and their sum a cardinal measure for all in this sense, even though utility scales differ from person to person. People often intuitively view per capita GDP (living standard) in this way.

If analysts waive these imponderables for reported GDP, and alternative virtual reality GDPs estimated for every configuration of r, s, t, then they can compare and assess potential "national utilities." Socialism could be objectively said to be better than capitalism or vice versa judged from the standpoint of diverse income recipients (via community indifference curves). If they do not waive these imponderables, socialism and capitalism are not definitively comparable.

Moreover, even under ideal sci-fi conditions, socialists and capitalists could reject any outcomes they dislike on ethical and sentimental grounds. Subjective utility is not a standard of supreme merit. It is just a hedonic indicator. If evildoers are happiest, virtuous people need not concede that wickedness is best.

All of these qualifications also apply to Bergson's W function, which includes utility generating outcomes like democracy, civil liberties, egalitarianism and institution shaped interpersonal relations outside the GDP framework.[7]

Many people assume that the systems they prefer on intuitive, sentimental, aesthetic and ethical grounds are objectively superior unaware that the facts they need to validate their judgments are mostly figments of their imagination. The belief, duty and wilfulness of some do not negate the counterviews of others. Utility, belief, duty and wilfulness all count in assessing social welfare. Bergson argued that critical discourse offers a useful tool for finding common ground and perhaps consensus. Most analysts ignore his advice (Bergson, 1976).

Finally, r, s, t parameters can be transformed into behavioral equations for those interested in studying political and sociological dynamics. Economic utility seeking in Bergson's world governs all aspects of human behavior.

Notes

1 The alternative to work is leisure, with the connotation of entertainment. Bergson chose to omit leisure time utilities as distractions from the E sub-function focus on commercially generated activities.

2 Some of the elements r, s, t may affect welfare, not only directly, but indirectly through their effect on (say) the amounts of x and y produced with any given amount of resources, e.g., the effects of a change in the weather. On the other hand, it is conceivable that variations in the amounts of commodities, the amounts of work of each type, and the amounts of non-labor factors in each of the production units also will have a direct and indirect effect on welfare; e.g., a sufficient diminution of x_i and y_j may be accompanied by regime change. But for relatively small changes in these variables, other elements in welfare, I believe, will not be significantly affected. To the extent that this is so a partial analysis is feasible. I shall designate the function E... .

3 The continuity assumption is not essential for rational decision making but is an integral aspect of the Paretian perfectly competitive ideal.

4 Pareto duality requires a perfect correspondence between the objective functions of both systems. Individual preferences must be the competitive ideal. Soviet planning did not satisfy this requirement. Planners' preferences ruled. Bergson understood the distinction.

5 Isaac Newton (1642–1727) invented the calculus in the mid- to late-1660s and formulated the theory of universal gravity. His *Philosophiæ Naturalis Principia Mathematica* transformed natural philosophy into modern physical science. Vilfredo Pareto (1812–1882), Paul Samuelson (1915–2009) and others attempted to accomplish the same feat for the economics branch of the soft social sciences.

6 Utility can be conceived as a quantum like an atom in physics. Jeremy Bentham believed that utilities could be counted and added. Bentham's ambition in life was to create a "Pannomion," a complete utilitarian code of law. He not only proposed many legal and social reforms, but also expounded an underlying moral principle that the greatest happiness of the greatest number is the ultimate measure of right and wrong. Utility can be quantified in some circumstances using probability and the theory of games, but complete estimation is infeasible. The utility transformation function in each individual is unique, and non-addable. The utility generated by a unit of q_i differs across individuals and cannot be summed across the population. Also, as is seldom noted, utility cannot be reliably stored and retrieved because memory is inexact. Consequently, the sum of individual experiences has no invariant effect on people's well-being, happiness and quality of existence. Utility is evanescent and mutable. It cannot serve as an infallible ethical guide.

7 See the Fourier section of Chapter 2, this volume on and institution shaped interpersonal relations.

References

Bentham, Jeremey. (1948). *An Introduction to the Principles of Morals and Legislation.* New York: Hafner Publishing Co.

Bergson, Abram. (1938). "A Reformulation of Certain Aspects of Welfare Economics." *Quarterly Journal of Economics.* Vol. 52, No. 1, 310–334.

Bergson, Abram. (1954). "The Concept of Social Welfare." *Quarterly Journal of Economics.* Vol. 68, No. 2, 233–252.

Bergson, Abram. (1976). "Social Choice and Welfare Economics under Representative Government." *Journal of Public Economics.* Vol. 6, No. 3, 171–190.

Dorfman, Robert, Paul Samuelson and Robert Solow. (1958). *Linear Programming and Economic Analysis.* New York: McGraw-Hill.

Graaff, Johannes de Villiers. (1957). *Theoretical Welfare Economics.* Cambridge: Cambridge University Press.

Neumann, John von and Oskar Morgenstern. (1944). *Theory of Games and Economic Behavior.* Princeton: Princeton University Press.

Samuelson, Paul. (1956). "Social Indifference Curves." *The Quarterly Journal of Economics.* Vol. 70, No. 1, 1–22.

Scitovsky, Tibor. (1941). "A Note on Welfare Propositions in Economics." *Review of Economics and Statistics.* Vol. 9, No. 1, 77—88.

Appendix 2
Marx, Lenin and Stalin

Karl Marx

Karl Heinrich Marx (1818–1883) was a German political economist, journalist and socialist revolutionary. Born in Trier, Germany in 1818, he studied law and philosophy at university. He irked authorities with his liberal views by opposing the German religious conservative establishment. He secularized Hegel's historicist philosophical concepts, applying them to the proletarian cause. Marx had no formal training in economics and never grasped the rudiments of classical microeconomic theory.

He became stateless and lived in exile in London for decades, where he develop his revolutionary socialist strategy in collaboration with Friedrich Engels. His best-known works are the 1848 pamphlet *The Communist Manifesto* jointly authored with Engels and the three volume-*Das Kapital* (1867–1883) dealing with class struggle–driven macroeconomic crisis theory. Engels was Marx's industrialist patron. He financed *Das Kapital*. Three of Marx's children survived childhood. Two of the three surviving daughters committed suicide: Jenny Laura (1845–1911) and Jenny Julia Eleanor (1855–1898) (Gilbert, 2012).[1]

Marx died in 1883. Thirteen people attended his funeral. He was a fringe figure when he passed away, but became a socialist icon in the 1890s.

The essence of Marx's contribution to socialism lies in his pioneering effort to link class struggle, radical trade unionism and revolutionary insurrection after 1871. Marx the man, political economist, journalist and factional leader are mostly interesting from the standpoint of the history of the socialist movement and revolutionary mythmaking.

Marx's march to socialist icon began in the mid- to late-1860s after the founding of the International Workingmen's Association (IWA), often called the First International (1864–1876), and his publication of *Das Kapital* (1867). His insistence on the vanguard principle occasioned in part by the suppression of the Second Paris Commune in 1871,[2] came to epitomize the battle line between future Marxist–Leninists and democratic socialists. Mikhail Bakunin's expulsion from the IWA at the Hague Conference in 1872 formalized the rift.[3]

It took 28 years between penning *Economic and Philosophical Manuscripts of 1844* and the IWA Hague Conference for Marx to reach the conclusion that the proletariat could only defeat capitalism and create a communist society through militant vanguard action. His concept of communism and its prospects evolved gradually during this interval starting as an "angry young man,"[4] an encounter with Friedrich Engels that acquainted him with the plight of the working class in 1843[5] and then slowly crystalized into a historicist theory of revolutionary class struggle.[6]

Marx from adolescence to the end of days (March 18, 1883) sought to grasp man's destiny and his own place in the great transformation unfolding before his eyes (Polyani, 1944),[7] during the Age of Metternich 1815–1848[8] and the first wave of globalization in 1870–1914 (Ferguson, 2004). He approached the problem by presuming a happy-ending for tomorrow's valiant workers.

Marx spun his conjecture as a messianic revelation, a materialist vision of an apocalyptic battle pitting workers against evil capitalists and nobles (Marx and Engels, 1848). Influenced by Pierre-Joseph Proudhon (1809–1865), Marx persuaded himself that property was theft (Proudhon, 1840), unjustly acquired and used to squeeze surplus value from workers.[9] He also came to believe that the oppressed sensing their plight were gradually committing themselves to seizing state power (Lukács, 2000; Hirschman, 1991).[10] Marx characterized this battle as a class struggle driven by a dialectical historical process that would ineluctably culminate in workers' permanent victory, the establishment of communism and the end of history. Communism meant nationalization of the means of production, criminalization of markets, egalitarianism, mutual support and harmony. Marx believed that although proletarian state seizure was essential as an interim measure, it would inevitably wither culminating in a harmonious self-regulating worker community (communism). People everywhere across the globe would interact without alienating intermediaries and fully actualize the quality of their existence.

Contemporary Marxists de-emphasize the Hegelian idealist roots of his dialectical materialism (Hegel, 1807) and self-regulating communalism. They stress economic and sociological aspects instead, while continuing to insist that Marxist prophecy is infallible. They are befuddled. The assumption that capitalists and nobles can increase their utility by exploiting the toiling masses does not mean that workers must be immiserated. It does not prove that a communist revolution is ineluctable, that criminalizing private property and markets will improve the masses lot, or that the vanguard of the proletariat will be beneficent. Marx wanted all these things to be true, but they are not.

Many contemporary academics venerate Marx as a scientific genius, sage and prophet. The attitude reflects a penchant to put radical politics in command over science. It constitutes a striking change of fortune for a mid-19th-century fringe figure who was on the cusp of slipping into oblivion in 1883 (Kengor, 2020).

Marx had few followers in Britain when he died, and was not a dominant figure in socialist circles during the Age of Metternich and the first wave of globalization, despite his sporadic stints as a professional journalist.[11] His stature grew thereafter because his concepts of class struggle, dictatorship of the proletariat and political activism appealed to alienated radicals,[12] militant labor unionists and insurrection-minded intellectuals (Aron, 2001). The demise of the Soviet

Union scotched Marxist enthusiasm for a decade after 1991. Few contemporary economists take Marx's pseudoscientific historicism seriously (Samuelson, 1967), but Marxism has made a comeback in the new millennium across the rest of the social sciences. Nostalgia for Marxist–Leninism is on the rise.[13]

Vladimir Lenin

Vladimir Lenin (1870–1924), founder of the Communist Party (Bolsheviks), leader of the Bolshevik Revolution (1917) and architect of the Soviet state, was born as Vladimir Ilyich Ulyanov in Simbirsk two years before the Hague Conference that committed the IWA to the goal of communist state seizure.[14] He grew up in a professional family during the turbulent period following the abolition of serfdom in 1861 and the revolutionary anarchist assassination of Tsar Alexander II in 1881.[15] Lenin displayed no signs of political activism until authorities hanged his 21-year old brother Alexander for plotting to assassinate Emperor Alexander III in 1887.[16] He read *Das Kapital* in 1889 and became a Marxist.

In 1895, his Saint Petersburg comrades sent him abroad to contact the Marxist philosopher Georgy Plekhanov and other Russian exiles in Western Europe.[17] Upon his return to Russia in 1895, he succeeded in unifying Saint Petersburg Marxist groups in the Union for the Struggle for the Liberation of the Working Class. The Union issued leaflets and proclamations on the workers' behalf, supported strikes and infiltrated education classes. Authorities arrested its leaders in December 1895 and exiled Lenin to Shushenskoye, Krasnoyarsk Krai in Siberia for three years.

Lenin elaborated his revolutionary Marxist theory of the party as the "vanguard of the proletariat" in his pamphlet *What Is to Be Done?* (1902), where he urged the creation of a highly disciplined, centralized party that would work unremittingly to infuse workers with socialist consciousness.

Lenin left Russia for Switzerland in September 1914 to organize Marxist opposition to World War I. His position was unpopular, but as the war dragged on, it attracted disaffected tsarist soldiers, facilitating the Bolshevik coup against the Constituent Assembly on January 19, 1918. Lenin ruled Russia thereafter.

Fanny Kaplan, a member of the Socialist Revolutionary Party shot Lenin three times on August 30, 1918. He was badly injured. The Cheka executed her.

Lenin was seriously ill by the latter half of 1921, perhaps attributable to syphilis (Lerner, Finkelstein and Witztum, 2004, 372). He suffered a stroke and died on January 21, 1924.

Joseph Stalin

Joseph Vissarionovich Stalin (1878–1953) was a Georgian Marxist revolutionary and Soviet politician who ruled the Soviet Union from the mid-1920s until his death in 1953. He served as the general secretary of the Communist Party of the Soviet Union (1922–1952) and premier of the Soviet Union (1941–1953). Initially governing the Soviet Union as part of a collective leadership, he consolidated power by the 1928.

Stalin joined the Marxist Russian Social Democratic Labor Party as a youth. He edited the party's newspaper, *Pravda*, and raised funds for Vladimir Lenin's Bolshevik faction through robberies, kidnappings and protection rackets. The authorities frequently arrested and exiled him. Stalin joined the Communist Party Politburo immediately after the Bolshevik revolution and assumed the position of general secretary (keeper of party secrets and cadre appointments) in 1922. He sought to build socialism in one country, initiated Five-Year Planning, collectivized agriculture, fostered rapid industrialization and created a centralized command economy. His policies precipitated the great famine of 1932–1933 killing approximately 5 million peasants (Conquest, 1986). Stalin launched the Great Purge Trials in 1936 to consolidate his authority, executing at least 700,000 through 1939.

His government promoted Marxist-Leninism abroad through the Communist International and supported European anti-fascist movements during the 1930s, particularly in the Spanish Civil War. In 1939, the USSR signed a nonaggression pact with Nazi Germany, resulting in the Soviet and German invasion of Poland. Germany ended the pact by invading the Soviet Union in 1941. Despite initial setbacks, the Soviet Red Army repelled the German incursion and captured Berlin in 1945, ending World War II in Europe. The Soviets annexed the Baltic States and helped establish Soviet-aligned governments throughout Central and Eastern Europe, China and North Korea. The Soviet Union and the United States emerged from the war as global superpowers. Tensions arose between the Soviet-backed Eastern Bloc and US-backed Western Bloc (Cold War). Stalin led his country through the postwar reconstruction, during which it developed a nuclear weapon in 1949. In these years, the country experienced another famine and anti-Semitic campaign peaking in the doctors' plot. After Stalin's death in 1953, Nikita Khrushchev denounced him and began de-Stalinizing Soviet society.

Widely considered one of the 20th century's most significant figures, Stalin was the subject of a pervasive personality cult within the international Marxist–Leninist movement, which revered him as a champion of the working class and socialism. After the dissolution of the Soviet Union in 1991, Stalin retained popularity in Russia and Georgia as a victorious wartime leader who established the Soviet Union as a major world power, even though Putin publically condemned his mass repressions, ethnic cleansing, deportations executions and famines that killed no less than 14 million people.

Notes

1 Jenny Laura died in a suicide pact with her husband in 1868. She was 66. Laura and her husband Paul Lafargue translated Marx's work into French. Jenny Julia Eleanor was a socialist activist. She committed suicide at the age of 43 by poisoning herself with prussic acid after discovering that her long-term partner Edward Aveling secretly married Eva Frye in June 1897.

2 A revolutionary uprising called the Paris Commune seized power in Paris after German forces defeated the armies of the Third Republic on January 28, 1871, concluding the Franco Prussian War of 1870. The commune held power for two months, until the regular French army suppressed it at the end of May 1871.

3 The Hague Congress was the fifth congress of the International Workingmen's Association (IWA), held from September 2 to 7, 1872, in The Hague, the Netherlands. Anarchist leaders Mikhail Bakunin and James Guillaume were expelled for protesting the vanguard principle. Mikhail Alexandrovich Bakunin (1814–1876) was a Russian revolutionary anarchist, socialist and founder of collectivist anarchism. His prestige as a revolutionary also made him one of the most famous ideologues in Europe, gaining substantial influence among radicals throughout Russia and Europe.

4 The "angry young men" were a group of mostly working- and middle-class British playwrights and novelists who became prominent in the 1950s. The group's leading figures included John Osborne and Kingsley Amis.

5 On August 28, 1844, Marx met the German socialist Friedrich Engels at the Café de la Régence, beginning a lifelong friendship. Engels showed Marx his recently published *The Condition of the Working Class in England in 1844*, convincing Marx that the working class would be the agent and instrument of the final revolution in history.

6 *The Condition of the Working Class in England in 1844* laid the foundation for Marx and Engels' most famous work, *The Communist Manifesto*. This new open political society was called the Communist League. Both Marx and Engels participated in drawing up the program and organizational principles of the new Communist League.

   In late 1847, Marx and Engels began writing what was to become their most famous work – a program of action for the Communist League. Written jointly by Marx and Engels from December 1847 to January 1848, The *Communist Manifesto* was first published on February 21, 1848. The *Communist Manifesto* laid out the beliefs of the new Communist League. The opening lines of the pamphlet set forth the principal basis of Marxism: "The history of all hitherto existing society is the history of class struggles." It goes on to examine the antagonisms that Marx claimed were arising in the clashes of interest between the bourgeoisie (the wealthy capitalist class) and the proletariat (the industrial working class).

7 Polanyi describes the social and political upheavals that took place in England during the rise of the market economy.

8 The 33 years after the end of the Napoleonic Wars are called in Austria – and to some extent in all of Europe – the Age of Metternich. The chief characteristics of this age are the onset of the Industrial Revolution, an intensification of social problems brought on by economic cycles of boom and bust, an increasingly mobile population, more demands for popular participation in government and the rising tide of nationalism, all governmentally managed to preserve the social, political and international status quo.

9 Marx defined surplus value was revenue earned by workers, but misappropriated by capitalists in the form of unearned profits.

10 The Hungarian Marxist philosopher György Lukács stressed the need to distinguish between class consciousness and the ideas or feelings actually held by the members of a social class.

11 Marx's principal earnings came from his work as European correspondent, from 1852 to 1862, for the *New York Daily Tribune*. The *New York Tribune* was an American newspaper, first established in 1841 by Horace Greeley. Greeley sponsored a host of reforms, including pacifism and feminism and especially the ideal of the hardworking free laborer.

12 During the decade of the 1840s, the word communist came into general use to describe those who hailed the left wing of the Jacobin Club of the French Revolution as their ideological forefathers. This political tendency saw itself as egalitarian inheritors of the 1795 Conspiracy of Equals headed by Gracchus Babeuf. The sansculottes of Paris which had decades earlier been the base of support for Babeuf – artisans, journeymen and the urban unemployed – was seen as a potential foundation for a new social system based on the modern machine production of the day.

13 Andrei Konchalovsky, "Dear Comrad," film 2020.

14 He adopted the pseudonym Lenin in 1901 during his clandestine party work after exile in Siberia.

15 Alexander II (1818–1881) ruled as emperor of Russia (1855–1881). A period of repression after 1866 led to a resurgence of revolutionary terrorism and to Alexander's assassination.

16 In 1886 Alexander Ulyanov became a member of the "terrorist faction," which was part of the Narodnaya Volya (People's Will) party that had assassinated Tsar Alexander II. Lenin's brother was one of the authors of the party's Marxism-influenced program. Acknowledging the working class as the nucleus of the Socialist Party, the program affirmed the revolutionary initiative of fighting autocracy through terrorism. Ulyanov and his comrades conspired to assassinate Alexander III of Russia. On March 1, 1887 (Julian calendar), the day of the sixth anniversary of Alexander II's murder (The Second First of March). Alexander Ulyanov served as the main ideologist of the group and bomb-maker. On May 8, he was hanged at Shisselburg together with Pakhomy Andreyushkin, Vasily Generalov, Vasili Osipanov and Petr Shevyrev.

17 Plekhanov opposed "democratic centrism" (unwavering devotion to the communist party line), a key element of Leninism.

References

Aron, Raymond. (2001). *The Opium of the Intellectuals*. New Brunswick: Transaction Press.

Conquest, Robert. (1986). *Harvest of Sorrow: Soviet Collectivization and the Terror-Famine*. New York: Oxford University Press.

Engels, Frederick. (1845). *The Condition of the Working Class in England in 1844*. Leipzig: Otto Wigand.

Ferguson, Niall. (2004). *Empire: The Rise and Demise of the British World Order and the Lessons for Global Power*. New York: Basic Books.

Gilbert, Mary. (2012). *Love and Capital: Karl and Jenny Marx and the Birth of a Revolution*. Boston: Back Bay Books.

Hegel, Georg Wilhelm Friedrich. (1807). *Phänomenologie des Geistes* (Phenomenology of Spirit). Cambridge: Cambridge University Press.

Hirschman, Albert. (1991). *The Rhetoric of Reaction: Perversity, Futility, Jeopardy*. Cambridge: The Belknap Press of Harvard University Press.

Hoffman, Robert. (1967). "Marx and Proudhon: A Reappraisal of Their Relationship." *The Historian*. Vol. 29, No. 3, 409–430.

Kengor, Paul. (2020). *The Devil and Karl Marx: Communism's Long March of Death, Deception, and Infiltration*. New York: TAN.

Lerner, Vladimir, Y. Finkelstein and E. Witztum. (2004). "The Enigma of Lenin's (1870–1924) Malady." *European Journal of Neurology*. Vol. 11, No. 6, 372.

Lukács, Georg. (2000). *History and Class Consciousness: Studies in Marxist Dialectics.* Cambridge: The MIT Press.

Marx, Karl and Frederick Engels. (1848). *Communist Manifesto.* London.

Polanyi, Karl. (1944). *The Great Transformation.* New York: Farrar & Rinehart.

Proudhon, Pierre-Joseph. (1840). *What Is Property? An Inquiry into the Principle of Right and of Government.*

Samuelson, Paul. (1967). "Marxian Economics as Economics." *The American Economic Review.* Vol. 57, No. 2, 616–623.

Appendix 3

Marxist Economics

Karl Marx was a political economist preoccupied with the issues of labor exploitation, concentrated wealth, economic crises, nationalization of the means of production and working-class seizure of state power. He constructed his economic theory to discredit capitalism, not to understand the logic of competitive utility seeking and optimization. Marx supported his narrative with one-sided microeconomic claims that ignored rational consumer, worker and producer choice in an interactive cybernetic system of demand and supply. He contended without proof that labor (working class) was the only source of value added, treating management services, entrepreneurial rewards, rents and profits as stolen labor income. This transformed a positive issue into an allegation of worker exploitation.[1]

Marx insisted that capitalists would drive wages down to subsistence levels, ignoring the productivity possibilities of science and technological progress. He contended that labor exploitation would impoverish the working class and trigger a series of acute crises, culminating in catastrophic collapse.

Market economies are prone to business cycles, and falling wages may sometimes contribute to depressions, but wage cutting is only one of many causes and hyper-depressions (black swans) are rare events (Talib, 2007). Marx's revolutionary political economy is not Newtonian science nor were subsequent developments in applied linear programming because neither he nor his successors developed an operational theory of individual consumer (worker) demand.

Marx knew that individual consumer demand played a role in the production of goods and services and retail sales. He liked caviar and purchased it instead of cheaper substitutes. He knew too that if everyone ceased purchasing caviar, producers would stop supplying it. However, he insisted that the value of products depended solely on direct and indirect labor time independent of demand.

The error was fundamental to his historicist political economy. He could not admit that he was wrong in neglecting individual consumer demand without moderating his war on capitalism. The error had pernicious consequences. Soviet economists guided by Marx's supply side thinking could not devise an individual worker-consumer demand guided theory of economic behavior. This is why Marxist–Leninists never fretted about criminalizing markets. It never dawned on them that satisfying individual worker demand was essential for maximizing worker utility. The same myopia prevented Marx and the Soviets from appreciating the roles that private ownership of the means of production and entrepreneurship play in enhancing worker utility.

Marx did not understand microeconomics. His ignorance invalidated his political economy and set Soviet socialism off on a wild goose chase.

Note

1 Robert Owen was unconcerned about labor exploitation. He advocated rewarding worker for their labor time, rather than the value of their marginal products on the grounds of "fairness."

Reference

Talib, Nassim Nicholas. (2007). *The Black Swan: The Impact of the Highly Improbable.* New York: Random House.

Appendix 4

Perfect Competitive Benchmark

The Soviet planned economy performed poorly. Technologies were inferior and factors misallocated. Goods were shoddy, tax transfers inefficient and the quality of worker existence was low. The democratic perfectly competitive standard illuminates these defects (Arrow, 1951; Sen, 1999). The figures in this chapter pinpoint the deficiencies of central planning.

Factor Space

Figure A4.1 is an Edgeworth-Bowley factor/production box. It illustrates the impact of Soviet command planning on what would otherwise be the efficient allocation of factors.

The ordinate represents variable capital (not the capital stock captured by the isoquants) and the abscissa labor for both activities. Factor supplies are the general competitive equilibrium volumes. The origin for guns is located at the southwest corner of the Edgeworth-Bowley box. The butter origin begins at the northeast corner. The space between the origins contains isoquants for the two goods. The isoquants are components of production functions (factor

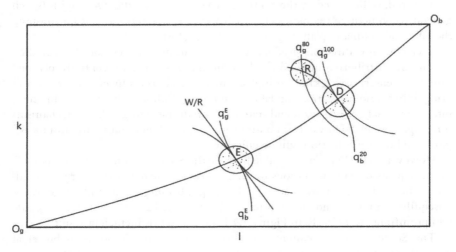

Figure A4.1 Factor Space

substitution sub-functions) that link varying amounts of capital and labor to output. There are two nested sets of isoquants, one for guns and the other butter:

$$q_g = F(k, l) \text{ and}$$
$$q_b = G(k, l),$$

where q_g represents guns and q_b butter; k is variable capital and l is labor. Variable capital includes intermediate inputs (fuels, raw materials) and tools with a service life of less than one year. The price of variable capital is r; the wage rate is w.

The superscripts on the isoquants represent output volumes (expressed in units). Output increases the further isoquants lie from their respective origins (the greater the volume of capital and labor utilized), given embodied technologies. The more productive the technology, the higher the superscripts. The embodied technologies in Figure A4.1 are the perfectly competitive ideals. They can also represent Soviet technologies by a scalar reduction of isoquant superscripts.[1] Isoquants are convex to their respective origins and nested (they do not intersect). They fill the entire production space and illustrate the possibilities for efficient factor substitution between the two activities.

Under perfect competition (Arrow and Debreu, 1954; Novshek and Sonnenschein, 1987), there exists one and only one equilibrium (E) [or a fuzzy set of possible E points in accordance with "bounded rationality" theory (the circular sets in Figure A4.1)] that reflects prevailing consumer demand. Fuzzy sets do not alter basic conclusions, given sensible assumptions about information sufficiency and people's ability to choose rationally (Rosefielde and Pfouts, 2014; Simon, 1957, 1988, 1991; Gigerenzer and Selten, 2002; Rubinstein, 1998; Tisdell, 1998; Kahneman, 2003). If consumer preferences change (demand), point E must adjust accordingly. Conjectured changes in consumer preferences are counterfactual. They could exist, but do not at the moment. The set of all equilibria, real and conjectured, is illustrated by the contract curve connecting the two origins (given generally competitive technology), which serves as a useful referent for grasping the effect of command planning on economic performance.

Soviet systems directors produce at point D using a variety of physical allocation and distributive methods.[2] These mechanisms include centrally planned directives, enterprises tekhpromfinplans, managerial bonus incentives, wage and price fixing, resource rationing, labor assignment, "khozraschyot" coordination, interministerial coordination and state bank credit rationing. These mechanisms shift capital and labor away from butter toward guns. Under ideal circumstances,[3] guns and butter production will be efficient.

However, point D is unachievable because the Soviet command economy inefficiently plans output and rations factors. Variable capital and labor are assigned, immobile and guided by state fixed disequilibrium rental and wage rates. Disequilibrium input and output prices set by the State Price Committee misguide tekhpromfinplans. Point R in Figure A4.1 illustrates this inefficient result.

The Soviet planned economy produces 80 guns and 20 sticks of butter at point R, but Figure A4.1 shows that planners could do better merely by sliding along the butter isoquant from R to D, where gun production increases to 100, without any reduction in butter. This Pareto superior outcome illustrates the general case where one party gains without the other losing. The Soviet command planning economy was intrinsically Pareto inferior. Its GDP, given the leadership's preferences, did not achieve the USSR's perfectly planned potential or the West's perfectly competitive ideal.

Production Space

Remapping the contract curve in Figure A4.1 in the production space (Figure A4.2) underscores this judgment. The ordinate represents government services, the abscissa butter. The highest concave curve to the origin is the Pareto production possibilities frontier (PPF). It is identical to the contract curve in Figure A4.1 (embodying the best Pareto optimal technologies). It represents the menu of guns and butter attainable if planning were perfect and Stalin's preferences determined the butter supply. The workers' community indifference curve U (the demand function) is tangent to the PPF (the aggregate supply curve) at point E. (Samuelson, 1956; Scitovsky, 1941). The double tangency at the price ratio p_b/p_g indicates a complete equilibrium of individual demand and supply. It is Pareto optimal and represents the ideal GDP when q_g is aggregate investment I and q_b is aggregate consumption C.

Feasible Soviet production at point R is suboptimal from both Stalin's and workers' perspectives because inefficient planning prevents systems directors from choosing best technologies. It misallocates factors, impairs factor productivities (reduced output) and forces workers to substitute guns for butter. The Soviet

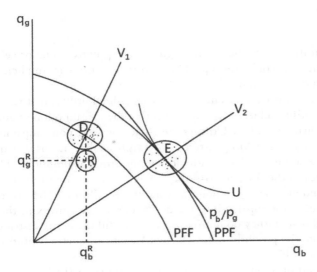

Figure A4.2 Production Space

Marxist–Leninist communist ideal (assuming that the leader knew and honored the people's preferences) is point E; the feasible best is D (given leaders' preferences), but production occurs at the inferior point R. The Soviet PFF depicted in Figure A4.2 lies below the PPF because restrictions placed by the planning system on technology diminish productivity (the isoquant superscripts in Figure A4.1). Soviet technology, anticompetitively developed in design institutes, is inferior because it is detached from consumer demand and leader preferences. Point R lies on a lower PFF (not depicted) because the misallocation of variable factors of production reduces productivity further.

Distribution Space

Soviet maldistribution of goods and services in wholesale and retail markets compounded utilitarian losses in the factor and production spaces. Figure A4.3 illustrates the essentials. It depicts the distribution of public services and butter to two purchasers: A and Z. The ordinate represents guns and the abscissa butter. The supply of both products is determined in Figures A4.1 and A4.2 at point R. The origin for individual A is located at the southwest corner of the Edgeworth–Bowley box; Z's purchases begin at the northeast corner.

The interior of the Edgeworth–Bowley distribution box contains A's and Z's iso-utility (indifference) curves for the two goods: q_g and q_b. The iso-utility curves are utility functions that link varying amounts of government services and butter consumption to utility. There are two nested sets of iso–utility curves: one for A and the other for Z.

$$u_A = F(q_g, q_b) \text{ and}$$
$$u_Z = G(q_g, q_b)$$

where U represents utility, q_g public services (guns) and q_b butter. The price of public services is p_g; the price of butter is p_b. These utility functions are implicit in Bergson's W function (see Appendix 1).

The superscripts on the iso-utility curves represent ordinal utility; that is, the ordinal magnitude of utility subjectively experienced in the consumption of guns and butter by individuals A and Z. Utilities are subjective and noncomparable (Bentham, 1948; Neumann and Morgenstern, 1944).[4] Ordinality means that the iso-utilities of A and Z are not addable without making strong assumptions. The degree of utility increases the further iso-utility curves lie from their respective origins, given each individual's psychological scale of sensibilities.[5] The greater the sensibility, the higher the superscript.[6] Iso-utility curves are convex to their respective origins and nested (they do not intersect). They fill the entire distribution space and illustrate the possibilities for efficient barter (product substitution) between individuals A and Z.

There exists one and only one Soviet consumer equilibrium (E) [or a fuzzy set of bounded rational E points (the circular sets in Figure A4.3)] that reflects

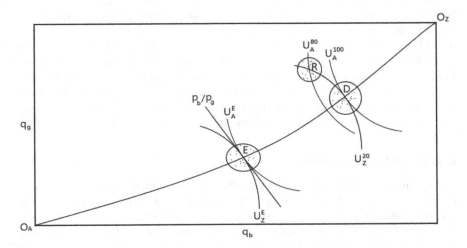

Figure A4.3 Distribution Space

prevailing consumer demand under perfect competition or perfect planning (Arrow and Debreu, 1954; Novshek and Sonnenschein, 1987). Fuzzy sets do not alter basic conclusions, given credible assumptions about sufficient information and rational choosing. If consumer preferences change, point E must adjust accordingly. Conjectured changes in consumer preferences are counterfactual. The contract curve connecting the two origins is the set of all equilibria, real and conjectured.

Soviet retail distribution operates inefficiently at point S. Soviet guns and butter were maldistributed from the individualist worker perspective. Marxist–Leninist principle requires setting wages without regard to competitive value added and stresses state egalitarian rationing. This warps the competitive distribution of worker income. The Soviets fixed prices according to embodied labor time without regard to consumer demand. This warped retail distribution. Soviet wage and price fixing and product rationing distributed too much to individual A and too little to individual Z at point R. Figure A4.3 shows that Soviet workers could do better merely by forcing Z to slide along its iso–utility curve at R to D, where individual A's utility increases from 80 to 100, without reducing individual Z's utility. This Pareto superior outcome illustrates the general case where one party gains, without the other losing. Soviet retail distribution was Pareto inferior from workers' and Bolshevik's perspectives.

The Soviets neither allocated resources nor distributed retail supplies efficiently. Moreover, Figure A4.3 shows that planning was inequitable from both meritocratic and purchaser utility points of view. A is inadvertently favored over Z. Consumers prefer retail distribution at point D, but the leader compelled them to choose point R.

The flawed Soviet retail distribution mechanism compounds the underproduction of consumer goods. If retail distribution markets were perfectly competitive or perfectly planned, the price ratio p_b/p_g in Figure A4.3 could increase, shifting distribution from R to D via the Walrasian excess-demand price adjustment mechanism. Soviet planning, however, cannot reach point D because Marxist-Leninism banned market price adjustment. Consumers are stuck at point R.

They are unable to reach point D in the factor-production space (Figure A4.1) from point E in part because Marxist-Leninism criminalized the Marshallian excess-price adjustment mechanism (competitive profit seeking).

Quality of Existence Space

The quality of existence depends on plan efficiency examined in Figures A4.1–A4.3 plus other utilities. The main component of workers' quality of existence is utilities derived from consuming goods and services, but people also benefit or suffer from conditions of labor, inequities, injustices, insecurities, illiberality, intolerance, discord and alienation. Job security, job quality, independence, cooperation, congeniality, team spirit, mutual support and solidarity generate nonpecuniary utilities unrecorded in national income accounts. Political, economic, social, religious and personal freedom, together with national security, full employment, social safety nets, psychological and spiritual health allow people to enjoy their incomes more fully. Supportive cultures, families, neighbors, communities and compatriots permit richer lives as do democracy, civil rights and fair income distributions. National income statistics do not capture these utilities and disutilities, nor a host of virtuous factors affecting the quality of existence (gains from refining individual consciousness (enlightenment), wisdom, compassion, morality and sensibilities). Individual utilities derived from GDP-based consumption are additive in value terms[7] and can be combined with non–GDP-generated utilities, assuming perfect optimization, even though there are no explicit monetary transactions.[8]

The quality of existence (M) is the sum of utility obtained from consuming butter $(u_{A1} + u_{Z1})$ and guns $(u_{A2} + u_{Z2})$ goods [Bergson's E function] plus other utilities (X) generated from learning, self-discovery, self-improvement and cultivating gratifying family, social and spiritual relations $(u_{A3} + u_{Z3})$ [such as nurture, security, equality, social justice, cooperativeness, amity, harmony, tranquility, romance and adventure experiences].[9]

W $(u_{A1} + u_{Z1} + u_{A2} + u_{Z2})$ and X $(u_{A3} + u_{Z3})$ involve opportunity costs and are substitutes in consumption. GDP excludes X because other utilities are generated from nonwork, leisure activities.

$$M = W + X$$

where

$$X = u_{A3} + u_{Z3}$$

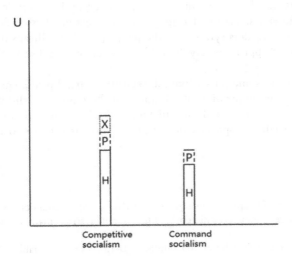

Figure A4.4 Quality of Existence Space

These other utilities are unobservable, even though consumers implicitly compute them if they comprehensibly utility maximize.

The quality of existence M measures individual cardinal utility in value terms. The magnitude of the quality of existence depends on the degree of individual optimization across all activities.

The highest quality of existence (all sources of utility) is not necessarily normatively best from all standpoints. The concept reflects individual feelings including utilities of conscience, but does not represent an ethical or sentimental judgment about aggregate merit. Ethical and sentimental judgments made about personal conduct differ because tastes and ethics vary from person to person. Puritans distain acquisitiveness. The Protestant Ethic repels hedonists. Nonetheless, the utilitarian measure M provides a sensible benchmark for judging systems merit from the standpoint of the sum of well-being and noncommercial utilities each individual feels from economic activities (Bergson, 1938).

Figure A.4.4 sheds light on precisely why command planning underperforms the Pareto benchmark. The diagram arrays quality of existence on the ordinate and two socialist systems on the abscissa: the competitive and command planning models. The vertical quality of existence bars contains utility derived from butter (H) and guns (P) for households (H) and the public (P) and other utilities (X). The quality of existence (M) is the sum of these three sources of utility.[10]

Liberal competitive socialism provides higher household utility than Soviet planning because consumers enjoy more degrees of freedom in determining the demand and supply of butter (H). The utility that the public derives from guns also is greater because competitive socialism is more efficient.

Liberal competitive socialism provides significant other utilities (X) too.

Command planning reduced workers' quality of existence by banning democracy, abridging civil liberties, criminalizing private ownership, laissez-faire and entrepreneurship. Soviet leaders tyrannized the people, herded millions into force labor camps and caused approximately 20 million civilian excess deaths. See Chapter 14.

Marxist–Leninists point to some pluses like job security, martial pride, egalitarianism, libertinism and the suppression of religion, but these positives did not outweigh the negatives, an outcome reflected in Figure A4.4 by the zero value assigned the command socialist X space. Command socialism is inferior to the competitive ideal.[11]

Notes

1 The productivity of the fixed capital converges to the Pareto ideal in tandem with improvements in resource allocative efficiency. This is not a strict mathematical necessity.

2 These allocative and distributive methods are included in Bergson's r, s, t variables. See Appendix 1.

3 Bergson's E systems function. See Appendix 1.

4 Utility can be conceived as a quantum like an atom in physics. Jeremy Bentham believed that utilities could be counted and added. Bentham's ambition in life was to create a "Pannomion," a complete utilitarian code of law, based on the principle that the greatest happiness of the greatest number. The utility function for each individual is unique. The utility generated by a unit of q_i differs across individuals and cannot be reliably retrieved because memory is inexact. The sum of individual experiences has an obscure effect on people's quality of existence. It cannot serve as an infallible ethical guide.

5 A and Z may have different "sensibilities," that is, appreciative capacities.

6 Individual sensibilities may increase or diminish intertemporarily.

7 GDP is a value metric. Individuals maximize their marginal utility under perfect competition. The prices they pay at the margin reflect their marginal utility. Value measures are cardinal. They are addable for each individual and are cardinal in this limited sense. They do not measure differences in individual subjective sensibilities.

8 The same principle hold for bounded rational cases.

9 Other utilities derive from the consumption of goods and services omitted from GDP, self-services, interpersonal, political, social, spiritual and aesthetic experiences. These include learning, self-discovery, self-improvement and cultivating gratifying family, social and spiritual relations.

10 Utilities are ordinal. They can only be summed across individuals in an aggregate context by making strong assumptions to establish a benchmark. If GDP is generated perfectly competitively (Pareto ideal) and noncommercial activities are perfectly planned and/or perfectly cooperative, then dollar values observed and imputed establish a numerical ideal benchmark that can be used to weigh comparative merit under alternative regimes. These dollar values are not transformable into cardinal psychometric values across individuals because ordinal utilities differ from individual to individual. Nonetheless, they are "quasi-cardinal" in the limited sense defined and can be used suggestively to compare the quality of existence under the alternative regimes depicted in Figure A4.4. The strategy can be extended to time series and

international comparisons across systems by making even stronger assumptions about the intertemporal and interspatial stability of individual utility preference functions. The perfect competitive assumption can also be relaxed by taking account of satisficing possibilities across individuals, time and space. Most economists do this intuitively with different degrees of rigor.

11 The utility on the ordinate is the sum of individual utilities. It is derived by computing per capita GDP and the estimated per capita dollar value of other utility-generating activities. The per capita sum is then transformed into utilities with transformation functions $u_A = F(q_g, q_b, q_x)$ and $u_z = G(q_g, q_b, q_x)$.

References

Arrow, Kenneth. (1951). *Social Choice and Individual Values*. New York: John Wiley and Sons.

Arrow, Kenneth and Gerard Debreu. (1954). "The Existence of an Equilibrium for a Competitive Economy." *Econometrica*. Vol. 22, No. 3, 265–290.

Bentham, Jeremey. (1948). *An Introduction to the Principles of Morals and Legislation*. New York: Hafner Publishing Co.

Bergson, Abram. (1938). "A Reformulation of Certain Aspects of Welfare Economics." *Quarterly Journal of Economics*. Vol. 52, No. 1, 310–334.

Gigerenzer, Gerd and Reinhard Selten. (2002). *Bounded Rationality*. Cambridge: MIT Press.

Kahneman, Daniel. (2003). "Maps of Bounded Rationality: Psychology for Behavioral Economics." *The American Economic Review*. Vol. 93, No. 5, 1449–1475.

Neumann, John and Oskar Morgenstern. (1944). *Theory of Games and Economic Behavior*. Princeton: Princeton University Press.

Novshek, William and Hugo Sonnenschein. (1987). "General Equilibrium and Free Entry: A Synthetic Approach to the Theory of Perfect Competition." *Journal of Economic Literature*. Vol. 24, No. 3, 1281–1306.

Proudhon, Pierre-Joseph. (1840). *What Is Property? An Inquiry into the Principle of Right and of Government*.

Rosefielde, Steven and Ralph W. Pfouts. (2014). *Inclusive Economic Theory*. Singapore: World Scientific Publishers.

Rubinstein, Ariel. (1998). *Modeling Bounded Rationality*. Cambridge: MIT Press.

Samuelson, Paul. (1956). "Social Indifference Curves." *The Quarterly Journal of Economics*. Vol. 70, No. 1, 1–22.

Scitovsky, Tibor. (1941). "A Note on Welfare Propositions in Economics." *Review of Economics and Statistics*. Vol. 9, No. 1, 77–88.

Sen, Amartya. (1999). "The Possibility of Social Choice." *American Economic Review*. Vol. 89, No. 3, 349–378.

Simon, Herbert. (1955). "A Behavioral Model of Rational Choice." *Quarterly Journal of Economics*, Vol. 69, No. 1, 99–118.

Simon, Herbert. (1988). "A Mechanism for Social Selection and Successful Altruism." *Science*. Vol. 250, 1665–1668.

Simon, Herbert. (1991). "Bounded Rationality and Organizational Learning." *Organization Science*. Vol. 2, No. 1, 125–134.

Tisdell, Clem. (1998). *Bounded Rationality and Economic Evolution: A Contribution to Decision Making, Economics, and Management*. Cheltenham: Brookfield.

Appendix 5

Soviet Statistics

Most socialists contend that the quality of socialist existence will be superior, perhaps even sublime. Soviet statistics support this expectation. If taken at face value, the dissolution of the Soviet Union is incomprehensible. Soviet GDP per capita grew more rapidly during 1950–1989 than the West, and the USSR's defense burden was a small fraction of the United States. Income inequality was low (Bergson, 1984; Alexeev and Gaddy, 1992),[1] and the state provided a comprehensive housing, transport, education and health care safety net. The discrepancy between impressions of communism conveyed by Soviet published statistics and citizen perceptions provides reasonable grounds for suspicion; nonetheless, socialists and most Western economists are inclined to assume that Soviet economic statistics are "reliable," including:

1 National product and income series based on enterprise output and payments.
2 Price and wage statistics.
3 Government budgetary expenditures.
4 Demographic data.
5 Prison, excess death and military statistics.

Abram Bergson elaborated the principal arguments for accepting the reliability of national income statistics in 1953 (Bergson, 1953, 1961; Treml and Hardt, 1972).

He asserted that Soviet leaders needed reliable statistics to administer and manage the USSR's centrally planned command economy. Planners, the state economic directorate and enterprise managers could not competently allocate factors, produce and distribute output to desired use with fraudulent data that compromised accountability, discipline and command control. Lenin replaced markets with administrative command planning to rid the Soviet Union of market anarchy. It seemed implausible that the Bolsheviks would license planned chaos by tolerating widespread statistical malfeasance (Mises, 1947).

Bergson acknowledged that the Soviets could conceivably have had their cake and eaten it by compiling two sets of books, one for systems managers and the other for public disinformation (putting lipstick on a pig), but brushed the possibility aside including weapons production and defense expenditures.

Reliability, as Bergson used the term, did not assure accuracy. It precluded free invention and intentional widespread falsification, but left ample room for mundane corruption, inept data processing, statistical anomalies and errors. His own research disclosed enormous discrepancies between recalculated Soviet GDP and official claims, even after allowance for index number relativity (Bergson, 1961), and did not dispose of two additional problems. First, the disaggregated physical production data Bergson used to reconstruct Soviet GDP might themselves have been inaccurate (overreported). Second, they might have been further distorted by hidden inflation (misreporting price inflation as value added by falsely claiming that physical units had been qualitatively improved) (Rosefielde, 2003, 2004). Enterprise managers, their supervisors and ministers had sound motives for embellishing production and real economic growth to earn bonuses and curry Politburo favor.

Gorbachev's 1989 revelation that the defense budget excluded weapons exemplifies the possibilities of Soviet statistical mischief. Bergson insisted in 1948–1988 that the official defense budgetary expenditure statistics included weapons but was mistaken. Soviet GDP statistics may have been reliable in some vague sense, but, nonetheless, significantly miss stated real achievements.

Worse still, they were opaque. The merit of economic systems as Bergson himself demonstrated in 1938 depends on the utility derived by individuals from national consumption of goods and services and other variables excluded from GDP (Bergson, 1938). See Appendix 1. Soviet consumers were not sovereign. Their preferences did not determine product characteristics, assortments and supplies. Most Soviet goods satisfied state demand and were rationed (forced substitution). A perfectly competitive economy would have manufactured other products with better characteristics and/or supplied desirable goods in different proportions. Valuing Soviet GDP in dollars or adjusted ruble-factor cost prices does not make Soviet and American per capita income comparable indicators of consumer utility. Whatever the form and substance of utility functions East or West, utilities experienced by Soviets for identical composites of equal monetary value was necessarily less than the metric suggested because Soviet citizens did not want and strongly disliked the goods they were compelled to consume. Forced-production and forced-substitution gave Soviet GDP performance statistics a patina of success that they did not deserve. The same principle holds for distribution. See Appendix 4. People in competitive economies pay for distribution services that enable them to improve their utility. The cost of distribution is included in GDP of planned and competitive economies. It always represents full value added under perfect competition, but never in Soviet planned economies. Soviet rationing cost expressed as accounting value added could easily overstate their utilitarian benefit. Most analysts implicitly assume that because individuals maximize utility under perfect competition, per capita GDP serves as a cardinal utility measure that permits serviceable intertemporal and international comparisons. This may be so for a small set of workably competitive economies but not for comparing anticompetitive Soviet planning with efficient markets.

Comparative GDP performance statistics also are incomplete. GDP statistics East and West omit important systems sensitive utilities. The Soviet Union was authoritarian, often despotic. It suppressed democracy, civil liberties, free speech, free thought and religion. Although, wages and wealth were relatively egalitarian, communist party insiders had privileged access to superior quality goods. Power and privilege were highly concentrated and a source of disutility for workers who resented their inferior access (Bulgakov, 1967).

During Stalin's reign, terror was rampant. Still communism had some compensating virtues. Unemployment was negligible and some people were enthused by Marxist ideology. The balance, however, was strongly negative as suggested by the Soviet Union's self-liquidation.

Finally, as Bergson himself stressed, statistics are not an adequate surrogate for morality. Even if Soviet GDP statistics were reliable, accurate and serviceable as utilitarian measures of comparative international economic performance, analysts can applaud or condemn the USSR from the standpoint of their personal ethics.

See Chapter 15 for further discussion of Soviet economic statistics.

See Chapter 14 for further discussion of Soviet demographic, prison, excess death and ethnic cleansing statistics.

Note

1 Gini coefficients using official data were low in the 1980s, approximately 0.28.

References

Alexeev, Michael and Clifford Gaddy. (1992). "Income Distribution in the USSR in the 1980s." *National Council for Soviet and East European Research*. November. www.ucis.pitt.edu/nceeer/1992-807-01-Alexeev.pdf

Bergson, Abram. (1938). "A Reformulation of Certain Aspects of Welfare Economics." *Quarterly Journal of Economics*. Vol. 52, No. 1, 310–334.

Bergson, Abram. (1953). "Reliability and Usability of Soviet Statistics: A Summary Appraisal." *American Statistician*. Vol. 7, No. 3, 13–16.

Bergson, Abram. (1954). "The Concept of Social Welfare." *Quarterly Journal of Economics*. Vol. 68, No. 2, 233–252.

Bergson, Abram. (1961). *The Real National Income of Soviet Russia since 1928*. Cambridge: Harvard University Press.

Bergson, Abram. (1984). "Income Inequality under Soviet Socialism." *Journal of Economic Literature*. Vol. 22, No. 3, 1052–1099.

Bulgakov, Mikhail. (1967). *The Master and Margarita*. London: Collins and Harvill Press.

Mises, Ludwig von. (1947). *Planned Chaos*. Irvington-on-Hudson: The Foundation for Economic Education, Inc.. https://cdn.mises.org/Planned%20Chaos_3.pdf

Rosefielde, Steven. (2003). "The Riddle of Postwar Russian Economic Growth: Statistics Lied and Were Misconstrued." *Europe-Asia Studies*. Vol. 53, No. 3, 469–481.

Rosefielde, Steven. (2004). "Postwar Russian Economic Growth: Not a Riddle – A Reply." *Europe-Asia Studies*. Vol. 56, No. 3, 463–466.

Treml, Vladimir and John Hardt. (1972). *Soviet Economic Statistics*. Durham: Duke University Press.

Index